*The Ibero-American Enlightenment*

# The Ibero-American Enlightenment

EDITED BY

## A. OWEN ALDRIDGE

UNIVERSITY OF ILLINOIS PRESS

URBANA   CHICAGO   LONDON

© 1971 by the Board of Trustees of the University of Illinois
Manufactured in the United States of America
Library of Congress Catalog Card No. 78-126520
252 00122 2

TO PROFESSOR MARCOS A. MORINIGO

PREFACE

This collection of essays grew out of a conference on the Ibero American Enlightenment held on the Urbana campus of the University of Illinois in May 1969, sponsored jointly by the University and the Hispanic Society of America. The most pertinent of the papers presented at that time have been supplemented by others written subsequently.

No previous attempt has ever been made to link the areas of North America, South America, and the Iberian Peninsula in an examination of the penetration of the thought of the Enlightenment. Not only do the papers in this collection reveal common trends in widely separated geographical areas, but they freely utilize the different perspectives of history, philosophy, and comparative literature. Taken together they offer valuable evidence to be used in deciding whether the Enlightenment was a movement limited to two or three national cultures with characteristics peculiar to each nationality or whether it was a general movement in Western thought transcending national boundaries. The method of diachronous comparative analysis as exemplified in this collection reveals that the phenomena usually associated chiefly with France and England in the eighteenth century developed also in other geographical areas in the same and in later chronological periods.

A. O. A.

CONTENTS

[ix]

### III. LATIN AMERICA

### IV. ANGLO-AMERICA

*¡Influya en la felicidad de los pueblos*
*iluminándolos, despertándolos, desengañandolos!*

Mercurio de Chile, 1822

# The Concept of the Ibero-American Enlightenment

### A. OWEN ALDRIDGE

THIS IS THE FIRST BOOK ever to be published devoted to the Ibero-American Enlightenment, that is, to the spread of liberal ideas in both North and South America and in the Iberian Peninsula. On the closely related subject of Latin America and the Enlightenment only one book has so far appeared, a collection of essays published in 1942 and reissued in a revised edition in 1961.[1] Its editor, Arthur P. Whitaker, contributes the present volume's lead essay, a look at the most recent scholarship concerning the Enlightenment in general and particularly in relation to Latin America.

It is strange that intellectual historians have neglected the Enlightenment in the New World. During the eighteenth century itself, Thomas Paine in *The Rights of Man* quoted Edmund Burke to the effect "that the people of America are more enlightened than those of England, or of any other country in Europe."[2] To be sure, Burke was referring only to the English colonies, and he and Paine did not agree for long on the meaning

[1] Arthur P. Whitaker (ed.), *Latin America and the Enlightenment* (Ithaca, N.Y., 1961).
[2] Part II, Chap.III. Philip S. Foner (ed.), *Complete Writings of Thomas Paine* (New York, 1945), I, 366.

[3]

of the concept of being enlightened, but the quotation establishes, nevertheless, that America in the eighteenth century was considered as a natural environment for rational philosophy.

The reasons the three geographical areas of North America, South America, and the Iberian Peninsula should be selected for joint study are historical and linguistic. Independent nations developed in both North and South America from a previous colonial status. A classic example of similarity in the two hemispheres is that of the exploration and development of the frontier and the resulting social and political changes. This parallel is especially close between the United States and Brazil.[3] The Southern hemisphere looked to the Northern for experience, if not leadership, in the evolution of systems of democratic government and popular education; the careers of Sarmiento and Francisco Bilbao supply ample proof. In language and cultural heritage, however, the ties of Latin America were, of course, with Spain and Portugal. Stressing the relationships between these three geographical areas does not in any way imply that the history of the Enlightenment's penetration in them should be studied without reference to the major streams in Europe, particularly in England and France. Professor Whitaker in his essay vigorously affirms, and quite properly so, that a full understanding of the Enlightenment in Latin America cannot be attained without taking the European prototype as a point of reference.

### DEFINING THE ENLIGHTENMENT

In some Spanish dictionaries the translation for *Enlightenment* is given as *Las Luces*; in others it is given as *Enciclopedismo*, referring to the doctrines reflected in the famous French *Encyclopédie* of Diderot and d'Alembert. The word *Ilustración*, often used, has recently been approved by the Spanish Academy and will be included in the next edition of its official dictionary. The definition of this word in the *Diccionario del uso del español*

---

[3] Vianna Moog, *Bandeirantes e pioneiros. Parelelo entre duas culturas*, 3d ed. (Rio de Janeiro, 1956).

of M. Moliner takes in a very narrow scope, much more limited than the concept of Enlightenment in France and England. According to Moliner, *Ilustración* represents the "movimiento ideológico que culminó en el Siglo XVIII en favor de la secularización de la cultura." One of the best and most comprehensive definitions to be found anywhere of the philosophy of Enlightenment is that of abbé Morellet, a friend of Franklin and Voltaire. Referring to the common ground occupied by the encyclopedists, Morellet wrote: "All of these men had an identical philosophy; it is this ardent desire to know, this mental activity which refuses to leave an effect without seeking its cause, a phenomenon without an explanation, an assertion without proof, an objection without a reply, an error without combatting it, an evil without seeking the remedy, a possible good without trying to attain it; it is this general movement of minds which characterized the eighteenth century and which will be its glory forever."[4]

In Chile a conservative spokesman for the Roman Catholic church spoke glowingly of that "wholesome, beneficial and re-generating philosophy, which taking for exclusive object the welfare of humanity, too long debased by the chains of despotism, has not lost the zeal to establish liberty of nations, prolific fountain of its felicity."[5] The conservative wing of the church could not go along, however, with the currents of deism and ecclesiastical reform which also played a dominant role in the Enlightenment, even in Catholic countries. A good estimate of the combined political and religious aims of the Enlightenment is found in the following sarcastic and strongly disapproving view of another Chilean priest: "All this fuss is to prove that sovereignty resides in the people, that kings receive authority from them through the social contract, that they are removable by the authority of the people, and that philosophy has been

[4] "Eloge de Marmontel," quoted by A. O. Aldridge in "Benjamin Franklin and the Philosophes," *Studies on Voltaire and the Eighteenth Century,* XXIV (1963), 43.

[5] *El Observador eclesiástico,* June 21, 1823. Quoted by A. O. Aldridge in "Apostles of Reason: Camilo Henríquez and the French Enlightenment," *Studies on Voltaire and the Eighteenth Century,* LV (1967), 66.

neglected for the period of eighteen centuries; however the dawn of its triumphs is impending, and beginning to raise its luminous and triumphant countenance—which means that impiety and error will prevail over the religion of Jesus Christ."[6] This perspective is perhaps too caustic to be useful as a criterion, just as that of abbé Morellet is too idealistic. A great many men participated in the Enlightenment who were neither deists nor encyclopedists.

It is obvious that great differences separated the intellectual milieux of Newton's London, Diderot's Paris, Franklin's Philadelphia, Feijoo's Oviedo, Pombal's Lisbon, and Camilo Henríquez's Santiago. Undoubtedly there was a much greater degree of intellectual freedom in the first three centers than in the latter three. One cannot deny Voltaire's aphorism that a man born in a despotic country has the same relationship to a man born free as a potted plant in a hothouse has to an orange tree in a grove.[7] An American historian has even raised the question whether the intellectual milieu of North America in the eighteenth century may legitimately be compared to that of England. In a paper entitled "The Myth of an American Enlightenment," Daniel J. Boorstin objects to the process of homogenizing carried on by some historians, that is, in making the assumption that since a certain complex of ideas existed in one geographical area the same climate of opinion must inevitably have existed in all other areas during the same period.[8] He particularly discredits as evidence of strong intellectual influence the presence of books from one country in libraries in another, a type of evidence, by the way, which has been heavily relied upon by scholars seeking to demonstrate Enlightenment tendencies in Iberian cultures. According to Professor Boorstin, the contents of a man's mind are not necessarily the same as the contents of his library. The works of Montesquieu and Voltaire, for example, may have cir-

[6] Melchor Martinez, *Memoria histórica sobre la revolución de Chile, desde el cautivero de Fernando VII, hasta 1814* (Valparaiso, 1848), pp.140–41.

[7] Theodore Besterman (ed.), *Voltaire's Correspondence*, Letter No. 613.

[8] Daniel J. Boorstin, *America and the Image of Europe* (New York, 1960), pp.65–78.

culated in North and South America, but this does not in itself prove that they fostered a spirit of toleration. Professor Boorstin's words of caution should not be ignored. One overzealous homogenizer, in struggling to prove "a spirit of reform and reinvigoration" at the University of Salamanca, affirmed in the preface to his book that "to that end Montesquieu was read." In the text of his book, however, he revealed quite to the contrary that Montesquieu was considered a "pestilential" author and was cited at the University merely as an example of the pernicious thought which law students needed to be protected against.[9] At the same time that we are against homogenizing historians, we should be alerted against the even worse distortions of provincial historians, those who fail to perceive the international currents that affect the local areas they are studying. A superb model for scholarly treatment of Enlightenment-oriented thinkers in an anti-Enlightenment environment is an article by Raphael Demos in the *Journal of the History of Ideas*, "The Neo-Hellenic Enlightenment (1750–1821), a General Survey."[10] Students of Ibero-America could well emulate this rational presentation, which makes no excessive claims and allows the evidence to speak for itself. Insofar as North America is concerned, a good case may be made that Enlightenment thinking originated as a native growth, but that it was still very much part of the spirit of the times as reflected in France and England. Professor Adrienne Koch has conclusively demonstrated the real existence of Enlightenment in North America in a brilliant analysis of the thought of Franklin, Adams, Jefferson, Madison, and Hamilton.[11] She has amply revealed that the foundations for the free society we know today developed from the vision and spirit of these political leaders. It was not part of her purpose to show the relations between the thought of these men and that of their counterparts in England and the Continent, but this would

[9] George M. Addy, *The Enlightenment in the University of Salamanca* (Durham, N.C., 1966), pp.viii, 198. See A. O. Aldridge, "The Cloudy Spanish Enlightenment," *Modern Language Journal*, LII (February 1968), 113–16.

[10] XIX (1958), 522–41.

[11] *The American Enlightenment* (New York, 1965).

be a legitimate enterprise of great value for some scholar of the future.

Historians concerned with Latin America and the Iberian Peninsula have a completely different problem. They must take into account the largely successful efforts at thought control exercised in these areas by both church and state. Enlightenment existed in these societies but it was different, both in degree and kind, from that in France and England. The scholar's obligation is to recognize differences, not to give the impression of uniformity when none exists. He cannot, moreover, circumvent these differences by applying to France and England a definition of Enlightenment, comprising its full spirit, one such as that of abbé Morellet, and to Spain and Portugal a narrower or more limited one.

The following four-point definition adapted from another study by Professor Koch has broad application; it is as relevant to the French encyclopedists as to the Spanish Sociedad de Amigos del País or to the Peruvian *Mercurio Peruano*.[12] The essence of the Enlightenment consists of:

1. "Hospitality to scientific inquiry" and acceptance of its discoveries even at the risk of displacing "all other *a priori* or intuitive or merely traditional beliefs with respect to matters of fact."

2. A struggle against "superstition, tribal idols, and irrational prejudices," particularly when these unfounded beliefs issue in "manifest human injustices and oppression."

3. A critical reconstruction and re-examination of basic beliefs.

4. A dedication to the work of social and economic reform.

Interpretations of Enlightenment philosophy and values differ widely. Historians of the last century such as Michelet and John Morley, together with those of the twentieth century such as Carl Becker, have stressed the humanistic and utopian idealism of the Enlightenment. In recent years other scholars have

12 "The Aftermath of the American Enlightenment," *Studies on Voltaire and the Eighteenth Century*, LVI (1967), 735.

reacted against this view, arguing that counter currents of irrationality, pessimism, and individualism also existed. Still others have stressed utilitarian ideals and the promotion of useful knowledge. Emphasis on the humanistic and utopian quality of the Enlightenment has never been unanimously discarded, however, and very recently has been attracting new support.[13]

THE DATES OF THE ENLIGHTENMENT

Traditionally the European Enlightenment has been considered as spanning the entire eighteenth century with a few outstanding thinkers such as Locke, Newton, and Bayle included as precursors. Peter Gay indicates the precise hundred-year period between 1689 and 1789 for Europe, and Adrienne Koch the fifty-year period between 1765 and 1815 for North America, representing, in the words of John Adams, "an age of revolutions and constitutions." In an article on "The Aftermath of the American Enlightenment," Professor Koch has presented the evidence of the survival of the ideals and methods of the Enlightenment into the midst of the nineteenth century in the writings of Emerson and the abolitionists. In French history, the terminal limit of the Enlightenment has traditionally been regarded as the outbreak of the French Revolution in 1789, but a significant study has just appeared, arguing that the *idéologues* of the Napoleonic era carried on the philosophic purpose of the great eighteenth-century thinkers and that no real philosophical distinction separates the eighteenth century from the First Empire. The nineteenth-century *idéologues*, in "what might be called their team action," carried on the methods and ideals of the encyclopedists, and the *Encyclopédie méthodique*, which came from the presses in the period from 1782 to 1832, represented a blending of the efforts of the last generation of the *philosophes*

---

[13] Robert Shackleton has vigorously praised the relevance of Carl Becker's *The Heavenly City of the Eighteenth-Century Philosophers*, 1932, in an address, "Traditional Survivals in the Enlightenment," given at the Eleventh Congress of the International Federation for Modern Languages and Literatures in September 1969 at Islamabad, Pakistan.

with those of the new *idéologues*.[14] There can be little objection, then, to the perspective of the articles in the present volume, which range from attitudes toward reason in sixteenth-century Inca writers to attitudes toward primitivism in nineteenth-century Latin American fiction. A recent article on "The Enlightenment in Two Colonial Brazilian Libraries," for example, extends the Enlightenment in South America to 1838.[15] Even though this article is based on the reprobated method of assuming an intellectual milieu on the evidence of library holdings, the author is to be commended for one felicitous phrase concerning the new science, describing it as "the progenitor of the Enlightenment."

### ENLIGHTENMENT AND DESPOTIC GOVERNMENTS

Although the historian who deals with liberal attitudes in Spain, Portugal, and Latin America may easily justify the chronological periods which he selects, he may have some difficulty in defending himself from the charge of artificially homogenizing his materials unless he frankly admits the differences in degree and in kind between the Enlightenment in his areas and that in such advanced countries as England and France. Voltaire may have exaggerated in affirming that for Italy and Spain "il y faut demander la permission de penser à un capucin,"[16] but opponents of received opinions in these countries certainly experienced more difficulty in publicizing their ideas than did the philosophical radicals of England, France, and Germany. In both Spain and Italy a large degree of intellectual activity was controlled by the Inquisition, which, to mention only one restriction, considered the notion of toleration as anathema. There was, to be sure, distinguished scientific investigation in Spain and Portugal, but most of it concerned botany, and it was tech-

---

14 Sergio Moravia, *Il tramonto dell'illuminismo: filosofia e politica nella società francesa (1770–1810)* (Bari, 1968). See the review by Alfred J. Bingham in *Comparative Literature Studies*, VI (1969), 212–16.

15 E. Bradford Burns, *Journal of the History of Ideas*, XXV (1964), 430–38.

16 Theodore Besterman (ed.), *Voltaire's Notebooks* (Geneva, 1952), II, 379.

nical rather than theoretical. There were no Iberian Newtons, Franklins, or Buffons.

When the French Academy of Sciences sent the La Condamine expedition to measure the longitude at the equator, "le conseil d'Espagne," to cite Voltaire once more, "a nommé quelques petits philosophes espagnols pour apprendre leur métier sous les nôtres."[17] Actually, these "quelques" consisted of merely two young men, Jorge Juan and Antonio de Ulloa. While they were inexperienced at the start, they learned quickly, worked independently during the eight years of the expedition, and published a book about it which was translated into English, French, and German. For this and other scientific achievements, they were elected members of the Royal Society (London) and other learned groups on the Continent. This is a concrete illustration of the true nature of Enlightenment in Spain.

Scholarship on the intellectual history of Spain, Portugal, and Latin America has frequently been vitiated by excessive claims. The articles in the present collection are unusual in their moderation and restraint. Professor Monguió, for example, prefaces his analysis of the eighteenth-century periodicals of Mexico and Peru with the admission that their contents were restricted by the boundaries set by orthodox belief. As he says, "What other Enlightenment could we really expect to find in the colonies of Catholic Spain?" A previous scholar has complimented the *Mercurio Peruano* by describing it as "dedicated to the dissemination of Enlightenment, especially in fields of pure science less likely to involve theological dispute."[18] Even with the qualification of the last phrase, this is excessive praise if we compare it to the realistic appraisal of the *Mercurio* given by a near-contemporary in Argentina: *"El Mercurio Peruano* publicó algunos papeles curiosos, mas no habló de política; y no pudiendo sus muy apreciables autores hablar una palabra acerca de los asuntos de más alto y trascendental interés, se vinieron a ver

17 Besterman (ed.), *Voltaire's Correspondence*, Letter No. 839.
18 John Tate Lanning, "The Reception of the Enlightenment in Latin America," in Whitaker (ed.), *Latin America and the Enlightenment*, pp.28–83.

precisados a escribir la historia de la fundación de los monasterios, y en fin, quedaron en silencio."[19]

To admit that the governmental authorities in Spain and Portugal and their American colonies did not support the Enlightenment, even if it is considered merely as the "movimiento ideológico . . . en favor de la secularizacion de la cultura," is doing no disservice to the phases of Iberian culture which are truly admirable and it allows for a distinction between the courageous leaders who rose above their milieu to condemn it and the vast majority of conformists who accepted or extolled it. Even the classic study of the Spanish Enlightenment, Jean Sarrailh's masterful survey, *L'Espagne éclairée de la seconde moitié du XVIII*^e *siècle*, is weakened somewhat by the generosity of the author, "who sees a free thinker in each cultivated Spaniard."[20]

A distinction should always be made between those Spaniards who merely took an interest in practical science or economics and those who worked for free inquiry or social reform. The two activities are not, of course, mutually exclusive or unrelated, but in all chronological periods, including the eighteenth century, some individuals have devoted themselves to one rather than the other. In Spain, particular attention should be given to those stalwart minds who rebelled against the system which forced them to "live in the ignorance of the truths most important to the human race." These are the words of a professor at the University of Salamanca during the eighteenth century, Dr. Ramón de Salas, in the preface to a pioneer work he circulated in secret and published after the Napoleonic invasion, *Lecciones de derecho público constitucional para las escuelas de España*. The greatest contribution of the Spanish Enlightenment may well have been the independent thought of indi-

---

[19] *Gaceta de Buenos Aires*, September 9, 1815, quoted by A. O. Aldridge in "Las ideas en la América del Sur sobre la ilustración española," *Revista Iberoamericana*, XXXIV (1968), 283–97.

[20] See the review by Pierre Van Bever in *Revue Internationale de Philosophie*, XI (1957), 469–71.

viduals rather than the economic reforms of government decrees and the adjustments of institutions, although scholars have been primarily concerned with the latter. Feijoo was one of the most original minds of the eighteenth century as well as one of the most paradoxical, an unusual combination of the progressive and the naïve. Important aspects of his work still await systematic study by historians of ideas. He was not the representative of official Spain, but neither was Voltaire the spokesman for received opinions in France. Feijoo was, moreover, a highly independent thinker, within, of course, the limits of his theology. He was an originator, not merely a transmitter of English or French ideas.

In Latin America the authorities could not police public opinion with the effectiveness they exercised on the Peninsula, either because of the physical vastness of the territory involved or because of the lesser degree of conformism in the people themselves. For this reason sporadic demands for intellectual freedom began to crop up throughout Latin America late in the eighteenth century, leading to the struggle for political liberation in the nineteenth. Men such as Camilo Henríquez, Rocafuerte, and San Martín were heroes of the Enlightenment as well as political leaders.

#### POLITICS AND THE ENLIGHTENMENT

This consideration gives rise to the question of the relationship of the wars of independence in Latin America. Do these struggles for liberation belong or not to the intellectual movement of Enlightenment? Part of the answer is to be found in comparisons with other geographical areas. Rousseau's *Contrat social* and the Revolutionary Declaration of the Rights of Man are obviously documents belonging both to the Enlightenment and to the French Revolution. The North American Declaration of Independence is certainly a philosophical document as well as a call to political action. Thomas Paine, author of *Common Sense* and *The Rights of Man,* is as much a participant in the American Enlightenment as he is a political propagandist. For all geographical areas, including Latin America, the Enlightenment may not have been, strictly speaking, part of a political movement, but the quest for political reform was a part of the Enlightenment. The relationship between ideology and political action in the independent movement in Latin America is a very complex subject, as Professor Whitaker reveals in his survey of historiography in the present volume. The article by Juan Marichal shows how a ray of Enlightenment thought relaxed the political control of religion in Spain, and Luis Leal describes the role which one outstanding Cuban philosopher played in the movement for independence in his country. It may seem paradoxical to ascribe to the Enlightenment a major role in the independence movement of Spanish America if the climate of opinion which prevailed there was hostile toward it. Official policy was indeed opposed to religious toleration and democratic reforms, but, as we have said, thought control could not be enforced as rigidly in the vast areas of Latin America as in the tightly knit communities of Spain and Portugal.

## INTELLECTUAL CURRENTS: EAST AND WEST

In discussing intellectual influences from Europe upon North America, one cannot escape the conclusion that these were almost entirely limited to British and French. Since this is a volume devoted to Ibero-American relations, the statement perhaps is relevant that Spanish thought had negligible significance in the English colonies, hardly any more than Chinese and less than Swedish. England contributed to its colonies the basic principles of deism and Whig politics, communicating them not only through books and periodical essays but also through liberalized forms of religion and practical government. In addition, England, through Bacon and Locke, developed and fostered empiricism, the emphasis upon experiments, the looking toward fruits and results. Franklin is clear proof of this in his *Experiments and Observations on Electricity*, 1751, and Jefferson in his *Notes on the State of Virginia*, 1787. An earlier and much less familiar example is John Winthrop, subject of one of the essays in this collection. Both Bacon and Locke, by throwing out metaphysics as the central content of philosophy, made way for a new emphasis on man, on human and social areas of knowledge and inquiry. The essence of Enlightenment thought is a blending of reason and experience which had not existed previously. The contribution of France, limited largely to the printed word, was less extensive, but important nevertheless; it can be clearly seen in the thought of Paine, Jefferson, and Madison. French thought made an impression upon North America, moreover, through the travel experiences of such men as Franklin, Jefferson, Paine, and Adams, who lived in Paris during the 1780's and were in almost daily touch with Lafayette, Condorcet, La Rochefoucauld, and others. The latter felt that these Americans brought to France more than they took away, but the era was one of mutual reinforcement and new lines of development.

The flow of ideas was by no means exclusively from east to west. Franklin's electrical experiments had important repercussions in the scientific societies of England and France, second only to the theories of Newton. The example of the American Revolution, if not all of its principles, did not fail to mold the ideas of many leaders in the French Revolution, particularly such moderates as Condorcet, La Rochefoucauld, and Du Pont de Nemours. Spain also felt the impact of New World liberalism in at least one concrete manifestation. The Inquisition in that country was disbanded partly because of a chain of events set off by Benjamin Franklin.[21] In 1788 a young Spanish priest, Antonio José Ruiz de Padrón, shipwrecked at Philadelphia, attended a weekly gathering of clergymen at Franklin's home. One day Franklin argued that religious convictions could not be changed by the use of torture and physical force, and he condemned the Inquisition for using them. Ruiz de Padrón, instead of defending the Inquisition, agreed with Franklin and disassociated that body from the Roman Catholic church, describing it as ex-

21 A. O. Aldridge, *Benjamin Franklin and Nature's God* (Durham, N.C., 1967), pp.245–49.

clusively an arm of the political authority. Returning to Spain and becoming a member of the Cortes, he delivered in January 1813 a *Discurso contra la Inquisición*, which blended with the sentiments of a commission of the Cortes that had already recommended stripping the Inquisition of judicial powers. That body was then condemned and dissolved, but was re-established almost immediately afterwards. Ruiz de Padrón continued his opposition into the decade of the 1820's and was heartily applauded for his stand by an article, "Tolerancia," in the Chilean periodical *El Interrogante y respondente*.[22]

Many of the scholarly works discussed by Professor Whitaker attribute a fundamental importance to Spain itself in estimating the influences on Enlightenment thought in Spanish America, and it is obvious that the major cultural heritage in the colonies was Spanish. Much of this evidence of Enlightenment thought in Spain itself obviously concerns the acceptance of the physics of Newton, the psychology of Locke and Condillac, and the political concepts of Montesquieu and Rousseau. Whether these ideas were disseminated in Latin America through Spanish channels or through books in their original languages, however, they still originated in countries other than Spain. In this sense, as most scholars have recognized, Spain was merely a transmitter.

INTELLECTUAL CURRENTS: NORTH AND SOUTH

One of the most hotly debated subjects in Latin American history is that of the relative influence of France and the United States on the independence movement in that area. In 1940 a Chilean historian made the unequivocal statement that "la influencia directa de la ideología revolucionaria francesa en la gestación de la independencia, en América, fue escasa y, en Chile nula."[23] The foremost propagandist in the Chilean movement for independence, however, Camilo Henríquez, left no doubt as to his opinion that the French *philosophes* were responsible for the

22 June 6, 1823.
23 Francisco A. Encina, *Revista Chilena de Historia y Geografía*, LXXXIX (1940), 31.

"new dawn of enlightenment." French thought, he felt, was the primary factor in its philosophical phase as the Revolution in North America was outstanding in its political phase. In his words, "Voltaire, Rousseau, Montesquieu are the Apostles of reason. They are the ones who have broken the arms of despotism, those who have elevated indestructible barriers against the enemy, those who, destroying compacts which had been dictated to weakness by strength in the midst of the horrors of war, have erased the names of master and slave; those who have restored to the tiara its regrettably lost humanity, and those who have thrown into hell intolerance and fanaticism."[24] Henríquez also recognized an intellectual debt to the United States by paraphrasing Paine's *Common Sense* in the first appeal for the independence of Chile to appear in print, an essay in *La Aurora de Chile*, June 4, 1812, in which every major concept is borrowed from Paine.[25] The question of whether France or the United States held priority in the Enlightenment of Latin America is an interesting one, but it is in a sense frivolous for it can never be answered. Questions of priority seldom can be. It is like asking whether influences from France take precedence over those from England in the Spanish Enlightenment or whether the English were more important than the French. In Latin America it is possible to separate the influence of the United States from the influence of France in the arena of practical politics and diplomacy, but in the arena of ideas the two forces tended to merge.

Professor Harry Bernstein, in expounding the concept of an "inter-American interest," has explored the intricacies of publishing and distributing books sharing a joint market in North and South America, and he has also traced the relations between scientific societies in both hemispheres.[26] Another aspect of "inter-American interest" which is related to the Enlightenment is that of education. Before the independence movement in Latin

24 *El Mercurio de Chile*, March 13, 1823.

25 A. O. Aldridge, "Camilo Henríquez and the Fame of Thomas Paine and Benjamin Franklin in Chile," *Inter-American Review of Bibliography*, XVII (1967).

26 *Making an Inter-American Mind* (Gainesville, Fla., 1961).

America, students in the Spanish and Portuguese colonies who sought a university education could choose from more than a dozen institutions, including the University of San Marcos in Lima and the University of Mexico, or they left the New World altogether to enroll in one of the more prestigious European centers of learning. Early in the nineteenth century, however, some students turned to the United States for their training, particularly in medicine. A professor living in Buenos Aires wrote to Santiago, Chile, in 1822, for example, announcing the great progress that had taken place at the University of Maryland, an institution which, in his opinion, could then be compared with the best universities of Europe. Since a native of Scotland, Dr. Granville Sharp Pattison, had joined the faculty as professor of anatomy, bringing with him a superb anatomical laboratory, the medical school had grown by leaps and bounds, and there were plans to annex a hospital to the University. These details were summarized in the periodical *El Cosmopolita* as a public service for those who would prefer, in seeking advancement in science as well as in ethics and economics, a trip to the country that had produced a Washington, a Franklin, and a Rush, rather than risking a tumultuous and perhaps dangerous residence in Europe.[27]

This example of inter-American interest is by no means intended to suggest that every favorable reference by a Latin American in the early days of independence was an endorsement of the Enlightenment. This would be as much of an error as that of many French authors who assume that every Afrancesado in Spain should automatically be placed in the ranks of liberal thought. To study the Enlightenment is to study ideas, not nationalities. At the same time it is obvious that the movement developed along different lines in different countries, both in Europe and in the Western hemisphere. This collection of essays concentrates on the development in Ibero-America of those great ideas "which characterized the eighteenth century and which will be its glory forever."

[27] October 11, 1822.

# I

## Definition and Intellectual Background

I

# Changing and Unchanging Interpretations of the Enlightenment in Spanish America*

### ARTHUR P. WHITAKER

Revisionism has been a marked feature of the increasing flow of historical writing about the European Enlightenment in recent years. The present paper seeks to determine to what extent the same trend has appeared in studies of the Enlightenment's Spanish American phase and what aspects of European revisionism are particularly pertinent to that phase.

Only works published since 1942 will be considered here. That starting point has been chosen because it was then that a little book of essays entitled *Latin America and the Enlightenment*[1] provided the first comprehensive account of the subject in any language. Also, the present survey omits Brazil, which is a special case. On the other hand, it includes aspects of the Enlightenment in Europe, particularly in Spain, the main channel or filter until 1808 through which the Enlightenment reached

*Grateful acknowledgment is hereby made to the following, who read this paper in draft and gave me the benefit of their criticism and suggestions: Harry Bernstein, Charles Gibson, Mathias Kiemen, Peggy Korn, John Tate Lanning, and Irving A. Leonard.

[1] New York, 1942; 2d ed., Ithaca, N.Y., 1961; both edited by Arthur P. Whitaker. The other contributors were: in 1942, Roland D. Hussey, Harry Bernstein, John Tate Lanning, Arthur Scott Aiton, and Alexander D. Marchant; in 1961, the same, except that Aiton was replaced by Charles C. Griffin.

Spanish America, but also in France and England, the center of the movement, from which it passed directly to Spanish America on a lesser but still considerable scale. In order to keep the task within reasonable bounds, only works regarded as significant for the interpretation of this transatlantic phenomenon are discussed here. No effort has been made to give a systematic account of the rise and spread of the Enlightenment, or even to cover the literature regarding the Spanish American movement's precursors such as Carlos de Sigüenza y Góngora of Mexico and Pedro de Peralta Barnuevo of Peru, to which Irving A. Leonard and others have made notable contributions, both before and since 1942.

If the present undertaking still seems rash, it is at least rational. The Enlightenment, though varying from one country to another, was marked by the same basic features on both sides of the Atlantic and underwent greater changes in crossing the Pyrenees into Spain than in crossing the Atlantic, mainly from Spain, to Spanish America. Yet historians of the European Enlightenment continue to slight Latin America when (as is usually the case) they do not omit it altogether. Conversely, Latin Americanists generally show too little familiarity with recent reinterpretations of the European Enlightenment, which have brought out more clearly than ever before the changes that took place in it from time to time and its rich diversity at all times. It is hoped that the present paper may help to bring historical writing about the two sides of the Atlantic closer together.

We begin with Spanish America since that is our main concern. This first section defines the problem, beginning with the old controversy over the Enlightenment's relation to the independence movement. The second and third sections examine works that deal, respectively, with specialized works on particular topics or individual countries, and with Spanish America in general. The fourth section discusses revisionist works on the Enlightenment in Europe that are deemed relevant to the Spanish American phase.

### DEFINITIONS: RELATION TO INDEPENDENCE

How much and how little interpretations of the Enlightenment in Spanish America have changed since 1942 is indicated by a succinct but suggestive passage in Charles Gibson's "Review of Two Decades" of Spanish American historiography, published in 1966. Regarding the late colonial period Gibson wrote:

> Here the definition of the Latin American Enlightenment and its relation to the European Enlightenment stand out as the principal problem that historians have sought to solve. The result has been a general rejection of the earlier belief in an immediate causal connection between the Enlightenment and independence, and a separation of the Enlightenment in Latin America as a distinct subject. The movement's intellectual, scientific, and economic features are now stressed for the mid- and late-18th century, and its political aspects are relegated to a late and rather contrived role. While these views undoubtedly represent gains in the accuracy of our understanding of the Enlightenment, they leave a certain vacuum at the point of transition to the independence movement. . . . Thus as frequently happens, an advance in information serves only partially to resolve a problem.[2]

One can agree heartily with much of the foregoing, and examples in support of some of its generalizations will appear below. But two questions may be raised about it: first, whether the vacuum in question still exists; and second, whether, as seems to be implied, the overarching problem in the study of the Latin American Enlightenment is its relation to the origins of the independence movement.

Let us examine the latter question first since it involves a major problem of interpretation. It has its counterpart in the

---

2 *Handbook of Latin American Studies*, No.28 (Gainesville, Fla., 1966), 61–62. Gibson's own conclusion, as stated in his *Spain in America* (New York, 1966), is that the Spanish Americans' "response to the Enlightenment involved a gradual intellectual reorientation rather than a sudden inclination toward subversion and liberty" (p.176).

interpretation of the European Enlightenment as a prelude to the French Revolution. Though no longer widely held as regards Europe, this view still characterizes much of the writing, particularly in English, about Spanish America. It has been criticized by some, including the present writer,[3] on the ground that it is a *post hoc* fallacy resulting in the teleological subordination of the Enlightenment to the political revolutions in Europe and America and that it produces a narrow, static, and misleading picture of that rich and ever-changing cultural movement. No one would deny that the relation of the Enlightenment to the independence movement is both a proper and an important subject of inquiry, and in fact it will be discussed below in these pages. What is objected to is that the excessive attention often paid to it leads to the neglect or distortion of the Spanish American Enlightenment's other and more characteristic aspects, which, though mainly cultural, were also economic and, in a limited and special way until after 1800, social and political. In its extreme form such treatment makes it seem that in Spanish America the independence movement was the one far-off divine event to which the whole Enlightenment moved.

Though in a much more moderate form, this treatment is well illustrated by two British historians, Robin Humphreys and John Lynch, in their introduction to a volume of readings, *The Origins of the Latin-American Revolutions, 1808–1826*.[4] Their views are well worth noting, for Humphreys has long been a leading authority on the history of Latin America in this period and the younger Lynch is on his way to becoming one. They devote five pages of their twenty-five-page introduction to answering the question, "To what extent did the Enlightenment

3 Particularly in "The Intellectual History of Eighteenth-Century Spanish America," *Relazzioni del X Congresso Internazionale di Scienzi Storiche*, I (Rome, 1955), 187–206, also published with an additional note in *Revista de Historia de América*, No.40 (Mexico City, 1955), 553–73, and in Howard F. Cline (ed.), *Latin American History: Essays on Its Study and Teaching* (Austin, 1967), II, 723–32; and "The Enlightenment in Spanish America," *Proceedings* of the American Philosophical Society, CII, No.6 (Philadelphia, 1958), 555–59.

4 New York, 1965.

penetrate to Spanish America and what was its effect?"[5] This is their own statement of the question, and it clearly goes beyond their immediate problem, the origins of the independence movement, to embrace the Enlightenment as a whole.

Yet the independence theme dominates their discussion of the question. It could hardly be otherwise, given their conception of the Enlightenment, which could be summed up as "no revolution, no Enlightenment." They contrast the Enlightenment in the Hispanic world with that north of the Pyrenees in ways that are questionable at least. They say, for example, that Spain "drained the Enlightenment of its ideology and reduced it to a program of empirical reform within the existing political and social order" and that its creole exponents similarly demanded reforms in the colonial regime but did not question the regime itself.[6] However true these propositions may be, they do not differentiate the Enlightenment in either Spanish America or Spain from that in Europe north of the Pyrenees, where they were equally true of many of its proponents, as will be shown below.

Again, Humphreys and Lynch apparently conceive of the revolutionary influence of the Enlightenment in the narrowly restricted sense of deliberate subversion of the existing order. Thus, although they stress the conservative, nonrevolutionary character of the movement in Spanish America, in almost the same breath they say that it was "characterized by a preference for reason and experiment rather than for authority and tradition."[7] The fact is that this preference for reason and experiment—and the spirit of innovation nourished by it—was the most revolutionary thing about the Enlightenment. It was far more revolutionary than the movement for political independence and came closer than anything else to providing a common theme for the multifaceted Enlightenment in Europe and Spanish America and in relations between the two areas.

[5] *Ibid.*, pp.10–15.
[6] *Ibid.*, p.10.
[7] *Ibid.*

In a negative way a similar view of the Enlightenment in Spanish America is represented by omission in the two-volume collection of readings, *Latin American Civilization*, edited by Lewis Hanke.[8] Though the book covers both the colonial and national periods and is described in Hanke's introduction as illustrating the social, economic, and cultural history of Latin America, not one of its scores of readings contains more than brief and fragmentary references to the Enlightenment. The most appropriate place for a discussion of it would have been the section on "Climax and Crisis in the Eighteenth Century,"[9] but of the five readings in this section three deal respectively with the army in New Spain, Tupac Amaru's revolt in Peru, and the Huancavelica mercury mine, while a fourth is an excerpt from Humboldt's "Political Essay on New Spain," and the last and most comprehensive, "The Fall of the Spanish American Empire," has nothing to say of the Enlightenment beyond such casual references as those to "the material and intellectual advance during the so-called century of enlightenment" and the efforts of "enlightened despotism . . . to rationalize and simplify the machinery of imperial administration."[10] In the absence of any explanation by the editor of his virtual omission of the Enlightenment, one seems justified in inferring that it reflects adherence to the older interpretation of that movement as an essentially political-revolutionary phenomenon and as of no particular consequence in the cultural, economic, or social history of Latin America.

A very different and much more accurate appraisal of the Latin American Enlightenment was given more than a decade ago by John Tate Lanning in his book on its manifestations in the University of San Carlos de Guatemala. Developing a thesis briefly stated in one of his earlier works,[11] and speaking of the Spanish American dominions at large, Lanning uses the term "intellectual revolution" to describe the Enlightenment's im-

8 Boston, 1967, 2 vols.
9 *Ibid.*, I, 454–97.
10 *Ibid.*, pp.485, 489.
11 *Academic Culture in the Spanish Colonies* (Miami, Fla., 1940).

pact on the creoles. What is more, he makes the perceptive observation that this intellectual revolution "depended very little upon the exuberant radicalism of the *philosophes.*" "The colonial professor," he says, "made thoroughgoing moderns of at least 95 per cent of his students without dependence upon prohibited books . . . [and] the whole creole element revised its ideas at home, openly and above board."[12]

As even this brief reference to it should suggest, Lanning's book has the important merits of differentiating both among various aspects of the Enlightenment in Europe and also between one period and another in the history of its impact on Latin America. These merits, all too uncommon, combine with an almost uniquely detailed and penetrating analysis of the particular case of the University of San Carlos to make Lanning's book one of the outstanding reinterpretations of the Spanish American Enlightenment since 1942.

Profiting by the studies of Lanning and many other scholars, Charles Griffin produced in 1961 a well-balanced, persuasive essay on the relation of the Enlightenment to the independence movement.[13] His achievement is all the more noteworthy because, as he explains, he was "not concerned primarily with the evaluation of the Enlightenment as a 'cause' of the later [i.e., post 1808] revolutionary movement," but rather with showing "the continued presence of various characteristics of the Enlightenment in the latter era."[14] Nevertheless, a substantial portion of his well-documented account deals with the pre-revolutionary era and the evidence assembled by him shows that, as regards politically subversive ideas, such as popular sovereignty, democracy, and anti-clericalism, the Latin American response to the Enlightenment was limited, spotty, and on the whole weak if

[12] *The Eighteenth-Century Enlightenment in the University of San Carlos de Guatemala* (Ithaca, N.Y., 1958), p.115. As regards Mexico, this interpretation was accepted in one of the best recent monographs on the period, Hugh M. Hamill, Jr., *The Hidalgo Revolt: Prelude to Independence* (Gainesville, Fla., 1966), pp.6–8.

[13] "The Enlightenment and Latin American Independence," *Latin America and the Enlightenment* (2d ed.), pp.119–43.

[14] *Ibid.*, pp.140–41.

not hostile. It also shows that the response was most favorable to other aspects of it, such as the liberation of philosophy from Scholasticism and the promotion of science and useful knowledge.[15] On the other hand, Griffin demonstrates the powerful impact of these same political ideas once the independence movement had begun.

One might conclude, then, that in its political aspects it was the independence movement that promoted the Enlightenment in Latin America, rather than the reverse. But this would be a tentative conclusion. Like so many other questions about the Enlightenment, it still needs further study.

The promotion of useful knowledge, which was an important aspect of the Enlightenment in both Europe and America, is admirably illustrated by Robert J. Shafer's *The Economic Societies in the Spanish World (1763–1821)*.[16] These societies were mostly of the *amigos del país* ("friends of the country") type. The first and most important of them was the Sociedad Vascongada de Amigos del País, established in 1764 at Vergara, Spain, by the Basque Society, from which it took its name. By the 1790's it had many members in the overseas dominions as well as in Spain. One of the many merits of this book is that it embraces both Spain and Spanish America, as is seldom done in studies of the Enlightenment that probe beneath the surface. It might perhaps have brought out more clearly the ultimately political significance of the initially economic and cultural *amigos del país* theme that ran through this movement—its significance in the growth of particularism through devotion to one's *país*, which was a flexible term but could be, and often was, disjunctive. To be sure, the members of these societies were, as Shafer points out, generally well-heeled and conservative, but people of that kind have often become patriots and even nationalists.

15 *Ibid.*, pp.120–30.
16 Syracuse, N.Y., 1958. For an earlier study of the promotion of useful knowledge in a particular case, see Clement Motten, *Mexican Silver and the Enlightenment* (Philadelphia, 1949).

### SPECIALIZED STUDIES

Many specialized studies still treat the Enlightenment as a prelude to Spanish American independence, but several have made notable advances in refining the relationship between the two. A very few have reversed it and made independence a reaction against the Enlightenment. The works in these various categories range in scale from Ricardo Donoso's short but substantial essay, "Antecedentes de la emancipación hispano americana,"[17] to the two sturdy volumes by Rafael Gómez Hoyos on *La revolución granadina: ideario de una generación y de una época.*[18]

The latter study of New Granada (the present Colombia) and a somewhat earlier one by Leopoldo Uprimny reverse the political role usually assigned the Enlightenment.[19] According to Uprimny, who stated the thesis more uncompromisingly, the Enlightenment led to independence, not by the converts it made, but by the hostile reaction it provoked among New Granada's conservative élite. To them, separation from Spain was a means of protecting their country against the contagion of the Enlightenment and the threefold revolution—political, religious, and moral—that it had already incited in the mother country. Few subsequent writers have accepted this thesis, but there has been increasing support for his less novel insistence on the key role of Spain as the main transmitter of the Enlightenment to Spanish America.

The nature of Spain's role is still being debated. Perhaps the most controversial proposition about it is to the effect that the radical idea of popular sovereignty was derived by Spanish Americans from Spanish medieval law and practice and from

[17] *Cuadernos Americanos*, CXIV, No.1 (1961), 179–218. See also his *Las ideas políticas en Chile*, 2d ed. (Santiago, 1967), pp.15–24.

[18] Bogotá, 1962.

[19] "Capitalismo calvinista o romanticismo semi-escolástico de los próceres de la independencia colombiana?" *Universitas*, No.6 (Bogotá, 1954), 87–148. Gómez Hoyos, *La revolución granadina*, I, 38, gives Uprimny's thesis general endorsement though he finds his style too polemical.

later writers, notably the seventeenth-century Spanish Jesuit Francisco Suárez. In one form or another this thesis has been sustained by some of the ablest Spanish American historians, including the Argentine Ricardo Levene, the Mexican Silvio Zavala, the Chilean Jaime Eyzaguirre, and the already mentioned Gómez Hoyos, and by a distinguished Spanish scholar, Manuel Giménez Fernández.[20]

As regards the idea of popular sovereignty and Suárez, the thesis has been combated by no less able Spanish American historians, including two Argentines, Tulio Halperín Donghi and Ricardo Zorraquín Becú,[21] and by Griffin and Humphreys-Lynch in the works already mentioned. The main contention of the critics is that the linkage with Suárez and earlier Spanish sources has not been demonstrated. In one of the most thorough and persuasive of these critiques, which deals with Argentina, Halperín Donghi presses the argument still further. There, he maintains, the idea of revolution grew out of local circumstances, which he describes at length; this idea had no precedent in the political tradition of Spain, nor in the dominant tradition of the rest of Europe; and consequently the search for "complicated ideological genealogies" of the Argentine revolutionary idea is a waste of time.[22] The critics' reasoning is so strong that, as regards Spanish America at large, the case for the Suárez thesis must be regarded as not proven, for the present at least.

But it should not be dismissed for all parts of Spanish America without further investigation. Regional probings are still needed and it is not impossible that they might bolster up the con-

[20] Ricardo Levene, *Historia de las ideas sociales argentinas* (Buenos Aires, 1947); Silvio Zavala, *La filosofía política en la conquista de América* (Mexico City, 1947); Jaime Eyzaguirre, *Ideario y ruta de la emancipación chilena* (Santiago, 1957) and *Historia de Chile: génesis de la nacionalidad* (Santiago, 1965); Manuel Giménez Fernández, "Las doctrinas populistas en la independencia de Hispano-América," *Anuario de Estudios Americanos,* XIV (Seville, 1956).

[21] Tulio Halperín Donghi, *Tradición política española e ideología revolucionaria de Mayo* (Buenos Aires, 1961); Ricardo Zorraquín Becú, "Algo más sobre la doctrina jurídica de la Revolución de Mayo," *Revista del Instituto de Historia del Derecho* (Buenos Aires, 1962), pp.13, 138–71.

[22] Halperín Donghi, *Tradición,* p.211.

clusions reached by the Uruguayan Edmundo M. Narancio in his brief but suggestive monograph on the Plata area.[23] Attempting a synthesis of old and new interpretations, Narancio found that the dominant political ideas in that area at the beginning of the nineteenth century had three main sources: first, traditional Spanish thought, including Suárez; second, Pufendorf's *De jure naturae et gentium*, which reached the Plata area during the Enlightenment, very probably through a French translation of 1759 and the *Encyclopédie*; and third and last, about 1810, Rousseau.

Subsequently, positions similar to Narancio's, though not identical either with his or with each other's, were taken by Jaime Eyzaguirre, his fellow Chilean, Ricardo Krebs Wilckens, and a British historian, Simon Collier. According to Eyzaguirre,[24] the subversive ideas of the French *philosophes* were much less effective in late eighteenth-century Chile than in Mexico and indeed were generally unknown to the Chileans of that period unless they had traveled outside the country, as the only proven possessor of the *Encyclopédie* in Chile had done. Among the writers who were influential in Chile, Eyzaguirre mentions Suárez, but he stresses much more strongly the "critical and reforming spirit" of several eighteenth-century Spanish writers, whose ideas were propagated in Chile without the least obstacle. Those most widely read there, he continues, were Benito Feijoo and Pedro Rodríguez, Conde de Campomanes, followed by Gaspar Melchor de Jovellanos. These Spanish reformers, he concludes, made a deep impression on the Chilean creoles and stimulated among them criticism of the existing order and resentment against it, though

---

[23] *Las ideas políticas en el Río de la Plata a comienzos del siglo XIX* (Montevideo, 1955).

[24] Eyzaguirre, *Ideario y ruta de la emancipación chilena*, pp.72–83. Walter Hanisch Espíndola, S.J., *En torno a la filosofía en Chile (1754–1810)* (Santiago, 1963), pp.109–15, describes Chilean thought in the latter part of this period as marked by a discriminating *modernidad* which was more traditionalist than modern and notes that the library of one of its chief exponents, José Antonio Rojas, who was reputedly a Voltairean, contained none of Voltaire's works. He admits that such evidence is not conclusive, and his book illustrates the paucity of evidence that is a striking feature of many works in this field.

at first (i.e., until about 1810) they were not inclined toward separatism and revolution.

Krebs Wilckens pursued this line of argument much further in his study of the historical, political, and economic thought of Campomanes, with special reference to Chile.[25] He finds that the three principal cultural bases of Campomanes' ideas were the Spanish cultural tradition, French ecclesiastical culture of the seventeenth century (meaning mainly Gallicanism), and "the rationalist and secularized Enlightenment of the eighteenth century."[26] The last-named element was the weakest of the three, for Campomanes did not accept the extreme ideas of the Enlightenment in matters of religion. Instead, he held that dogmatic faith and critical reason should be kept rigorously apart and that science should be limited to natural phenomena.[27] Nevertheless, in other respects Campomanes' thought, as Krebs describes it, was strongly marked by the spirit of the Enlightenment, notably as regards its stress on utilitarianism, the cult of happiness, and philanthropy.[28] In addition, despite his conservatism in matters of religion, there was a definite secular bias in his writings, in the sense that, mainly under the influence of the French physiocrats, he conceived of the state as a mundane institution whose duty it was to increase its power and wealth and promote the happiness of its subjects.[29]

For our purposes, Krebs's most important conclusion is that Campomanes represented the "Christian Enlightenment" that developed not only in Spain but also in all the Catholic countries of Europe,[30] and, we might add, in Spanish America at large. To

---

25 *El pensamiento histórico, político y económico del conde de Campomanes* (Santiago, 1960).

26 *Ibid.*, p.62.

27 *Ibid.*, p.63.

28 *Ibid.*, p.277.

29 *Ibid.*, p.120.

30 *Ibid.*, p.277. As a particularly good account of the *ilustración cristiana* Krebs here cites, in note 1, Mario Góngora, "Estudios sobre el Galicanismo y la 'Ilustración Católica' en América española," *Revista Chilena de Historia y Geografía*, No.125 (1957).

deny that this Christian Enlightenment was a part of the "true" Enlightenment would be to identify the latter wholly with the extremism of its later phases, mainly in France, to the exclusion of most of Europe and America.

While building on the work of his predecessors and dealing mainly with the quarter-century after 1808, Simon Collier clarified two important developments in Chile in the generation before 1808, the creoles' "rising patriotism" and the emergence of a "small group of economist-precursors" of independence.[31] Both developments were related to the Enlightenment; both were confined to the creole leaders; and neither was consciously aimed at independence. Collier describes the rise of patriotism in a way that suggests comparison with the similar findings of Bernabé Navarro in Mexico, to be discussed below. Among the ingredients of the Chilean creoles' patriotism was identification with their country's "noble savages," the Araucanian Indians, whose heroic resistance to the Spanish conquerors was described in Ercilla's still popular epic poem of the sixteenth century. Another ingredient was a growing alienation from Spain as a result of the latter's misgovernment and neglect of Chile. In the latter connection, creole leader Juan Egaña, who obviously knew more about Chile than about Russia, complained in 1804 that "Russia had taken full advantage of the Enlightenment, while Chile [meaning Spain in Chile] had failed to do so." As for the "economist-precursors," Collier shows that they were well acquainted with "enlightened Spanish thought on economic matters" and urged various economic and social reforms. Yet he makes it clear that before 1808 their "reformist zeal" was not deliberately revolutionary; their only political proposal was that the Spanish monarchy should take a more active hand in Chilean affairs.

Conclusions similar to those of Krebs and Collier had already been reached by historians in Mexico, which since 1940 has led Latin America in the study of the Enlightenment. Though Mex-

[31] *Ideas and Politics of Chilean Independence, 1808–1833* (Cambridge, 1967), pp.27–29, 40–41.

ican interest in the movement already existed, it was quickened thereafter by the stimulus that two émigrés from Republican Spain, José Gaos and José Miranda, gave to the history of ideas through seminars at the Colegio de México and the National Autonomous University of Mexico. Of the many excellent works produced by this group, only two can be discussed here: one by Bernabé Navarro, the other by Miranda himself.

Navarro's conception of the Enlightenment is set forth in a collection of his essays written between 1947 and 1963,[32] in which he acknowledges his special indebtedness to José Gaos, Samuel Ramos, and Gabriel Méndez Plancarte. In these essays Navarro performs the unusual feat of meticulously analyzing the Enlightenment in Mexico both as an eighteenth-century cultural development and also as a prime factor in the subsequent movement for independence; most writers concentrate on one of these aspects and slight the other.

Defining the Enlightenment narrowly as "philosophical work relating to the *Encyclopédie*," he classifies it as a variant or species of the genus *modernidad* (modernity), which had its sources in the philosophers and scientists of the seventeenth century, such as Bacon, Galileo, Descartes, Newton, and Leibniz.[33] In the Hispanic countries, including Mexico, still another variant appeared in the form of "eclecticism on a Christian base"—a phenomenon that Krebs and others have called "Christian Enlightenment." Its emergence is explained on the ground that modernity and the Enlightenment gained acceptance in the Hispanic world only insofar as strongly rooted religious and philosophical traditions permitted. This was the case in Mexico, where the product was "modernity with a touch of Enlightenment."[34]

Navarro has given the Jesuits great credit—too much credit, it has been objected—not only for introducing this modern current of thought into Mexico but also for "laying the ideological

---

32 *Cultura mexicana moderna en el siglo XVIII* (Mexico City, 1964).
33 *Ibid.*, p.171.
34 *Ibid.*, pp.172–73.

foundations for our [Mexican] emancipation."[35] In saying this, he is not seeking to perpetuate the exploded myth that the Jesuits undertook to destroy the Spanish empire after their expulsion from it in 1767. Instead, he argues that the movement for autonomy among any subject people must begin, not in the political and economic fields, where the dominant power is strongest, but in the minds and spirit of the people, which are far more difficult for government to control; and once the first stage has been accomplished, "the force of ideas naturally leads on to complete autonomy."[36] In Mexico, he holds, the Jesuits were principal agents in this process of emancipation.

Perhaps their greatest contribution to the process was made after their expulsion, through the persistence of their doctrines and the action of their disciples. Among their doctrines Navarro includes the affirmation of liberty, of a Mexicanism embracing mestizos and Indians as well as creoles, and of popular sovereignty. Chief among the Jesuits' disciples were two whom Navarro discusses at length: José Antonio Alzate, who represented "the culmination of the enlightened spirit" and was foremost in forging "the new *patria*," and Miguel Hidalgo y Costilla, who started the independence movement in 1810.[37] Navarro certainly left no vacuum between the Enlightenment and the independence movement, at least as regards Mexico, the most populous of Spain's dominions at that time. Whether his findings could be matched in the other dominions, he does not undertake to determine, and, like most Spanish American historians, he makes few references to the works of historians in other countries.

José Miranda gives a broader definition of the Enlightenment

---

[35] *Ibid.*, p.188. For a different view, see Rafael Moreno, "La filosofía moderna en la Nueva España," in Miguel León-Portilla *et al.*, *Estudios de historia de la filosofía en México* (Mexico City, 1963), p.184, note 41, where he objects, among other things, to "la importancia concedida a los Jesuitas frente a las otras órdenes, el clero diocesano y la Universidad." Among the other orders, the importance of the Franciscans has been stressed by several historians.

[36] Navarro, *Cultura mexicana*, p.196.

[37] *Ibid.*, pp.192–200. There is also a separate chapter each on Alzate and Hidalgo.

than Navarro's in *Humboldt y México*,[38] published a few years before his death. Also, as regards Mexico his definition is less political. Instead of identifying the Enlightenment with encyclopedism, Miranda says that it was not a system of thought nor the work of a single philosophical school. Rather, it expressed a natural or human conception of the world that was given practical application in social and political affairs and at the same time was based on a mystical, veritably religious faith in rationalism.[39]

In describing its Mexican phase he agrees with Navarro that this began about 1750 and was mainly the work of the Jesuits in its first stage, which lasted a quarter of a century and was characterized by the emergence of "Christian philosophical modernism."[40] But, he continues, in its second stage, 1775–1800, during which the Enlightenment spread rapidly in Mexico, its main focus shifted from philosophy to science. In the latter connection Miranda notes that in 1792 Mexico accounted for one-eighth of the total membership of Spain's leading "economic society," the Basque Society discussed above. In Mexico City alone it had almost as many members as the largest center in Spain, Madrid (132 and 137 respectively), and in addition there were respectable numbers of them in other Mexican centers, such as Puebla (25) and Chihuahua (24).[41] And a considerable part of Miranda's study is devoted to justifying Humboldt's oft-quoted tribute to Mexico's scientific institutions as he found them on his visit there in 1803–1804.

Another Mexican historian, Luis Villoro, has brought out a different aspect of the problem by showing that by the beginning of the nineteenth century there had developed in Mexico an "enlightened middle class," or intelligentsia, composed mainly of members of the liberal professions and the middle and lower

---

38 Mexico City, 1962. The first one-fourth of this book recapitulates and refines the ideas that *maestro* Miranda and his students had developed about the Enlightenment in the preceding twenty years.

39 *Ibid.*, p.12.

40 *Ibid.*, pp.22, 31.

41 *Ibid.*, pp.30–31.

clergy.[42] The principal sources of their ideas were, in point of time, first, the natural law rationalism of Grotius and Pufendorf; second, the doctrines of the "enlightened Jesuits" who followed Suárez in the affirmation of popular sovereignty; and, finally, a related group of new influences such as the economic societies of "friends of the country," writers like Jovellanos who tried to reconcile modernity with Spanish tradition, and, last of all, the ideas of the French *philosophes*.[43]

Studies of other parts of Spanish America reinforce one important point which is suggested by a comparison of the cases of Mexico and Chile as described above, and which may merit more attention from historians than it has so far received. This is the fact that the Enlightenment developed in a different way in each of the principal cultural centers of the area. The differentiating factors could be one or more of several, including the time of the Enlightenment's arrival, the environment in which it developed, its sources and agents or carriers, the aspects of it that were stressed, and the response it met with.

A few illustrations must suffice. A historian of philosophical ideas in Argentina tells us that Scholasticism remained dominant there until the end of the eighteenth century and that the Enlightenment, in the form of a combination of French encyclopedism with English ideas, arrived late, just in time to become "the philosophy of emancipation."[44] In the present Uruguay, on

---

[42] "Las corrientes ideológicas en la época de la Independencia," in León-Portilla *et al., Estudios,* pp.203–42, summarizing and updating Villoro's book of 1953, *La revolución de independencia.*

[43] Villoro, pp.205–206.

[44] Coriolano Alberini, *Problema de la historia de las ideas filosóficas en la Argentina* (La Plata, 1966), pp.81, 124. José Luis Romero, *A History of Argentine Political Thought,* trans. Thomas F. McGann (Stanford, 1968), discusses the Enlightenment in the Plata area before 1808 in one short paragraph (pp.42–43), in which he says that its liberal influences bore fruit in creating "an atmosphere of rebelliousness among small but determined groups of creoles." This is preceded by four pages on the Enlightenment in Europe and is followed by six pages (pp.67–75) in which he develops the thesis that the "Revolution of May [1810]" in Buenos Aires was the work of men "educated in the principles of the Enlightenment" (p.69).

the other hand, it seems that "modern rationalism" began to operate earlier, about the same time as in Mexico but through the agency of the Franciscans rather than, as in Mexico, the Jesuits, who played a brief and very minor role in Uruguay.[45] Our authority, Arturo Ardao, also holds that this religious rationalism was inseparable from the political revolution to which it led and that the "solidarity" of these two phenomena is best illustrated by freemasonry.[46] The former proposition is quite familiar, the latter much less so.

Another case, that of the celebrated Andrés Bello, brings out another factor in the Enlightenment, just mentioned with regard to Argentina but, as regards the period before 1808, seldom discussed by Spanish American historians, namely, the influence of English thought upon it. Until 1810 Bello lived in his native Venezuela and at an early age he was weaned away from Scholasticism by the writings of Bacon, Locke, and Hume as well as Condillac; his long residence in England after that date only confirmed his devotion to British empiricism.[47]

How the "new philosophy" had gained a foothold in the University of Caracas in the late eighteenth century has been shown in a well-documented study by a promising young historian, Ildefonso Leal.[48] In the prologue to it Eduardo Arcila Farías makes several noteworthy points of broader scope: that the Spanish American universities were the principal centers of reception of the Enlightenment's "revolutionary ideas"; that the ground these universities provided for the new ideas, though good, was "less fertile" than has been generally believed; and that these ideas came by way of Spain, both in the writings of the best Spanish authors from Feijoo to Jovellanos, and more particularly in royal ordinances and the reports of "enlightened" Spanish offi-

45 Arturo Ardao, *Racionalismo y liberalismo en el Uruguay* (Montevideo, 1962), pp.105, 108–109.

46 *Ibid.*, p.23.

47 Sergio Fernández Larrain (ed.), *Cartas a Bello en Londres* (Santiago, 1968), pp.xxii–xxiii, xxxiii.

48 *Historia de la Universidad de Caracas (1721–1827)* (Caracas, 1963), pp.135–59.

cials. "Our Enlightenment," he concludes, "was fundamentally Hispanic."[49]

SPANISH AMERICA IN GENERAL

The works considered so far have been specialized studies dealing in most cases with individual Spanish American countries. The next three are samples of generalizations about the area at large. Each is significant in its own way, but all three tend to free the Enlightenment there from its long servitude to the nineteenth-century movement for independence.

First we have the thirty-page introduction by the Mexican Raúl Cardiel Reyes to his anthology, *Los filósofos modernos en la independencia latinoamericana.*[50] According to him, the revolutionary principles of the Enlightenment were not a cause of the movement for independence, but only a justification for it in its culminating stage, after purely indigenous, domestic factors had built it up among the people at large during what Reyes joins Mariano Picón Salas in calling the *época de revueltas* of the latter half of the eighteenth century. During most of this period, Reyes insists, the Enlightenment (which he generally refers to as "modern philosophy") was an eclectic movement confined to the upper classes and aimed at promoting the sciences, the useful arts, and economic activities such as agriculture and commerce.

A similar conclusion was reached by a different route in the Argentine Enrique de Gandía's book, *La independencia americana, ensayo.*[51] His starting point was a proposition adopted by the first Congreso Hispanoamericano de Historia, held in Madrid from October 1 to 12, 1949, in which he took part. This proposition (called a "general conclusion") was to the effect that the Spanish American independence movement was not an isolated episode whose explanation should be sought in the sudden opera-

49 *Ibid.,* p.11.
50 Mexico City, 1964.
51 Buenos Aires, 1961.

tion of one or more causes, but a total spiritual process, linked with universal history, whose understanding requires a profound knowledge of pre-revolutionary history.[52]

After brooding about this proposition for a dozen years, Gandía made a slashing attack on it in the book in question and then went on to set the record straight. His argument may be summarized as follows: The Spanish American independence movement was not a revolution but an essentially political civil war provoked by Napoleon's intrusion into Spain in 1808. The movement was not the product of the political ideas either of the eighteenth-century Enlightenment or of the French Revolution, the latter of which was generally abhorred in Spanish America; and in fact the two sets of ideas differed greatly from each other, though historians have too often confused them. Even when Napoleon's intervention in Spain led to an interregnum in Spanish America and a conflict among its leaders over filling the power vacuum, those who advocated local autonomy were at first guided mainly by traditional Spanish thought and the doctrines of St. Thomas Aquinas. (Here Gandía takes his stand with the Chilean historian Eyzaguirre, though he rejects the thesis of the influence of Suárez as propounded by Giménez Fernández and others.) But once innovation had been started, it could not be stopped. Soon after the establishment of autonomy in 1810, the movement for complete independence took shape rapidly; and it was at this point that non-Spanish ideas, including those of the encyclopedists and Rousseau, at last came into play.[53]

Third and last in this group is a section of French historian Pierre Chaunu's book, *L'Amérique et les Amériques*.[54] First well known for his multivolume history of *Séville et l'Atlantique*, Chaunu in this later work skillfully sums up and interprets in a single volume the history of all the Americas through five centuries.

In the section of it that concerns us, Chaunu labels "a stereo-

[52] *Ibid.*, p.9.
[53] *Ibid.*, pp.9–26.
[54] Paris, 1964.

type" the interpretation of the Enlightenment (*les lumières*) as a prelude to the Spanish American independence movement.[55] While the subtitle of this section calls it "a useful stereotype," the discussion that follows makes it clear that he regards its usefulness as extremely limited. To be sure, he says, the participation of Latin America in the Enlightenment is not open to question, but one may doubt that it was wide or deep among the 2 to 3 per cent of the population that made up the creole élite, particularly in view of the fact that "the scholastic edifice of the Spanish American *colegios* remained still intact a century later."[56] Here he is obviously in agreement with Gandía, though without citing him, as he is also in saying that far too much has been made of foreign influences in general on this independence movement, that the essential factor was Napoleon's invasion of Spain in 1808, and that the Spanish American war of independence was essentially a civil war.

Chaunu's own explanation of the independence movement,[57] though fresh and persuasive, need not detain us here. We should note, however, that he explains it mainly in social and economic terms, without further reference to the Enlightenment, the elimination of which as a significant factor in the gestation of that movement he thus completes. Though he makes out a strong case, he may have overstated it, for he does not take into account the profoundly unsettling effect of the Enlightenment in Spanish America, which Bernabé Navarro and other recent writers have demonstrated and which Lanning goes so far as to call an "intellectual revolution." Moreover, while Chaunu is right in saying that the Latin American Enlightenment was confined to a very small élite minority, the same was also true, though in lesser degree, of the Enlightenment in Europe, and no one has proved that the difference in degree was sufficient to constitute a difference in kind.

For that matter, no one has yet made a comprehensive, detailed

55 *Ibid.*, p.192.
56 *Ibid.*, p.193.
57 *Ibid.*, pp.195–211.

comparison of the Spanish American with the European Enlightenment. Until that has been done, the distinctive character of the former cannot be determined, for, despite its local variations, it was only a branch of the European movement. Therefore, in studying the Enlightenment's Spanish American aspects we must take the European prototype as their point of reference. If they departed from the norm, that fact can be ascertained only by comparing them with it.

### THE ENLIGHTENMENT IN EUROPE: REVISION

Revision of the Enlightenment's history at its center in Europe has been so extensive in recent years that those of us who in the 1930's and 1940's rather fancied ourselves among the avant-garde of Latin Americanists because we had got the last word about Europe from Carl Becker, Ernst Cassirer, Daniel Mornet, and Paul Hazard, find that today they are becoming outmoded. This is not the place for a comprehensive account of that process, but the present paper would not be complete without a discussion of those developments in the revision that seem particularly pertinent to Spanish America and Spain.

An early example of the rising tide of revisionism was provided a decade ago by Alfred Cobban, who is also editor and co-author of a book on the age of the Enlightenment published in 1969, with a chapter on the Enlightenment itself by Robert Shackleton.[58] Becker's views, says Cobban, are fundamentally opposed to his own, and Cassirer, whose account of the Enlightenment begins with Leibniz and ends with Kant, does not seem to him to be writing about the same movement.[59]

Both Cobban and Shackleton stress the Enlightenment's diversity as well as its unity, its pragmatism as well as its idealism, and in this and other ways both define it in terms relevant to

[58] *In Search of Humanity: The Role of the Enlightenment in Modern History* (London, 1960); *The Eighteenth Century: Europe in the Age of the Enlightenment* (New York, 1969).
[59] *In Search of Humanity*, p.7.

Spain and Spanish America. To give only one example, after noting the seventeenth-century origin of the Enlightenment's basic ideas and commenting on a tendency among its historians to regard Britain as "somehow not a part of the general European movement," Cobban says: "It seems to me on the contrary that such thinkers as Bacon, Newton, Locke, Hume, and Bentham occupy key positions in the whole evolution of 'enlightened' Europe."[60] This promises to be a fruitful line of thought for the Hispanic world, where it needs further development. It has already had some. As regards Spanish America, brief reference has been made above to the influence of a few British writers. To these we may add Adam Smith's *Wealth of Nations*, which Cobban describes as belonging to the Enlightenment "both in its empirical basis and its utilitarian ends,"[61] and which finds a place in Reyes' anthology mentioned above. Further research should greatly enrich this part of the Spanish American story.

How important a factor England was in the Enlightenment in Spain itself has recently been shown by John H. R. Polt's admirable study of the sources in English of the thought of Gaspar Melchor de Jovellanos.[62] Jovellanos, Polt tells us, was the "high point" of that eighteenth-century era at its end, as Father Benito Feijoo had been at its beginning, and both men were profoundly influenced by British writers. The influence of the latter on Spain in that era, he says, has until recently been "somewhat obscured by the more spectacular and undoubtedly more widespread influence of things French," but in our own time the balance is shifting in favor of British sources. Thus, in a book published in 1953, Luis Sánchez Agesta concluded that Feijoo regarded France with suspicion and reserved "all his devotion for English culture and English thought."[63] Now, Polt has

60 *Ibid.*, p.8.
61 *Ibid.*, p.132.
62 *Jovellanos and His English Sources. Economic, Philosophical, and Political Writings*, in *Transactions* of the American Philosophical Society, new series, LIV, Part 7 (Philadelphia, 1964).
63 *Ibid.*, p.6.

demonstrated the deep indebtedness of Jovellanos to "English sources"—by which he means sources in English, including the works of Scots such as Adam Smith and Americans such as Benjamin Franklin.[64]

Jovellanos never succumbed to Anglomania, Polt says, and indeed the influence of France on his thought was paramount until he reached middle age in the 1780's, and continued in some respects until the end of his life. But about 1784, when he was forty years old, it began to give way to English influence, first in economics. Jovellanos had the highest esteem for Francis Bacon as the founder of modern science, but science was not his special field. His principal English sources were John Locke, Adam Smith, and Adam Ferguson.[65] Locke's *Essay on Human Understanding* was one of the two chief sources of his epistemology (Condillac was the other). Smith's *Wealth of Nations* shaped his economic thought after 1784, and he was never a follower of the French physiocrats (unlike his early patron Campomanes). Ferguson's *Essay on the History of Civil Society*, with its organic concept of society, strengthened his devotion to reform of the existing order as against revolution. Summing up the influence of English thought on Jovellanos, Polt declares that it "allied him to the British political heritage and separated him from the radicalism of the French Revolution," which disgusted him by making a "mockery of the ideals of the Enlightenment."[66]

Polt does not discuss Jovellanos' important role as a transmitter of the Enlightenment to Spanish America, but that was not called for by his plan. With the addition of the transatlantic theme, his excellent monograph could well serve as a model for studies-in-depth of the thought of leading Spanish American writers of this era.

A recent study of Benito Feijoo by J. A. Pérez-Rioja provides further evidence of English influence on the Spanish Enlightenment, and another by Arturo Ardao describes Feijoo as a pre-

64 *Ibid.*, p.11 and note 30.
65 *Ibid.*, pp.67, 68.
66 *Ibid.*, p.68.

cursor of that movement rather than a participant in it.[67] From the start, Pérez-Rioja tells us, Feijoo's voluminous writings were marked by an Anglophilia that was due in large measure to the superiority of the British in science at that time. As a result, Feijoo looked at the world in much the same way as the British and was perhaps the "most British" of all Spanish writers. Moreover, an examination of the French writers who influenced Feijoo (there were such, after all, beginning with Bayle and Fontenelle) shows that several of them were not exponents of encyclopedism, but of modernized traditionalism.[68]

The latter point is emphasized even more strongly by Ardao in defining Feijoo's position. Rejecting earlier characterizations of Feijoo as a Spanish Diderot and "the representative *par excellence* of the Spanish Enlightenment," Ardao maintains that the many elements in Feijoo's writings that later turned up in the Spanish Enlightenment were derived by him from the "classical modernity" (*modernidad clásica*) of the seventeenth century that he imbibed in his formative years about 1700 and clung to the rest of his life. Among these "elements" were independence from tradition, empiricism tinged with skepticism, devotion to science, and hostility to superstition. Times changed, but Feijoo did not. When he learned late in life, after 1750, that the exponents of "the Enlightenment properly speaking" were carrying things too far and propagating a materialist philosophy and subversive ideas, he condemned it strongly from the point of view of his "philosophical classicism and religious orthodoxy." Nevertheless, Ardao insists, the developments to which Feijoo objected were implicit in his own spirit of rational criticism,

[67] José Antonio Pérez-Rioja, *Proyección y actualidad de Feijoo (ensayo de interpretación)* (Madrid, 1965); Arturo Ardao, *La filosofía polémica de Feijóo* (Buenos Aires, 1962). Pérez-Rioja states that while Feijoo's name was formerly written with an accent (Feijóo), the unaccented form has now gained almost universal acceptance, and that Feijoo himself usually omitted the accent (pp.48–49). His importance, widely recognized in Spanish America as well as Spain in the eighteenth century, was generally lost sight of thereafter until the 1920's, when Agustín Millares Carlo began his rehabilitation.

[68] Pérez-Rioja, *Feijoo*, pp.40–41, 163.

and the "enlightened Spain" of the late eighteenth century would never have been the same without him.[69] We may conclude, then, that the eighteenth-century Feijoo was one of the finest minds of the seventeenth century and a precursor of the Enlightenment *malgré lui.*

To return from Spain to the mainstream of the European Enlightenment, revisionism was strongly stressed by Robert Niklaus in a review article published in 1967 in a *festschrift* for Theodore Besterman.[70] It is Niklaus who states most explicitly the proposition, mentioned above, that the study of the Enlightenment is in a state of flux at the present time and that the leading authorities of a generation ago, such as Mornet, Hazard, and even Cassirer, are now being questioned on matters of principle as well as detail.[71] As a result, he concludes, in the study of the Enlightenment "philosophy, the philosophical and critical spirit can no longer be separated from science, history, jurisprudence and politics, or confined to the realm of abstract speculation."[72] Another new interpretation, but one which he (like others) considers less well sustained, makes the Enlightenment a principal source of nineteenth- and twentieth-century totalitarianism.[73] This seems to be an extension of the much older interpretation suggested by Marx and Engels in their assertion that modern socialism has its roots in the fundamental principles of the eighteenth century.

Prominent revisionists among United States historians of the Enlightenment include Peter Gay, Frank Manuel, Adrienne Koch, and Bernard Bailyn.[74] Since space is limited, Gay's two-

---

[69] Ardao, *Polémica*, pp.115–21.

[70] "The Age of Enlightenment," in *The Age of Enlightment: Studies Presented to Theodore Besterman* (Edinburgh and London, 1967), pp.395–412.

[71] *Ibid.*, p.410.

[72] *Ibid.*, p.412.

[73] J. L. Talmond, *The Origins of Totalitarian Democracy* (1952); L. G. Crocker, *An Age of Crisis: Man and World in Eighteenth Century French Thought* (Baltimore, 1959).

[74] *The Enlightenment: An Interpretation*, Vol.I, *The Rise of Modern Paganism* (New York, 1966); Vol.II, *The Science of Freedom* (New York, 1969). Gay had

volume study has been chosen for discussion here as the most thoroughgoing and recent large-scale work of this kind. A sharp critic of his predecessors, particularly of Carl Becker (though elsewhere than in this book), Gay undertakes to correct what he calls "the simplistic interpretations [of the Enlightenment] that have served [historians] for so long and so badly—interpretations that treat the Enlightenment as a compact body of doctrine, an Age of Reason." This, he well says, "is to strip the Enlightenment of its wealth and then complain about its poverty."[75]

Accepting the traditional time limits of the Enlightenment—the hundred-year span ending in 1789—he divides it into three generations: first, the generation of Montesquieu and Voltaire, which did most of its great work before 1750; next, the generation which, reaching maturity about mid-century, "fused the fashionable anticlericalism and scientific speculations" of its predecessors "into a coherent view of the modern world" (this was the generation of Diderot, d'Alembert, Condillac, Hume, Rousseau, Buffon, and Franklin, all born between 1706 and 1717); and third and finally, the generation of Turgot, Lessing, Kant, and Jefferson, which "moved into scientific mythology and materialist metaphysics, political economy, legal reform, and practical politics." There was no great change, he holds, in the basic ideas of the Enlightenment, which he identifies as the uses of antiquity, devotion to modern science, and hostility to Christianity. "What changed," he continues, "was the balance of forces within the philosophic coalition" and the range of criticism, which became "deeper and wider, more far-reaching, more uncompromising," so that by the 1770's the

begun his revisionist work much earlier, e.g., in "The Enlightenment in the History of Political Theory," *Political Science Quarterly*, LXIX, No.3 (September 1954), 374–89. Frank Manuel's works include *The Age of Reason* (Ithaca, N.Y., 1951 and 1967); *The Eighteenth Century Confronts the Gods* (Cambridge, Mass., 1959); and a volume of selections from eighteenth-century writers, *The Enlightenment* (Englewood Cliffs, N.J., 1965). Adrienne Koch, *Power, Morals, and the Founding Fathers: Essays in the Interpretation of the American Enlightenment* (Ithaca, N.Y., 1966). For Bernard Bailyn, see below, note 95.

75 *The Enlightenment*, I, x.

*philosophes* "had grown intensely radical in their program."[76]

Gay's analysis could be quite useful to Latin Americanists in many ways, particularly for its fresh treatment of problems with which all students of the Enlightenment have to deal, and for its richly furnished bibliographical essays; but I have two reservations about its usefulness to them. The first concerns his identifications of "hostility to Christianity" as one of the basic and unchanging ideas of the Enlightenment.[77] This proposition seems to me too sweeping. He himself admits in a footnote that "some exceptional philosophes, notably Montesquieu, Turgot, and Lessing," assigned Christianity a privileged place among religions.[78] There must be something wrong with a rule that has to admit of such major exceptions as these, to which some of us would add others, beginning with Rousseau, Kant, and Jefferson, on the ground that "hostility" is too strong a word in this context. Consequently there seems to be no reason why the failure or refusal of Spanish and Spanish American intellectual leaders of this period to attack Christianity should be made a ground for excluding them from the Enlightenment.

Yet Gay leaves Spain and Spanish America almost completely out of account. Hence my second reservation about the book's usefulness for historians of the Hispanic world. To be sure, his first volume also leaves the United States largely out of account, or "on the sidelines," as he puts it. This omission he explains by saying, "I did not wish to overload the book—or myself, for that matter—with material, and I have thus drawn my examples primarily from Europe."[79] This consideration did not, however, prevent him from devoting the last chapter of his second volume to the American Revolution and describing that revolution, not the French, as the Enlightenment's "program in practice."

Spain, on the other hand, despite its strong French ties and well-known Bourbon reforms in the eighteenth century, gets

---

76 *Ibid.*, pp.17–19.
77 *Ibid.*, pp.18, 373.
78 *Ibid.*, p.373, note 2.
79 *Ibid.*, p.442.

only a very few passing references in either of Gay's two volumes; and in this case he does not explain the omission. Nevertheless, the explanation can be inferred on three grounds, in addition to his stated unwillingness to overload the book or himself. The first is that Spain's Bourbon reforms were largely a product of Enlightened Despotism, which he, unlike many of his predecessors, divorces *a mensa et thoro* from the Enlightenment. The second is his differentiation, in the preface of the second volume, between "the two Enlightenments—the philosophic movement and its environment," the Age of the Enlightenment, and his statement that "the organizing principle of these two volumes is the Enlightenment taken in its narrow sense—the Enlightenment of the philosophes." Since he identifies the *philosophes en bloc* with "hostility to Christianity," it is clear that Spain did not qualify for inclusion in his plan. The third and most obvious ground is a passage in the bibliographical essay at the end of his second volume in which he writes: "Doubtless the best place to study the other side of the eighteenth century—the victory of stagnation and clerical conservatism—is Spain." In this connection he cites recent works on the Enlightenment in Spain by Jean Sarrailh and Richard Herr, from which some of us would draw a different conclusion.[80]

As for Spanish America, it is not discussed at all in Gay's volumes, though he had several appropriate occasions to speak of it. The most obvious are those involving writers of the Enlightenment in whose works Spanish America bulked large and whom Gay discusses. Thus he speaks of William Robertson several times but never mentions Robertson's notable *History of*

---

[80] *Ibid.*, II, 490–93 (Enlightened Despotism); ix, x (Preface); p.593 (Spain), citing Jean Sarrailh, *L'Espagne éclairée de la seconde moitié du XVIIIᵉᵐᵉ siècle* (Paris, 1954), and Richard Herr, *The Eighteenth-Century Revolution in Spain* (Princeton, 1958). He might have added Luis Sánchez Agesta, *El pensamiento político del despotismo ilustrado* (Madrid, 1953), and an article originally published in 1947 by Vicente Palacio Atard, "Spanish Enlightened Despotism," in Troy S. Floyd (ed.), *The Bourbon Reformers and Spanish Civilization* (Boston, 1966), which distinguishes between the Enlightenment and Enlightened Despotism without divorcing them completely (pp.31–35).

*America.* Similarly, though Raynal is given six index entries, mainly in connection with his famous *Histoire philosophique des Deux Indes*, and though Spanish America formed the largest bloc in the "Two Indies" at that time, Gay tells us nothing about Raynal's account of Spanish America except to say, without specification, that each of the book's several editions after 1770 was "more radical than its predecessor."[81] Such treatment is all the more surprising in view of the well-known fact, which Gay notes,[82] that Raynal's book "was the work of perhaps a dozen philosophes," including Diderot—a fact which would seem to indicate that the leaders of the European Enlightenment attached considerable importance to Spanish America. Further evidence that they did so is not hard to find. Voltaire himself, for example, had a good deal to say about Spanish America in his *Essai sur les moeurs* and other writings, and Diderot was the first biographer of Pablo de Olavide,[83] one of the outstanding figures of the Enlightenment in the Hispanic world.

Gay's interpretation of the Enlightenment widens the gap that has always existed between the European core and the Hispanic periphery, but in this respect it is not typical of revisionist writing on the subject. More frequently, recent interpretations are applicable to Spain and Spanish America even when they are not discussed. Examples among the writings already mentioned are those of Cobban, Shackleton, and Polt. To these should be

---

81 Gay, *The Enlightenment*, I, 19.

82 *Ibid.*, p.176.

83 Marcelin Defourneaux, *Pablo de Olavide ou l'afrancesado (1725–1803)* (Paris, 1959), p.viii and Appendix I, pp.471–72. This appendix reproduces the text of Diderot's brief biography of Olavide, prefaced by a bibliographical note stating that it was written in late 1779 or 1780. In Olavide, Spanish America made a reverse contribution to the Spanish Enlightenment. Born and brought up in Lima, Peru, he came to Spain in 1767 as governor of Seville, took an active part in the reform movement, and was imprisoned by the Inquisition for possessing and lending prohibited books, and other offenses, but escaped to France. He played a significant role in spreading the Enlightenment in Spain. For example, Polt, *Jovellanos*, p.7, says that Jovellanos' "first and most decisive encounter with the thought of the French and English Enlightenment took place through Olavide and his circle" in Seville between 1768 and 1776.

added three recent monographic articles on the European Enlightenment—by Roger Hahn, Werner Krauss, and Bernard
Plongeron—all of which bring out points of special interest to
historians of Spain and Spanish America.

Roger Hahn's article, "The Application of Science to Society:
The Societies of Arts,"[84] begins by paraphrasing a proposition
adopted in 1779 by the Geneva Society of Arts to the effect that
"after having conquered the intellectual realm during the century of the scientific revolution, enlightened man turned to the
pressing question of his material well-being." The rest of the
article develops this thought with special reference to the "societies of arts," a term in which he includes the "economic
societies" discussed in Shafer's book on Spain and Spanish
America. Covering the whole of Europe as well as America,
Hahn lists as the earliest societies of arts those in Edinburgh
(1723), Paris (1726), and Dublin (1731).[85] Those in Edinburgh
and Paris, he says, though short-lived, "established patterns that
were almost immediately imitated in other countries and became
the operating procedures for all Societies of Arts."[86] Later societies included those in London (1753), New York (1764), our
Basque Society in Vergara, Spain (1765), and Geneva (1776).

All these societies aimed at "the improvement of the *practical*
arts, including crafts, industries, agriculture, and husbandry."[87]
Here again the facts do not support the thesis that the Latin
American Enlightenment's concern with "empirical reform
within the existing order" differentiated it from the Enlightenment in Europe. The European societies of arts had the same
concern, and they were, or at any rate believed themselves to be,
an authentic expression of the Enlightenment. Also of interest
to Latin Americanists is the fact that some of these societies used
the word *patriotic* in their titles, or else, as in the case of the

84 In *Studies on Voltaire and the Eighteenth Century*, XXV (Geneva, 1963),
829–36.
85 *Ibid.*, p.832.
86 *Ibid.*, p.835.
87 *Ibid.*, p.831.

prototypical Edinburgh society, called its members "lovers of their country"[88]—a phrase which was, of course, an exact equivalent of *amigos del país* in the title of the Hispanic world's prototypical Basque Society.

That after about 1750 *patriot* became a key word of the European Enlightenment is Werner Kraus's main contention in a very recent article, " 'Patriote,' 'patriotique,' 'patriotismo,' à la fin de l'Ancien Régime."[89] The predilection of the Enlightenment for the conception of patriot, he says, is shown by the titles of an infinity of books published in and after 1750; and in 1757 the word received the accolade of acceptance in the *Dictionnaire de l'Académie Française*.[90] The *philosophes* gave the word a new connotation, which was that of a reform of all sectors of society in the interest of national progress.[91] In support of this assertion he cites d'Alembert and Diderot, who were surely among the most authentic spokesmen of the Enlightenment. In conclusion he shows that from France this concept of patriotism passed into Spain as well as Germany with the same linkage with the idea of national progress that the *philosophes* had given it.[92]

These findings should be stressed. If valid—and they are at least plausible—they provide a needed corrective for the erroneous but widespread belief that the Enlightenment was fundamentally and everywhere internationalist and hence anti-patriotic, not to say anti-nationalist. Though true of some of the enlightened, it was not true of others, and further research may show that, through the influence of the latter, one result of the Enlightenment's transmission overseas was to sow the seeds of the rudi-

---

[88] *Ibid.*, p.833.

[89] In *The Age of the Enlightenment: Studies Presented to Theodore Besterman*, pp.378–94. Krauss is a member of an Enlightenment research group in East Berlin.

[90] *Ibid.*, p.388.

[91] *Ibid.*, p.390.

[92] *Ibid.*, p.394. Though without reference to the Enlightenment, Stanley J. and Barbara H. Stein use such terms as "extremely nationalistic" and "proto-economic nationalism" in describing the policies of Spain and Portugal in the late eighteenth century: *The Colonial Heritage of Latin America: Essays on Economic Dependence in Perspective* (New York, 1970), pp.98–101.

mentary nationalism that soon cropped up in the new Spanish American states. Proof still needs to be provided on this as on several other points that have been made in the preceding pages.

In the most recent of the three articles under discussion Bernard Plongeron examines the history of the Catholic *Aufklärung* in Western Europe from 1770 to 1830.[93] He recognizes that the very existence of such a thing has been denied on the ground that Catholic and *Aufklärung* are mutually incompatible, but he concludes that it not only existed but was not limited to Germany, as its name might suggest. Rather, he finds, it brought together, mainly between 1770 and 1815, men of talent from all parts of Western Europe, including Spain, in an effort to adapt Christianity to the problems of the times. Did they not, asks Plongeron, thereby express the confused aspirations of many believers who thought it *néfaste et dépassé* that the Church should be divorced from the Enlightenment (*les lumières*)? At the end of his documented fifty-page article, he modestly leaves this and certain other questions, presumably less rhetorical, for future settlement by research-in-depth. Yet even so, his article can hardly fail to give heart to those historians in the Hispanic world who, as we have seen, identify the particular form taken by the Enlightenment in their countries as Catholic or Christian.[94]

[93] "Recherches sur l'"Aufklärung' catholique en Europe occidentale (1770–1830)," *Revue d'Histoire Moderne et Contemporaine*, XVI (October–December 1969), 555–605. The author is identified as *chargé de recherches* in the Centre de la Recherche Scientifique, Paris.

[94] A similar view had already been expressed by Franklin L. Ford in his briefer and more general but very substantial essay, "The Enlightenment: Towards a Useful Redefinition," in R. F. Brissenden (ed.), *Studies in the Eighteenth Century: Papers Presented at the David Nichol Smith Memorial Seminar, Canberra 1966* (Toronto, 1968), pp.17–29. Noting the many national and other variations in the Enlightenment and taking religion as an example, Ford says that Peter Gay's emphasis on "paganism" seems excessive until it is recalled that he is writing mainly about the French Enlightenment. The German *Aufklärung*, continues Ford, had some skeptical ideas, but it was also Christian in many of its concerns, and in the United States the leading exponents of the Enlightenment "never even approached the range or intensity of French social or anticlerical criticism." Summing up this aspect of the whole movement, he concludes that "the *lumières*" were neither "smug rationalists" nor "systematic skeptics."

SUMMARY AND PROSPECT

In conclusion, we may answer the question stated at the beginning of this paper by saying that the current revisionist trend in the historiography of the European Enlightenment has also been strong in studies of its Spanish American phase published since 1942. But it seems clear that, taken as a whole and with some notable exceptions, the latter have not achieved the breadth and depth of their European counterparts and that the results have not yet been sufficiently assimilated to produce a consensus on all major points among workers in the field.

Perhaps the most important result of the revisionists' labors, and one that has come close to gaining general acceptance, has been to lay to rest the myth of the Enlightenment as a "cause" of the independence movement through the creole leaders' deliberate application of the subversive ideas of Rousseau and company. These, it now seems clear, had little effect in Spanish America before, but great effect after, Napoleon's invasion of Spain in 1808 threw her empire into disarray and opened the door to revolution in her American dominions.

This points to the tentative but plausible conclusion, suggested above, that considered as a force for deliberate political subversion, the Enlightenment in Spanish America was not only not a "cause" but rather a consequence of the independence movement. On the other hand, even before 1808, as Navarro, Lanning, and others have shown, the Enlightenment made a deeply unsettling impact on Spanish America, which may have contributed indirectly to the independence movement—perhaps in some cases by the hostile reaction it aroused among conservatives—and also to patriotism and the rudimentary nationalism that soon emerged in the new states.

Other major revisions have been the promotion of Spain to front rank as channel or filter for the transmission of the Enlightenment to Spanish America before 1808 and the more precise definition of the Enlightenment in Spain and Spanish

America as "Christian" or "Catholic." To some the latter point seems a contradiction in terms, which only proves that there was no true Enlightenment in either Spain or its colonies. But as Krebs Wilckens and Bernard Plongeron point out, a similar Christian Enlightenment took shape at the same time in all the Catholic countries of Europe. Even in France the *philosophes* who preached the new paganism did not speak for the whole Enlightenment, which had many voices there as elsewhere. How many of these were English and how greatly they influenced the Hispanic world, historians are beginning to note. If in Protestant and complacent England the *écrasez l'infame* spirit was relatively weak, the Enlightenment in Spanish America and Spain, for all its residual Catholicism, was marked by an increasingly secular spirit, and it is submitted that this secularism came closer than hostility to Christianity to characterizing the European Enlightenment at large.

The order of business now awaiting revisionists of the history of the Enlightenment in Spanish America is not a short one. There is need for studies in depth of its sources and leaders in that area like those already made of such Spanish writers as Feijoo, Campomanes, and Jovellanos; for more searching studies of individual countries such as Mexico has begun to produce; for more attention by historians in each country to what has been and is being done in the rest; and for differentiating between the Spanish American Enlightenment before and after 1808. There is also need for broadening the concept of the Enlightenment along lines indicated by European revisionists, so as to include not only politics, religion, and philosophy, but also economics, science, jurisprudence, history, and humanitarianism. Then the Spanish American record should be checked against this list, by specification rather than generalization.

Above and beyond all these needs is the one for a clearer vision of the Enlightenment as an unfolding historical process in Spanish America as compared with other areas. A particularly useful comparison would be with the Enlightenment in another peripheral area, the United States, as described by Bernard Bailyn.[95] According to Bailyn, the "writings of [European] Enlightenment rationalism" were only one of several factors that were "influential in shaping the thought of the Revolutionary generation" in the Thirteen Colonies before 1776. At that time the Enlightenment's following in these colonies was so far from being confined to radicals that conservatives and loyalists, too, cited the European rationalists as authoritative and were not outdone by colonial radicals in denouncing "opponents of Enlightened rationalism" such as Hobbes, Filmer, and Mainwaring. Moreover, Enlightenment ideas conflicted with two other factors shaping English colonial thought at that time. These were "covenant theology," which derived political principles from divine intent, and the English common law as "an unbroken tradition evolving from time immemorial."

As Bailyn well says, "Nothing could have been more alien to the Enlightenment rationalists" than the English colonists' veneration for the common law tradition, for it was "precisely the heavy crust of custom," the "accidental inheritance of the past," that they wanted to throw off, so that the unfettered power of reason could create better institutions. How then were this and other incongruous elements in the English colonial thought of the period reconciled? Bailyn finds the answer in the powerful tradition of opposition thought that stemmed from the English Civil War and Commonwealth, flourished in the colonies in the eighteenth century, and brought together Enlightenment ideas, common law precedents, and the other elements in the "comprehensive theory of politics" with which the colonists responded to English impositions after 1763.

Comparison of this process with the one in Spanish America

95 *The Ideological Origins of the American Revolution* (Cambridge, Mass., 1967), pp.26–35, 43, 54. Bailyn had already written, in "Political Experience and Enlightenment Ideas in Eighteenth-Century America," *American Historical Review*, LXVII (January 1962), 351, that "Enlightenment ideas . . . did not create new social and political forces in America. They released those that had long existed, and vastly increased their power. This completion, this rationalization, this symbolization . . . this was the American Revolution."

before 1808 suggests important analogies as well as at least one profound difference. In Spanish America, too, enlightened ideas were widely circulated, for many years were not identified with radicalism, and became so identified only under external pressure (in the Spanish American case, pressure from the French Revolution and Napoleon). Also, two of the other factors in the Anglo-American cluster of ideas had counterparts in Spanish America: for "covenant theology," Catholic theology, and for English common law, the tradition of Spanish law reaching far back into the Middle Ages. But the Spanish American situation differed profoundly from the Anglo-American in that the colonists (creoles) had no counterpart for the powerful tradition of opposition thought which, in the United States, had brought contradictory elements together in a comprehensive theory of politics by the time its war for independence began. The lack of such a unifying factor in Spanish America may help to explain the widely different course of its history after the politically radical ideas of the Enlightenment began to come into free play there about 1808.

Much of the foregoing is hypothetical, but it may be that probing such hypotheses will help historians to answer the many questions that still remain open about the Spanish American Enlightenment, both in itself and in relation to its European homeland.

# II

# The Philosophical Concept of Enlightenment

### ROBERT N. BECK

AMONG THE MANY CHARACTERIZATIONS of the Enlightenment, perhaps none has been more widely read than that of Immanuel Kant. "Enlightenment," he said in his well-known introductory paragraph,

> is man's release from his self-incurred tutelage. Tutelage is man's inability to make use of his understanding without direction from another. Self-incurred is this tutelage when its cause lies not in lack of reason but in lack of resolution and courage to use it without direction from another. *Sapere aude!* "Have courage to use your own reason!"—that is the motto of Enlightenment.[1]

In amplifying these thoughts in his essay, Kant connected reason to the concepts of freedom, science, and religion. And while he refused to call his century an enlightened age, he did believe that he lived in an Age of Enlightenment.

Written in 1784, Kant's essay is in many ways both an interesting summary of some Enlightenment sentiments and yet a misleading guide to its philosophy. The ties of reason to science,

---

[1] "What is Enlightenment?," in *Critique of Practical Reason and Other Writings in Moral Philosophy*, trans. and ed. Lewis White Beck (Chicago, 1949), p.286.

freedom, and a new morality are surely present in the great thinkers of the period, and Kant emphasized them. But his main concern was psychological, even moralistic—men should think for
themselves, and they should live in a society which provides for
the free expression of their thoughts. Kant's own philosophy,
to be sure, did not really encompass the Enlightenment, but it
had its foundation there. As Jaspers has noted, the critical
philosophy, "by opening new horizons, limited, defined, and
justified the attitudes and achievements of the Enlightenment."[2]
And yet Kant's observations are a starting point, for an emphasis
on reason—or more accurately, a new conception of reason, born
in the seventeenth century and continued into the eighteenth—
is surely at the heart of the Enlightenment. The subsequent
marriage of reason with morals, politics, and religion came as
the almost inevitable consequence of that birth: a youthful
marriage, to be sure, expressing the boundless enthusiasms of
the men of Enlightenment to find the natural and the rational
in every nook and cranny of the world. The special, even defining, impulse of the Enlightenment was to discover a rational
foundation for every field of human interest, so that thought
and action would be independent of religious revelation and
speculative metaphysics. And indeed, by the eighteenth century,
as Carl Becker has written, "the words without which no enlightened person could reach a restful conclusion were nature,
natural law, first cause, reason, sentiment, humanity, perfect-
ibility (the last three being necessary only for the more tender-
minded, perhaps)."[3] Reason in the seventeenth and eighteenth
centuries was looked upon as the expression of free and enlightened individuals, and free and enlightened individuals
were made so by reason.

Thus the philosophical concept of Enlightenment—or the
basic concept for the Enlightenment, as my paper might more
accurately be titled—is a special view of reason. Indeed, this view

[2] Karl Jaspers, *Kant*, ed. Hannah Arendt (New York, 1962), p.151.
[3] Carl Becker, *The Heavenly City of the Eighteenth-Century Philosophers*
(New Haven, 1932), p.47.

of reason is more fundamental even than nature, the word with which reason was so often coupled. Though his neo-Kantianism sometimes colors his interpretations too much, Ernst Cassirer has written that " 'Nature' therefore does not so much signify a given group of objects as a certain 'horizon' of knowledge, of the comprehension of reality."[4] And again, "In one and the same intellectual process of emancipation the philosophy of the Enlightenment attempts to show the self-sufficiency of both nature and intellect. Both are now to be recognized as essential and to be firmly connected with one another."[5] It is the meaning of reason, and the philosophical perplexities connected with that meaning, that constitute the central concern of this paper.

The Enlightenment, as most historians judge it, is both the spiritual consequence of science and a step toward modernity. The most direct source of the spirit of Enlightenment (I am suppressing here some details of interpretation and influence) was the scientific writing of Newton. As is well known, Newton had proceeded by a rational, mathematical method to demonstrate truths or "laws" about the physical universe. Both aspects of his work, method and conclusions, became widely influential. The mathematical systematization of scientific thought had been the means for Newton's synthesis, which offered a picture of nature as thoroughly orderly, lawful, and rational. The Enlightenment understandably drew the implication—with hints from Newton himself—that the mathematical-scientific method could and should be used to reach secure conclusions or laws in all fields of human concern. The search for the reasonable and the rational thus led to a scientific study of man, including his history, his religion, his ethics, and his politics. Here too regularities and certainties seemed available to the rational mind. The rational was taken as the natural, and the natural as the lawful.

4 Ernst Cassirer, *The Philosophy of Enlightenment,* tr. Fritz C. A. Koelln and James P. Pettegrove (Princeton, 1951), p.39.
5 *Ibid.,* p.45.

Small wonder that John Locke would write that he believed that even the truths of ethics are capable of demonstration—as in fact Spinoza had been attempting to do on the Continent.

This mathematical-demonstrative model of reason, so often written of in the seventeenth century, provides the clue for unraveling the concept of reason of the Enlightenment—even though one finds a more inductivist model of knowledge at work in eighteenth-century science. Buffon's study of animals, in fact, almost established a new type of natural science, and sensationalistic epistemologies were typical of the century. One might even agree that the essential genius of eighteenth-century science lay in its combination of conceptualization and experimentation. Yet within this model of knowledge, reason remained as Locke's "power to repeat, compare, and unite" simple ideas. First of all then, reason in the Enlightenment is understood as calculation. Descartes spoke (sometimes dimly) of intuition, Locke of the agreement of ideas, Leibniz of a universal algebra, but few philosophers were as direct—or as accurate of seventeenth-century scientific reason—as Hobbes, for whom thought is simply computation or a "reckoning with consequences."

Historically viewed, this "reckoning with consequences" was a polemic weapon. Greek and medieval natural philosophy had, after all, gone wrong in their inability to explain inertia, or to accept the telescope. The assumptions of that philosophy could obviously, therefore, not be trusted. Indeed, nothing could be less trustworthy for acquiring knowledge than final causes and mere contemplation. To be certain one had to *make* sure by reckoning, and make *sure* by dealing with what human thought can deal with, namely consequences. Such sureness or certainty was purchased at a price: as Whitehead has so clearly noted, the pursuit of scientific reason in the seventeenth century contained, paradoxically, an anti-rationalistic strain: "It is a great mistake to conceive this historical revolt as an appeal to reason. On the contrary, it was through and through an anti-intellectualist movement. It was the return to the contemplation of brute fact;

and it was based on a recoil from the inflexible rationality of medieval thought."[6] The development of epistemological theories in the Enlightenment, many of them touching on the problem of the limits of human knowledge, reflect this same emphasis. In a way, perhaps, one can go beyond Whitehead to say that a double paradox is involved. The limitation of reason to calculation was the basis for the expansion of scientific knowledge; but this expansion in turn led to limitations in the visions of man and of the human condition.

This latter limitation may be seen as we "reckon with the consequences" of defining thought by this phrase. Utilitarianism in ethics and politics is an almost inevitable development. John Locke's thought provides documentation of this implication (and Locke with his fellow Englishmen Bacon and Newton remains the formulator of Enlightenment thought, however much the French were its propagandists). As Alfred Cobban summarized it, Locke, by extending scientific analysis to the mind,

> asserted that man is a part of nature and subject to the same empirical investigation. By concentrating his attention on problems of epistemology, he let metaphysics go the way of religious dogma. By insisting that all we can really know is what is of use to us, he justified the growing utilitarian spirit and its concern with practical consequences.[7]

Most of the national Enlightenment movements produced utilitarian theorists, although the flirtation with utilitarianism was perhaps longest and strongest in Britain and France. (Interestingly, as contemporary philosophy has become a logico-linguistic handmaiden of contemporary science, this flirtation has been renewed.) But utilitarianism is a perplexing doctrine, to say the least, for it is caught in an unending chain of means and ends without ever arriving at a principle which could justify the whole category of means and ends. The inability of man to find such justification, or even to assert his humanity within a utili-

[6] Alfred North Whitehead, *Science and the Modern World* (New York, 1925), p.12.

[7] Alfred Cobban, *In Search of Humanity* (New York, 1960), p.73.

tarian perspective, is nowhere better shown than in the rapidity with which even the Enlightenment itself replaced simple utility with the "greatest happiness principle."

"Reckoning with consequences" was of course to serve a purpose, and that purpose was announced early in the period by Bacon's "knowledge is power." Reason is an active agency, and the betterment of the human condition is its aim. But reason becomes an agent primarily through the instrument or tool (was it not a tool, the telescope, that opened the heavens to Galileo?), and therefore Enlightenment man set about to produce the tools for the conquest of both natural and social forces that would create here and now the heavenly city Augustine reserved for the hereafter. But in doing so, he began to define himself, as Benjamin Franklin said, as a tool-maker, and therewith he adopted the mentality of the tool-maker. The world is instrumentalized, the means-ends category is given a universal range, the principle of utility is used in the attempt to understand human motivation and to justify every value, the sense of human sovereignty is the basis for regarding everything as material (had not Hobbes seen even society as "body"?), and the sense of instrumentalism is the ground for contempt of all thought that is not a first step toward power and the control of nature and society.[8]

But reckoning with consequences is only a first characterization of the view of reason held by the Enlightenment. A second may, provocatively, be taken as a subjectivist conception of reason. The legitimate use of such an adjective may be difficult to establish, for above all else the Enlightenment seems to stand for the autonomy of reason, for its ability to grasp objective structures in nature and society, and for an objective value system rooted in the rationality of man and nature. And yet there are tensions within the Enlightenment which suggest the very opposite of such objectivity. Descartes's meditations on knowledge, while directed toward establishing a firm and certain basis for

[8] So Hannah Arendt's summary in *The Human Condition* (Garden City, N.Y., 1959), p.279.

knowledge, in fact initiated a kind of alienation between reason and the world. Eighteenth-century epistemological debates centered on the subject-object relation—reflecting doubts, perhaps, that subjects are related to objects. Even the discussions of the primacy of will and intellect (and in the end, with Hume, of the passions and the intellect) carried a sense of threat to reason as the mirror of an objective rational order. Kant himself, when he wrote of the Enlightenment, had already developed a phenomenalistic epistemology.

To trust the telescope, the social contract, or a political system of checks and balances—all of them tools—is, despite protestations to the contrary, ultimately to distrust reason, and in fact to subjectivize it. Confidence rather must be placed in man's hands, for it is through them that nature in man and nature in the cosmos meet. And indeed they did meet, with another implication, in the hands of some of the radical Enlightenment thinkers. If man knows nature through the agency of his machines, and if perhaps nature is herself machine-like, then why should not man himself be considered a machine? It was the English moralist Hartley who completed the trend toward the elimination of creative elements in the operations of the mind by his theory of automatic, formalistic association of ideas. But then thought itself, as a reckoning with consequences, can be viewed as a mere function of the brain. And while the Enlightenment did not have the technology to accomplish it, the modern computer and some interpretations given it here received their philosophic groundwork. The computer can fulfill the functions of reckoning infinitely better than man's brain ever could; and therewith the modern world is *tending*, at least, toward drawing the conclusion initiated by the Enlightenment, namely the irrelevance of human beings to the human enterprise.

The third character I find in the Enlightenment's view of reason is its formalism—its view of reason as calculating form. Indeed, the first of my points above, namely reason is calculation, may have foreshadowed this character. And once again, it may be somewhat paradoxical to charge the Enlightenment with a formalistic view of reason. The history of the period might rather be read as including a developing recognition that reason apart from experience is only empty form. This was the actual sequence of events, to be sure, and the men of Enlightenment turned to experience everywhere—in the spirit of the laws, in the parts of animals, and even in the composition of a critical dictionary. Reason needed experience, as Locke presumably had proven for the Enlightenment in his rejection of innate ideas. Still, even if the forms of reason need content, the reason needing that content is a formal one. The point is not much changed.

The skeptical drive showing the inadequacy of reason alone was not to stop with reason alone: David Hume, whose philosophy is relevant here not because of any influence it had but as an indication of the skepticism latent in Enlightenment ideas, was soon to show that the appeal to experience is in no way to avoid skepticism, for it too is subject to skeptical disillusion. Perhaps—and I am suggesting more—the step from Newton to Hume was inevitable. Nevertheless, Hume could exist and enjoy his backgammon, partly perhaps because the civilities of life in Britain could sustain him (what if his skepticism were really to turn to them?). But a half-century later a melancholy Dane, still retaining a formalistic conception of reason, was agonizing over the question of existing, and was finding resolutions only in religion.

Kierkegaard did not learn much from Hegel about the inadequacies of a formalistic conception of reason—or if he did, he rejected Hegel anyhow; but he saw, in his own way but with Hegel, the materialistic view of man implied by the Enlightenment view of reason as formalistic. This materialism is not Marxist, or even directly metaphysical; it is primarily a view of man as object, even as an element in calculation. Hegel once suggested that the Absolute or God viewed without qualification (as is said, all predicates are inadequate to Him) is no different from matter; and similarly an anthropology which allows no or only inadequate ascription of "human" or subject predicates to man is sheer materialism. But the error of this materialism, as

Hannah Arendt has pointed out,[9] however powerful it was in some respects (and new conceptions of reason did lead to new insights, even as the new utilitarianism aided the attempt to eliminate pain and cruelty from human affairs), is not difficult to find. It overlooks the inevitability with which men disclose themselves as subjects, as unique and distinct persons, even when they are completely committed to pursuing some material good.

The fourth characteristic I ascribe to the Enlightenment is its view of reason as function. Reason, that is, is not so much a body of principles as a kind of energy, a force; and what it can do is known through its functioning—which, as we have seen, is the power to combine and dissolve. Another way of stating this point is to say that reason became for the Enlightenment a concept of agency, not of being. And so put, a number of consequences and observations made by Enlightenment thinkers are immediately obvious. As Diderot and Fontenelle, with Bacon and even the remote Descartes, announced to the world, science ascribes a new function to the mind, and therefore the spread of science must depend on and bring about a new way of thinking. The characteristics noted above describe part of this "new way," but under the present heading the new element is the "practicality" of reason. Turning away from reason as an agency of being, scorning in many ways the contemplative life (at least as it had been understood), and indeed reversing the traditional notion that doing and making should serve contemplation, the Enlightenment rather viewed reason as the handmaiden of action. Doing, so to speak, is the ultimate meaning for the sake of which thinking is to be performed. This, I think, accounts for the fact that much of the criticism of religion in the Enlightenment, for example, was directed more toward the *deeds* of religion—priestcraft, inquisition, moral decline, etc.—than toward theological

9 *Ibid.*, p.163. Sir Isaiah Berlin has written widely on the problem of freedom and its interconnections—necessary to their very existence—with our ordinary moral categories. By extension of his argument, I am indicating that a materialistic view of man is inconsistent with the categories we ordinarily use in describing and understanding ourselves as human. See his *Four Essays on Liberty* (New York, 1969).

issues. Even the paganism of Hume (as Peter Gay has called it) rests largely on this type of observation, though his epistemology had, to be sure, ruled out the possibility of theology. Similarly, the common and strongly worded objections to metaphysics derived in large measure from the "impracticality" of metaphysical thought. And the ethical thought of the Enlightenment is also colored by this new function of reason. To be sure, ethical thought needed content, needed experience, and it found an empirical content in pleasures and pains. Thought would combine and separate, that is, calculate about this content, and the value of the calculation is found in the changes wrought in the individual and social lives of men. Rousseau, uncharacteristic as he is of much of the Enlightenment, believed that his thinking could remove men from their birth in chains, and Carl Becker summarized the entire notion in observations about the heavenly city of the eighteenth century, to be achieved by men through the instrumentality of a practical reason. In sum, processes—experimentation, the founding of nations, the use of instruments—more than ideas became the guide for things to come; and the ideals of productivity and creativity, so pervasive in the modern world, were given birth.

The philosophical concept of Enlightenment, as I have sketched it, is a concept of reason whose chief characteristics involve calculation, subjectivism, formalism, and functionalism. Taken as a view of reason, however, these characteristics are, as I have been suggesting, inadequate. Thus to criticize the Enlightenment, however, is not to overlook the fact that we are all more or less children of the Enlightenment, and that it contains one of our deepest ties to the rest of humanity. But however much we owe it—and many of its values remain values for modernity—we must at the same time, I am afraid, charge it as the origin of many of our twentieth-century ills.

In the present context the chief of these ills is, as Max Weber so clearly recognized, the problematic character of scientific rationality in the Western world. Weber was not alone in his worry: Whitehead wrote of the vicious abstractionism of early scientific thought, and more recently Hannah Arendt has developed the theme of world alienation as a consequence of seventeenth-century thought. I think these critics are essentially correct, and the seeds of the break between reason and reality, between reality and appearance, are present in Enlightenment thought from its beginning in Descartes and Galileo to its end in Hume and Kant. Descartes separated appearance and reality, then united them through his metaphysics and God. But his successors dropped in turn metaphysics and God, and the possibility of the original separation returned. If, as Hannah Arendt has said,

> Being and Appearance part company forever, and this—as Marx once remarked—is indeed the basic asumption of all modern science, then there is nothing left to be taken upon faith; everything must be doubted. It was as though Democritus' early prediction that a victory of the mind over the senses could end only in the mind's defeat had come true, except that now the phenomena themselves seemed to have won a victory over both the mind and the senses.[10]

Scientific rationalism has turned out to be unreal, and realism has become irrational.

The alienation of reason and reality begun in Enlightenment thought can be observed in two further ways. First, regarding philosophy itself, which has perhaps suffered more from modernity than any other field of human interest. The Enlightenment began and remained a philosophic movement, and modern philosophy owes its content and direction to specific scientific discoveries more than any previous philosophy. Yet the basis for the impoverishment if not destruction of philosophy is contained in Enlightenment thought. Peter Gay has argued that the Enlightenment defined philosophy as the organized habit of criticism. By way of this definition, it was led to doubt the value of metaphysics—which, as Voltaire said, is only like a

---

10 *Ibid.*, p.250.

minuet in which the dancer displays much agility and grace but ends where he starts. But criticism neither constructs nor proposes. Even Hegel had to write that "the owl of Minerva begins its flight when dusk is falling," and philosophy has become a phenomenal second-order reflection on scientific achievements, where all the action is. The Enlightenment, paradoxically, had increased man's power by mitigating his claims; and metaphysics —indeed philosophy itself—was to suffer in the mitigation. A second observation derives from or is inspired at least by a contemporary technological development that I have mentioned before, the computer. Some interpretations of the computer—those equating it with reason, primarily—are derived from Hobbes's formalistic conception of reason as "reckoning with consequences." But if we do make the equation of reason and calculation, are we not led by the experience of alienation with the whole of our culture? Surely Marx and Bergson were right in seeing this kind of intelligence merely as a function of the life process itself, or, as Hume put it, a "slave of the passions." Yet it is open to serious doubt whether such brain power is capable of erecting or sustaining a human, cultural world of values, meaning, and artifacts.

These comments largely center on the alienation of abstract reason and reality, but the last of them touches on the question of the view of reason and the human condition held by the Enlightenment. Here too—and in spite of the fact that the Enlightenment was a moralistic and political age—the development of implications from the concept of Enlightenment lead only to alienation. To be sure, such ideals as tolerance, personal integrity, and social equity have remained a precious part of our inheritance from the Enlightenment, but a concept of reason developed finally into a "slave of the passions" is hardly likely to support or justify them. If there be no base for values except such a concept, then there is no real base at all. Little wonder that contemporary youth seem to find no root for value except in personal creativity and in confrontation—and here they may be only following Sartre. The Enlightenment conviction that man knows only as he does, that so-called higher faculties like reason depend on doing, may further suggest the notion that violence and values are directly related.

Is the Enlightenment's concept of reason capable of maintaining the public space necessary for associative and cultural life? The Enlightenment itself had a heritage of Greek, medieval, and Christian thought on which to maintain its public space. But the implications of its view of reason, when developed by Hume and even more by contemporary philosophers of science, suggest that the Age of Reason could not supply such a basis from its own resources. A public space, a world of culture, is above all else a world of objects or artifacts which shield man from the ceaseless flux of nature and provide the stabilities necessary for meanings and values. But the scientific view of reason fails at just this point, for it has no need of objects, natural or cultural, and does not in fact even admit the category of objects. The alienation between science, technology, and the human condition —though having many sources to be sure—has its epistemological base in seventeenth-century science.

We can turn to literature for more concrete illumination of the concerns and problems I have sketched out here. And I have concentrated on problems. Surely the successes of Enlightenment thought, and they are many, need no apology. But there is a sense, as I have tried to suggest, in which the Enlightenment did fail miserably. Its conception of reason, and therewith its view of human nature, have provided modernity a very ambiguous inheritance. Whether we can overcome those ambiguities remains an open question—the owl of Minerva, unfortunately, is still flying at dusk.[11]

11 In addition to the works cited above, the following studies, and through them their vast sources, have been especially important to me in preparing this paper: Peter Gay, *The Enlightenment: An Interpretation* (New York, 1967); H. Stuart Hughes, *Consciousness and Society* (New York, 1958); Herbert Schneider, *A History of American Philosophy* (New York, 1946); and Basil Willey, *The Seventeenth-Century Background* (New York, 1934).

# The Diccionario of Antonio de Alcedo as a
# Source of Enlightened Ideas*

ISAÍAS LERNER

ABSTRACT

Don Antonio de Alcedo was born in Quito, Ecuador, probably
in 1734, the son of don Dionisio de Alsedo y Herrera, President
of the Real Audiencia de Quito. Alcedo's family returned to
Spain in 1752, where Antonio completed his studies, entered the
army, and soon rose in the ranks. As a soldier, he was apparently
more interested in administrative matters than in military
strategy; late in his career he became Gobernador Militar and
Mariscal de Campo in La Coruña.

Like his father, he devoted a great deal of time and energy
to the study of American history and geography; father and son
collaborated in the recollection of sources and documents related

*Editor's Note: This essay, concerning, as it does, a work published in Spain
and associated with Spain, but written by a native of Ecuador about the American
continent, presents a problem in classification. A similar problem exists concerning Ercilla's epic poem La Araucana, written by a native of Spain about Chile.
Should it be ranked with the literature of Spain or with that of Chile? Instead
of trying to solve the problem of the nationality of the Diccionario of Alcedo, I
am classifying the present discussion of many of the most important ideas which
it contains under the heading of "Intellectual Background." Because of the close
dependence of this article on the Spanish text of the Diccionario, it is printed in
Spanish rather than in English translation.

to the Spanish conquest and government in the colonies. An eighteenth-century version of the ideal Renaissance blending of the man of letters and the soldier, Alcedo directed his intellectual efforts toward works of erudition and encyclopedic reference.

His *Diccionario Geográfico-Histórico de las Indias Occidentales o América*, published in Madrid (1786–1789) in five volumes, was considered by his contemporaries to be the most important reference work concerning America, and notwithstanding some inconsistencies in the usage of sources of information, it still remains the most accurate compilation of historical and geographical documentation of the Spanish eighteenth century—far more complete and interesting than others of its kind, like the *Dizionario storico geográfico* by the Italian Jesuit Juan Domingo Coleti (Venice, 1771). In many ways it is comparable to the famous *Histoire philosophique et politique des établissements et du commerce des européens dans les deux indes* of the abbé Raynal. The book earned recognition outside Spain and was soon translated into English by G. A. Thompson (London, 1812–1815), who added more information, mainly about the United States.

The Spanish government considered that the work was a source of strategic information which should be concealed for military and economic reasons, and the book was eventually banned. Both the original and the English versions became, therefore, bibliographical rarities, and the book was practically forgotten by scholars. It was not until 1966 that the *Diccionario* was reprinted in the *Continuación* of the *Biblioteca de Autores Españoles* (Madrid, 1967, Vols.205, 206, 207, and 208). Certainly, the practical information it offers is now outdated, but it is still a priceless work for the study of ideas in Spain of the eighteenth century. Although Alcedo intended his book to be primarily a reference work, he nevertheless established quite clearly his position on many disputed issues of his time, namely the problem of race and intellectual differences; the contrasts between Spanish conquest and English colonization; the character of the Indians; the institution of slavery and the treatment of Negro slaves; the defense of human rights; and the possibilities of multiple answers to the question of the meaning of a civilized society.

A careful reading of Alcedo's *Diccionario* will show the involvement of the author in these and other issues of his time. His opinions were expressed, however, with the restrictions that this kind of work demanded. His rationalism and humanitarianism have specific Spanish characteristics which should be related not only to the philosophical movement of the eighteenth century, but also to the long Spanish tradition originating in Las Casas.

Alcedo's sources are still a matter of study; the recent, though practically unobtainable, edition of a companion work, his monumental *Bibliotheca Americana* (Quito, 1965), makes clear his intellectual debts, especially to Jesuit authors for whom Alcedo showed affection and sympathy.

El *Diccionario Geográfico-Histórico de las Indias Occidentales o América* comenzó a publicarse en Madrid en 1786 y el último y quinto tomo apareció en la misma ciudad en 1789. El primero salió de la imprenta de Benito Cano; el segundo (las letras D—L), de 1787, y el cuarto (letras P—S) y quinto (letras T—Z y *Vocabulario*), de 1789, se inprimieron en la imprenta de Manuel González; el tercero, de 1788, en la de Blas Román. La obra tuvo buen recibimiento general e inmediato aprecio por el vasto material seleccionado[1] y aparentemente fue prohibida su circulación y exportación al extranjero en virtud de la abundante información estratégica que ofrecía.[2] Algún eco de esta prohibición,

[1] Alcedo mismo señala en las *Adiciones y Correciones a este primer Tomo* (I, 753–54 de la primera edición) "la buena acogida que ha tenido la obra, así en todo el Reyno como en la América y Países extrangeros," al mismo tiempo que se defiende de los que "se han contentado con criticar algunos Artículos del primer Quaderno y pudiéramos convencer a alguno del poco fundamento con que lo ha hecho, nos hemos propuesto no entrar en contextación" (*ibid.*)

[2] Ya su traductor inglés G. A. Thompson (London, 1812–1815) señalaba las dificultades para conseguir ejemplares; cf. J. de Onís, *Los Estados Unidos vistos*

que naturalmente se extendía a todo el continente americano (adonde con seguridad llegó buen número de ejemplares)[3] se halla en una carta que José Joaquín de Araujo escribió al Dean Funes, fechada en Buenos Aires, el 26 de junio de 1802: "Con la orden de V.S. quité yo *El Nuevo Diccionario* de Alcedo y substitui el *Padre Guerrera y Rui-Diaz.*"[4]

El *Diccionario* no volvió a editarse hasta 1967 en que la Continuación de la Biblioteca de Autores Españoles publicó la nueva edición a cargo de don Ciriaco Pérez-Bustamante, autor también del *Estudio Preliminar* (pp.xi–xxxix);[5] esta nueva edición se publica en cuatro tomos y ha incorporado al texto las adiciones y correcciones de los tomos I (753–86) y III (426–96) de la edición original (*Estudio Preliminar*, p.xxxiii), aunque no se hace la advertencia en cada caso;[6] en cambio no se creyó necesario

---

*por escritores americanos*, Ed. Cultura Hispánica (Madrid, 1956), p.75, publicada originalmente en inglés, *The United States as Seen by Spanish American Writers (1776–1890)* (New York, 1952). A los datos aportados agréguese, todavía en 1862, M. Paz Soldán, *Geografía del Perú* (Paris, corregida y aumentada por su hermano Mariano Felipe Paz Soldán), I, 718.

3 Por lo pronto, en la *Continuación de la lista de Suscriptore*s (I, 787 y ss. de la primera edición) ya aparecen los nombres de don Manuel de Florez, teniente general de la Real Armada y virrey de Nueva España; don Francisco Joseph Bernal, Contador de ejército en el puerto de la Guayra; don Manuel de Arredondo, Regente de la Real Audiencia de Buenos Aires; don Joseph Ignacio del Pumar, vecino de la ciudad de Barines en América; don Justo Pastor de Asteguieta y Sarralde, residente en México; el doctor don Manuel de Florez, secretario del Ilmo. Sr. arzobispo de México; don Pedro Joséph de Lemus, vecino de México; el R. P. Fr. Juan Fiayo, del Orden de San Francisco, Predicador General en su Convento de Cartagena de Indias; don Antonio Bergosa y Jordán, Inquisidor de México; don Isidro Limonta, coronel de infantería, teniente del Rey de la plaza de Cuba.

4 *Archivo General de la Nación*, Doc. 0545, legajo 176. Debo el dato al prof. Raúl Moglia.

5 *Biblioteca de Autores Españoles. Continuación*, v.205, 206, 207, 208, Ed. Atlas (Madrid, 1967). Las citas corresponden a la primera edición; dado el orden alfabético de la obra la consulta es indistinta para ambas ediciones y por ello se ha suprimido mención de tomo o página; se ha conservado la ortografía de la primera edición, de donde transcribimos las citas.

6 Así, se transcriben y comentan textos correspondientes a la página que prologa las *Adiciones y Correciones* (I, 753–54) en el *Estudio Preliminar* (p.xxxi) que no parece haberse impreso en esta edición. El detalle no se señala por hacer

reproducir la interesante *Lista de Suscriptores* (t.I, pp.xi–xvi) ni su *Continuación*, ya mencionada en la nota 3. El *Estudio Prelimi-nar* está dedicado en buena parte al padre de nuestro autor, don Dionisio de Alcedo y Herrera (pp.xvii–xxii), al siglo XVIII en la América española (xii–xvi) y a la familia Alcedo (xvi–xvii) de la que ya había señalado ilustres antecedentes don Justo Zaragoza.[7] Para la biografía de nuestro autor, el prologuista agre-ga muy útiles datos sobre su desempeño en la Academia de Historia.[8] Echamos de menos en esta muy esperada edición, una bibliografía más completa que tuviera en cuenta nuevos aportes[9] y un índice de nombres y lugares citados que habría

presente un descuido editorial sino porque en la citada página, Alcedo da el nombre de las personas que contribuyeron con datos al perfeccionamiento de la obra y son sólo las seis que anota Pérez-Bustamante como parte de una serie mayor.

[7] Justo Zaragoza, *Piraterías y agresiones de los Ingleses y de otros pueblos de Europa en la América Española desde el siglo XVI al XVIII deducidas de las obras de D. Dionisio de Alcedo y Herrera* (Madrid, 1883).

[8] Conviene aquí señalar discrepancias de detalle en cuanto a algunos datos. No es segura la fecha de nacimiento de don Antonio de Alcedo; el acta de bautismo correspondiente al 14 de marzo de 1735 que publicó Pedro Fermín Cevallos en *El Iris* parece ser la de un hermano; probablemente nació en 1734 (cf. I. J. Barrera, *Historia de la literatura ecuatoriana*, Ed. Casa de la Cultura Ecuato-riana [Quito, 1954], II, 219). Tampoco puedo asegurar que "usó, como su padre, los apellidos Alcedo y Herrera" (cf. *Hispanic American Historical Review*, XXXI [1951], n.3, p.531) aunque lo hiciera su hermana Leonor, como consta en la partida bautismal arriba mencionada; en todo caso, el *Diccionario* y la *Biblio-theca Americana*, como los documentos que transcribe el propio Pérez-Bustamante registran la forma simple; en el texto de la *Bibliotheca* correspondiente a su propia biografía el nombre completo es Antonio de Alcedo y Bexarano. No estuvo casado con doña Blanca Seoane (p.xxiii del *Estudio Preliminar*) sino, como él mismo lo dice en la ya citada biografía de la *Bibliotheca*, con doña María Ignacia Codallos, camarista del príncipe Carlos (según se había señalado certeramente seis páginas antes: *Estudio Preliminar*, p.xvii).

[9] Aparentemente, Pérez-Bustamante ha seguido las indicaciones de Roberto J. Paez (cf. infra), que resume el estado de la bibliografía sobre Alcedo hasta 1957, pero que no toma en cuenta sino las obras más importantes; agréguese también Camilo Destugue, *Album biográfico ecuatoriano* (Guayaquil, 1903), p.88, que se basa en el *Diccionario* de José D. Cortés. Véase también la ya citada *Historia de la literatura ecuatoriana* de I. J. Barrera en la que se le dedica un capítulo (pp.219–26 del segundo tomo, con bibliografía) y el trabajo de Gonzalo Zaldumbide pub-licado en la *Biblioteca ecuatoriana mínima*, publicación auspiciada por la

facilitado el estudio de las fuentes de mención directa en esta obra singular.[10] Singular no sólo por su interés histórico y

Secretaría General de la Undécima Conferencia Interamericana (Quito, Ecuador, 1960), *Prosistas de la Colonia*, pp.524–49, en donde se comenta y discute el artículo de J. de Onís en la *Hispanic American Historical Review* y su traducción por Roberto J. Paez (*Boletín de la Academia Nacional de Historia* antes *Sociedad Ecuatoriana de Estudios Históricos Americanos*, XXXVII [1957], n.89, pp.90–102). A los datos que este último trae conviene agregar que el artículo de Pedro F. Cevallos, fechado el 5 de abril de 1862, apareció en *El Iris*, según Barrera y Zaldumbide, en la entrega 16, correspondiente al 20 de junio de ese mismo año. El artículo fue reproducido en *La Revista de Buenos Aires*, VII (1870), n.87, t.22, pp.433–41, y lleva al final la siguiente nota al pie: "Este artículo debió publicarse en la entrega once de *El Iris* de Quito, mas el autor contuvo su publicación aguardando otros datos que tenía pedidos a Panamá. La espera ha sido inútil, porque las investigaciones han sido siempre burladas." No hemos podido consultar *El Iris* de Quito; si los datos de Barrera y Zaldumbide son los correctos, el trabajo de don Diego Barros Arana publicado en el segundo tomo de la misma *La Revista de Buenos Aires*, a.I (1863), n.8, pp.533–64, y reproducido luego en las *Obras completas* (Santiago de Chile, 1910), II, 35–44, habría recogido gran parte de su información de Cevallos. Agréguese también, sobre el *Diccionario*, Ariosto González, "América en la obra de Antonio de Alcedo," *La Nación* de Buenos Aires, 19 de junio de 1965, y también "El *Diccionario* de Alcedo: América en orden alfabético," *ibid.*, 25 de julio de 1965. En cuanto a don Dionisio de Alcedo, habría sido útil tener en cuenta el trabajo de Carlos Manuel Larrea, *El presidente de la Real Audiencia de Quito, Don Dionisio de Alsedo y Herrera*, Ed. Casa de la Cultura Ecuatoriana (Quito, 1961), 52pp. El título exacto del *Plano* publicado por C. A. González Palencia (Hispanic Society of America, Madrid, 1915) con el título *Descripción Geográfica de la Real Audiencia de Quito* es: *Plano Geográfico y Hidrográfico del Distrito en la Real Audiencia de Quito, y Descripciones de las Provincias Goviernos y Corregimientos que se comprehenden en su jurisdicción y las Ciudades, Villas, Assientos y Pueblos que ocupan sus territorios*. Finalmente, el *Compendio histórico de la provincia . . . de Guayaquil* fue nuevamente impreso en 1789 con un examen crítico por don Pedro Carbo; reimpreso en Guayaquil, en la imprenta Gutenberg de E. A. Uzcategui en 1938; y de la edición de 1741 hay una reproducción fotostática en edición numerada de cien ejemplares con nota explicatoria de E. Juliá Martínez, publicada en Madrid, Tip. Clásica Española, 1946; cf. *Handbook of Latin American Studies* (1948), n.1995.

10 Aparte de las fuentes señaladas por Alcedo en las *Adiciones y Correcciones* al tomo primero, la nota 19 del *Estudio Preliminar* trae algunos nombres de autores recogidos al azar, sin mención de lugar. Sin proponernos agotar la lista y sin modificar grafías, agréguese: Mr. de Anvile (s.v. *Beni*); el *Diccionario* de Cornelio (s.v. *Camsuare*); Conde Pagani (s.v. *Camsuare*); los padres Acuña y Fritz (*ibid.*) o Friz (s.v. *Marañón*) o p. Samuel Fritz (s.v. *Tarma*); Las Casas (s.v. *Santo Domingo*); Rochefort (s.v. *Dominica*); Juan Martínez (s.v. *Dorado*); el padre Joseph Gumilla (s.v. *Dorado*); los dos hermanos Zanis, nobles venecianos (s.v. *Estotiland*); Bau-

geográfico sino también léxico. En efecto, el *Vocabulario de las voces provinciales de la América* que Alcedo preparó "como parte precisa para la inteligencia de muchas voces usadas en aquellos países"[11] es de los primeros, si no el primero en su género y ofrece buen número de interesantes datos léxicos que no han sido estudiados aun suficientemente.[12] Además, la obra de Alcedo

chene Guin, Roggers, Frecier y Le Maire (s.v. *Fuego, Tierra del*); don Juan de la Cruz (s.v. *Fracatoa*); el comandante Byron (s.v. *Gigantes*), cuyo *Diario* tradujo don Casimiro de Ortega; F. Antonio Zamora, don Francisco Antonio Moreno Fiscal de la Audiencia de Santa Fe y don Basilio Oviedo (s.v. *Granada*); Ovalle (s.v. *Guasco*); Mr. Cartúr (s.v. *Hochelaga*); Ellis (s.v. *Hudson*); Uringe (s.v. *Honduras*); Fr. Gregorio García (s.v. *Indios*); Jusieu, botánico (s.v. *Loxa*); Monsieur de L'Isle (s.v. *Mamore*); Jasón (s.v. *Manoa*); doctor don Juan José de Eguiara (s.v. *México*); el barón de Tuy (s.v. *Misisipi*); el padre Tomás Gage (s.v. *Mixco*); fr. Juan Menchero (s.v. *Nauajoa*); el barón de la Hontán, el p. Hennepin y el señor Bowen (s.v. *Niágara*); Mr. Page de Pratz (s.v. *Osages*); el p. Manuel García (s.v. *Magallánicas* en *Adiciones y Correcciones*, t.III); don Martín del Barco (s.v. *Mahomas* en *Adiciones y Correcciones*, t.III); el piloto don Joseph Amich y el capitán de fragata don Cayetano de Langara (s.v. *Otahiti* en *Adiciones y Correcciones*, t.III); Gemeli (s.v. *Pachuca*); la *Colección General de Documentos para el Extrañamiento de los Jesuitas* y el dean de Albarracín, Dr. Xarque (s.v. *Paraná*); la *Gigantología* (1756) del p. Torrubia, d. Próspero del Aguila, el caballero Hans-loane, el *Diccionario* de Chambers (s.v. *Patagones*); Nicolás Rosende (s.v. *Rio Grande*); Seixas (s.v. *San Sebastián*); el almirante Pedro Sarmiento (s.v. *Sedger*); María Sibila Merian, natural de Francfort (s.v. *Surinam*); *Diario* de Fernando de Quirós (s.v. *Taumaco*); el ex-jesuita don Antonio Julián, autor de una *Historia de Santa Marta* (s.v. *Tayronas*); Molly (s.v. *S. Thomas*); Percy (*ibid.*); Walter Raleigh (s.v. *Trinidad*); p. Pedro Lozano, *Historia del Chaco* (s.v. *Tucumán*); *Carta* del Poncho Chileno (s.v. *Verde*).

11 V. el prólogo al *Vocabulario* al final de la obra.

12 Ciro Bayo, en el prólogo a su *Vocabulario Criollo-Español sudamericano* (Madrid, 1910), señala que "El primero, quizás, que escribió un diccionario de vocablos particulares de Indias fue el Conde de Lemus en la *Relación de la provincia de Quixos*" pero tal vez haya error: *La descripción de la provincia de Quijos* hecha por el conde de Lemus en 1608, publicada en el tercer tomo (pp.88–101) de los *Documentos anexos a la memoria del Perú* por Mariano H. Cornejo y Felipe de Osma (Madrid, 1905), no trae diccionario ni vocabulario alguno. M. de Toro y Guisbert advierte que el *Diccionario provincial casi razonado de voces cubanas* (1836) de Esteban Pichardo "fue la primera de su clase que se publicó en América" (*Americanismos* [Paris, 1912], p.190). Cf. E. Rodríguez Herrera, prólogo al *Pichardo novissimo*, Ed. Selecta (La Habana, 1953), p.xv. Ninguno de los dos recuerda a Alcedo, aunque es cierto que su obra no se había publicado en América; tampoco la tuvo en cuenta E. S. Zeballos en el prólogo a las *Notas al castellano en la Argentina* de Ricardo Monner Sans (Buenos

se destaca, dentro de las de erudición características de Ilustración española, no sólo por la reconocida eficacia de su información sino porque refleja, aun en campo tan poco apto para ello, muchos de los debates doctrinales de su tiempo; así, es posible rastrear en el *Diccionario* las influencias ideológicas y las posiciones asumidas por nuestro autor, sobriamente reveladas en la ingente masa de datos y cifras de la obra.

En efecto, entre las polémicas suscitadas en el siglo XVIII, la entonces candente acerca de la inferioridad del continente americano, está directamente relacionada con nuestro libro.[13] Alcedo no permaneció ajeno a ella y mantuvo correspondencia con el ex-jesuita Francisco Iturri, autor de la *Carta crítica sobre la Historia de América del Sr. Juan Bautista Muñoz.*[14]

---

Aires, 1903), que menciona el primero referido al inglés de los Estados Unidos: "El Dr. Witherspoon publicó en Filadelfia el primer trabajo orgánico sobre americanismos en una serie de escritos recopilados con el título *The Druid* (1761)" (p.xvi). Tampoco aparece mencionado Alcedo en la muy completa lista final de Y. Malkiel, "Distinctive Features in Lexicography. A Typological Approach to Dictionaries Exemplified with Spanish," *RomL.*, XII (1959), n.4, pp.366–99, y XIII (1959), n.2, pp.111–55.

[13] Cf. el notable libro de Antonello Gerbi, *La disputa del Nuovo Mondo. Storia di una polemica 1750–1900* (Milano, 1955). Hay traducción española de Fondo de Cultura Económica de México, que no me ha sido accesible. Gerbi cita de paso (p.338) el *Diccionario* de Alcedo, a propósito de una mención errónea del rector de la Universidad de San Marcos, Lima, don José Dávila Condemarín, quien, en una lista de eruditos americanos que desmiente la tesis de de Pauw, incluye el "Diccionario de América de Salcedo."

[14] Cf. J. de Onís, "The Letter of Francisco Iturri, S.J. (1789). Its Importance for Hispanic-American Historiography," *The Americas*, Academy of American Franciscan History, VIII (1951), n.1, pp.85–90. No señala el autor cómo ha obtenido el documento. De la carta transcripta se deduce que mantenía correspondencia con Alcedo: "No me contesta Vmd. sobre el elogio de mi paysano Buenaventura Suárez, qᵉ deseo en su último tomo" (p.89). Sobre Iturri, v. Guillermo Furlong, S.J., *Francisco Javier Iturri y su "Carta Crítica"* (Buenos Aires, 1955), quien, no obstante el entusiasmo y celo patriótico puestos en su trabajo (que no es el primero suyo sobre Iturri), no parece conocer el artículo de Onís, ni la amistad con Alcedo (pp.70–71 sobre la correspondencia de Iturri con "personas eruditas de su época"). Para el paisano de Iturri, el cosmógrafo Buenaventura Suárez, que no recordó mencionar Alcedo en su obra, v. Ricardo Rojas, *Historia de la literatura argentina*, Ed. La Facultad (Buenos Aires, 1918), II, 242–43, y también G. Furlong, *Glorias santafecinas* (Buenos Aires, 1920), pp.79–140. Aunque, como hemos dicho, Alcedo no mencionó directamente a Suárez en su *Diccionario*, sí

La carta de Iturri a Alcedo que nos interesa es ocho años anterior a la *Carta crítica*, publicada en 1797, y también es anterior a la *Historia* de Muñoz, de 1793; fue escrita al recibo del primer tomo del *Diccionario*; es muy elogiosa, le promete a Alcedo ayuda de todo tipo y la colaboración de otros eruditos; se extiende en la crítica de los detractores de América en boga por entonces y nos ofrece un valioso documento que anticipa la viva polémica posterior a la que Alcedo aportó la estricta elocuencia de los datos de su *Diccionario*.

Ya se había ocupado en España el padre Feijóo de las calidades intelectuales de los criollos en su Discurso sexto "Españoles americanos" que apareció en 1773, en el cuarto tomo del *Teatro Crítico Universal*.[15] En él ataca el error común acerca de la temprana pérdida de las facultades intelectuales entre los criollos y ejemplifica la opinión suya con mención de nombres ilustres. No debió desconocer el *Discurso* Alcedo, pues en muchos casos coincide con Feijóo en el reconocimiento de los americanos famosos.[16] Naturalmente, de esta coincidencia no es justo inferir fuentes ya que Alcedo tenía una frecuentación de datos de este tipo mucho mayor y superior a la de Feijóo, que escribía de oídas; pero la coincidencia sirve, sobre todo, para acercarnos al ambiente intelectual español de entonces y a los nombres que sonaban, según palabras de Feijóo, aun "en un rincón del mundo, qual es el que yo habito y otros semejantes, donde apenas se ve jamás un Español nacido en la América."

lo incluyó en su *Bibliotheca Americana* en donde transcribió los datos enviados por Iturri en la carta mencionada (s.v. *Ventura Suarez*).

[15] Para Feijóo y América, cf. A. Millares Carlo, "Feijóo en América," *Cuadernos Americanos*, III (1944), n.3, pp.139–60, y los trabajos de Abel Calvo y Emilio Carilla en *Fray Benito Jerónimo Feijóo y Montenegro*, Estudios reunidos en conmemoración del II centenario de su muerte, Facultad de Humanidades y Ciencias de la Educación, Universidad de La Plata (La Plata, 1965).

[16] Sin pretender agotar las coincidencias, Alcedo también recuerda encomiásticamente a F. Antonio de Monrroy (s.v. *México*), don Pedro Corvete (s.v. *Lima*), don Pedro de Peralta y Barnuevo (s.v. *Lima*) al que también elogiara Concolorcorvo en el *Lazarillo de ciegos caminantes* (cf. el trabajo de Carilla citado en la nota 15, p.299), el marqués de Villarrocha (s.v. *Panamá*) pero sin la estima que muestra Feijóo, y don Joseph Pardo de Figueroa (s.v. *Lima*).

A lo largo de la obra y aun antes del elogio de Iturri, Alcedo hace mención oportuna del ingenio de los "naturales," los "criollos," o simplemente de los habitantes de cada región o ciudad. Son dignas de señalarse las listas de celebridades que transcribe para Cartagena, Santa Fé de Bogotá, patria de "muchos sugetos ilustres cuyo catálogo sería dilatado y por eso expresaremos solamente los que han sobresalido y dexado eterna memoria de su mérito"; Guamanga, cuyos "naturales son corteses, liberales y capaces así para las ciencias como para el manejo de sus negocios," entre los que cita a "Doña María Teresa Cruzategui y Munive, Marquesa de Feria, dama de singular talento y erudición con que se distingue, poseyendo la latinidad, filosofía, letras humanas y diferentes lenguas"; Lima, que "ha producido muchísimos sugetos ilustres en virtud y letras cuyo catálogo sería muy dilatado y así nos contentaremos con hacer memoria de los más sobresalientes" y pone en lista más de treinta nombres encabezados por Santa Rosa de Lima; en ella no se olvida de establecer paralelos y puntos de referencia con Europa, como en el caso de Fr. Miguel de Lima, capuchino, llamado antes don Tomás de la Concha, "cuya inmensa sabiduría y monstruosa memoria asombró en Roma"; no menos impresionante es la lista preparada para México y su Universidad, que ha producido "muchos sugetos insignes en virtud, ciencia y artes en todos los tiempos." No falta el elogio cálido a su propia patria, Quito; en efecto, allí "los criollos son dóciles, humanos, corteses, liberales amantes de los estrangeros, inclinados a la piedad y de despierto ingenio y capacidad" y asimismo es "patria de muchas personas ilustres en virtud, armas y letras"; también registra ilustres hijos para Popayán, Santiago, y Truxillo, para los que puntualiza virtudes especiales, entre los muchos ejemplos que pueden señalarse. Pero Alcedo no se queda en las listas o elogios generales; también arriesga explicaciones y justificaciones, siempre en el tono de mesura y con la brevedad que la obra le exige; en efecto, s.v. *Perú* hace mención de sus habitantes en estos términos: "Los españoles se establecieron desde la Conquista, cuyos descendientes llaman Criollos y Peruleros, son hábiles, valerosos, dóciles,

de genio suave, de excelente ingenio y muy amantes de los fo-
rasteros: les ha faltado la instrucción y el premio con lo qual
hubieran hecho prodigiosos progresos en la literatura y las artes
habrían florecido en este país, pues sin embargo de lo dicho
nunca han faltado entre los criollos algunos hombres sobresalientes en las armas y en las letras. Los españoles europeos se llaman
chapetones y casi todos se aplican al comercio; algunos se estable-
cen allí y fundan nuevas familias, otros se vuelven a Europa con
ricos caudales adquiridos a costa de muchas fatigas y riesgos por
tierra y mar." El comentario es interesante en todos sus aspectos;
así, la imagen del indiano rico que vuelve a España sigue tan
viva a fines del siglo XVIII como lo era en los años en que Lope
de Vega la incorpora a los personajes de sus comedias; o aun
antes, cuando preocupan a Santa Teresa sus veleidades y osten-
taciones.[17] Ahora, y por conocerlo por propia experiencia, se
valorizan las "fatigas y riesgos" de estas fortunas y también se
ofrece una explicación social de algunas características de la
Colonia. Se trata de la capacidad natural y general de todos los
seres humanos para progresar por la educación y la cultura,
capaces de crear el espíritu de emulación y premiar el esfuerzo;
se trata de hacer llegar a estos hombres naturalmente ingeniosos
las ventajas del saber.[18] En efecto, solo la permanente ejercita-
ción de los beneficios de la educación y la cultura hacen del
hombre, de cualquier hombre, un ser de razón; y lo ejemplifica
el caso de la población de Ximbura, de la que dice Alcedo en el
artículo correspondiente: "Ximbura, pueblo de la provincia y co-
rregimiento de Loxa en el Reyno de Quito anexo al curato del
de Cariamanga, situado en una montaña retirada y fragosa donde
va el coadjutor del cura una vez al año y hace las funciones y
ceremonias de Párroco, sus naturales pueden servir de humilla-
ción a las naciones más cultas de Europa considerando a lo que

---

[17] Cf. Marcos A. Morínigo, *América en el teatro de Lope de Vega* (Buenos
Aires, 1946), pp.149 y ss., y A. Alonso, *Estudios lingüísticos. Temas hispanoamericanos* (Madrid, 1953), pp.70-71.

[18] Cf. J. Sarrailh, *L'Espagne éclairée de la seconde moitié du XVIII siècle*
(Paris, 1954), pp.145 y ss.

pueden llegar los hombres abandonados a la naturaleza; en su color, barba, trage y lenguage corrompido muestran sin la menor duda ser descendientes de Españoles, pero tan rudos e incultos que son de peor condición que los indios más bárbaros . . . apenas se hallan en ellos vestigios de Religión ni de la lengua Española y su trage mueve al mismo tiempo a compasión y risa, pues no es posible comprender su extraordinaria rusticidad sino considerando lo contentos que viven en aquel estado, prefiriéndolo a otro que sea correspondiente a su origen, aun después que lo saben."

Abandonado a la naturaleza el hombre no sólo vuelve al estado primitivo, sino que pierde la noción de los valores y puede llegar a contentarse con su estado de degradación y aceptarla con conocimiento de ello. Por el contrario, cualquiera sea su origen, el hombre puede elevarse a los más altos méritos como lo prueba el "célebre mulato zapatero" Miguel Enríquez (s.v. *Puerto Rico*).

Seguramente hay acá, en mezcla ecléctica, algo de la visión idealizadora de la vida del salvaje, pero en este caso se trata de presuntos españoles. Por cierto, las ideas de Alcedo acerca de los indios, abundantemente documentadas en toda la obra, reflejan muchas de las tendencias de la época y también el lastre de viejas opiniones y la originalidad de su propia experiencia. En efecto, Alcedo dedica un artículo entero (s.v. *Indios*) a la consideración de las características generales de los indios; en él se halla presente su opinión personal pero "como no es posible reducir a un artículo toda la historia de los indios, el que quisiere instruirse de ella enteramente puede ver lo que dicen el Cronista Antonio de Herrera, Fr. Gregorio García, Don Antonio de Ulloa y el p. Laffiteau." Las fuentes van desde las *Décadas* de Herrera (1601–1615), "la primera y única gran crónica mayor de Indias,"[19] hasta los más recientes estudios etnográficos defensores de las costumbres indígenas como el de Laffiteau (*rectius* Lafitau) de 1724.[20]

19 Cf. Rómulo D. Carbia, *La Crónica Oficial en las Indias Occidentales* (La Plata, 1934), pp.150–79.

20 *Moeurs des sauvages ameriquains comparees aux moeurs des premiers temps*

A este último debe mucho el artículo de Alcedo mencionado, sobre todo el capítulo *Idée ou caractere des sauvages en general* (I, 103–108) del que Alcedo toma en cuenta la opinión de Lafi- tau sobre los rasgos de carácter pero descarta las extravagantes referencias al físico del jesuita francés, imponiendo los datos de su propia experiencia. Sobre todo, el artículo de Alcedo propone, siguiendo a Lafitau, un retrato que tenga en cuenta los elemen- tos de juicio contradictorios que ofrecen los indios para su carac- terización[21] y más que calificaciones de orden moral, propone una presentación en que cualidades y defectos considerados generales, permitan una evaluación más científica y objetiva; pero contrariamente al francés no intenta una defensa de la cultura indígena como forma de crítica a la complejidad de cuestionable eficacia de la cultura europea. No obstante, en el artículo citado asoma la posibilidad de una valorización parcial de la simplicidad de la vida indígena: "Si la indiferencia absoluta de los indios en las cosas temporales no fuese igual en las espiri- tuales, serían dignos de llamarse felices." Y ya Lafitau: "Mais leur rusticité et la disette où ils sont presque de toutes choses, leur donnent sur nous cet avantage, qu'ils ignorent tous ces reffinemens du vice, qu'ont introduit le luxe et l'abondance" (p.106) y más adelante: "nous serions sans doute plus heureux, si nous avions comme eux cette indifference qui leur fait mépri- ser et ignorer beaucoup de choses dont nous ne sçaurions nous passer" (p.107).[22]

_____

(Paris, 1724). Cf. sobre este autor, Silvio Zavala, *América en el espíritu francés del siglo XVIII* (México, 1949), pp.160 y ss. Para las opiniones iniciales de los historiadores de Indias y sobre todo las de G. Fernández de Oviedo, v. A. M. Salas, *Tres cronistas de Indias*, FCE (México, 1959), pp.117–34.

[21] "Le caractère de leur génie et de leur esprit est plus difficile à prendre, et semble même renfermer quelques contradictions" (pp.104–105).

[22] Las coincidencias podrían acumularse; Alcedo conviene con Lafitau en los siguientes rasgos de carácter: seriedad, frialdad de carácter, hospitalidad, crueldad con los enemigos; vengativos "disimulan sus sentimientos aparentando amistad hasta que tienen ocasión de vengarse, aunque pasen muchos años . . ." ("vindicatifs et d'autant plus dangereux qu'ils sçavent mieux couvrir, et qu'ils couvent plus long-temps leurs resentiments," p.106); "flema, indiferencia falta de cólera, respeto de los ancianos, tranquilidad inalterable en todos los accidentes prósperos y

En ambos se nota un parejo interés por comprender la manera de vivir indígena como un problema de adaptación cultural; para Alcedo su "educación se dirige sola a hacer sus cuerpos adaptados al método que tienen de vivir y acostumbrar el ánimo a sufrir el peso de los mayores males" (*loc. cit.*); Lafitau por su parte había usado razonamiento semejante para condenar la falta de moderación de la cultura europea (p.107).

Alcedo también se pregunta por el talento natural de los indios y su respuesta trata de conciliar las ideas tradicionales con datos propios: "es digno de admirar que siendo los indios de una estupidez increíble (que obligó a los principios a controvertirse entre los sabios si eran especie de irracionales) pues muchas veces les falta aun el instinto que tienen estos, se advierta en varios asuntos el discernimiento más vivo y las ideas más bien concertadas." Sin otra intención que la de la información científica y sin voluntad polémica, ajena a la de la presentación de los mejores datos posibles, Alcedo se aleja de las defensas de los indios impulsadas en el siglo XVIII por sus admirados jesuitas (el citado Lafitau, el padre Clavigero, etc.).[23] Pero en este pasaje archiva en el pasado ("a los principios") toda discusión acerca de la naturaleza irracional de los habitantes primitivos de América, y a lo largo de la obra ensayará explicaciones para su manera de ser que reflejan su posición en las polémicas contemporáneas. En efecto, Alcedo rechaza la teoría de la innata debilidad de los indios (Buffon, de Pauw, etc.): "era una de aquellas [naciones] cuyo carácter desmiente los defectos que a todos los indios imputan generalmente algunos filósofos, pues aunque habitaba un clima muy cálido no era débil ni desnervada, sino vigorosa, robusta y de grandes fuerzas . . . sin que obstase . . . el habitar en la zona ardiente para ser una de las

---

adversos de la vida" ("une egalité que les contretemps et les mauvais succès n'alterent point," p.106). Ciertamente son estos rasgos poco novedosos; en lo que a vicios se refiere parecen repetición, con diversidad de matices, de lo dicho ya por los cronistas del siglo XVI hasta la *Monarquía indiana* de J. de Torquemada (1615).

23 Cf. A. Gerbi, *o.c.*, sobre todo el capítulo V.

más guerreras y valerosas" (s.v. *Yaguache*). Tampoco cabe dudar acerca de las capacidades intelectuales ante el ejemplo del "ilustrísimo señor don Nicolás del Puerto, indio, célebre jesuita que mereció llegar a la dignidad de obispo de Oaxaca, varón de tanta sabiduría y ciencia que destruyó la opinión de que los indios no eran capaces de los conocimientos de los europeos" (s.v. *Mixteca*).[24] Alcedo expone su admiración por la arquitectura indígena, especialmente la incaica a la que dedica sus mejores elogios (s.v. *Cuzco* y *Guamalíes*, entre otros) y no deja de recordar a Las Casas con ecuanimidad; en efecto, mal podía caer en olvido Las Casas en el siglo XVIII para nadie que se interesara en los asuntos de América;[25] por lo menos tres veces cita Alcedo al obispo de Chiapas en el *Diccionario*; en la primera lo menciona, cautelosamente, como fuente para sus datos sobre la primitiva población indígena de Santo Domingo (s.v. *Santo Domingo*): "estaba tan poblada de indios que el obispo de Chiapa, Fr. Bartolomé de Las Casas dice (si su cálculo no es exagerado) que tenía más de tres millones."[26] La prudente reserva se basa en los datos de autores que no concuerdan con Las Casas y son fuente también de Alcedo; pero es curioso que en otros casos admita sin discusión las abultadas cifras de Torquemada, de quien debió tomar sin duda los datos sobre las epidemias en los indios de México: "ha padecido varias pestes en que han perecido millares de indios, particularmente la del año de 1545 en que murieron 800.000 y en la que experimentó el año de 1756 [*sic*], que duró hasta la mitad del siguiente, más de dos

24 En la lista de "Obispos que ha habido en Oaxaca" (s.v. *Oaxaca*) no había mencionado Alcedo su origen indio.

25 Así lo suponía don Ramón Menéndez Pidal, *El padre Las Casas. Su doble personalidad*, Espasa-Calpe (Madrid, 1963), pp.360–65. Cf. M. Gutiérrez Fernández, "Sobre Bartolomé de Las Casas," *Anales de la Universidad Hispalense*, XXV (1964), n.2, p.60, para el rechazo de esta opinión. V. también para las afinidades de los pensadores del siglo XVIII y Las Casas, Silvio Zavala "¿Las Casas esclavista?," *Cuadernos Americanos*, III (1944), n.2, pp.149–54.

26 Cf. *Brevissima relación de la destruyción de las Indias*, edición facsimilar, Biblioteca Argentina de Libros Raros Americanos, III, 9; para este y otros textos de Las Casas, cf. A. Rosenblat, *La población de América en 1492*, El Colegio de México (1967), pp.11 y ss.

millones."[27] Cabe aquí recordar que en 1723 habían vuelto a
ser impresos los *Veinte i un libros rituales i Monarquía indiana*
que ya en el siglo XVII se habían hecho una rareza biblio-
gráfica (Fr. Juan de Torquemada, *Monarquía indiana*, selección, introducción, y notas de Miguel León-Portilla [México,
1964], p.vii).

La otra cita de Las Casas aparece s.v. *Ciudad Real*: "Es cabeza
de obispado erigido el año 1538 y tiene la gloria de haber sido
su primer obispo don Fray Bartolomé de las Casas o Casaus del
Orden de Santo Domingo que se hizo célebre en el mundo así
por su virtud como por el zelo y empeño con que tomó la defensa de los indios para liberarlos de las vejaciones que padecían
por los conquistadores." Pero el recuerdo de Las Casas se da
también en forma menos explícita; así, Alcedo no oculta las in-
justicias del trabajo en las minas (s.v. *Desaguadero*): "allí se
juntan los indios mitayos que van al trabajo de las minas de
Potosí, celebrando una gran fiesta que termina en llanto, por el
sentimiento de los parientes al despedirse, creyendo que no se
han de volver a ver, como sucede ordinariamente por los muchos
que mueren en aquella fatiga"; o a la codicia de los españoles,
que le sirve también para explicar la expulsión de los jesuitas
(s.v *Mamalucos* en *Adiciones y Correcciones*, III, 437): "No sufrí-
an menos que los indios los españoles del Paraguay por su culpa,
pues no tenían más que sostener las reducciones contra los ma-
melucos, que nunca habían podido forzar esta barrera; pero el
interés los cegó porque juzgaron estas nuevas iglesias como
dique opuesto a su codicia." A Las Casas también se debe remon-
tar la idea de la capacidad de los indios para asimilar la doctrina
de la fe,[28] remozado el método con las ideas de su tiempo (s.v.

27 La segunda fecha es errata (que no corrigió la edición de BAE) por 1576
según se comprueba en Torquemada (primera parte, libro 5, c.22: "El año de
1576 gobernando este Virrey sobrevino a los naturales indios una mortandad y
pestilencia que duró por tiempo de más de un año . . . y hallóse que habían sido
los muertos más de dos millones que parece cosa increíble que excedió esta
mortandad a la pasada del año de 1545 en doce veces cien mil personas. Porque
en la pestilencia del Año 1545 murieron ochocientas mil personas.")

28 Cf. textos en A. M. Salas, *o.c.*, p.237; por lo demás, las semejanzas entre las

*Omaguas*): "Los reduxo a la religión católica el año de 1686 el padre Samuel Fritz alemán, de la extinguida compañía, célebre misionero y gran matemático y encontró en ellos alguna idea de cultura y civilidad: encubrían su desnudez, vivían en sociedad lo qual y un método racional contribuyeron mucho a su reducción convencidos con la luz natural de la verdad y propiedad de la Doctrina que se les enseñaba y de los males que eran consecuentes con su método y barbarie."

En cuanto a los vicios y virtudes enumerados a lo largo de la obra, no se muestra original Alcedo (si en asunto como éste cabe la originalidad); su valor bélico le merece constante alabanza siempre que se practique contra otros indios (s.v. *Saramissues, Iroqueses, Darién, Yaguarcocha*), pero puede convertirse en reprobable ferocidad y salvajismo (s.v. *Paraguay, Moxos*); cierto es que no son los únicos feroces en el continente y a veces contribuye a su criminalidad la compañía de otros bandidos nada recomendables (s.v. *Mamalucos*): "sacudieron el yugo de la autoridad divina y humana, aumentándose con haberse establecido entre ellos infinitos bandidos de varias naciones: portugueses, españoles, italianos y holandeses fugitivos de la justicia que los perseguía por sus delitos"; tampoco faltan "muchos criollos y mulatos foragidos que se les han agregado" con los que "tienen varios pueblos y habitaciones de donde salen a talar y destruir los de las jurisdicciones de Mendoza y de Córdoba" (s.v. *Mendoza*).

Aparte de la frecuente mención de su pereza e indolencia, de su embriaguez y su lascivia, el rasgo negativo que con mayor persistencia se señala es su antropofagía (s.v. *Guaticas, Mariquites, Masteles, Cuzco, Guamba, Guarayos, Guatemala, Puna, Tapuyes*). A veces los llama *antropófagos*, otras veces son *come-*

ideas sobre la igualdad de los hombres de Las Casas y las del siglo XVIII tienen que establecerse dentro de ciertos límites que deben tener en cuenta el proceso de secularización de Europa. No se trata de la perfección por la fe, sino mediante la buena educación, así sea dirigida a propagar la doctrina cristiana. Cf. Silvio Zavala, *La filosofía política en la conquista de América*, FCE (México, 1947), pp.117 y ss.

*dores de carne humana*; por lo menos tres veces cree necesaria la explicación de la palabra "antropófagos o comedores de carne humana" (s.v. *Chiriguanos, Guarayos, Guaticas*) aunque según Corominas la palabra ya aparece registrada a mediados del siglo XVI; tal peculiaridad gastronómica de los indios da lugar a comentarios pintorescos: "comen la carne humana con mucho apetito" (s.v. *Tapuyes*), texto que seguramente no conocía el Borges de *Fundación mítica de Buenos Aires*; "después de reducidos a christiandad y policía, pasó el obispo de Truxillo a corregir sus errores y abominables vicios y en odio de su apostólico zelo le quitaron la vida con veneno y después de sepultado el cadáver le desenterraron sigilosamente, purificaron la carne de la infección del tósigo y se lo comieron renovando los cruentos banquetes de su gentilidad" (s.v. *Puna*); "don Fray Vicente de Valverde . . . muerto a manos de los indios de la Puná en el gobierno de Guayaquil quando volvía a España y se lo comieron asado" (s.v. *Cuzco*, "Obispos que ha tenido").

Los de nobles virtudes y costumbres también son señalados (s.v. *Guajiros, Loreto, Natchez, Salivas, Sechúra*) y tales virtudes están directamente unidas a su talento para aceptar la doctrina cristiana (*Nebome, Illinois*). Hay pues, un carácter que puede considerarse típico y que nos permite hablar sobre los indios en general; hay también diferencias de grado en el equilibrio de vicios y virtudes; y el hecho irrefutable de su capacidad para cambiar, asimilarse a las costumbres europeas y vencer las características naturales negativas. A esta conclusión llega Alcedo desde su propia experiencia limitada y a través de las numerosas fuentes que le suministran datos; falta todavía hacer un riguroso análisis de esas fuentes pero en su transcripción y selección, Alcedo se compromete como erudito y como hombre de opiniones. En efecto, el tema de la esclavitud despierta en nuestro autor un violento celo emancipador a tono con el espíritu filantrópico de su época al tiempo que hace posible su defensa de la conquista española comparada con lo que ingleses y portugueses llevan a cabo en sus colonias. Dedica Alcedo un artículo de su *Diccionario* a los *Negros* como había hecho para los indios;

en él hallamos la tercera mención del "célebre" Fr. Bartolomé de Las Casas quien fue el que "con zelo indiscreto propuso para libertar a los indios de la servidumbre, llevar negros esclavos para el trabajo, como si esta parte del género humano debiera carecer de los privilegios de la humanidad por la diferencia del color que les da el nombre." Ciertamente, Alcedo se basaba en las propias palabras de su bien leído Las Casas (*Historia de las Indias*, l.III, c.102) y se adelantaba a lo que sería pocos años después renovada polémica sobre si el obispo de Chiapas había sido o no esclavista;[29] este positivo interés por la situación de los negros en América es de larga tradición en la orden de los jesuitas que tanto admiraba Alcedo, de modo que no debe sorprender el tono polémico de los textos en los que, como ya se ha señalado, juega también su papel el factor político.[30] Así, s.v. *Negros*, Alcedo denuncia que "los compran en las costas de Africa y los llevan por esclavos, donde [América, los dominios de España, Portugal, Francia, Inglaterra, Holanda, etc.] son tratados con el mayor rigor e inhumanidad como si no fueran de la especie racional." Acusa a los ingleses, holandeses, y portugueses de "este infame comercio" y recuerda el derecho a conseguir la libertad "que dispuso sabiamente el gobierno español", denuncia las dificultades para ponerlo en práctica pues "no suele tener efecto por lo que elude el interés y dureza de los dueños." Cierto es que "el carácter general de los negros es de malísimas costumbres" pero todo se debe admitir pues "aboga en su disculpa el amor de la libertad y la sinrazón de la esclavitud"; no olvida señalar Alcedo que son muchos "en quienes se observan virtudes morales" y recuerda que son los españoles, entre todas las naciones "los que los tratan menos mal." Es a partir del tercer tomo del *Diccionario*, publicado en 1788 (comienzo de la letra *M*) que hallamos referencias a la defensa de la conquista de

[29] Cf. el artículo de Silvio Zavala citado en la nota 25. Para la esclavitud en América y una defensa de Las Casas por los cargos de esclavista, v. José Antonio Saco, *Historia de la esclavitud de la raza africana en el Mundo Nuevo y en especial en los países hispanoamericanos* (Barcelona, 1889), I, 100 y ss.

[30] V. F. Ortiz, "La *Leyenda Negra* contra fray Bartolomé," *Cuadernos Americanos*, LXV (1952), n.5, pp.146–84, sobre todo pp.180–82.

América por España y no sólo con respecto al trato dado a los esclavos sino también por su actitud con los indios.[31] En las *Adiciones y Correcciones* al final del tomo tercero añade Alcedo nuevos datos sobre los negros en América que no tenía o no se había decidido a poner en la obra originalmente; da como primera fecha de llegada de esclavos negros a América el año 1523 por concesión del emperador Carlos V a su mayordomo Lorenzo Garrebood (*sic*). En verdad, la fecha de la real cédula es 1518 y el nombre del mayordomo del rey fue Lorenzo de Gouvenot o Gavorrod; sin embargo el texto es interesante porque además de datos y generalidades sobre usos y costumbres más o menos pintorescas, Alcedo recuerda con orgullo la abolición de la marca de fuego por decreto de Carlos III (1784), "cuyo piadoso corazón es protector de la humanidad"; según Alcedo la abolición de esta "horrorosa práctica en una nación culta y católica" influyó en el gobierno inglés, que intentó eliminar el "infame comercio" sin más resultados que "providencias para su mejor trato y condición"; Alcedo no era un reformador o un revolucionario pero creía en los necesarios cambios de la sociedad: "Muchos Ingleses, Franceses y Españoles convencidos de las razones que en un siglo ilustrado como el presente se han hecho públicas, han dado libertad a todos sus esclavos y podemos esperar el día en que esta clase miserable de hombres goze como todos los demás este derecho de que no los excluyó la naturaleza." No es mejor la situación de

31 V. por ejemplo, s.v. *Massachussets* (en la primera edición en III, 457, *Adiciones*): ". . . a este padrón tan feo [prohibición de la vacuna antivariólica] se añade otro peor de esta provincia en el premio que asignó a qualquiera que matase un indio, y el año de 1724 se entregó la cantidad que era de 2250 libras sterlinas a Juan Lovvevvel, que con una compañía de facinerosos que había formado para salir a caza de estos infelices, como si fuesen fieras, dio muerte a diez que encontró durmiendo alrededor de una hoguera: blasonen con este borrón de humanidad los ingleses y declamen contra las pretendidas crueldades de los españoles en la América, que aunque fuesen ciertas, no llegan a esta barbarie, que no tiene exemplar en Nación alguna." La traducción inglesa de Thompson mantuvo sin cambios el texto y aun añadió otros datos nada edificantes a propósito de John Lovewell (que en la edición de BAE es Liwewel, por errata), ubicando el hecho que narra Alcedo en el año 1725 (III, 35).

los esclavos en Brasil y Alcedo denuncia esta injusticia (s.v. *S. Salvador*): "las calles están llenas de negros esclavos de ambos sexos que están casi desnudos sudando con la fatiga y gimiendo baxo de la más cruel e insoportable esclavitud; pero lo que causa más admiración a los que tienen humanidad, es ver varias tiendas abiertas y otros parages llenos de estos miserables, desnudos, expuestos a venta pública como si fuesen bestias, sobre los quales tienen sus dueños la misma autoridad que sobre los animales, y muchas veces los tratan con la misma ó más inhumanidad."

No falta tampoco un artículo dedicado a los *Mulatos*; está también en las *Adiciones y Correcciones* del tomo III (1788). En él, Alcedo señala que la abundancia de mulatos en América es "fruto del libertinage de los Europeos y de la lascivia de las negras a que se agrega el dominio de aquellos sobre sus esclavos que les facilita este comercio criminal." Con rara destreza reparte vicios y virtudes y añade: "se puede asegurar que en los vastos dominios del Rey de España en la América no tiene mejores soldados ni más malos hombres." No olvida nuestro autor la ejemplificación edificante: "sin embargo de las malas calidades que tienen los mulatos, se han visto algunos que por tenerlas muy buenas han merecido singular aprecio y distinciones de los Virreyes, Obispos y personas de carácter y distinción como Miguel Angel de Goenaga, Capitán de milicias en la ciudad de Portovelo cuya honradez y virtudes le grangearon la distinción con que fue tratado de todos y en las colonias Inglesas, Francesas y Holandesas tenía una firma suya el mayor crédito; y en Puerto-Rico otro llamado Miguel Enríquez, que aunque zapatero de oficio era tan honrado y hizo tantos servicios al Rey, que mereció ser condecorado de su Real Orden con una medalla de su efigie y el distintivo de Don, bastando estos para ver lo poco que influye el color en los dotes del espíritu." Ya hemos visto que Enríquez había aparecido s.v. *Puerto Rico*, pero aquí el texto ilustra la opinión de Alcedo y no la fama de un lugar.

Salvados así de la condena arbitraria los indios, negros, y mulatos, los esquimales (s.v. *Esquimaux* y *Labrador*) pasan a ser la nación "que mejor corresponda a la voz *salvages*" cuya raza de pigmeos es la "más miserable" del mundo y parecen "distintos de todos los indios de la América."

Como se ha visto, faltan las estridencias polémicas en el *Diccionario*; es claro también que en compendios de esta índole no es lo frecuente encontrarlas, pero las firmes ideas filantrópicas de su tiempo y un principio de aproximación antropológica al estudio de la población de América están presentes en esta obra de esforzada erudición. Es notable también el empeño por desvirtuar fábulas persistentes desde el descubrimiento de América como la de la existencia de gigantes (s.v. *Chunianis; S. Elena, Tucumán; Tula; Vilcas*); o la de indios con talones hacia adelante (s.v. *Marajo*); o la de la ilusoria existencia de El Dorado "donde perecieron muchos sin otro fruto que conocer países áridos, montuosos, con grandes fatigas y trabajos" (s.v. *Coropa; Manoa*); o la de las amazonas "delirios y sueños de algunos que han querido publicar maravillas para acreditar sus viages y relaciones" (s.v. *Marañón*; v. también s.v. *Guacares*). Alcedo pone en tela de juicio la leyenda de la presencia de Santo Tomás en América (s.v. *Itoco, Mañacicas* en *Adiciones y Correcciones* del tomo III, *Pai-Zuma*) aunque se siente inclinado a aceptarla como posible cuando se trata de confirmar la información de una fuente jesuítica como s.v. *Paraguay*. Prudentemente relegados a la fuerza de la tradición, quedan los testimonios de la presencia del apóstol Santiago (s.v. *Querétaro*) y de San Bartolomé (s.v. *Ubaque; Viscas*).[32] Asimismo, Alcedo recoge numerosas tradiciones milagrosas en todo el territorio americano sin más comentario que la simple mención de su existencia y la práctica de ritos, pero a veces pone a salvo su prescindencia en la materia o arriesga la probabilidad de una explicación naturalista, como en la profecía del hundi-

[32] A propósito de la presencia de San Bartolomé en América, Alcedo se permite un comentario irónico sobre la destrucción de lo que podía ser prueba documental de la presencia del santo: "en su inmediación hay una piedra como una mesa en que han creído algunos la tradición vulgar heredada entre los indios de que allí se recostaba el apóstol San Bartolomè, tenía antes esculpidos unos caracteres que mandó picar un visitador del Arzobispado por razones que le parecieron suficientes."

miento del pueblo de Lagunilla que la "tradición general de padres a hijos" atribuye a San Francisco Solano (s.v. *Lagunilla*); no es la intención de este trabajo el registro minucioso de las creencias, curiosidades, milagrerías, y cultos anotadas en el *Diccionario* que muchos servicios prestaría a los folkloristas, pero cabe destacar que junto a este interés se nota en su obra un paralelo entusiasmo por la libertad de conciencia y cultos que observa en las poblaciones de la colonización inglesa, convertidas ahora en nación independiente; por ejemplo, en los artículos dedicados a *Boston*; a *Charlestown* "la libertad de conciencia que concedieron a poco tiempo de su fundación la hizo hacer una población numerosa, que ha crecido cada vez más por su gran comercio y estas y otras muchas qualidades la constituyen por una de las mejores poblaciones de la América"; o a *Pensilvania*: "siendo digno de admiración que en tanta diversidad de naciones, lenguas y creencias reyne la harmonía y unión en que viven todos; y sin embargo de que cada uno siente que los demás no sigan su secta y procura por todos medios persuadirlos, no por eso se apartan de la unión de afectos, de que resulta que viven si no en la misma secta, en la misma religión christiana con la mayor fraternidad."

Falta aun un estudio de las fuentes de Alcedo que ahora se verá facilitado por la publicación de su monumental *Bibliotheca Americana*; de tal estudio resultará más segura la evaluación de su capacidad crítica y su criterio de investigador.[33] En nuestro trabajo hemos querido poner de relieve el interés de esta figura poco conocida y bien representativa de la Ilustración en Hispanoamérica y España; parejo interés ofrece para los que estudien la influencia de Norteamérica en los movimientos liberales de las colonias españolas que contribuirían tan profundamente a los procesos de independencia. Resulta irónico que las excelencias de las informaciones y datos de su *Diccionario* hicieran acreedor a este quiteño ilustre de la paradójica gloria del olvido.

[33] El nuevo editor del *Diccionario* se atiene todavía a las opinones muy generales y vagas de don Diego Barros Arana, escritas en 1863 (*Estudio Preliminar,* p.XXXIII).

# II

## Iberian Peninsula

IV

# From Pistoia to Cádiz:
# A Generation's Itinerary 1786–1812

## JUAN MARICHAL

THERE IS AN ANECDOTE, often told in Spanish universities, of
a well-known professor of Roman law who always began his
courses by saying, "El derecho romano empezó por no existir"
("Roman law began by not existing"). The Spanish and Hispanic American Enlightenment began also by not existing—not
existing, that is, in the writings of historians. It is true also that
many Spaniards—and perhaps as many Hispanic Americans—
*did not want* the Enlightenment to have existed. In the eighteenth century itself a great Spanish conservative called his own
times, with emphatic disdain, "siglo de ensayos" ("century of useless experiments"). Later Spanish conservatives called the three
liberal years of 1820–1823 "los mal llamados años"—"the
improperly called years"—and they thought probably of the
entire eighteenth century as "the century that wasn't." Not so
many years ago one of the greatest minds of the Spanish-speaking
nations, Ortega y Gasset, said that there was in the history of
Spain a considerable gap: the absence of an entire century, the
eighteenth. But, in spite of Ortega, it can be maintained today that there *is* indeed an eighteenth century in the Spanish-
speaking nations: in short, the Spanish and Hispanic American
Enlightenment *is here to stay*, though it cannot be denied that

it began by not existing—by not existing *in fact* in the early 1700's; and it took about half its age to become itself. Spaniards were actually seen as unfit for the century in its first quarter, while in the 1760's some of them were considered as the very embodiment of their own times' intellectual temper. Three texts on Spain and on Spaniards by the great trinity of the French Enlightenment—Montesquieu, Voltaire, and Rousseau— bear witness to that becoming itself of the Spanish eighteenth century.

In 1721 Montesquieu said in his *Lettres persanes* (letter 78): "Voyez une de leurs bibliothèques, les romans d'un côté et les scolastiques de l'autre; vous diriez que les parties ont été faites et le tout rassemblé par quelque ennemi secret de la raison humaine" ("Look at their libraries, novels on one side and scholastic philosophy on the other; one would say that all these books were written and brought together by some secret enemy of human reason"). Forty years later, in 1762, Jean-Jacques Rousseau—thinking certainly of his close friend Manuel de Altuna—wrote in his book *Emile ou De l'éducation*:

> Je ne connais guère que les Espagnols qui voyagent de cette manière . . . l'Espagnol étudie en silence le gouvernement, les moeurs, la police et il est le seul . . . qui de retour chez lui rapporte de ce qu'il a vu quelque remarque utile à son pays [Spaniards are the only ones who travel in this manner . . . they are the only ones who quietly observe the government, the way of life, the administration of justice, and they are indeed the only ones who use their observations upon returning to their country].

Six years after the publication of Rousseau's book, Voltaire was visited at Ferney by a son-in-law of the Spanish prime minister, Count Aranda. And he wrote about both: "Je vous réponds qu'il aidera puissament le comte Aranda á faire un nouveau siècle" ("I can tell you that he will help Count Aranda to make a new century").

Spain, or at least some representative Spaniards, had thus gone a great distance from 1721 to 1768, from Montesquieu's disdain to Voltaire's confidence. Spain began by being out of the century and fifty years later it was expected to be a seminal agent of the Enlightenment. Of course, Voltaire's exaltation of Count Aranda was meant, first of all, as the accolade given by the *philosophes* to Charles III and to the extraordinary group of intellectual executives brought into power by him—men who indeed wanted *to make a new century* in Spain and in Hispanic America. And that is why those thirty years of the Caroline Age, 1759–1788, became a retrospective national utopia for Spaniards of later times. It could be said that when Jovellanos spoke, in one of his poems, of "los amenos carolíneos valles" ("those pleasant Caroline valleys")—referring to the towns and plantations founded by Olavide in Sierra Morena—he was obviously hoping that the Caroline Age would transform all of Spain into a continuous pleasant valley. Or as Olavide himself put it in 1796, despite so many years of persecution and exile: "¡Ah quién tuviera a su encargo toda la tierra del reino para hacer un jardín de toda España!" ("If one could control all the land of this kingdom to make a garden of all of Spain!") The death of Charles III—December 14, 1788—had seemed to close that "garden." On the road to El Pardo there was a small tree to which Charles was particularly attached and in the walks of his last years he was often heard to say: "Cuando yo muera ¿quién cuidará de ti, pobre arbolito?" ("When I die, who will take care of you, my poor little tree?") *144728*

I have chosen as my subject for this paper the quarter of a century between the death of that king and the establishment of a constitutional monarchy by the Cortes of Cádiz in 1812. My final purpose is to show that the Spanish Enlightenment finally became *itself that year*: because those men of Cádiz and their 1812 constitution did play a considerable rôle in the making of the new century, of the new liberal Europe. And I submit that the younger among them—the generation of 1812, those in their early thirties—were the intellectual and political culmination of the Caroline Age. I should add that the generation of 1812 was strictly speaking the class of 1792 at the College of Arts of the

University of Salamanca. The second purpose of this paper, then, is to expound what Miguel de Unamuno wrote, in 1902, about the Salamanca of the 1780's: "era esta Universidad foco de liberalismo . . . dominaba en esta Universidad la preocupación de ir al compás de Europa, de *europeizarse*, como hemos dado en decir por acá . . . aquí se fraguaron algunos de nuestros *doceañistas*" ("this University was a center of liberalism . . . this University did not want to stay behind the rest of Europe and it tried to *Europeanize* itself as we say now . . . here were shaped the minds of some of the men of 1812").

The recovery by the oldest Spanish university of its national leadership was the effect of the reforms started there in 1771 by Charles III. The royal decrees of February 1771 did aim at changing the social composition of the University and they have been studied by three historians: the late Luis Sala Balust, with one of the best examples of recent Spanish historical research and scholarship (*Visitas y reformas de los Colegios Mayores de Salamanca en el reinado de Carlos III*, Valladolid, 1958); Professor George Addy, who has included the Spanish text of the 1771 University Reform Plan in his book *The Enlightenment in the University of Salamanca* (Durham, N.C., 1966); and Francisco Aguilar Piñal, who recently has published a documentary volume, *Los comienzos de la crisis universitaria en España* (Madrid, 1967). I will not therefore discuss the social transformation of the student body and of the faculty at Salamanca, though it obviously had immediate intellectual and political consequences. I am rather concerned here with the long-range effects of the 1771 university reforms in the quarter of a century following the Caroline Age, because very seldom do we find in Spanish history a university generation so influential as the Salamanca graduates of 1792: they were both the children of the Caroline Age and its faithful legatees in the unceasing struggle of the two Spains in the first two decades of their intellectual manhood.

The temper of the Salamanca students in the 1790's is precisely described by Jovellanos in the entry of his so-called sixth diary, dated March 20, 1795:

. . . Liaño, bueno; pasamos el tiempo en preparativos y con-versación. Toda la juventud salamantina es *port-royalista*. De la secta *pistoyense*: Opstraët, Zola, y sobre todo Tamburini, andan en manos de todos; más de tres mil ejemplares había ya cuando vino su prohibición; uno solo se entregó. Esto da esperanza de que se mejoren los estudios cuando las cátedras y gobierno de la Universidad estén en la nueva generación. Cuando manden los que (ahora) obedecen. Cualquiera otra reforma sería vana. Como la de los frailes. Los de Calatrava, en la última corrupción.

My comments on this Jovellanos text will be a sort of expanded translation. But I need to quote again from the same diary, from the entry of April 16, 1795: "Visita de tres colegiales benedicti-nos que pasan al monasterio de Nájera; larga conversación con ellos de estudios . . . hay ya (entre ellos) muchos *port-royalistas* y *tamburinistas*. La mudanza está hecha, porque las nuevas y buenas ideas cundieron por los jóvenes; serán viejos y ellas con ellos." Jovellanos expresses in these two entries of his journal that he is certain that the universities and Spain will change when the new generation of students becomes the new generation of teachers and national leaders: he knows that reforms of insti-tutions are useless unless there are new minds to implement them. That is why he alludes to the waste of time spent in trying to improve existing academic institutions and refers to the im-possibility of innovation within a group such as "the friars of Calatrava." Jovellanos had been involved for some years in the government effort to improve the Salamanca colleges of the Mili-tary Orders—Alcántara, Calatrava, and Santiago—and in 1790 he was commissioned to visit the Calatrava College and to pre-pare a report. (This document, *Reglamento para el Colegio de Calatrava*, Gijón, 1964, has been edited by José Caso González, the most dedicated *jovellanista* of the post–Civil War literary historians of Spain.) In October 1791 Jovellanos arrived in Salamanca to proceed on his *visita*, and on the thirteenth of that month he wrote in his journal, "Se empezó la visita secreta . . . por la tarde a Alcántara; a la librería de Alegría; compra del Tamburini. . . ." Jovellanos thus bought his copy of Tamburini at a Salamanca bookstore—I would guess Alegría was the 1791 Salamanca equivalent of our own León Sánchez Cuesta—probably because it was already being read by many students and faculty members.

But why Tamburini? And why Opstraet and Zola? The answers appear, implicitly, in the title of this paper: Pistoia, 1786. That old walled Italian town in Tuscany, not far from Florence, had given previously to our civilization a weapon that still carries its toponymic origin: *pistòla*, pistol. In the 1780's it became famous after its bishop, Scipione De' Ricci, asked all ecclesiastics of his diocesis to meet at a synod to consider fundamental administrative, liturgical, pastoral, and ethical matters of the Catholic church. Two well-known theologians—teaching then at Pavia and both prominent leaders of Italian Jansenism—Pietro Tamburini (1737–1827) and Giuseppe Zola (1739–1806), were also invited, Tamburini becoming, in fact, the guiding mind of the Pistoia ecclesiastical assembly. The proceedings were published in 1788 and distributed by the tens of thousands throughout Catholic Europe. In Spain, according to a contemporary document, the Pistoia proceedings were seen as "a holy book" and a translation in Spanish was duly authorized and printed. These proceedings recommended that the study of the theological writings of Melchor Cano should be replaced by those of Jean Opstraet (1651–1720), a Belgian Jansenist. The three authors mentioned by Jovellanos as being in the hands of students at Salamanca in the 1790's—Opstraet, Zola, and Tamburini—appeared in the "required" Pistoia reading list. The Vatican, a target of critical views at the Pistoia synod, reacted rather slowly, six years later, with the condemnatory bull *Auctorem fidei* of August 28, 1794. But the royal authorities of Spain did not accept that bull or give orders to implement its instructions until January 9, 1801. Jovellanos, who was arrested March 10, 1801, wrote the following passage in his journal, January 9, 1801: "Correo. Decreto para admitir la bula *Auctorem fidei*. Orden para su observancia. Azotes al partido llamado jansenista. ¡Ah! ¡Quién se los da, Dios mío! Pero ya sabrá vengarse . . ."

("Mail. Royal decree accepting bull *Auctorem fidei*. Orders for its implementation. Blows against the so-called Jansenist party. Alas! And the one who does it, oh my God! But [that party] will take vengeance for it . . ."). I should add that the so-called Jansenist party at the University of Salamanca was able to survive the government offensive against them, as the bishop of Pistoia was writing in February 1804 in a letter to the so-called constitutional bishop, the famous French revolutionary Henri Grégoire: "Je suis bien surpris qu'un pays d'Inquisition comme l'Espagne vous devance en zèle et en intérêt pour la religion. . . . L'Université de Salamanca a un grand évêque [Tavira] à la tête et des braves professeurs . . . la vérité aura la dessus ("I am quite surprised to see that an inquisitorial country such as Spain is ahead of you in spiritual matters. . . . The University of Salamanca has a great bishop at its head and very brave professors . . . truth will prevail"). And indeed truth, or rather the principle of the free search for truth, did prevail when some of those brave Salamanca professors went to the Cortes of Cádiz in 1810 and put an end to the inquisitorial institutions of Spain. But were they Jansenists? Can those students of the 1790's who were reading Opstraet, Tamburini, and Zola be called "Jansenists"? That party—"llamado jansenista" ("called Jansenist") as Jovellanos said—is it truly "Jansenist"? We come here to an issue in Spanish and Hispanic American intellectual history still clouded, to say the least, by political beliefs and by hard-headed attitudes. Most of the bibliography in Spanish on the so-called Jansenists suffers from what I propose to call "the Menéndez Pelayo syndrome": that historian adopts the *Auctorem fidei* approach and tries to show that the so-called Jansenists deserved their pontifical condemnation of 1794. The other side, in this twentieth-century debate of deaf monologists (generally non-Spanish and most often French), comes to the rescue of the "Jansenists" by making of them good and almost mimetic *afrancesados*. The recent book by Emile Appolis, *Les jansénistes espagnols*—the first one truly on this specific field, including a section on the Hispanic Americans —cannot prevent itself from concluding that it confirms "combien l'influence française a été forte sur les Espagnols cultivés de cette époque" ("how strong has been the French influence on the Spanish élite of that period," meaning mostly the eighteenth century). But if it is imperative to save Spanish "Jansenists," historically speaking, from Don Marcelino's scholarly flames, it is nonetheless equally important not to transform them into a Gallican fifth column: because if Menéndez Pelayo reduces them to heretical ashes, Sarrailh and Appolis do not succeed in raising them to credible personalities. Unamuno's Hippocratic precept for historians—"No hay opiniones sino opinantes" ("There are no ideas but holders of ideas")—comes back perennially to our minds and to our daily tasks. Let us take an Unamunian look at these "Jansenist" Spanish "ashes."

I should indicate, first of all, that to be a *pistoyense* (as Jovellanos calls the student reader of Tamburini and Zola) in 1795 was in many ways to be a forerunner of the conciliar temper of the post–John XXIII Catholic church. The Synod of Pistoia and the recent Vatican Council have much in common: the ecclesiastics assembled at the Tuscany town proclaimed the need to return to a less centralized church and to considerable increase in episcopal autonomy. They emphasized the pastoral nature and obligations of all priests, and they asked for respectfulness for other Christians and other religions. It was therefore decidedly anti-inquisitorial. The Pistoia synod was also totally against the monastic orders, and that is why the *pistoyenses* will be called in Spain "monacómacos," "monk-fighters." All these ecclesiastical views of the Pistoians could not be traced exclusively, of course, to Cornelius Jansenius. Nor were the Salamanca students of the 1790's primarily interested in the traditional Jansenist theological positions concerning faith, grace, and free will. Emile Appolis maintains that "pure" Jansenism reaches Spain only in the 1780's and becomes after 1812 an individual anachronism, but he has not persuaded this reader that the Salamanca followers of Tamburini and Zola were reading them as "pure" Jansenists. I would even deny that Tamburini and Zola should be called "Jansenists" without strong attenuations and qualifications. Actually, Emile

Appolis' great contribution to the history of the eighteenth century is his book *Le 'thiers parti' catholique au XVIIIᵉ siècle* (*The Catholic 'Third Party' in the 18th Century*), in which he uses a very appropriate historical designation (the "third party") to cover the wide intermediate domain of the new Catholic thought and attitudes between the two traditional extremes of the Jansenists and the so-called Zelanti, the most dogmatic of the Vaticanists.

The "Jansenist" Spaniards of the quarter of a century between the death of Charles III and the Cádiz constitution of 1812 should be placed also within that "third party" of Catholic Europe described so carefully by Emile Appolis, though their singularity could be somehow lost by that historical affiliation. Strictly speaking, there were only two ideological and ecclesiastical "parties" in Spain at the end of the eighteenth century: the inquisitorial and the anti-inquisitorial. It is therefore understandable that a term such as "Jansenist" should have been used by the inquisitorials first of all, and with patent derogatory intentions, to designate a variety of approaches and views on religion and national life. But it is obvious that "Jansenism" in Jovellanos' Spain was much more an intellectual attitude than a theological—or even philosophical—doctrine: that is, I would suggest that "Jansenism" was the indispensable gesture of the mind that wanted to break away from the intellectual mortmains of church and society. Ettore Rota, in his book *Giuseppe Poggi e la formazione del patriota moderno (1761–1843)* (Piacenza, 1923), has put that gesture of the eighteenth-century mind in words that can be extended to the Spaniards: "Chi nasce ribelle, nel settecento, è giansenista." It should be added, however, that the impact of the Pistoia synod was not due only to this need, in all of Latin Europe, for a philosophical disentailment, for a new logistics of the intellect, even for a new logic—and let us recall that the Jansenists of Port-Royal were great logicians and grammarians (many readers will be acquainted, of course, with Noam Chomsky's *Cartesian Linguistics* and his references to the Port-Royal Jansenists)—but the thinking impulsion that was embodied, so to say, in Tamburini and the other Pistoians would not have been so influential if it had not been oriented toward the concrete social and political problems of Latin Europe. I cannot go into what Italian historians call "Democratic Jansenism" now; instead I shall simply mention a recent book by Carmelo Caristia, *Riflessi politici del giansenismo italiano*, and the already classic work by Arturo Carlo Jemolo, *Il giansenismo in Italia*, but it should be kept in mind that the Pistoia synod, and particularly Tamburini, did accentuate the equality as much as the solidarity of men on this earth. And we should not forget that by a quasi-astrological coincidence the Pistoia proceedings were published in 1788, not only the year of the end of the Caroline Age in Spain, but above all the eve of the French Revolution. The Pistoians' impact does show that they were ready for all the challenges of that historical situation, and also that their ideas were relevant for the new post-1789 Europe. In spite of the fears expressed by Voltaire twenty-five years before— "Les jansénistes gouvernent donc Paris! C'est bien pire que le règne des jésuites. . . . Les jansénistes sont impitoyables" ("The Jansenists in control of Paris! That's much worse than the Jesuits' control. . . . The Jansenists are pitiless")—in spite of those fears of the *philosophes*, the Jansenists, or rather the Pistoians, made possible for many European Catholics the active participation in the making of the new century. This was precisely the Spanish case: the young Salamanca Pistoians of the 1790's became twenty years later the Liberal leaders of the new Spain. That connection was seen, as it happens often in history, first of all by a ferocious enemy of both: Father José Vidal, a Dominican and theology professor at the University of Valencia, whose book has a self-explanatory title: *Idea ortodoxa de la divina institución del estado religioso contra los errores de los liberales y pistoyanos monacómacos* (abbreviating it: "The errors of the Liberals and Pistoians, both monk-haters"). I should mention also a paper by a Franciscan friar, Isidoro de Villapadierna, "El jansenismo español y las Cortes de Cádiz," published in *Analecta Gregoriana* (Vol.LXXI, 1954; the entire volume is dedicated to studies on Jansenism). His conclusion is the following: "The Jansenists—who became important in Spain only after Pistoia—joined the Liberals of Cádiz to achieve the principal aim of their program, the national resistance against Pontifical authority." But let us now go to Cádiz, to the conclusion of a generation's itinerary. There at the Cortes, some of the Spaniards who were fighting against Napoleon's armies wrote a constitution, the almost legendary constitution of 1812. And they baptized the new ideologies by calling themselves *Liberals*. To Cádiz corresponds thus what I would call the semantic originality in the history of liberalism. The terms *liberal* and *liberalism* acquired there a political meaning. This has been more or less accepted in general by nineteenth-century encyclopedias and some history texts. Let us begin by quoting what a great liberal, Benedetto Croce, said regarding this semantic change in his history of nineteenth-century Europe: "It is not without irony that the new ideological advance received its baptism in the most unlikely place: in the country which more than any other in Europe was closed to the eighteenth-century philosophy, the country that was by essence scholastic and medieval, clerical and absolutist." And Croce added that Spain had given a new political meaning to the adjective *liberal*.

I should say at once that Croce was wrong in this, because the Spanish innovation consisted actually in the semantic transformation of a *noun*, not of an adjective. *Un liberal*, "a liberal," had been used in Spanish since the Renaissance, but not surely in other European languages, with the same connotation as the adjective. That is, *un liberal* meant in Spanish "a generous man," and, in a sense, it was the condensation of the ideal of the gentleman.

On the other hand, several prominent *diputados*, among them the rector of Salamanca University, used constantly the expression "liberal ideas" when they were speaking in favor of a new constitution. This expression had already a concrete political meaning, imported into Spain. It has been said that the men from Cádiz, the deputies of 1810–1812, were deeply influenced by French thinkers. And this is a fact. But it should be pointed out that that influence was particularly strong among the Liberals and that this influence came specifically from the French intellectuals called by Bonaparte, *in a negative sense,* "ideologists." That is, the group of intellectuals who were against Robespierre and who finally became victorious in their struggle to preserve the Revolution by emphasizing its moderate aspects; in short, by recovering the Revolution for the class that had started it, the bourgeoisie. Or to put it in another way, by making of the French Republic what one member of this group, Mme. de Staël, called "the property owners' republic." Or as another leader of this same group, Benjamin Constant, put it, "to have the Republic replace at last the Revolution." In the writings of this group, between 1795 and 1799, there are constant uses of "progrés libéraux et politiques," "idées libérales," "républicain inébranlable et libéral." All of these uses point out that they did employ the adjective *liberal* as meaning "anti-Jacobin," "anti-clerical," and "anti-Royalist." That is, as a synonym of "middle of the road" of the Republic. We must remember that these intellectuals were behind the 1799 coup d'état when Napoleon took by force the government of France. Those intellectuals saw Napoleon as the strong man who could preserve the bourgeois character of the Republic. Thus in the 1799 message of Napoleon to the French people, to justify his overthrow of the previous government, he even said he was doing it "in the name of the conservative and liberal ideas of the Revolution." This paradoxical, almost comical, coupling of *conservative* and *liberal* had a clear historical and political reason. Napoleon knew what he was doing: his message was probably written by one of the "ideologists" from the brain trust of his fellow conspirators. By coupling *conservative* and *liberal* he meant that he was giving political expression to the need for preserving the Revolution between its two dangers, the Left (the Jacobins) and the Right (the Royalists). That is, Napoleon was using *conservative* and *liberal* as synonyms. And from then on most of the French intellectuals of the early nineteenth century thought of "liberal ideas" as meaning "moderate ideas," ideas of change but within very strict limits. In short, the adjective *liberal*, in French use, was actually being dissolved into a general qualifier of all achievements under the Revolution. Napoleon himself was called—liked to be called—"the prince of liberal ideas." And that is why he also used the term *liberal* when addressing himself to Spaniards. At his headquarters in Madrid, he signed a proclamation to Spaniards on December 7, 1808, telling them: "Spaniards . . . I have broken the fetters which hampered the people. I have given you a liberal constitution . . . and a limited and constitutional monarchy."

If we go back now to Cádiz, to the Spanish Constitutional Convention of 1810–1812, we see that the term *liberal* was never coupled with *conservative*. And I am sure that the 1810 Spaniards of the Liberal group knew very well the writings of the French "ideologists." I assume therefore that the Spanish *Liberales*, when they used the expression *liberal ideas*, knew what they were doing. That is, they were trying to convey something *quite different* from what Napoleon and his group meant when they spoke of "idées conservatrices et libérales." The Liberals were intent on defining in more strict terms, in *more radical terms*, their position.

We know that the first person to use the term *liberal* in England, but in its Spanish plural form, *liberales*, Lord Castlereagh, said in Parliament on February 15, 1816: "The [Spanish] *Liberales* were politically a French party of the very worst description. The *Liberales* were a perfectly Jacobinical party." And I would say that Lord Castlereagh was somehow right, though not exactly as he believed. I do maintain that the *Liberales* gave to other Liberals from Europe a new strength, a real source of political hope. That is why the Spanish constitution of 1812 was translated into many languages. In short, Cádiz gave its semantic birth to liberalism—and it thus helped to make a new century.

What Jovellanos had said—that the new ideas would become rooted in Spain as the young of the 1790's grew older—was confirmed by history. The Pistoians of Salamanca, the children of the Caroline Age, had become the Liberals of 1812. Pistoia had been the starting point for that Spanish generation, and Cádiz became also a point of departure for the new generation of Latin Europe. The Spanish eighteenth century became finally itself in 1812—and its contribution should not be forgotten. It asked men to be "justos y benéficos": not a novelty but not useless.

V

# Enlightenment Philosophy
## and the Emergence of Spanish Romanticism

RUSSELL P. SEBOLD

O<small>N THE ONE HAND</small>, my title would seem to promise too much. In the space available here, I could scarcely enumerate all the currents of Enlightenment philosophy that contributed to the genesis of Romanticism in Spain or any other Western country. On the other hand, although I am going to look at only one aspect of Enlightenment philosophy—sensationalism—it is the most typical, and it leads directly to the Romantic *sine qua non*: the metaphysic that distinguishes the literary trend commonly called Romanticism from all those that preceded it.

According to James Thomson, Sir Isaac Newton observed nature, which "Stood all subdued by him, and open laid/Her every latent glory to his view." But nature revealed her secrets to the great physicist only after he had resisted the temptation to sit down and dream what the poet calls "romantic schemes."[1] Voltaire worries that "Peut-être je gâte à la fois/La poésie et la physique./Mais cette nouveauté me pique."[2] The Spanish poet

[1] Thomson, *To the Memory of Sir Isaac Newton* (1727), vv.24, 37–38. The same poet's *The Seasons* will also be quoted by verse numbers, inserted in parentheses in the text, as will Pope's *Essay on Criticism* and Horace's *De Arte Poetica*.

[2] Voltaire, *Épitre XLVII. Au Prince Royal de Prusse*, quoted by Ralph B. Crum, *Scientific Thought in Poetry* (New York, 1937), pp.92–93.

Meléndez Valdés expresses his envy of a friend who is to have the chance to see the botanical and zoological marvels of the New World: "¡Oh, a tu mente curiosa qué de objetos/van a ostentarse, cuánta maravilla/A ese tu genio observador aguarda!/. . ./Sacia la ardiente sed: admira, estudia/la gran naturaleza, y con divina/mente su inmensidad, feliz abarca;/sus vínculos descubre, y un hallazgo/sea cada paso que en sus reinos dieres."[3] One of the eighteenth-century Spanish translators of the Swiss poet Salomon Gessner commented, "Gessner is the author of the loveliest descriptions because he knew the countryside scientifically."[4]

At the beginning of the nineteenth century, the kind of poet we call Romantic still stands in essentially the same semispiritual, semi-materialistic relationship to the world about him as these figures because, according to Américo Castro, "what essentially is called Romanticism is a sentimental metaphysic, a pantheistic concept of the universe, whose center is the ego . . . a special value was attributed to all those works and all those situations in which it could be seen that man was acting upon his milieu, or was determined by it."[5] Professor Castro's definition is the most exact that has been given by a historian of any Western literature because almost every other trait commonly mentioned in connection with Romanticism—subjectivism, idealism, suicide, local color, melodrama; macabre, sepulchral, necromantic, and medieval elements and themes, tubercular heroines, heroes of mysterious origins, the violation of the unities—every one of these can be found as readily in other times as in the so-called Romantic period. Professor Castro has very appropriately viewed Romantic literature in terms of Schelling's philosophy of identity whereby nature becomes dynamic, visible spirit, and spirit becomes invisible nature. The blood of Shelley's Alastor, after all, "ever beat in mystic sympathy/With nature's ebb and

3 Juan Meléndez Valdés, *Poesías*, in *Biblioteca de Autores Españoles*, LXIII, 204b. Page references to this and other volumes of the BAE will subsequently be indicated in the text.

4 Salomón Gessner, *Idylios*, trans. M. A. Rodríguez Fernández (Madrid, 1799), p.xcv.

5 Américo Castro, *Les grands romantiques espagnols* (Paris, 1922), p.13.

flow."[6] I should like now to show, step by step, how the egocentric pantheism Professor Castro rightly regards as the *quid* of Romanticism emerges from a philosophical and scientific curiosity about nature such as that shown by the poets I have quoted above. I am primarily interested in the emergence of Romanticism in Spain, but again I think we shall come across influences and lines of development that have *not* been considered in studying the evolution of Romanticism in any other Western country either. I shall have to ask the reader's indulgence as I lead him through some preliminary reflections on poetics and descriptive poetry. With these preliminaries, I hope to demonstrate the freedom of the eighteenth-century poet to follow new paths, as well as give some indication of the sensitivity of nature and the sensitivity of the soul as they appear in eighteenth-century Spanish poetry—indispensable factors in the birth of the egocentric pantheism of the Romantics. Through all these considerations we shall have the thread of sensationalism to guide us.

Without the mediation of sensationalist doctrine, poetics would have militated against the representation of the universe in such a way as to permit the kind of interaction between the psyche and its physical circumstances that Professor Castro sees as typical of Romanticism. The technique of French literature during the seventeenth century precluded a convincing representation of an individual's milieu because of a marked tendency to reason from the general to the particular in the construction of descriptions, as Gustave Lanson demonstrated a number of years ago in his "L'Influence de la philosophie cartésienne sur la littérature française."[7] In seventeenth-century Spanish literature, description was also largely based on preconception rather than on the observation of nature, as one can see from a significant passage in Luis Alfonso de Carballo's *Cisne de Apolo* of 1602: "And when the poet knows what he is to describe, so that his description will be perfect, he must inform himself very well

---

[6] Percy Bysshe Shelley, *The Complete Poetical Works*, bound with the *Works of Keats* (New York, n.d), p.16.

[7] See Gustave Lanson, *Études d'histoire littéraire* (Paris, 1929), pp.58–96.

about what he is to describe and represent it in his phantasy *as if he had seen it with his eyes,* and according to the image of it he may have *conceived,* he will convey it in the most appropriate words he may find."[8] The poet was to describe "as if he had seen," *not* "having seen."

In classical antiquity, poetics was essentially naturalistic, that is to say, it was based on nature variously defined as the world about us, natural inspiration, or the nature of the creative process and literature. Aristotle's *Poetics* is an analysis of the works of poets who wrote following the dictates of their natural genius long before there were any rules. In their writings Aristotle *discovered* the rules. For example, he tells us: "Once dialogue had come in, *nature* herself *discovered* the appropriate measure. For the iambic is, of all measures, the most colloquial." He also considers the play's "limit as fixed by the *nature* of the drama itself."[9] Similarly, Quintilian insists that "most rules must be altered to suit each case, the circumstances of time and place . . . the precepts are not established by law or public decrees, but expediency *discovered* whatever is contained in them."[10] *Observation* was the byword of the ancient littérateur in creation and in criticism.

Later the habit of observation is lost in the literary arts, as it is in other spheres, when, as one of the first Spaniards to take part in the Quarrel of the Ancients and the Moderns tells us, "people won't believe their own eyes in order not to disbelieve Aristotle's."[11] Hence the often mentioned practice in seventeenth-century literature of imitating Homer rather than nature. The superstitious preference of another's observations over one's own contributed as much as Cartesian influence to the rise of a sterile

---

[8] Luis Alfonso de Carballo, *Cisne de Apolo,* ed. Alberto Porqueras Mayo (Madrid, 1958), II, 72–73. The italics are mine.

[9] Aristotle, *On the Art of Poetry,* trans. S. H. Butcher–Milton C. Nahm (New York, 1950), pp.7, 12. The italics are mine.

[10] Quintilian, *Institutio Oratoria,* Bk.II, Chap.13, secs.2, 6 (*mutantur pleraque [praecepta] causis, temporibus, occasione. . . . Neque enim rogationibus plebisve scitis sancta sunt ista praecepta, sed hoc quidquid est utilitas excogitavit*). The italics are mine.

[11] See Olga Victoria Quiroz-Martínez, *La introducción de la filosofía moderna en España* (Mexico City, 1949), p.36.

aesthetic *idealism,* as Jovellanos called it. In his *Elogio de las bellas artes,* the great eighteenth-century Spanish statesman and writer takes note that "the artist used to look for beauty in his mind, and going round and round in this circle, where it existed not, he exhausted himself in vain without finding it" (BAE, XLVI, 352a).

One of the most commonly misunderstood phenomena of literary history is the fact that slowly, under the influence of Francis Bacon's inductive, observational philosophy, Newton's empirical physics, and most notably Locke's and Condillac's sensationalist epistemology, poetics regained its own empirical, naturalistic bent and capacity for individuation. In his *Investigaciones filosóficas sobre la belleza ideal,* the eighteenth-century Spanish aesthetician Esteban de Arteaga says that the "work our Spain needs" is one that "would occupy in literature and the fine arts the same place as the [*Novum*] *Organum Scientiarium* of Bacon of Verulam in the sciences."[12] William Guthrie asserted in 1747 that "dramatic poetry stands upon the same footing with our noble system of Newtonian philosophy."[13] "Torricelli, Newton, Kepler, Galilée,/Plus doctes, plus heureux dans leurs puissants efforts,/A tout nouveau Virgile ont ouvert des trésors," André Chénier wrote later.[14] Also addressing Newton and alluding to the poetic implications of his science, Meléndez Valdés avows, in a poem entitled *A mis libros*: ". . . y si tu mente alada,/Sublime Newton, al Olimpo vuela,/Raudo te sigo" (BAE, LXIII, 199a). Cadalso, before Meléndez, seems to have known both Newton's *Principia* and his *Opticks.*[15] Cadalso knew Locke in the original as well as in French translation; and Meléndez, who also owned the complete works of Condillac, wrote of Locke in a personal letter to Jovellanos: "One of the first books they put in my hands,

---

12 Esteban de Arteaga, *La belleza ideal,* ed. Miguel Batllori (Madrid, 1943), p.159.

13 William Guthrie, *Essay upon English Tragedy* (London, 1747), p.6.

14 André Chénier, *L'Invention,* in Jacques Charpier and Pierre Seghers, *L'Art poétique* (Paris, 1956), p.187.

15 José Cadalso, *Los eruditos a la violeta,* in one volume, with *Cartas marruecas* (Madrid, 1944), pp.373, 375, 376.

and I learned it by heart, was that of a highly learned English-man. To the *Essay Concerning Human Understanding* I owe and shall owe all my life what little ability I have to think."[16] On yet another occasion, Meléndez addresses one of the great natural-ists of the century as though he were a muse: "Buffon, natura, tu sublime manto,/A alzar me enseñe . . ." (BAE, LXIII, 211b).

The deep imprint these philosophical and scientific works made on poetics in the eighteenth century is underscored by the reappearance of a verb that had not been used in arts of poetry and criticism since the days of Aristotle and Quintilian. In the *Essay on Criticism*, Pope affirms that "those rules of old *discov-ered*, not devised,/Are nature still" (I, 88—89). In l'abbé Charles Batteux's *Les Beaux Arts réduits à un même principe,* which Meléndez and many other eighteenth-century Spaniards read, the verb *discover* occurs in a context with other equally signif-icant words like *seek, observe,* and *observer*. "Let us suppose," Batteux says in 1746, "that there were no rules, and a philosoph-ically inclined artist were commissioned to seek them and establish them for the first time. . . . Before establishing the rules he will be an observer for a long time. . . . [Poets] merely *discover* what already existed; they are only creators by what they have observed, and conversely they are only observers in order to get into the right frame of mind to create."[17] Tomás de Iriarte, ap-parently influenced by Dr. Warburton's commentaries on Pope as well as by Pope himself, proclaims that "those laws were not *in-vented*, but *discovered*, for nature yields them up from herself."[18] The implication of all these passages is very clear: just as a New-

16 Cadalso, *Eruditos,* p.377; Georges Demerson, *Don Juan Meléndez Valdés et son temps (1754–1817)* (Paris, 1962), p.65; BAE, LXIII, 73.

17 Charles Batteux, *Las bellas artes reducidas a un principio,* in Batteux, *Principios filosóficos de la literatura, o Curso razonado de bellas letras y de bellas artes,* trans. Agustín García de Arrieta (Madrid, 1797), I, 15, 70–73. The French original is not available to me.

18 Tomás de Iriarte, *Los literatos en Cuaresma,* in *Colección de obras en verso y prosa* (Madrid, 1805), VII, 73. In the monumental edition of 1751, Dr. Warburton comments as follows on the lines of Pope quoted a moment ago: "These *Rules of Art* . . . were not *invented* by abstract speculation, but *discovered* in the book of Nature."

ton might uncover new physical principles that still lay hidden in the infinite bosom of nature, eighteenth-century Europeans like Guthrie were confident that the same source would give them infinite new rules of poetry: for example, those "other particular rules that must be drawn from the substance of the subject itself," as Batteux calls them.[19]

Pope has described the discovery of a new rule in the lines: "If, where the rules not far enough extend/(Since rules were made but to promote their end),/Some lucky license answer to the full/The intent proposed, that license is a rule" (*Criticism*, I, 146–49). According to the Spaniard Feijoo, the gifted artist creates "following a superior rule . . . different from those common ones that are taught in school . . . which he came upon thanks to his boldness." In another place, Feijoo refers directly to those "new precepts" required by the infinite "combinations of situations and circumstances" one finds in the arts (BAE, LVI, 353a, 507a). The much-touted new freedom of the nineteenth-century Romantics from all restrictions save those of universal nature actually evolved in the context of eighteenth-century Neoclassicism under the influence of sensationalism and the new science. The new freedom of eighteenth-century poetics played a major role in the evolution of the new forms we are going to talk about now, but it itself is also one of the more striking proofs that the course from Neoclassic to Romantic was *evolutionary* rather than revolutionary, and that that evolution was simply one of many signs of a total shift in the European *forma mentis*.

In philosophy this shift was signaled by the enshrinement of inductive in place of deductive rationalism, and in poetics by the acceptance of an open, organic concept of the rules, in lieu of a closed, mechanistic one. It is not new to use the terms *mechanistic* and *organic* to distinguish between Classic and Romantic, but the birth of literary organicism occurred much earlier than we have thought, and it is more intimately tied to the patterns of Western intellectual history than it is commonly thought to be. Nor does the advent of organicism in poetics herald the rejection

[19] Batteux, *Principios,* trans. Arrieta, I, 91.

of the notion of rules, as historians of literature are wont to tell us. As I have demonstrated on another occasion, the rules are merely a description of the human psychological phenomenon known as the creative process, and the formulation of new rules simply means that the description of the creative process is going to be more accurate. In 1718, in his *Complete Art of Poetry*, Charles Gildon says that the rules of poetry are not "so firmly establish'd, that it is impossible to add anything to them . . . all the new *Discoveries* are so far from destroying this Establishment, that they do nothing more than confirm it."[20]

Among the accomplishments of the philosophically liberated Neoclassical school, the invention of descriptive poetry occupies an important place. The invention of a new genre is always a significant event in itself, but the real importance of descriptive poetry is that with its advent a line of development is initiated that leads directly to the egocentric Romantic metaphysic, as we shall see. Often confused with the traditional pastoral forms, which continued to be cultivated in the eighteenth century, the descriptive or nature poetry of the Enlightenment seems, nevertheless, considerably more realistic.

In his *Ensayos literarios y críticos* of 1844, Alberto Lista became one of the few critics to insist upon the distinction between the two genres and upon the recentness of the "descriptive poem" as a form that "was not cultivated until around the middle of the last century."[21] However, one of the first, perhaps the first, to call attention to the innovation in the Romance countries was the Marquis de Saint-Lambert, in the "Discours préliminaire" of *Les Saisons* (1769), and in so doing he went a long way toward identifying both the sources and the national origins of the new genre: "Bucolic poetry has been enriched in this century with a genre that was unknown to the ancients. . . . The language of philosophy, having been received in good society, has now also been received in poetry; it has become possible to undertake

20 Charles Gildon, *Complete Art of Poetry*, in *Critical Essays of the Eighteenth Century*, ed. Willard Higley Durham (New Haven, 1915), p.67.

21 Alberto Lista, *Ensayos literarios y críticos* (Seville, 1844), II, 48.

poems that require a broad knowledge of nature. . . . The English and the Germans [that is, Haller, Gessner, and Thomson] have created the genre of descriptive poetry." Saint-Lambert also observes that bucolic poetry in the eighteenth century "no longer has the false ring to it that it had in earlier centuries," that the art of the new genre consists in part in "observing man in his relationships to nature," and that in composing his own descriptive poem "it was a pleasure to me to paint those objects that made an impression on my senses."[22] It is evident from Saint-Lambert's words that a significant step had been taken in the direction of the Romantic's psychic relationship with material nature. Now, concretely, what role do the senses play in the newly observed "relationships" between man and nature? But, first, what do the senses have to do with the convincing quality Saint-Lambert has remarked in the word landscapes of his contemporaries?

Thomson tells us that it is for him an exquisite pleasure to "converse with Nature," whether it be "Where the deer rustle through the twining break," or when "refracted from yon eastern cloud,/Bestriding earth, the grand ethereal bow/Shoots up immense; and every hue unfolds,/In fair proportion, running from the red/To where the violet fades into the sky," or, finally, while walking by an "extended field/Of blossom'd beans" that "Breathes through the sense, and takes the ravished soul" (*Spring*, vv.94, 203–207, 499–500, 502; *Summer*, vv.1381–82). This, Samuel Johnson tells us in his *Life of Thomson*, is the technique of a man "with a mind that at once comprehends the vast and attends to the minute. . . . Nor is the *naturalist* without his part in the entertainment; for he is assisted to *recollect* and to *combine*, to arrange his *discoveries*, and to amplify the sphere of his contemplation."[23] Dr. Johnson's observation on the relationship between the comprehension of the minute and the comprehension of the vast in Thomson is an indication of the presence of the

[22] Saint-Lambert, *Poésies* (Paris, 1826), pp.4, 9, 21.
[23] Samuel Johnson, *Lives of the Poets* (New York, n.d.), II, 327. The italics are mine.

inductive thought pattern of the new mentality in poetry as well as in philosophy. With the terms *naturalist* and *discoveries*—discoveries in content now as well as in technique—Dr. Johnson recognizes the influence of the new science on poetry. But most important for us, the verbs *recollect* and *combine*, typical Lockean terms, used in the *Essay Concerning Human Understanding* to describe the process whereby we join old and new sense impressions to form abstract ideas, remind us of the sensationalist basis of the new science that influenced the sensuous descriptive poetry of the eighteenth century, poetry which "Breathes through the sense and takes the ravished soul." To my knowledge, the only critic who has posited the influence of Locke on the style and mood of poetic description in the eighteenth century is the English Hispanist Ronald M. Macandrew, in an essay on Meléndez Valdés, but it is a mere suggestion *en passant*.[24] In any case, those scholars who attribute the birth of eighteenth-century descriptive poetry solely to the inflence of Newton's *Opticks* are clearly wrong.[25] The *Opticks* illuminated more vividly the objects of sight. But it could not unlock the sense of sight, much less the other four senses, and all five senses play major roles in eighteenth-century descriptive poetry.

Not only can a great deal more be said about the influence of sensationalism on eighteenth-century poetry, but Meléndez Valdés is not the first Spaniard whose poetry was influenced by it, as Macandrew wrongly supposes. Cadalso, whom Macandrew does not mention at all in his book on naturalism in Spanish poetry, composed several Lockean descriptive poems in the years 1768–1770, precisely the same period in which Saint-Lambert composed and published his *Les Saisons,* so that the new poetic mode reached France and Spain simultaneously. Cadalso's deep knowledge of the English language and broad acquaintance with Eng-

24 See Ronald M. Macandrew, *Naturalism in Spanish Poetry from the Origins to 1900* (Aberdeen, 1931), pp.100–114.

25 This viewpoint is advanced, for example, by Marjorie Hope Nicolson, *Newton Demands the Muse. Newton's "Opticks" and the Eighteenth-Century Poets* (Princeton, 1946).

lish authors were significant factors.[26] In the *Carta a Augusta,*
Cadalso extols the myriad graces of nature that beckon the philosophically inclined matron to trade the court for their consol-
ing effects. The riot of colors may very well be owing to the
influence of Newton's *Opticks,* but the active role of the senses
can be attributed to the influence of Locke and Condillac, and
there is also some influence of Rousseau here.

> Pues ¡qué de las sabrosas
> Riquezas de los troncos que he plantado!
> ¡Qué peras tan gustosas!
> ¡Qué pero tan hermoso y colorado!
> Tendrás en mi verjel melocotones,
> Naranjas, brebas, limas y melones.
>   Después que hayas comido,
> Si buscas el descanso y el reposo,
> Ya te tengo escogido
> Un paraje encantado y delicioso
> En una parte del jardín de casa,
> Por donde el Ebro en miniatura pasa.
>   Los árboles, cargados
> De flores olorosas, hacen techo
> Con ramos enlazados,
> Con que el furor del sol queda deshecho.
> Mil pájaros, gozando la frescura,
> Se burlan de su ardor en la espesura.
>   Al pie de un mirto ameno
> Te pondré con mis manos una cama,
> No de pluma relleno,
> Sino de azar, jazmín y verde grama;
> A sus lados dos fuentes van tocando,
> Que los van defendiendo y refrescando. (BAE, LXI, 259b)

The nature that is in poetry before the eighteenth century the
reader can comprehend with his mind; but he cannot read the
new nature poetry without being conscious of his body—and of

[26] As examples of Cadalso's remarkable mastery of English, see the English-
language letters in Nigel Glendinning, "Cartas inéditas de Cadalso a un P. jesuita
en inglés, francés, español y latín," *BBMP,* XLII (1966), 97–115.

the continuous imprint that light, sound, texture, taste, and odor from the vegetable, animal, and human world make upon his physical being through his senses. The cardinal concern of the poet now is, to use Saint-Lambert's words, that of "observing man in his relationships to nature." The most convincing demonstration of the philosophical origins of the sensuousness of eighteenth-century nature poetry is to be found in two short paragraphs of the next to the last chapter of Condillac's *Traité des sensations*, a work that influenced the nature poets of the Continental countries almost as much as Locke's *Essay* did.

The statue in Condillac's celebrated allegory, having finally been endowed with all five of the bodily senses, stands in ecstatic wonder before the beauty of the countryside and then yields to the voluptuous pleasure of running up and down to inhale, taste, hear, see, and feel one beautiful natural object after another. In effect, Condillac's statue itself becomes a nature poet and indeed sounds very much like Thomson, Saint-Lambert, Parini, Cadalso, or Meléndez Valdés:

> It seems to me that with each object I study, I discover a new way of seeing and regale myself with a new pleasure. Here is a vast plain. . . . There is a country that is intersected and more limited. . . . Carpets of verdure, groves, flowers, clumps of trees where the sun scarcely penetrates, waters that flow slowly or rush violently beautify this landscape. . . . Moved by curiosity, I eagerly traverse the places whose first view enraptured me, and I love to recognize with my hearing, my sense of smell, taste, and touch the objects that everywhere catch my eye. All my sensations seem to fear the possibility of having to yield to their fellows. The variety and vividness of the colors vie with the fragrance of the flowers; the birds strike me as more admirable for their shape, their movement, and their plumage than for their songs. And what is the murmur of the waters compared to their winding courses, their cascades, and their crystalline glimmer![27]

27 Abbé de Condillac, *Traité des sensations* (Pt.IV, Chap.8), in *Oeuvres* (Paris, 1792), III, 276–77.

I do not think that this passage has heretofore been considered in connection with the history of descriptive poetry. In any case, it suggests an essential point about eighteenth-century poetry: namely, that its "realism" depends less on the poet's ability to describe nature with photographic accuracy than on his capacity to capture the sensations he has felt when in contact with the various natural objects he has decided to represent. Beginning with eighteenth-century descriptive verse, sensation has provided the source, the process, and the substance of much of modern poetry. Bécquer, for example, tells us, in his *Cartas literarias a una mujer*, that he composes after inspiration has passed, working from the memory of former sensations—essentially a Lockean procedure—and a number of more recent poets, like Melville Cane, have affirmed that they do the same. Sensation has become the determinant of the subject-object relationship between poet and nature, and also between reader and poem. For example, in an apparently early Anacreontic entitled *A una fuente,* Meléndez Valdés establishes the tie between visible spirit (nature) and invisible nature (his own spirit) by interlacing several sensorial and sensorially stimulated spiritual phenomena: "¡Oh! ¡Cómo en tus cristales,/Fuentecilla risueña,/Mi espíritu se goza,/Mis ojos se embelesan!" (BAE, LXIII, 93c).

Jovellanos considers the new rapport between man and nature to be primarily English in origin, and he rightly attributes it to the influence of the new philosophy of observation on the arts, an influence which he describes in his own words as "the insistent study of nature, and the inspired investigation of the relations that exist between nature and art . . . and between the latter and the sentimental faculty of our souls." In the same retrospective critical letter of 1805, Jovellanos calls poets and other writers who have followed the lead of Locke *naturalistas,* to distinguish them from the Cartesian-like *idealistas,* whose art held so little attraction for him; and thanks to the efforts of the *naturalistas,* he concludes, "poetry and the art of eloquence have also become graphic. The poems, novels, histories, and even philosophical works of modern times are full of descriptions of objects and natural, moral acts which enchant the reader with their truth, their grace, and, above all, with their power to awaken the sentiments of the heart" (BAE, LXXXVII, 379ab). I think it is significant that Jovellanos emphasizes description and nowhere mentions Rousseau in this letter on man, nature, and the tender emotions of the heart. Rousseau's influence on the themes and style of individual works was of major importance in Spain during the so-called Pre-Romantic period, but there is still a tendency to overestimate his general influence on the emergence of Romanticism in all countries. A number of years ago, the French scholar Louis Reynaud pointed out that Rousseau's idea of the innocence of life in the state of nature and a number of the Genevan's other notions about man are to be found already in Pope's *Essay on Man*.[28] Nor was Rousseau the first *promeneur solitaire* to describe his walks in touching tones.

By 1730 Thomson already found it difficult to "forbear to join the general smile/Of Nature" because "she alone,/Heard, felt, and seen, possesses every thought,/Fills every sense, and pants in every vein," providing "My sole delight; as through the falling glooms/Pensive I stray," weeping now and then a "heart-shed tear, the ineffable delight/Of Sweet humanity," all the while thanking God for "thy Locke/who made the whole internal world his own" (*Spring*, vv.871, 1113–15; *Summer*, vv.196–97, 892–93, 1558–59). In 1744, Mark Akenside went further: abroad, under the "mighty frame/Of universal being," he discovered his "afflicted bosom" to have been "decreed/The universal sensitive of pain,/The wretched heir of evils not its own."[29] (Is this not already *Weltschmerz*?) The tender psychological ties between man and nature, and man and man, that we still think of as being Rousseauist in origin are really not so. Rousseau was simply one of the most talented among the first Romance authors to reap the artistic advantages of the total shift of direction of

28 See Louis Reynaud, *Le romantisme. Les origines anglo-germaniques* (Paris, 1926), pp.102-104.

29 Mark Akenside, *The Poetical Works* (London, 1867), pp.28–29.

the European mentality signaled by Locke and his first followers like the Earl of Shaftesbury. It should be remembered that Rousseau did not publish his *Nouvelle Héloïse* until the same decade in which poets like Giuseppe Parini, the Marquis de Saint-Lambert, and José Cadalso published similar works in verse.

Thomson had good cause to thank God and Locke for his ecstatic delight at how nature "alone/Heard, felt, and seen, possesses every thought,/Fills every sense, and pants in every vein." This enumeration of diverse sensorial experiences resulting in a deeper awareness of one's own being is pure Locke. The philosopher observes that "when we see, hear, smell, taste, feel, meditate, or will anything, we know that we do so. Thus it is always as to our present sensations and perceptions; and by this everyone is to himself that which he calls *self*."[30] As I have shown elsewhere, this idea of Locke supplied the philosophical basis for a prototype of the naturalistic novel that was created in Spain in the eighteenth century,[31] but it was just as effective in stimulating "melting sentiments of kindly care" in Pre-Romantic poets who walked abroad in pristine nature to observe and catalogue her beauties, for the great sensationalist was simply saying that whatever one's surroundings may be, they impress themselves upon his soul through the agency of his senses and largely mold his psyche.

In short, the first poet who applied the philosophy of Locke Castro's words. But this subservience to the mood of nature is to the description of nature also took the first step toward creating that psychological bond between the Romantic and his milieu that enabled him to be "determined by it," in Professor largely characteristic of the first phase of Romanticism when the poet is still far less afflicted than he is curious: if nature shows him a joyful face, chances are he will forget any sorrows he may have, and on the other hand if ominous storm clouds gather, he can just as readily put aside his own joy to share in the universal lament. Saint-Lambert, who does not go much beyond this first

[30] John Locke, *Essay Concerning Human Understanding*, Bk.II, Chap.27, par.9.
[31] See Chap.4 of the introduction to José Francisco de Isla, *Fray Gerundio de Campazas*, ed. Russell P. Sebold (Madrid, 1960–1964), I, lx–xciii.

phase, writes in his preliminary remarks: "There is a certain analogy between our situations, the states of our soul, and the sites, phenomena, and states of nature."[32]

However, there is also a more important second phase to which Professor Castro may have been alluding when he talks about those situations in which the poet "was acting upon his milieu." This is the point at which the sensitive soul and sensitive nature finally move into their new egocentric pantheistic relationship. Nature, no longer the determinant of the poet's feelings, becomes an extension of his consciousness, a material reiteration of his spirit. This too is foreshadowed in the pages of the great English sensationalist, who changed the course of Western literature as much as he did that of Western philosophy and science. While analyzing another aspect of our notions of personal identity and self, Locke states: "That with which the *consciousness* of this present, thinking thing can join itself makes the same *person*, and is one *self* with it . . . and so attributes to it *self*, and owns all the actions of that thing as its own, as far as that consciousness reaches." Personal identity depends then solely on consciousness, "whether it be annexed solely to one individual substance, or can be continued in a succession of substances."[33]

The importance of Locke's idea of identity to the evolution of the Romantic metaphysic cannot be overstressed, but it will also be useful to consider two passages of Condillac's *Traité des sensations* in which the still broader Romantic projection of the consciousness onto the entire universe and the cause for such a projection—a universal malaise—are suggested. Condillac's animated statue—hence man, for man is merely matter with the five senses added—has a "sense . . . of its extent [that] is vague. . . . It views itself as a being that is endlessly multiplied, and not knowing anything beyond itself, it is, from its standpoint, as if it were immense: it is everywhere, it is everything."[34] The pantheistic

---

32 Saint-Lambert, *Poésies*, p.17.
33 Locke, *Essay*, Bk.II, Chap.27, pars.10, 17.
34 Condillac, *Traité* (Pt.I, Chap.11), *Oeuvres*, III, 88.

concept of the self that was to characterize Romanticism is pre-
figured in Enlightenment philosophy. But this new homogeneity
of human spirit and extrapersonal reality would never have become the matrix for the majority of Romantic metaphors if it
had not reflected a vitally important new human situation.

Before the advent of sensationalism, God was the source of
consolation for man's troubles and the source of all his knowledge: man "saw everything in God," as Malebranche and his
contemporaries said, emphasizing the role of the divinity in the
Cartesian doctrine of innate ideas. But Locke cut off the path of
knowledge between God and man by teaching that all our ideas
are born of sense impressions. And once the way of knowledge
was cut, it was not long before the rest were also intersected, the
way of consolation among them. When post-sensationalist man
was afflicted, he went out from himself in search of consolation,
as he was accustomed to do, however not by the heavenly way any
longer, but by the five lower highways that had replaced it. His
God having been taken from him, he reacted in his despair like
Condillac's statue, which had never known God.

Having been endowed with all five senses (which for Condillac is the same as having a "soul"), the statue begins to conceive certain superstitions in connection with its milieu. "It
addresses itself after a fashion to the sun. . . . It addresses itself
to the trees. . . . In a word, it addresses itself to all the things on
which it believes itself to depend. If it suffers without discovering
the cause in those objects that strike its senses, it addresses its
own anguish as if it were an invisible enemy that had to be ap-
peased. Thus the universe becomes filled with visible and invisible beings that it entreats to work for its happiness."[35] The
understanding the newly vivified statue expects to find in each
of the myriad beings about it is, of course, a projection of its own
tormented psyche. Condillac not only anticipated the universalization of the Romantic poet's ego through its metaphoric projection on all things; the plight of his statue in 1754 also foreshadows,

[35] *Ibid.* (Pt.IV, Chap.4), *Oeuvres,* III, 254–55.

for example, that of the poet Meléndez Valdés in a Pre-Romantic—no, I shall say Romantic—poem written twenty-three years later: Condillac's statue standing expectantly before the infinite universe also clearly thought of itself as "Huérfano, joven, solo y desvalido."

As we focus more directly on Spain now, we should bear in mind that the majority of Spanish poets of the second half of the eighteenth century knew and owned the works of poets like Thomson and Saint-Lambert; but, as we have seen, the writings of Locke, Condillac, Buffon, and other philosophers and naturalists were also well known in Spain—Locke since about 1727—and much of the poetic evolution we have traced occurred independently in the country that interests us here. I think the reader will see further evidence of this as we proceed. One of the first examples of the new egocentric pantheism in Spanish poetry and also one of the clearest examples of the influence of sensationalism on the evolution of Spanish Romanticism is an Anacreontic —an Anacreontic in name and form only, because it is a threat to the very bases of the pacific pastoral genre to which it purports to belong. We owe Cadalso the first prose manifesto of Romantic principles and techniques: not a theoretical manifesto, but all the same in practice a manifesto. I am referring, of course, to his brilliant *Noches lúgubres*, which he said should have been printed on black paper with yellow ink. The Anacreontic I have mentioned was published in Cadalso's *Ocios de mi juventud* in 1773, when he had very possibly not yet finished the *Noches lúgubres*.

Of far less artistic quality than the *Noches*, the Anacreontic is nevertheless brilliant in its concept and amazingly radical for the Europe of 1773. Moreover, it contains in symbolic form some very shrewd critical reflections on the innovation that its treatment of nature constitutes. This Anacreontic will tie together what we have said earlier about the double influence of sensationalism in liberalizing Neoclassic poetic theory and in opening the eyes of the poet to dynamic nature. Entitled *A la muerte de Filis*, and inspired by the death of the actress María

Ignacia Ibáñez, this poem might well be thought of as the "Romantic Manifesto of 1773":

> En lúgubres cipreses
> He visto convertidos
> Los pámpanos de Baco,
> Y de Venus los mirtos.
> Cual ronca voz del cuervo
> Hiere mi triste oído
> El siempre dulce tono
> Del tierno jilguerillo.
> Ni murmura el arroyo
> Con delicioso trino;
> Resuena cual peñasco
> Con olas combatido.
> En vez de los corderos,
> De los montes vecinos
> Rebaños de leones
> Bajar con furia he visto.
> Del sol y de la luna
> Los carros fugitivos
> Esparcen negras sombras
> Mientras dura su giro.
> Las pastoriles flautas,
> Que tañen mis amigos,
> Resuenan como truenos
> Del que reina en Olimpo.
> Pues Baco, Venus, aves,
> Arroyos, pastorcillos,
> Sol, luna, todos juntos
> Miradme compasivos,
> Y a la ninfa que amaba
> Al infeliz Narciso,
> Mandad que diga al orbe
> La pena de Dalmiro. (BAE, LXI, 275a)

The senses of sight and hearing—the latter directly mentioned as "mi triste oído"—are the principal actors in this drama of chiaroscuro images and jarring sounds that Dalmiro has created to express his sorrow upon the loss of his beloved. The entire history of the influence of sensationalism on eighteenth-century poetry is suggested in the verses: "Cual ronca voz del cuervo/ Hiere mi triste oído/El siempre dulce tono/Del tierno jilguerillo." First in the descriptive poetry of the Enlightenment, sensationalism made possible a more acute perception of the physical and affective qualities of natural objects: "El siempre dulce tono/Del tierno jilguerillo." Then later in the century, as I have said, the direction of this emotional transference was reversed as the senses became the avenue for the projection of the poet's anguished consciousness onto nature: the provenance of the crow-like "ronca voz" is obvious: it is a sensorial extension of the poet's state of mind: *ronca* is to *voz* as *triste* is to *oído*. The reshaping of the universe in the image of the poet's ego and the emergence of the egocentric pantheism that was to characterize Romantic poetry become more and more striking as one after another the various features of Neoclassic nature are negated by sensorial projections of other features that are their opposites: the vine leaves yield to the cypresses, the voice of the goldfinch to that of the crow, the murmur of the creek to the shattering rush of waves against crags, the lambs to the lions, the light of the sun and moon to black shadows, and the music of the shepherds' flageolets to thunderclaps.

The Supreme Being occasionally addressed in Dalmiro-Cadalso's prose works is obviously of little comfort to him while, like Condillac's godless statue, he stands disconsolate before the wide world calling on all the creatures in sight—"aves,/Arroyos, pastorcillos,/Sol, luna"—and implores of them, "todos juntos/ Miradme compasivos." On an artistic level, to be sure, Dalmiro, like the statue, has begun to conceive "des égarements et des superstitions" respecting his mileu. For Dalmiro also, "l'univers se remplit d'êtres visibles et invisibles." And all these creatures, having been entreated by Dalmiro, are to help him pour out his troubles by in turn intervening with the nymph Echo for her assistance: "Mandad que diga al orbe/La pena de Dalmiro."

"Que diga al orbe la pena de Dalmiro"—this, as far as can be determined, is the first occurrence in Spanish literature of a new phenomenon: world grief, *Weltschmerz, mal du siècle,* for which in 1794 Meléndez Valdés was to invent the first name this emotion was given in any language (*fastidio universal*), as I have shown in a recent study.[36] The universalization of the Romantic poet's grief has many causes: eighteenth-century humanitarianism, for example, is an important factor; but it is evident that one indispensable cause is the sensorial projection of the poet's mood onto all the faces of the universe.

Now the autocritical reflections contained in this Anacreontic on the death of Phyllis take the form of a symbolic discussion of poetic license. Cadalso is fully aware of the extent of his technical innovation. "En vez de los corderos,/De los montes vecinos/ Rebaños de leones/Bajar con furia he visto." These lines are an allusion to the second example in Horace's admonishments about the excessive use of poetic license. Poets must be given license to follow inspiration's soaring flight, Horace grants, in his *Art of Poetry,* "But never to mix the wild and placid,/To mingle snakes with birds, tigers with lambs" ("*Sed non ut placidis coëant immitia, non ut/Serpentes avibus geminentur, tigribus agni*") (*De Arte Poetica,* vv.12–13). By alluding to Horace's precept while in the very act of contravening it, Cadalso suggests the view that the old idea of license is too stringent to permit the expression of the new era's feelings. Cadalso was thoroughly conversant with Feijoo's writings, and there can be no doubt that he also knew Pope's *Essay on Criticism,* but in any case he was very familiar with the new, liberal poetics of his century. And bringing the lions and the lambs together was his attempt to formulate a "new rule," a way whereby he might, after Pope, "boldly deviate from the common track" and "snatch a grace beyond the reach of art," or, after Feijoo, soar "por su valentía" up beyond the "reglas comunes" in pursuit of a "sublime idea" (*Criticism,* I, 151, 153; BAE, LVI, 353a). Cadalso had at least one model for his forbidden mixture of the wild and the placid, in Isaiah 11:6, wherein it is prophesied that the wild beasts and

[36] See my "Sobre el nombre español del dolor romántico," *Ínsula,* No.264 (November 1968), pp.1, 4–5.

the domesticated ones shall dwell and lie down together; and this biblical influence would explain the substitution of *lions* for *tigers* in Cadalso's Horatian allusion, as both cats appear in Isaiah together with lambs and other gentle creatures.

With the ferment in poetics and poetry toward the end of the eighteenth century, poets were more and more haunted by Horace's example of excessive license, sometimes as they tried to ward off the new tendencies in their art, sometimes as they tried to clarify and advance them. In Fable I, which serves as a prologue to his celebrated *Fábulas literarias* (1782), the ever Neoclassical albeit not illiberal Tomás de Iriarte introduces two opposing bands of animals (writers that are never to mingle), one group being captained by the lamb and the dove, the other by the tiger and the poisonous serpent. In *The Tyger*, written as the French Revolution was starting, William Blake asks the fiery-eyed cat: "Did He who made the Lamb make thee?" In an earlier poem, which Cadalso probably wrote between 1768 and 1770, the harsh element in nature already "destruye el rebaño/de tristes corderos" (BAE, LXI, 270a). Cadalso is not only an innovator in his attempt to understand the new organic tendency in poetry in terms of poetics; he is so intent upon finding an explanation that the reader can even find him musing about it in his more Neoclassical compositions. For instance, in the *Desdenes de Filis*, he employs the Horatian figure of the tiger and the lamb, and it may be significant that he at the same time refers to the Rousseauist-Romantic theme of the enmity between the innocent soul and society. Than that his adored shepherdess could be unfaithful, Dalmiro reflects, "Más fácil parecía/Vivir el tigre fiero/Con el manso cordero,/. . ./Y andar el inocente/Seguro por ciudades engañosas" (BAE, LXI, 254b).

I suppose someone might now say: *Tutto questo è bene trovato, ma forsè non sia vero.* Isn't this egocentric pantheism after all the same thing as the well-known figure of pathetic fallacy, which is to be found in all literatures since antiquity? I don't think so. First of all, it seems significant that the first name this figure received was coined in England, in precisely the period

we are talking about: in his *Elements of Criticism* (1762), Henry
Home, Lord Kames, called it "passionate personification."[37] I
think it is equally pertinent to note that the generic term still
in current usage—"pathetic fallacy," at first a derogatory term—
was proposed in the third volume of John Ruskin's *Modern
Painters*, published in 1856, when the influence of Romanticism
was certainly not altogether played out. Quite obviously, this
figure would not have been the object of such particular critical
attention at these times if there had not been something radically
new about the way European poets and readers experienced it
from about 1730 on.

A comparison between another example from Cadalso's poetry
and a similar passage from the Renaissance poet Garcilaso de la
Vega will show what is new about Romantic pathetic fallacy.
In a verse letter, written from a village in Aragón, Cadalso con-
fides that while weighed down with tedium—"Cargado de tedio"
—he has looked about him and seen that

> El cielo se muestra
> Airado y tremendo,
> Las yerbas sus verdes
> Matices perdieron,
> Las aves no forman
> Sus dulces conciertos
>
> .   .   .
>
> Sólo oigo la ronca
> Voz del negro cuervo. (BAE, LXI, 269b)

The earlier example with which we shall compare these verses
is drawn from Garcilaso's first eclogue:

> Con mi llorar las piedras enternecen
> Su natural dureza y la quebrantan;
> Los árboles parece que se inclinan;
> Las aves que me escuchan, cuando cantan,
> Con diferente voz se condolecen.[38]

[37] Henry Home, Lord Kames, *Elements of Criticism* (New York, 1838), pp.353ff.
(Chap.20, sec.1).

[38] *Garcilaso de la Vega y sus comentaristas. Obras completas del poeta acom-*

As one ponders these similar figures, it becomes very clear that there is one fundamental difference between them: in the Renaissance poem, there are four clearly defined, separate psychological identities: the stones, the trees, the birds, and the poet, each one of which reacts to the situation in its own manner; whereas in the eighteenth-century poem, there is but one psychological identity, that of the poet, because the mood and aspect of all nature's beings and even heaven's dome above them are assimilated to those of the solitary sufferer. In the metaphor, or simile (*parece*), in Garcilaso's eclogue, the poet is conscious of the *seeming* sympathetic attitude of the natural objects around him as of an attitude existing in *those* beings outside himself; in Cadalso's metaphor, the poet is only conscious of his own consciousness, within himself and as he projects it on the forms and other phenomena within his sight and hearing. In the Renaissance poem, the compassion the natural beings show is merely a deferential concession to the mood of the human interlocutor with whom circumstances have confronted them at a particular moment, and some of the words Garcilaso has selected to describe the way they express their grief (*natural dureza, inclinarse, con diferente voz*, etc.) imply that they will again assume their usual attitude after the poet has moved on. (In the Anacreontic we analyzed earlier, the vine leaves and myrtle did not at a given moment merely *look like* drear cypresses; they were "converted" into drear cypresses, that is, they *became* a part of sad Dalmiro's universal visage.)

In Cadalso's verse letter from an Aragonese village, nature does not sympathize with the poet; it psychologically reiterates him. In the verse letter, the lugubrious aspect of nature has a stated *terminus a quo* ("Desde que del hado,/Conmigo severo,/La mano tirana/Firmó mi decreto"), which is stated in the lines just preceding those that were quoted before, but there is no stated or even implicit *terminus ad quem* because the poet's ego

---

*pañadas de los textos integros de los comentarios,* ed. Antonio Gallego Morell (Granada, 1966), p.144.

has not only reshaped all nature in its own image, it has absorbed it all. Only a few years later, Meléndez Valdéz talked about being alone "en medio del universo" (BAE, LXIII, 149a). But Cadalso was already the hub of his world in the verse *Carta* we have been analyzing: he does not imagine that the stones momentarily soften *their* natural rigidness ("enternecen/Su natural dureza"—third-person forms); he is controlling the universe from within himself, through the agency of his senses: "Sólo *oigo* la ronca/Voz del cuervo," in which the key word is the first-person form of the verb of perception, italicized here. Pathetic fallacy, as it is found in the Romantics, is not so much a rhetorical figure as it is a *Weltanschauung*. Moreover, in Romantic pathetic fallacy, the influence of the new materialist philosophies led to a total fusion of *natura naturans* with *natura naturata* and thus to a naturalistic pantheism from which theologians and humanists of the Renaissance would have shrunk in horror.

Generally speaking, critical evaluations of literary works of the medieval, Renaissance, and Counter-Reformation–Baroque periods seem more firmly grounded than those of eighteenth- and nineteenth-century works because for the earlier periods clearly demonstrable parallels have been worked out between the various literary techniques and the notions of man and his universe that successively shaped the European mentality (Scholasticism, Neo-Platonism, Post-Tridentine asceticism, Cartesianism, etc.). The "Romantic traits" which critics usually mention can be considered authentically Romantic only in those works in which they are found as functions of a Romantic cosmology, and the fact that we have (1) discovered in certain Spanish poems written between 1768 and 1773 a relationship between man and the universe that is exactly the same as that found in the so-called Romantic works of the nineteenth century, and (2) established the philosophical basis for this relationship in the thought of the Enlightenment means that we are justified in considering those poems Romantic and in dating the emergence of Romantic poetry in Spain in the early 1770's. I could have analyzed poetry

[135]

of more artistic value if I had chosen my examples from Meléndez Valdés, but I have preferred to use the works of Cadalso because I was interested in determining the approximate date of the first appearance of the Romantic metaphysic in Spanish poetry. The existence of Cadalso's more obviously Romantic prose *Noches lúgubres*, finished by 1774, indicates that there is nothing extravagant about the date I have suggested, and at the same time the identification of the Romantic metaphysic in Cadalso's poetry indicates equally clearly that the *Noches lúgubres* is not an isolated chance phenomenon in the Spain of the 1770's, as has usually been thought.

The fact that the writings of many later European writers were characterized by a heavier concentration of the purely ornamental, accidental features of Romanticism does not make them more Romantic since the poet's *Weltanschauung* remained the same as in the earlier works that are usually called Pre-Romantic. Rather than distinguishing between Pre-Romanticism and Romanticism, it might be more germane to talk in terms of Romanticism in the final decades of the eighteenth century, and conscious Manneristic Romanticism in the nineteenth century. The very adjective *romantic*, which, we are told, is used in the eighteenth century only to describe the irregular, unkempt aspect of the natural landscape, seems nevertheless in some eighteenth-century contexts to be struggling hard to connote more. In several verses of Thomson's *Spring*, the association of *romantic* with harbingers of the new egocentric pantheism such as the phrases "sympathetic glooms" and "pensive dusk" at least from our distance seems to suggest a great deal about its future meaning: "Sudden he starts,/Shook from his tender trance, and restless runs/To glimmering shades, and sympathetic glooms;/Where the dun umbrage o'er the falling stream,/Romantic, hangs; there through the pensive dusk/Strays, in heart-thrilling meditation lost" (*Spring*, vv.1024–29).

In France and Germany, in the 1760's and 1770's, *romantique* and *romantisch* were applied to the landscape. I believe there are no known examples of the use of the Spanish adjective *romántico* in any sense before the nineteenth century, but Spain did have a name for Romantic grief long before the turn of the century, thirty-nine years before France had a name for it, and fifty-three years before Germany had one, as I have demonstrated in the article mentioned above. Moreover, when the literary texts are examined in the light of the reigning philosophical currents of the eighteenth century, it is clearly evident that the beginnings of Romanticism are as early in Spain as in her Continental neighbors. According to Van Tieghem, Cadalso's *Noches lúgubres* is characterized from its opening words by "un romantisme fort accentué et très rare en Europe vers 1770."[39] But we have seen that the *Noches lúgubres* is not an isolated example, as Van Tieghem thought. Spain has seldom led the Western world in the formulation of new philosophical and scientific thought, but she has usually remained abreast of her neighbors, often anticipated them, in the artistic use of new intellectual patterns. In the last decade of the eighteenth century, the Spanish translator of Gessner surveyed the progress of poetry in the years immediately preceding and concluded: "Philosophy improved this art as it did the others . . . and in short it seems that regenerating the imagination and sensitivity of Apollo's children, she at length revealed to them a new poetry."[40]

Now, before closing, what does all this imply about present-day historiographical criteria for the study of Romanticism? A student of mine once entitled a senior thesis on certain eighteenth-century literary figures "The First Spanish Romanticism," and recently a graduate student at another institution wrote to ask how my views on the origins of Spanish Romanticism can be reconciled with the reigning concepts of periodization for Romanticism, and if we are now to consider that there are three Spanish Romanticisms. I have never been partial to the practice of cutting centuries, styles, and often the works of individual writers up into neat, tight little divisions. It is presumptuous of

[39] Paul Van Tieghem, *La poésie de la nuit et des tombeaux*, in *Le préromantisme* (Paris, 1930), II, 165.
[40] Gessner, *Idylios*, pp.lxiii–lxiv.

scholars to assume that such inflexible criteria can at any time in history serve to describe the endless possibilities open to human nature, much less to human creativity. Literature develops in large, general trends, in response to the gradually shifting focus of the human mentality, with much overlapping of the old trends on the new, and many fruitless attempts by dissidents to initiate counter-trends. For this reason, to replace the usual idea of a Pre-Romantic "period" followed by a Romantic "period," I have suggested a distinction between Romanticism and Manneristic Romanticism, that is, between a trend and its accentuation.

According to Jovellanos, as we have seen, modern literary history was shaped by two major trends: that of the *idealistas*, slowly supplanted by that of the *naturalistas* from the early eighteenth century on, as the new sensationalist, inductive bias of the European mentality began to influence the arts more and more profoundly; and I am convinced he was quite justified in his view. It is significant that all the major literary styles of the nineteenth century (Romanticism, Realism, Naturalism) are merely variations on the same concept of man as a sentient material being in dialogue with a material universe. Ten years ago I pointed out that the Rousseauist-Romantic hero determined by pristine nature and the crippled characters of French Naturalism determined by their squalid proletarian milieu differ only as the positive and negative interpretations of a single philosophy differ, with Realism forming something like a mean between extremes.[41] Romanticism was simply the first fully achieved literary manifestation of the new European *forma mentis*; but there is still a great deal of Romanticism in the novels of Galdós, just as there was already much Realism in Rousseau's *Nouvelle Héloïse*. It is impossible to distribute pieces of such a broad, various, and on-going trend among the neat pigeonholes of conventional literary history, and I shall not attempt to reconcile my ideas on the origins of Spanish Romanticism (or Romanticism in general) with the usual concepts of periodization for Romantic literature because I consider the latter to be inherently false.

41 Isla, *Fray Gerundio*, I, lxxxi.

The most one can accurately do is indicate that toward a certain date in history one of the major styles representing the post-Lockean inductivist approach to literary creation emerges for a time as more dominant than the others.

From the viewpoint of literary technique, it is just as false to subdivide Romanticism along the lines of the several political and religious ideologies that come into play during its long sway, as it is to subdivide it by the external events of literary history. It is manifestly foolish, for example, to suppose that the return of a handful of exiles from England, upon the death of an illiberal king, could overnight plunge Spain into full-blown Romanticism. We are told that the ethic of nineteenth-century Romanticism is fundamentally Christian, yet in a play like Rivas' *Don Alvaro* the cloister proves a convenient place to conceal or conceive every manner of heinous crime. In Zorrilla's *Don Juan Tenorio*, society, not the deceiver himself, is responsible for his crimes (this is the very same materialist concept of man's determination by his milieu that was born of sensationalist theory during the Enlightenment), and the doctrine of original sin is implicitly negated as Doña Inés, metaphorically related in the play to Eve, leads the deceiver back to paradise, as it were, reversing the role of the first woman toward the first man. The ideas of a thinker like Sanz del Río, who comes at the very end of the so-called Romantic period, are, in many respects, nothing but an attempt to rediscover God without, however, abandoning the basic metaphysic that had been dominant since the eighteenth century because the founder of Spanish *krausismo* stresses the notion that with the advent of modern science man has finally realized he is a combination of nature and spirit. (The Romantic philosopher Schelling defined man's constitution in almost exactly the same terms, as I mentioned earlier.)

Moreover, with the exception of Locke and probably Condillac, individual philosophers are less important as influences that shaped Romanticism than as illustrations of the larger inductivist pattern of the European mentality that shaped philosophy, literature, and all the other arts from the eighteenth century on.

(Jovellanos, after all, said that "the poems, novels, histories, and even philosophical works of modern times are full of descriptions of objects and natural, moral acts which enchant the reader with their truth.") The pattern that characterized the Western mentality after its shift from deductivism to inductivism was broad enough to encompass both sides of numerous ideological disagreements and violent polemics in both philosophy and literature, but underlying all such differences the subject-object relationship between man and the universe—the authentic basis for all artistic representations of reality—remained essentially the same materialist, pseudo-spiritual, sensorially supported one we have studied here. (After the establishment of such an all-pervasive pattern in the European literary mind, it is obviously unnecessary to posit that later generations of Romantics were particularly familiar with the writings of Locke and Condillac, or would necessarily even agree with them on secondary questions.)

The appearance of the new inductivist mentality and the new sensationalist-derived subject-object relationship in Spain in the eighteenth century is what permitted Spanish literature to *evolve* in the direction of Romanticism, as I have shown. However, the scope of the Spanish Romantic *evolution* and the utter falsity of our present notions about the chronology of Spanish Romanticism will not become fully evident until Hispanists begin to study the profound—though often denied—influence of the eighteenth-century Spanish Romantics on the nineteenth-century Spanish Romantics.

VI

# The Internationalism of the Portuguese Enlightenment: The Role of the Estrangeirado, c. 1700–c. 1750

MANOEL CARDOZO

## I

THE EIGHTEENTH CENTURY was for the educated classes of Portugal, more than it was for those of Italy, France, and England, a period of crisis and change. To what extent the *crise mental* (to borrow Hernani Cidade's phrase)[1] was felt by the intelligentsia for the century as a whole is hard to determine, and the generalizations covering large segments of time may be more intuitive than documented. If the century were of one piece, the task would be simple; we could then assume that what characterized the reign of King John V (1706–1750) also characterized the reigns of his son and granddaughter.

Erudite pamphleteers of the stature of Antero de Quental,[2]

[1] Hernani Cidade, *Ensaio sôbre a crise mental do século XVIII* (Coimbra, 1929). The fifth enlarged edition of this seminal essay has been published as Vol.II of his *Lições de cultura e literatura portuguesas* (Coimbra, 1968); the latter edition will hereafter be cited as Cidade.

[2] I refer to his *Causa da decadencia dos povos peninsulares nos ultimos seculos. Discurso pronunciado na noite de 27 de Maio, na sala do Casino Lisbonense* (Porto, 1871).

Oliveira Martins,[3] and Teófilo Braga[4] were not conscious of this problem, and assumed that the Portuguese eighteenth century was uniformly bad; they allowed their doctrinaire liberalism to color their understanding of the past. Today the simplistic view of the eighteenth century, as held by the liberal historians, is no longer credible, and we must instead entertain the possibility that during the Age of Enlightenment Portugal was not, after all, truly isolated from the rest of Europe, that the Portuguese were in some way aware of their realities, as they were of the revolutionary thought that had transformed European philosophy and science.

The Portuguese were saddled, to be sure, with a Baroque establishment that had been fashioned largely in the seventeenth century, and it was not easy for unconventional people to manipulate or operate within it. They were cognizant of the rigidities of the philosophical system that had stemmed from the Council of Trent's concern for orthodoxy. They were impatient with the war on heresy, the relentless ferreting out of Jews and lapsed Catholics by the Inquisition, the censorship of the printed and spoken word, the absolutism of the state, the privileges of the clergy, the attempt at making Portugal an island of purity in a Europe that was inflamed with the ideas that Descartes, Locke, Bacon, Newton, Copernicus, Kepler, Galileo, and Vico had unleashed. Yet even in Portugal, the heated animadversions of foreign and domestic observers to the contrary notwithstanding, the intellectual was somehow able to make himself felt, and to create for himself, as for those who shared his view of life, areas of refuge where it was safe to discuss the *crise mental* that affected the country.

## II

Europeans of the modernized fringe of the Continent, beyond the Pyrenees, especially the British and the Protestants, treated

[3] See for example J. P. de Oliveira Martins, *A History of Iberian Civilization*, trans. Aubrey F. G. Bell (New York, 1969).

[4] *Historia de Universidade de Coimbra nas suas relações com a instrucção publica portugueza*, 4 vols. (Lisbon, 1892–1902).

the Portuguese and their culture with egregious contempt; this in itself is symptomatic of their tendentious ignorance of the Portuguese scene. Sir Richard Fanshawe, the English diplomat who translated the *Lusiads* into English for the first time and had warm praise for the poem,[5] called the language of Camões "so *uncourted* a *language*" that people would hardly believe that such a language could boast of a poet that rivaled Tasso.[6] Another seventeenth-century author, James Howell, looked upon Portuguese as a kind of sub-dialect of Spanish.[7] And John Stevens, whose book appeared in 1702, called the Portuguese language "Harsh and Barren" and considered it difficult "to refine the small Latin Remains from the Rubbish it is mixed with."[8]

Twenty-four years later Charles Brockwell repeated the libel against Portuguese and added a touch of his own flamboyance. "The *Portuguese* Language," he remarked, "is an uncough *Spanish*, or rather a Rude Resemblance of that Polite Tongue, with a Mixture of barbarous obsolete *Latin*, some *French*, more *Arabick*, a little *Greek*, to which is added some remains of the *Gothick*, and other Northern Nations that subdued them."[9] The author of a French gazeteer on Portugal, published in 1730, described Portuguese as a mixture of French and corrupted Spanish,[10] while Joseph Barretti, whose impressions of his visit to Portugal in 1760 were also published in English, held Portuguese literature

---

[5] Luís de Camões, *The Lusiads in Sir Richard Fanshawe's Translation*, ed. Geoffrey Bullough (Carbondale, Ill., 1963). See also Anne Fanshaw, *Memoirs of Lady Fanshawe, wife of the right hon. Sir Richard Fanshawe, Bart. ambassador from Charles the second to the court of Madrid in 1665: To which are added, extracts from the correspondence of Sir Richard Fanshawe* (London, 1829).

[6] Camões, *Lusiads*, p.33.

[7] Félix Walter, *La littérature portugaise en Angleterre a l'époque romantique* (Paris, 1927), pp.24–25.

[8] *Ibid.*, p.25.

[9] Charles Brockwell, *The Natural and Political history of Portugal. From its First Erection into a kingdom by Alphonso Son of Henry Duke of Burgundy, Anno 1090 down to the present time* (London, 1726), p.103.

[10] *Description de la ville de Lisbonne, où l'on traite de la cour, de Portugal, de la Langue Portugaise, & des Moeurs des Habitans; du Gouvernement, des Revenus du Roi, & de ses Forces par Mer & par Terre; des Colonies Portugaises, & du Commerce de cette Capital* (Paris, 1730), p.88.

in such low esteem that he believed the losses in books occasioned by the Lisbon earthquake of 1755 would be regretted only in Portugal.[11]

An ignorance of the Portuguese language which some Englishmen publicly and unashamedly professed is all the more remarkable when we realize that a considerable number of Englishmen at the time must have known Portuguese, if only to conduct their commercial and diplomatic relations with areas of the non-Portuguese world. In the days of Sir Thomas More, the Portuguese navigator with the uncommon name of Raphael Hythloday had to be invented for the voyage to Utopia. Later both Robinson Crusoe and Gulliver were with equal propriety provided with a knowledge of Portuguese. Gulliver in particular speaks of how he was found by Portuguese seamen: "One of the seamen in Portuguese bid me rise, and asked me who I was. I understood the language very well, and getting on my feet, said, I was a poor Yahoo."

Brockwell's animus was not limited to the language of Portugal. He found the country itself "more pleasant than profitable," affording the "Delicacies" rather than the "Necessaries of Life." There was much truth, or so he felt, in the old witticism about the wisdom and foolishness of the Latins. "The *Spaniards* seem wise, but are Fools; the *French* seem Fools, but are wise; the *Italians* seem and are wise; but the *Portuguese* neither seem to be wise, nor are so."[12] Oliver Goldsmith, without wondering whether or not any Englishmen had a sound moral base to stand on, shared the enlightened English feeling about the Inquisition. In one of the "Chinese Letters" that he wrote for *The Public Ledger*, he described the Portuguese as cruel and their *autos-de-fé* as wicked.[13]

In 1766 Charles-François Dumouriez, who later would become

---

11 *Voyage de Londres à Gênes. Passant par l'Angleterre, le Portugal, l'Espagne, et la France*, trans. from the 3d English edition (Amsterdam, 1777).

12 Brockwell, *History*, pp.12–13.

13 The letters appeared daily in *The Public Ledger* from January 1760 to August 1761. I have quoted from letter no.5. (I owe this reference to Professor Arthur Fenner.)

a general in the French revolutionary forces, was as sharply critical of Portugal as any Englishman. He blamed "the extreme
sloth and apathy of its inhabitants; they neither travel, write, nor
communicate with foreign nations"—for the obvious fact that
Europeans did not write about them. He was aware of "this cloud
of oblivion which covers Portugal, this national stupor." This
was true even of "the English travellers, those diligent observers
of men and things," who "seem to have neglected Portugal, or to
have despaired of finding in it any object that could repay their
trouble, or satisfy their spirit of philosophic research."[14] And of
the French: "The French, so remarkable for their curiosity,
vivacity, boldness, and acuteness of research; who make reflections and write upon all subjects, have nevertheless left Portugal
untried."[15] As also of the Spanish: "The Spaniards, though they
have a thousand notions of policy, rivalship, and hatred, to urge
them to a scrupulous examination of the neighbouring kingdom,
are yet more indifferent than the English."[16]

Dumouriez described the character of the Portuguese as bear-
ing a strong resemblance to that of the Spaniards: ". . . they possess the same disposition to idleness and superstition, the same
kind of courage, the same pride, but more politeness and deceit,
which arises from the rigour of their present government; the
same national zeal, and, above all, a decided spirit of independence, which incites the most violent hatred towards the Spaniards,
who have been their tyrants, and the English, who are their masters."[17] He expressed his disgust at the scandalous behavior of
the clergy, "which lessens the veneration of the people" and was
more "injurious to religion than the continual railleries of the
English, the introduction of philosophical books, and the quarrels with the court of Rome."[18] Indeed, "there is no catholic

---

[14] *An account of Portugal, as it appeared in 1766 to Dumouriez; since a celebrated general in the French army. Printed at Lausanne in 1775* (London, 1797),
pp.2, 5.

[15] *Ibid.*, pp.4–5.

[16] *Ibid.*, p.3.

[17] *Ibid.*, p.154.

[18] *Ibid.*, p.174.

country whatever, in which a more superstitious devotion is paid to saints, relics, miracles, and other religious mummeries; because no people stand more in need of expiations for their low and filthy debaucheries, and for the avarice and revengeful spirit which continually agitates the soul of a Portuguese."[19]

Still another Englishman, Sir Joseph Banks, in his journal of 1768–1771, took the Portuguese to be "without exception, the laziest as well as the most ignorant race in the whole world."[20] Arthur William Costigan had no better opinion of the Portuguese a decade later. They were to his mind a useless, ceremonious, false, impertinent, and cowardly race; the effects of ecclesiastical despotism were more fatal to Portugal than to Spain.[21] Only Giuseppe Gorani, the kindly Italian who lived in Portugal from 1765 to 1767, seemed to have been aware of the fact that "there was no people in Europe whose character has been so little known as that of the Portuguese, who, in general, are known through the accounts of Spanish writers." Gorani knew that even though Spanish authors were worthy of appreciation, they never wrote about the Portuguese with impartiality. "For that reason one must mistrust all Spaniards in general when they speak of the Portuguese nation, against which they nurture such bad will."[22]

The Lisbon earthquake of 1755, which destroyed a part of the city and killed no less than 10,000 people, sent waves of horror throughout Europe, but foolish moralists gloated over the punishment that God had wreaked upon the wretched Portuguese. So much holy fuss was raised in England over the destruction of the Portuguese capital that an anonymous writer felt obliged to

19 *Ibid.*, p.177.

20 Sir Joseph D. Hooker (ed.), *Journal of the right hon. Sir Joseph Banks bart., K.B., P.R.S. during Captain Cook's first voyage in H.M.S. Endeavor in 1768–71 to Terra del Fuego, Otahite, New Zealand, Australia, the Dutch East Indies, etc.* (London, 1896), p.42.

21 Arthur William Costigan, *Cartas de Portugal 1778–1779*, trans. Augusto Reis Machado, II (Lisbon, n.d.), 134, 136.

22 José Gorani, *Portugal a côrte e o país nos anos de 1765 a 1767*, trans. from the Italian with a preface and notes by Castelo Branco Chaves (Lisbon, 1945), p.96. My translation is from this Portuguese text.

raise a reasonable note: "A presumptuous forwardness in pronouncing on extraordinary events we leave to raving designing monks, methodists, and ignorant enthusiasts."[23] The remark may have been directed, among others, at John Wesley, the Methodist divine, who published his *Serious thoughts occasioned by the great earthquake at Lisbon* within a month after the catastrophe.[24] Although Wesley did not believe that the sins of the Portuguese explained the action of a just God in visiting vengeance upon them, he was too much of a moralist not to use the occasion to indict the depravity of mankind as a whole.

Elsewhere in Europe the news of the earthquake was received with mixed feelings. In Versailles, Madame de Pompadour's brother-in-law, M. de Baschi, the French ambassador to Lisbon in 1755, was delightfully humorous about the death and destruction that he had witnessed—he kept the Court roaring with laughter with his stories of the disaster.[25] Despite his cynicism, Voltaire posed the intelligent question for Frenchmen:

> Lisbonne, qui n'est plus, eut-elle plus de vices
> Que Londres, que Paris, plongé dans les délices?
> Lisbonne est abîmé, et l'on danse à Paris.[26]

In the Calvinist United Provinces of the Free Netherlands, where frivolity was frowned upon and freedom was somewhat of a myth, there was "little doubt but that the earthquake was an awesome example of the wrath of the Living God, and that Lisbon's addiction to 'Romish idolatry' had brought the visitation upon her."[27]

Fortunately for the sanity of the Portuguese, the ignorance of their country by Europeans, especially by Englishmen and Frenchmen, and the disrepute in which they were held by foreigners during the eighteenth century was as much contrived as

---

[23] T. D. Kendrick, *The Lisbon Earthquake* (London, 1956), p.161.

[24] Cited by C. R. Boxer, "Some Contemporary Reactions to the Lisbon Earthquake of 1755," *Revista de Faculdade de Letras* (Lisbon), XXII, 2d ser., No. 2 (1956), *passim*.

[25] *Ibid.*, p.17.

[26] "Poeme sur le désastre de Lisbonne, ou examen de cette axiome: Tout est bien," *Oeuvres complètes de Voltaire*, II (Paris, 1835), 508.

[27] Boxer, "Earthquake," p.17.

it was justified. Portuguese who had lived abroad and were experienced in the ways of men must have realized that foreigners ran no risk in attacking a politically defenseless country and that, moreover, their dwelling upon the evils of Portugal made it easier for them to overlook their own. Surely perceptive Portuguese knew that the restrictions against non-Catholics at the University of Coimbra were matched by the restrictions against Catholics at Oxford and Cambridge. It was easy to berate the Portuguese for establishing Scholasticism as the official philosophy of the schools while forgetting that the libraries of the University of Coimbra, the religious congregations, and the nobility were stocked with the very books that the Inquisition considered dangerous. The Count of Ericeira had a splendid collection of 18,000 volumes, while the King's library was one of the largest of Europe.[28]

Despite the legal restrictions under which they labored, the professors of the colleges and schools of the University of Coimbra were no boobs. They were obliged by law to follow the ancient routines, to teach the physics of Aristotle and the natural history of Pliny, but they were nonetheless "abreast of all the modern discoveries and in turn told their students about them, so that even in astronomy the theories of Copernicus, Kepler, Galileo, and Newton were known there."[29] Gorani, in fact, was delighted with the Coimbra students who had befriended him, and he concluded from their conversation "that in the University of Coimbra there were most able professors of literature and full of discernment."[30]

If modern languages were not taught in the secondary schools of Portugal before the opening of the Royal College of Nobles of Lisbon in 1766,[31] they were not normally taught in the official schools of Europe, or in Harvard College. Even so, it was possible

[28] António Alberto de Andrade, *Vernei e a cultura do seu tempo* (Coimbra, 1966), p.82. Hereafter cited as Andrade.

[29] Gorani, *Portugal*, p.40.

[30] *Ibid.*, p.35.

[31] Rómulo de Carvalho, *História da fundação do Colégio Real dos Nobres de Lisboa (1761–1772)* (Coimbra, 1959), *passim*.

to learn French, as many people did, from private teachers in Lisbon who tutored their pupils without interference from the authorities, and undoubtedly used Dom Luís Caetano de Lima's grammar of the French language published in 1710.[32] Indeed, French was so fashionable by 1738 that the Marquis of Valença observed that the children of the nobility customarily learned French before Latin.[33]

For all the vaunted backwardness of the study of science in Portugal, it remained for the Portuguese to send two Jesuit priests, Diogo Soares and Domingos Capassi, to Brazil in 1729 on the first geographical and cartographic mission to the New World subsidized by a European government.[34] The invidious distinctions between Old and New Christians were not abolished until 1773 and 1774, but Catholics in England had to wait until 1829 to vote and sit in Parliament. Certainly the health of Portuguese culture was not good in a society that discouraged change and dynamism, but it did not keep the Royal Society of London from electing Portuguese nationals to its membership.[35] Even King John himself became a member of the Academy of Arcadians (*Academia dos Árcades*), whose Maecenas he was, and to which many of his subjects also belonged.[36]

Insofar as historiography was concerned, the Portuguese eighteenth century was a notable one,[37] and in the quality of historical writing it compared favorably with the production of scholars in France, England, Italy, Spain, and the Germanies. As António Ferrão observed, "Portugal, far from being indifferent...reflected very well not only the developments abroad that in that period descriptive history—religious or ecclesiastical, political and lit-

---

[32] Andrade, p.79.

[33] *Ibid.*, p.80.

[34] *Ibid.* See also Luís de Pina, "Os Portugueses e a exploração científica do Ultramar," *Boletim Geral das Colónias*, XII, No.131 (May 1936).

[35] See Rómulo de Carvalho, *Portugal nas Philosophical Transactions nos séculos XVII e XVIII* (Coimbra, 1956).

[36] See especially Andrade, pp.63, 64, 123, 139.

[37] António Ferrão, "Os estudos de erudição em Portugal nos fins do século XVIII," *Boletim da Segunda Classe*, Academia das Ciências de Lisboa, XVIII, 22.

erary—had made, but also those that characterize the processes of investigation and criticism, and those that involve the auxiliary sciences of history, such as diplomatics, paleography, sigillography, etc."[38] The establishment of the Royal Academy of Portuguese History in 1720 is an indication of the importance that the Portuguese attached to the study of their past, and the scientific character of many of the projects sponsored by the Academy speaks highly of the concern for a national historiography free of fable and legend.[39]

In short, "not everything in Portugal was decadence and corruption," as Jaime Cortesão felicitously expressed it: "The common people, concentrated in their hovels in field, valley, and mountain, even in the presence of a shortage of males, kept intact the inherited virtues. In the small middle class of artisans, bureaucrats, and university graduates, civilian or military, many wholesome traits and vigilant minds were found. And the nobility itself, to which we add the higher clergy, but in greater proportion, the untitled nobility, had not lost the consciousness of the nation's essential, specific reason for being."[40]

## III

At the pinnacle of Portuguese society, the House of Bragança maintained itself with the dignity that Europe admired, and negotiated family alliances that reflected the reputation it enjoyed. By means of these marriages, the presence of another Europe, beyond the Peninsula, must assuredly have made itself felt. Queen Maria Francisca Isabel of Savoy, who married Peter II in 1668 and died in 1683, maintained a household so French in character that her daughter, the Infanta Isabel Luiza Josefa, was

38 *Ibid.*, pp.21–22.

39 In addition to what Ferrão says about the Academy in the work cited above, see Fidelino de Figueiredo, *Historia da litteratura classica continuação da 2.a epocha: 1580–1756. 3.a epocha: 1756–1825*, 2d ed. (Lisbon, 1930), pp.7–26.

40 Jaime Cortesão, *Alexandre de Gusmão e o tratado de Madrid*, Parte I, Tomo I (1695–1735) (Rio de Janeiro, 1952), p.90. Hereafter cited as Cortesão.

educated in the French manner and could write and speak French with ease.[41] When Peter married a second time, in 1687, he again chose a foreign bride, Maria Sofia Isabel of Neuburg.

His sister Catherine was married to Charles II of Great Britain. Returning to Portugal in 1693, after her husband's death and the success of the Glorious Revolution, Queen Kate established her new residence in Lisbon, at Bemposta, where her former subjects were wont to pay her court. The marriage had been a religiously strange mating, between a Catholic princess brought up to respect orthodoxy in the strict post-Tridentine manner, and the roué sovereign of a Protestant country that had produced Bacon, Locke, and Newton and was then in the forefront of the intellectual revolution. The Catherine that Lisbon saw, until her death in 1705, served on two occasions as regent of the realm, and reminded everybody, by her presence, that life among heretics did not require the sprinkling of holy water to make it worthwhile. Peter's son, and Catherine's nephew, the magnanimous John V, also went outside the Peninsula for a bride, and Maria Ana of Austria, daughter of the Holy Roman Emperor, became Queen of Portugal. Their son, Joseph I, reverted to the tradition of a Spanish marriage, but his principal minister, the Marquis of Pombal, who ruled Portugal with an iron hand, married Leonor de Daun of the Austrian nobility.[42]

We may assume that the mind and heart of John V, who ascended the throne in 1706 as a boy of seventeen, must have been shaped by his mother, the German second wife of Peter II, and by his aunt, the Dowager Queen of Great Britain, women who had lived abroad before settling in Portugal, but it is idle to speculate on his moral and intellectual formation. The fact remains that the young man who found himself suddenly on the throne of Portugal turned out to be the patron *par excellence* of

[41] Cidade, p.36.

[42] See in this connection Maria Alcina Ribeiro Correia, *Sebastião José de Carvalho e Mello na corte de Viena de Áustria elementos para o estudo da sua vida pública (1744–1749)* (Lisbon, 1965).

science and the arts, a man of sensitivity and good taste who, by opening windows upon the wider world of Europe, helped to make possible the subtle changes of the Portuguese eighteenth century. As Eduardo Brazão observed, King John was the sovereign who "marked for Portugal its reentry into Europe, from which it had been absent a long time."[43]

In an age dominated by Louis XIV and the memory of his sumptuous style, it was no mean achievement for John, from his isolated Western arcady, to make his presence felt among his contemporaries. John appears on the international scene during the Age of Gold in Brazil, when the wealth of Minas Gerais gave the mother country the cornucopia of abundance that enabled him to play his role, but another monarch might have played a different role. In 1760, ten years after the death of King John, Baretti foresaw the day when the Portuguese would be delivered from their ignorance and superstition and place themselves on the level of the other Catholic nations.[44] A little later Dumouriez was encouraged by the appearance of many books in Portugal that were translated from foreign tongues. He believed that by this means "a taste will be formed in this country, and the Portuguese will quit their state of ignorance much sooner than the Spaniards."[45] It is a waste of time to dwell upon the impertinence of these remarks. What is important is that they indicate that progress, as Baretti and Dumouriez understood the word, had been made. Both thought that Portugal had a chance to redeem itself. Would the progress, however tenuous, have been apparent to these observers if John V had not appeared? In this sense King John, the favorite target of liberal historians of the last century,[46] stands out as the royal hero of the intellectual modernization of Portugal.

43 Eduardo Brazão, *D. João V subsídios para a história do seu reinado* (Porto, 1945), p.53.

44 Baretti, *Voyage*, I, 284.

45 Dumouriez, *Account of Portugal*, p.193.

46 For example, J. P. de Oliveira Martins, *História de Portugal*, 2 vols., 11th ed. (Lisbon, 1927), II, 159 *et seq.*

## IV

When John asked Dr. Jacob de Castro Sarmento (1691–1762), the eminent physician, what he should do to improve the study of medicine in Portugal, the distinguished expatriate advised him to publish a translation of Francis Bacon (as a means of making available to the Portuguese the principles of the new science) and send young people to be trained abroad.[47] The advice did not fall on deaf ears, and King John, following the practice of his predecessors in the sixteenth century, began again to subsidize the education of young Portuguese in the academies and universities of Europe. The policy was maintained until the end of the *ancien régime*, the last notable example of the crown's largesse being no less a person than José Bonifácio de Andrada e Silva. The man who is now known as the patriarch of Brazilian independence spent many years of his life in northern Europe as a student of metallurgy. When he returned to Portugal, the Brazilian-born scientist became superintendent of the mines of the mother country, professor of metallurgy at the University of Coimbra, a member of the judiciary, and secretary of the Royal Academy of Sciences. Ultimately, he repaid the favors that he had received from the crown by contributing decisively to the independence of his homeland, a political risk that Castro Sarmento could hardly have envisaged.

Fortunately for King John, the people who profited from his bounty did not lead subversive political movements—the French Revolution and doctrinaire liberalism were still in the future. They contributed instead to the glory of his reign. He was served well by his protégés, the *estrangeirados* or cosmopolites that he was attracted to, Portuguese who had experienced life abroad and been informed by it. He was also well served by the Portuguese expatriates, voluntary exiles for the most part who lived in Rome, Paris, and London, who could function as the King's eyes and ears in the progressive countries of their residence. These

[47] Cidade, pp.49–50.

Portuguese, who made their careers abroad and never returned home, remained loyal to the country of their birth; they carried Portugal so much in their hearts that they gladly took advantage of opportunities that King John gave them to help their fellow Portuguese achieve modernization. Men like Castro Sarmento were a different breed from the liberal emigrés of 1828–1832, who fled their country to await the overthrow of the hated absolutist regime of Dom Miguel.[48] The emigrés of the earlier century, however much they may have opposed the rigors of Portuguese society, and especially the Inquisition, were not prepared as were the later liberals to throw out the baby with the bath water.

Dom Luís da Cunha, the remarkable diplomat of the first half of the eighteenth century, was hardly an emigré in the sense described. In common with the expatriates of later generations, he spent most of his life abroad, but he spent it in the diplomatic service of his country. He did not pursue a career independent of the state. He became, like so many of his contemporaries, an *estrangeirado*, a man who saw Portugal from abroad, but again his experience did not deracinate him. His solutions to Portuguese problems were obviously affected by his knowledge of the freer societies that gave him shelter, but they were not intended to destroy the basic fabric of life. Despite the length of his uninterrupted residence in England, the Low Countries, and France, he never lost touch with his own country. He made his influence felt among his fellow countrymen through personal contacts, through correspondence (notably with Diogo de Mendonça Corte-Real), and through works from his pen that circulated in manuscript form.[49]

48 Vitorino Nemésio, *Exilados (1828–1832) história sentimental e política do liberalismo na emigração* (Lisbon, n.d.).

49 For biographical details, see Diogo Barbosa Machado, *Bibliotheca Lusitana Historica, Critica, e Cronologica. Na qual se comprehende a noticia dos authores Portuguezes, e das Obras, que compuzéraõ desde o tempo da promulgaçaõ da Ley da Graça, até o tempo prezente*, III (Lisbon, 1752), 92. There are many intelligent and reflective references to Dom Luís da Cunha in Cortesão, pp.7–330, *passim*. The only published work of Cunha that I have seen is António Lourenço

Born in Lisbon in 1662, Dom Luís da Cunha received the doctorate in canon law from the University of Coimbra. He was appointed *Desembargador do Porto* in 1686 and in 1688 was promoted to the House of Supplication, one of the courts of final appeal. He began his diplomatic career in 1696, when he was appointed envoy extraordinary to the Court of London. He remained in England until 1712 when John V sent him as ambassador extraordinary to the Congress of Utrecht. He was then named the King's envoy to the Congress of Cambrai and afterwards ambassador to France, a post that he held until his death in 1749, at the age of eighty-seven. In Portugal, he briefly held an archdeaconry (*Arcediago do Bago*) in the Cathedral Church of Évora and, onward from 1723, one of the fifty chairs of the Royal Academy of Portuguese History.

In his "Instrucção Politica" written in 1737 for Marco António de Azevedo Coutinho, who was named Secretary of State for Foreign Affairs and War in 1734,[50] Dom Luís da Cunha, at a time when the gold and diamond mines of Brazil were at their peak of development, said bluntly that men are "the true Mines of a State."[51] Yet because of the multiplicity of convents for friars and nuns, there was a population shortage in Portugal. If the young people, he said, who now join convents married instead, "you will see that in two generations they could populate another Portugal, and if not, consider how many were needed to populate the world twice, the first time with only one Adam, and only one Eve, and the second time with only the children of Noah."[52] He thought that the King should restrict the number of novices

Caminha (ed.), *Obras ineditas do grande exemplar da sciencia do estado, D. Luiz da Cunha, a quem o Marquez de Pombal, Sebastião José de Carvalho e Mello, chamava seu mestre. Embaixador Extraordinario, e Plenipotenciario do Senhor Rei D. João V., de eterna memoria, na Corte de Londres, e Congresso de Utrecht. Commentadas, e consagradas ao muito alto e poderoso D. João VI., rei do reino unido de Portugal, Basil, e Algarve,* Vol.I (Lisbon, 1821).

50 I have used the manuscript copy (No.21) in the Oliveira Lima Library, The Catholic University of America, Washington, D.C. I have also used a second copy of the same work (No.22) which is likewise in the Oliveira Lima Library.

51 No.22, p.81.

52 No.22, p.44.

who are allowed to enter religious life,[53] and that nobody should be permitted to take solemn vows before the twenty-fifth birthday.[54]

If the excess of friars and nuns was, in his opinion, prejudicial to Portugal, it was more so in the overseas territories, where people were desperately needed.[55] And he condemned the Inquisition precisely because it obliged many people to leave Portugal; it got rid of a laboring class that added to the wealth of England and Holland.[56] It was the Inquisition, he added, that destroyed "the [Jewish] houses and families" of the province of Trás-os-Montes, forcing industrious people who manufactured silk to leave the country and take their skills elsewhere.[57] The evils of the ecclesiastical establishment would not be so great "if the commonwealth profited in some way from so many fat Benedictines, so many ignorant friars of the Order of St. Bernard, so many proud members of the Monastery of the Holy Cross of Coimbra, and so many deaf *Brunos*, who are in their Abbeys, perturbing public Society, with their partialities, and sending much money to Rome to get what each one wants, which is to govern the others."[58] There were, in short, too many friaries filled with "men with mouths to eat, and without arms to work."[59] Dom Luís da Cunha opposed the traditional pious practices of the Portuguese people, the excessive number of religious holidays, bull fights held in connection with religious celebrations, dances and comedies on feast days to honor Our Lady and the saints. "What do we mean by the bulls of St. Anthony?"[60] Because of a plethora of religious holidays, the Portuguese were gainfully employed only a third of the year, despite the fact that God had only sanctified Saturday (now Sunday) as the day of rest.

[53] No.22, p.48.
[54] No.22, p.51.
[55] No.22, p.49.
[56] No.22, p.55 *et seq.*
[57] No.21, fol.158.
[58] No.22, p.45.
[59] No.22, p.42.
[60] No.21, fol.153 and verso, 154.

These abuses, which the Protestant countries did not have, encouraged to his mind the natural laziness of the Portuguese.[61] Besides, Protestant religious services made more sense, for the people heard the Gospel explained to them. In Portugal, parishioners complained if Mass lasted more than half an hour.[62]

Dom Rafael Bluteau did not express himself in this demeaning way against the clergy and religion of Portugal, but like Dom Luís da Cunha he was no less an *estrangeirado*, a cosmopolite, no less influenced by foreign cultures, no less anxious to modernize the Portuguese; he too was patronized by King John.[63] He was, even so, a special kind of *estrangeirado*, for he was not a Portuguese at all but a foreigner who spent fifty-six years of his life in Portugal. Barbosa Machado, the learned author of the *Bibliotheca Lusitana*, the four-volume bio-bibliographical dictionary that appeared between 1741 and 1759, does not include him for this reason, but Bluteau was too much identified with Portugal to belong in any other *galère*.

Born in London in 1638 of French parents, Bluteau studied humanities in Paris, earned the doctorate in theology in Rome, and became a Theatine in 1664. In 1668 the Father General of his order sent him to Portugal, where the order had been established fifteen or twenty years earlier. In 1680 he accompanied Dr. Duarte Ribeiro de Macedo on a special mission to Turin whose purpose was to arrange the marriage between the heiress presumptive of the throne and the Duke of Savoy. With the death in 1683 of the Queen, who had protected him, life became difficult for him and he moved to France. He returned to Portugal in 1704 at an unfortunate time, when Portugal and France were fighting on opposite sides in the War of the Spanish Succession, and he was suspected of French sympathies. He was now separated from society and ordered to live at the Cistercian Abbey

61 *Ibid.*

62 No.21, fol.154 and verso.

63 See Inocêncio Francisco da Silva, *Diccionario bibliographico portuguez*, Vol. VII (Lisbon, 1862), and Cidade, pp.29–47. A comprehensive biography of the man remains to be written.

of Alcobaça, a blessing in disguise, for it enabled him to finish a number of literary works that he had under way and gave him access, for this purpose, to the Abbey's excellent library. He was allowed to return to Lisbon in 1713, after peace was declared. From now on he received the special favor of John V, who paid for the publication of his works and made him a member of the Royal Academy of Portuguese History at the time of its creation in 1720. At the time of his death in 1737 at the age of ninety-five, the eminent scholar, who knew English, French, Italian, Portuguese, Castilian, Latin, and Greek, had spent a total of six years in England, five in Italy, twenty-eight in France, and fifty-six in Portugal. No other *estrangeirado* could equal that record.

Bluteau was proud of the fact that he had served as preacher to the Queen of Great Britain and to Henriette Marie of France, but his real claim to fame was his *Vocabulario portuguez*, the first dictionary of the Portuguese language, which he published in eight volumes and in two supplementary volumes between 1712 and 1728. On the title page of his ambitious work, which he dedicated to King John V, he described in a series of adjectives what it was about. The *Vocabulario* was meant to be Portuguese, Latin, Aulic, Anatomic, Architectural, Bellic, Botanic, Brazilic, Comic, Critic, Chemic, Dogmatic, Dialectic, Dendrological, Ecclesiastical, Etymological, Economic, Floriferous, Forensic, Fructiferous, Geographical, Geometrical, Gnomonical, Hydrographical, Homonymical, Hierological, Ichthyological, Indic, Iphagogical, Laconic, Liturgical, Lithological, Medical, Musical, Meterological, Nautical, Numerical, Neotherical, Orthographical, Optical, Ornithological, Poetical, Philological, Pharmaceutical, Quidditative, Qualitative, Quantitative, Rhetorical, Rustical, Roman, Synonymical, Symbolical, Syllabical, Theological, Therapeutical, Technological, Uranological, Xenophonic, and Zoological.[64] The works of two Frenchmen, the *Grand Dic-*

---

[64] The first two volumes appeared in Coimbra in 1712, the third and fourth in Coimbra in 1713, all printed by the College of Arts of the Society of Jesus. Volumes V through VIII were published in Lisbon and printed by Pascoal da Sylva, printer to His Majesty: Vol.V in 1716, Vols.VI and VII in 1720, and Vol.VIII in 1721. The

*tionnaire Historique* of Louis Moréri (1643–1680), of which the
1759 twentieth edition, in ten volumes, is the best, and the *Dictionnaire Historique et Critique* of Pierre Bayle (1647–1706),
served in some way as guides; but Bluteau's contribution was
more of a dictionary and less of an encyclopedia than either Moréri's or Bayle's. Bluteau chose the dictionary format because "of
all books . . . the Dictionaries are those that more quickly and
easily instruct those who consult them."[65] Moreover, he was determined to make his dictionary as complete as possible: "Of
all the things that came to my notice, the said Vocabulary
makes mention. . . ."[66] At the same time, he wanted to lead
the untutored reader "without tripping to the Temple of
knowledge. . . ."[67]

The dictionary was therefore what Bluteau said it was on
the title page of its first volume. Inocêncio Francisco da Silva,
the bibliographer of the nineteenth century, pointed out that
one of the defects of the dictionary was the "inopportune digressions" that Bluteau took "to show off his erudition."[68] Yet it was
precisely his digressions that show us to what extent he was
aware of the new science and philosophy, and to what extent his
work served the interests of the Enlightenment in Portugal.
Here and there in the pages of his dictionary he tells what authors he consulted: the *Dictionnaire universel* by the Jesuits of
Trévoux, Bayle's dictionary, which the Roman Inquisition
placed on the index of prohibited books in 1698, Kepler's study
on the theory of the planets, Deschales's mathematical and astronomical world, Boyle's *Natural History*, Johnson's *Lexicon*

---

first part of the *Supplemento ao vocabulario portuguez, e latino, que acabou de
sahir á luz, Anno de 1721. Dividido em oito volumes, e dedicados ao magnifico rey
de Portugal D. João V* was published in Lisbon in 1727 and printed by the printer
of the Royal Academy. Part II also appeared in Lisbon, in 1728, and was printed
"Na Patriarcal Officina da Musica." I have used the volumes in the Oliveira Lima
Library.

65 Bluteau, *Supplemento,* I, a iii, verso.

66 *Ibid.,* [a iv].

67 *Ibid.,* prologue.

68 Inocêncio Francisco da Silva, *Diccionario,* VII, 43.

*Chymicum.* He tells the reader about Sturm's experiments in London, cites Descartes's theory of the vortex. Gassendi and Newton, as Hernani Cidade observed, are spiritually present in the Theatine's cell, along with Vives and Erasmus, Galileo and Huyghens, Cassini, Mariotte, and Boile.[69] Yet in the midst of this diversity he is careful not to offend orthodoxy or go beyond the limits of theological propriety as defined by the Holy Office. For example, in explaining the meaning of the word "Systema," he points out the three systems of the universe that were held in his day: the Ptolemaic, the Copernican, and the Thyconican. In the Copernican system the sun, not the earth, is the center of the universe. He advises the reader that, since there is no proof of Copernicus' theories, "it is better to ignore them with docility, and obedience, rather than sustain them with obstinacy and little respect for the Decrees of two Supreme Pontiffs, Paul V and Urban VIII."[70]

With his customary perspicacity, Hernani Cidade describes the pioneering significance of Dom Rafael Bluteau:

> We believe that we may consider this episode of intellectual activity of the eighteenth century the first shock—and therefore the first spark—between the tendencies of realism of the Enlightenment of the Century of Light, and the formalism, the taste for abstractions of the previous period. Orthodox Portugal, fearful of *dangerous speculations*, establishes again a more intimate contact with free France, and through France, with England, freer still. After substituting in a vast area of the dominions of science many *truths* that were ascribed to Revelation as *truths of reason*, Philosophy is now going to substitute more than ever the *truths of reason* by those of *experience*.[71]

Bluteau reflects, however modestly, "the curiosities that led his contemporaries of his own or following generations—Fontenelle, Voltaire, Rousseau himself and others—to exchange *literary im-*

69 Cidade, p.45.
70 Bluteau, *Vocabulario*, VII, 824.
71 Cidade, pp.45–46.

*agination* for *scientific observation.*"[72] Cidade pays Bluteau a
final compliment by asking a question he leaves unanswered:
"Is it not true that this cleric, French in origin, English by birth,
and, by cultural formation, English, French, Italian, and Portuguese, endowed with an encyclopedic knowledge acquired in
various schools, libraries, and countries, constitutes what one
might call the symbol, at the beginning of the *Experimentalist
Century*, of the vast and confused syncretism in which the total
renovation of the world, mental and moral, is prepared?"[73]

Like Bluteau, Manuel de Azevedo Fortes was formed intellectually during the reign of John's father, King Peter II (1667–
1706), and, as in Bluteau's case, served Portugal primarily as an
*estrangeirado* under John V.[74] He was born in Lisbon in 1660. At
the age of ten he began the study of humane letters at the Imperial
College of Madrid. Later he attended the University of Alcalá
de Henares, where he studied the "severe sciences." From Spain
he went to France. At the Collège du Plessis he studied "the system of modern philosophy"[75] as well as theology and mathematics. Subsequently he served two three-year terms as professor
of philosophy at the University of Siena. When he returned to
Portugal on a visit, Peter would not allow him to go back to
Italy. To keep him in the country, the King made him a captain
in the infantry, then promoted him to colonel. John V showed
his own esteem for the man by naming him chief engineer of
the realm in 1719 and by offering him a coveted membership in
the Royal Academy of Portuguese History. He also honored him
in 1739 by his presence when Azevedo Fortes demonstrated the
astronomical instruments he had acquired in Europe and which
were to become part of the observatory that was built at the Jesuit
College of Santo Antão of Lisbon.[76] He died in 1749.

[72] *Ibid.*, p.46.
[73] *Ibid.*
[74] Barbosa Machado, *Bibliotheca Lusitana*, III (Lisbon, 1752), 186–88.
[75] *Ibid.*, p.186.
[76] Cidade, p.47.

Azevedo Fortes was the author of many works, and his writings, as António Alberto de Andrade says, are gently impregnated with "a renovating spirit . . . which contributed very much to an effective knowledge of the European mentality."[77] His interest in mathematics led him to publish in 1744 a major work entitled *Logica nacional, Geometrica, e Analitica,* described by Barbosa Machado, who knew the author personally, as a "most useful work, and absolutely necessary to enter any science whatsoever, and even for all men, who in any particular may want to make use of their knowledge, and explain their ideas by means of clear, proper, and intelligible terms." In this book, according to Hernani Cidade, "scholastic logic is reduced to the clear simplicity of the geometric method."[78] More than a manual designed for engineers and even ladies, it is, again as Cidade points out, a work "that exalts the modern philosophers and believes Scholasticism to be a deformation of the philosophy of Aristotle through Arabic translations."[79] Though he does not refer to Descartes, Azevedo Fortes recognizes that doubt is the point of departure for certainty and thus becomes the first writer in Portugal to adopt publicly some fundamental Cartesian postulates.

Among those who also brought the new natural philosophy to Portugal was Francisco Xavier Leitão, who until his death in 1739 was recognized as an outstanding medical scientist.[80] Born in Lisbon in 1667, he became a Jesuit novice in 1682. After studying with the Jesuits in Évora, Leitão decided that the religious life was not for him; he returned to Lisbon and married in 1691. He then became a student of medicine at the University of Coimbra. Upon graduation he was appointed director of the Hospital of Our Lady of Light on the outskirts of Lisbon. Eventually he gave this up and returned to Lisbon in 1702, where he became the favorite physician of the nobility and the religious

77 Andrade, p.67.
78 Cidade, pp.47–48. There is a copy of the work in the Oliveira Lima Library.
79 *Ibid.,* p.48
80 Barbosa Machado, *Bibliotheca Lusitana,* II (Lisbon, 1747), 285–87.

communities. John V named him "physician of his chamber" and attached him to the entourage of the Marquis de Alegrete when the latter left in 1707 to arrange the King's marriage with Archduchess Maria Ana of Austria. The journey gave him the opportunity of meeting the great scholars of his profession in England, Holland, and Germany. Returning to Portugal, Leitão, now a widower, was ordained to the priesthood in 1720. In 1721 he accompanied Cardinal da Cunha to Rome for the conclave to elect the new pope. While the Cardinal took care of his ecclesiastical obligations, Leitão enjoyed the company of the physicians of Rome and of the Court of Turin. In Paris he observed other things of interest to a medical man. He became a member of the Royal Academy of Portuguese History in 1736 and in 1738 chief surgeon of the realm. Unfortunately, the manuscripts of his unpublished works are lost, and what we know of his learning is what Barbosa Machado wrote of him: "Even though he always venerated the ingenious artifice of the Dialectic of Aristotle, he was a stubborn follower of the Philosophy of René Descartes, in whose System he discovered solid principles for the Medicine that he professed."[81]

Actually, quite a few Portuguese of the eighteenth century were attracted to medicine, and a number of physicians were known for their espousal of the ideas of the Enlightenment. Jacob de Castro Sarmento, who has been mentioned before, was one of them, a celebrated expatriate who contributed from abroad to the modernization of Portuguese intellectual life during the Century of Light.[82] Born in 1691 in Bragança, a remote town in the far northeast corner of Portugal where many Jewish families had sought refuge from the Inquisition, Castro Sarmento studied Aristotelian philosophy at the University of Évora, where he obtained the degree of master in arts in 1710. He then

81 *Ibid.*, p.286; see also Andrade, pp.73–74.

82 The latest biography is by Rómulo de Carvalho in Joel Serrão (ed.), *Dicionário de história de Portugal*, III (Lisbon, 1968), 799–800. See also Cidade, pp.49–51. There is an incomplete biography in Barbosa Machado, *Bibliotheca Lusitana*, II, 469–71.

enrolled in the medical school of the University of Coimbra and graduated in 1717 with a bachelor's degree in medicine. Fearing the consequences of being a practicing Jew in his own country, he left in 1721 for London, where he established his permanent address. Here he became rabbi of the Portuguese Jewish community, a votary of the new philosophy (particularly as it was expounded by Newton), and a distinguished scientist. In 1725 he was admitted to the Royal College of Physicians of London, in 1730 to the Royal Society. The University of Aberdeen, finally, awarded him the doctor's degree in 1739.

Aware not only of his position in British medical circles but also of his loyalty to Portugal, King John V asked Castro Sarmento for advice on the reform of medical studies. As we have suggested earlier, Sarmento made it clear to the monarch that what existed in Portugal could not be salvaged, that an improvement could be expected only by translating Francis Bacon into Portuguese (as a means of preparing the mind for the study of medicine) and sending Portuguese students abroad. Sarmento obviously believed that these students would become imbued with an infectious enthusiasm for the new natural philosophy and contribute to the overthrow of Aristotelianism. By this means Portugal would once again become part of enlightened Europe.

Sarmento did in fact begin a translation of Francis Bacon, and the first fruits of his effort appeared in London in 1731 under the title of *Obras Philosoficas de Francisco Baconio Baraõ de Verulaõ Visconde de Santo Albano com Notas para explicaçaõ do que he escuro*. This truncated work (which was never finished) undoubtedly found its way to Portugal, but Sarmento was more interested in Newton and in the application of Newton's ideas to medicine. Three of his treatises, written in Portuguese and published in London between 1735 and 1737, strongly bear this out. The first was entitled *Materia Medica Physico-Historica-Mecanica, Reyno Mineral* and dedicated to Marco António de Azevedo Coutinho, the envoy extraordinary and plenipotentiary who had been named Secretary of State for Foreign Affairs and War. According to António Alberto de Andrade, the preface, addressed "to the Professors of Medicine of the Kingdom and Dominions of Portugal," was in effect a summary of the history of medicine by Dr. François Chiffon.[83] The book praised the "Mechanical Physicians" and their system as being the only true system in the "present and happy century." Sarmento explains his partiality in these words:

> This is the present experimental Sect of Philosophers, who, in matters speculative, instead of conjectures, base all their knowledge on experience, nor do they admit anything else that they cannot prove through demonstration and evidence, rounded out with philosophical, chemical, and anatomical experiments; and to the general Principles which do not suffer the least doubt, they call Mechanical Principles or Laws of nature. . . . Innumerable are the English, French, Italian, and German Authors who have written by this true and solid method; but, especially, the famous Hollander Boerhaave . . . organized the best and most concise System of Mechanical Medicine that has ever been seen.

He therefore followed Boerhaave while taking advantage of the "experimental or Newtonian Natural Philosophy" in place of the Aristotelian system which, insofar as he was concerned, was based on imagination.[84] His regard for Newton is evidenced even more clearly in two other works, *Cronologia Newtoniana epitomizada*, which he dedicated to Dom José, Prince of Brazil, and *Teórica verdadeira das marés*, on tides, which included a laudatory biography of the "incomparable gentleman Isaac Newton."[85] Both of course represent a reaction against Cartesian philosophy, but the important thing to focus on is that it takes place in Portugal at about the same time that it does in Europe generally. Castro Sarmento, along with so many of his colleagues

83 Andrade, pp.127–28.
84 *Ibid.*, p.128.
85 *Ibid.*, p.127.

in the field of science, had rejected the metaphysics and physics of Descartes and held that the truths of geometry and physics did not depend upon the existence of God.

As to the second part of Sarmento's advice to the King, the person who profited from it immediately was Bento de Moura Portugal (1702–1766),[86] who would shortly begin at John's expense a prolonged study tour of London and other European cities that may have lasted eight years. But Moura Portugal was an engineer, not a medical man, and one of his tours of duty was a trip to South America as a member of the commission charged with the demarcation of the boundaries of Brazil. He must have been an engineer of recognized achievement for in 1741 he was elected to membership in the Royal Society of London, to whose *Philosophical Transactions* he contributed a paper on the improvement of the steam engine.

In matters of orthodoxy, his reputation, from the point of view of the Inquisition, was bad.[87] Although a graduate of the law school of the University of Coimbra (and not of theology), he acquired a taste for joking about Holy Writ to show, as it was said, the sharpness of his mind and to test the mettle of his listeners. His stay in England and Holland got him into the habit of discussing matters of religion. He questioned miracles and the canonizations of the church. He denied the existence of Hell and of demons. He refused to take the books of Moses seriously and denied their divine inspiration. He made fun of the Catholic religion, the Supreme Pontiff, and the cardinals. To him all religions were equally good. Bento de Moura's friendship with Alexandre de Gusmão, the King's private secretary, did not save him from the Inquisition, in whose claws he tragically found himself as early as 1743, and his trial and imprisonment underscored the incompatibility of Baroque Catholicism and the new learning.

Portugal was not, after all, a free society, as England was, and

---

86 Rómulo de Carvalho is the author of his biography in *Dicionário de história de Portugal*, III, 451–52.

87 For this side of his career, see Andrade, p.290 *et seq.*

the *estrangeirados* of the eighteenth century had to learn to toe the line. Most knew how to adjust and thereby preserve their relative freedom of action, but a few, like Bento de Moura Portugal and Diogo de Mendonça Corte-Real, were made to suffer for their temerity or their independence. They were the notable examples that encouraged others to live in peace with the establishment. The case of Diogo de Mendonça is especially sad, for he had risen higher in the government and fell correspondingly lower. He was born out of wedlock in Madrid sometime between 1693 and 1703, when his father, the elder Diogo de Mendonça Corte-Real, represented Peter II at the Court of Madrid, and in due time he received the doctor's degree in canon law from the University of Coimbra. He completed the course with such distinction that in 1716 he was admitted to the College of St. Paul. In 1722 King John chose him as envoy extraordinary to Holland and he was in The Hague at least as late as 1727. In 1729 he became a member of the Royal Academy of Portuguese History. He served as principal treasurer of the Collegiate Church of Barcelos, councilor of the Exchequer, superintendent (*provedor*) of India House, and deputy of the Junta of the House of Bragança. On August 3, 1740, the new king, Joseph I, made him Secretary of State for Overseas Affairs. In 1756, however, he was summarily removed from office, the victim of the political intransigence that developed in Portugal following the earthquake of 1755.[88]

Perhaps the most tragic of the Portuguese expatriates of the eighteenth century was Francisco Xavier de Oliveira (1702–1783), generally known as the Chevalier de Oliveira from the knighthood in the Military Order of Christ that John V awarded him in 1721 as a token of appreciation for his father's services to the crown.[89] After completing his studies in Lisbon, he en-

[88] Diogo de Mendonça Corte-Real is mentioned in Barbosa Machado, *Bibliotheca Lusitana*, I, 677. Inocêncio Francisco da Silva also includes him in his *Diccionario*, II, 165–66.

[89] The information on the controversial Chevalier is abundant. Even Barbosa Machado, II, 296–97, lists him. The best source continues to be António Gonçalves

tered the royal service as an employee of the Tribunal of Accounts in 1717. For a number of years he led the life of ease and pleasure of the petty nobility. He married late, in 1730—there were to be two other marriages in his life—and a short time later left Portugal on his first trip abroad, to Madrid, where his uncle, the Reverend Manuel Ribeiro, was chargé d'affaires. He suffered the first of his many disasters in 1733, the death of his wife, to whom he was devoted, and at the beginning of 1734, the second, the death of his father, secretary of the Count of Tarouca, the Portuguese minister in Vienna.

Under the circumstances, it is logical that Tarouca should have asked young Oliveira to take his father's place, and this will explain why Francisco Xavier left Portugal for a second time in 1734. This time he would never return. The old Count soon realized that Oliveira was not the sort of man he wanted and dismissed him from his service. Without powerful friends to intercede for him in Portugal, with his honor compromised, and without a salary, the Chevalier de Oliveira began an existence that remained precarious until the end. From Austria he went to Holland, where he lived for three and a half years and began the literary career for which he acquired notoriety.

His first book, *Memoires de Portugal, avec la Bibliothèque Lusitane*, appeared in Amsterdam in 1741 and, with a changed title page, again in 1743.[90] Having lived long enough in foreign countries, and having read widely in many languages, Oliveira was aware of the "extravagances of the prejudices" that foreigners had about the Portuguese[91] and the "pure lies" against his

---

Rodrigues, *O protestante lusitano estudo biografico e critico sobre o cavaleiro de Oliveira MDCCII–MDCCLXXXIII* (Coimbra, 1950). The latter work will hereafter be cited as Rodrigues.

90 The 1741 edition is listed by Rodrigues, p.299. I have used the 1743 edition in the Oliveira Lima Library: *Memoires historiques, politiques, et litteraires, concernant le Portugal, et toutes ses dependances; avec la bibliotheque des ecrivains et des historiens de ces etats: par Mr. Le Chevalier D'Oliveyra, Gentil-Homme Portugais*, 2 vols. (The Hague, 1743).

91 *Ibid.*, I, fol.5 and verso of the "Epitres dedicatoire."

people that their books contained.[92] In writing his *Memoires,*
what he had in mind was to produce a substantial book that
would give European readers a more exact and complete account
of the history, geography, literature, and religion of Portugal
and its overseas possessions. It is by and large a patriotic work,
intended to give justice to his countrymen. Occasionally he describes Catholicism in an unfavorable way and bears hard upon
the Inquisition. It is a curious *mélange* of information, gleaned
from innumerable sources, put together in a simple manner, a
format that Europeans were accustomed to.

In 1741 he published a second book in Amsterdam, this time
in Portuguese, *Memorias das viagens de Francisco Xavier de
Oliveyra, Cavalleyro Prophesso da Ordem de N. S. Jesus Christo,
Cavalleyro Fidalgo de Caza de sua Magestade, Official do Numero
dos Contos do Reyno e Caza, e Secretario do Conde de Tarouca
Plenipotenciario de Portugal na Corte Cesarea,*[93] a lively account of what he saw and heard in the Germanies, Holland,
France, and England. In the prologue to the reader, Oliveira
justifies his work in these words: "These memoirs of my Travels,
if they do not have gentleness, have novelty, and the latter has always been applauded. This kind of book is rare in Portugal. The
Portuguese undertook some travels to India and others to the
Holy Land, and I knew that [in Portugal] they are kept in the Libraries with great respect because of their antiquity, and my
[Memoirs], which are also the work of a Portuguese, undertaken
in such different parts of Europe, why will they be thrown out
because they are modern, instructive, and necessary. . . ."[94] The
book, however, is much more than an impressionistic account of
his travels. He describes the cities that he visited, their population, the Portuguese synagogue of Amsterdam, important people
he met. He tells of incidents out of his life, furnishing us with
data that every biographer of the Chevalier has had to use. And

92 *Ibid.,* unnumbered p.1 of the preface.
93 I have used the copy in the Oliveira Lima Library.
94 Page 5.

he writes with a style that is in itself revolutionary, singularly free of the *culteranismo* of Baroque rhetoric, limpid in its flow, natural and rational, making clear to us today why he continues to have a place in Portuguese literature.

His years in Holland were singularly productive. In 1741 Volume I of his *Cartas familiares, historicas, politicas e criticas. Discursos serios e jocosos. Dedicados á Excellentissima senhora Condessa de Vimioso* appeared in Amsterdam; in 1742 Volumes II and III appeared in The Hague.[95] The literary qualities that distinguish his first book in Portuguese distinguish the *Cartas familiares* even more. To a person brought up in the Court of John V, where rationalism and irony were surely not openly admired, the Chevalier's bouncy letters strike an exotic note. "Despite his defective language," as Fidelino de Figueiredo observes, "our literature does not boast another epistolographer with such salt of grace, such spiritual versatility, such flexible and clever digression, so personal in his judgments and so advanced over his time and also so isolated in it."[96] Fidelino is impressed with the knowledge of ancient and modern authors that the letters reflect, with the author's erudition, with his sense of humor expressed at a time when the Portuguese were bound to a Baroque *gravità*, his power of incisive and moderate speech. His enormous talents add up to the most individual style of any Portuguese writer of his generation, a style as unique in his day as Eça de Queiroz' was a hundred and fifty years later.[97]

The Inquisition was not interested in Oliveira's literary qualities but in his orthodoxy, and it took exception to the Chevalier's remarks on marriage.[98] "It is true," he wrote, "that in the first Centuries of Christianity there were some Fathers of the Church

95 I have used the Lisbon edition in three volumes published in 1855. There is a copy in the Oliveira Lima Library. Aquilino Ribeiro, whose scholarship leaves much to be desired, published selected letters in the Colecção de Clássicos Sá da Costa, Cavaleiro de Oliveira, *Cartas familiares*, 2d ed. (Lisbon, 1960).

96 Figueiredo, *Historia*, p.116.

97 *Ibid.*, pp.112–13.

98 Vol.I, Letter LVI, pp.291–304, of the Lisbon edition of 1855.

who, carried by certain principles (borrowed one might say from Pagans who had recognized the excellence of Celibacy), preferred this State to that of Matrimony. Some of these Holy Doctors formed such . . . ideas in this matter, that they went so far as to declare that *Matrimony was an illegitimate, and impure thing.*" But, he added, "I do not find anything in Sacred Writ that supports this opinion, and I make bold to say . . . that Matrimony is the only means to preserve chastity, and the singular remedy that there is to put out the fires of concupiscence, since not everybody has the humor, or the taste of the blessed St. Francis of Assisi, who used to retire to beds of snow and brambles to extinguish the impetuous movements of the flesh, and to preserve the tunic of chastity from the flames of lasciviousness."[99] This was the ostensible reason why the Inquisition prohibited the sale and circulation of his works in Portugal. The real reason, as Gonçalves Rodrigues says, was more political than religious, and it had to do with the unflattering remarks that the Chevalier de Oliveira, in a moment of pique, made about his old boss the Count of Tarouca in his book of travels.[100] Unfortunately for the outspoken Oliveira, nothing could have hurt him more in the eyes of Portuguese society than the censure of the Inquisition, and he never recovered from the blow.

Four other works came from his pen during the remainder of his residence in Holland, among them the inconsequential *Viagem à Ilha do Amor* (1744), a free translation of Paul Tallemant's work of substantially the same title that had appeared anonymously in 1663 and in a new edition in 1742, which the Chevalier palmed off as his own composition.[101] Having spent his time in Holland writing for publishers, he left for England in 1744, hopeful no doubt of improving his lot and destined to spend the rest of his life there. The change did not really matter, for his existence continued to be precarious. Twice he was

99 *Ibid.*, pp.291–92.
100 *Memorias das viagens*, cited above, pp.3 and 133; Rodrigues, pp.115–16.
101 Rodrigues, p.103.

charged with trespass before the courts, in 1746 and 1747, and once he was "committed to his Majesty's prison of the fleet."[102] In 1746 he formally abjured Catholicism and became an Anglican, but his change of religion did not lead to a change of fortunes. It would be foolish, as one of his biographers says, to look upon Oliveira's conversion as a supreme act of freedom of conscience; his heterodoxy was "bourgeois and without greatness, encouraged on the one hand by his misunderstandings with Portuguese officialdom and on the other by the necessity of adapting to the Protestant world in which he was to live for the rest of his life."[103] He continued to write, for that is what he was best fitted to do, but in the writings of his English period the anti-Catholicism of his new-found Protestantism was propounded with the virulence of the convert. In 1751 he published his *Amusement Périodique*, a serial in French that was meant to appear in January, February, March, and April, three duodecimo volumes all told with over 1,200 pages of text.[104]

The Lisbon earthquake of 1755 affected him, as it did Wesley, but while the Methodist divine believed that the depravity of mankind as a whole rather than the sins of the Portuguese was responsible for God's wrath, the Chevalier de Oliveira held the Portuguese strictly accountable. The year after the great tragedy he published his *Discours Pathétique au sujet des calamités présentes arrivés en Portugal* as well as an English version of the same work, *A Pathetic Discourse on the Present Calamities of Portugal*. Each was offered for sale at one shilling. There was a second edition in the same year, sequels in the two languages in 1757, and two additional French editions, the first possibly in 1759, the second in 1762.[105]

---

102 The document is published in Rodrigues, p.359.

103 José María Cossío, "El Caballero de Oliveira (Documentos para la biografía de Don Juan)," *Revista de Occidente*, XXI (March 1925), quoted by Rodrigues, pp.145–46.

104 Rodrigues, p.301. There is a Portuguese translation by Aquilino Ribeiro published in 1922 by the Biblioteca Nacional of Lisbon in two volumes under the title *Recreação Periodica*.

105 These editions with their complete titles are listed by Rodrigues, pp.301–

Having been raised in the Romish faith and aware of its evils, the Chevalier exhorted his countrymen to give up Catholicism as he had and accept the truth as the Gospels as they were expounded by Protestantism. He denounced the Inquisition and the persecution of the Jews. He made clear that with Catholicism and the Inquisition Portugal would never move forward. The Inquisition again did not remain silent in the presence of the Chevalier's attacks. First the *Discours Pathétique* was condemned and burned. Next he was formally called upon to recant. When all avenues of persuasion had been exhausted, the Chevalier de Oliveira was burned in effigy at a public *auto-de-fé* held on September 20, 1761, in the cloister of the Dominican Convent of Lisbon as a "Heretical apostate of our Holy Catholic Faith," the author of a work that was declared to be "heretical, schismatic, seditious, erroneous, injurious to the Roman Catholic Church, and contrary to the Dogmas of our Holy Faith which he is endeavoring to ruin."[106]

Safe in his English asylum, where the justices of His Most Faithful Majesty could not touch him, the persistent and needling expatriate replied with *Le Chevalier d'Oliveyra brulé en effigie comme hérétique. Comment & Pourquoi? Anecdotes & Réflexions sur ce Sujet, données au Public par lui-même* (London, 1762). In 1767 he returned to the attack on the Catholic religion for the last time with a combative essay entitled *Reflexoens de Felix Vieyra Corvina de Arcos, Christam Velho Ulyssiponense: Sobre A Tentativa Theologica, composta pello Reverendo e douto Padre Antonio Pereyra, da Congregaçam do Oratorio de Lisboa*, published in London.[107] The two authors were poles

303. The 1762 French edition was reproduced in Oporto in 1893. A copy of the Oporto edition was reproduced in 1922 by the University of Coimbra Press, Vol.I of its *Biblioteca de Século XVIII*, with a bibliographical note by Joaquim de Carvalho.

106 See the 1922 edition of the *Discours Pathétique*, pp.106–16. The Chevalier's inquisitorial process was published by Anselmo Braancamp Freire in *Archivo historico portuguez*, II (1904), 281–320.

107 I have used the new edition with a preface by Eduardo Moreira published by the University of Coimbra Press in 1929, Vol.III of its *Biblioteca do Século XVIII*.

apart in their doctrine but they agreed on the independence of the Portuguese church. As Eduardo Moreira writes, "The *Tentativa* [which appeared in 1766] tries to resuscitate our ancient regalism, or nationalize Gallicanism; the *Reflexoens* dream about a National Reformed Church."[108]

*The Gentleman's Magazine* took note of Francisco Xavier de Oliveira's death, and he was buried in the parish cemetery of St. John's Church, Hackney. The inscription on his gravestone, as recorded for posterity by Daniel Lysons, was, as Gonçalves Rodrigues appropriately says, "the last revindication of his rights, and the last satisfaction of his pride":[109] "Sacred to the memory of Francis de Oliveyra, Knight of the Order of Christ in Portugal; which country, together with the reward due to the services which he had rendered his king, he sacrificed to the dictates of his conscience, by abjuring the Roman Church. Deprived by this step of the support of his relations and countrymen he found protection in England, where he was patronized by the eminently great and good and died respected and beloved, the 18.th of October 1783, aged 81 years."[110]

The efforts of the Chevalier de Oliveira to change the country of his birth, however well intentioned, were, after all, counterproductive. The Portuguese *estrangeirados* found him more galling than helpful, separated from them by his apostasy, without prestige or influence in Portugal. In time the Inquisition was changed, its powers curbed, but the Chevalier had nothing to do with it. Even here, where his influence might have been felt, a heterodox would not do. This was, ultimately, the greatest tragedy of his life, that so fruitful a mind as his, and so nimble a pen, were not able together to have the impact that they deserved.

With Dr. António Nunes Ribeiro Sanches, an expatriate like the Chevalier, the same did not happen. Respected by his col-

---

108 *Ibid.*, pp.v–vi.

109 Rodrigues, p.25.

110 Daniel Lysons, *The Environs of London being an Historical Account of the Towns, Villages, and Hamlets within twelve miles of that Capital*, II (London, 1795), 507–508.

leagues in Europe as distinguished in the medical sciences, he did not burn his bridges when he left Portugal, or for that matter at any time during his life. By maintaining good relations with his countrymen, he exercised from Paris a considerable influence upon them. In this sense he was more helpful to the cause of the Enlightenment in Portugal than Francisco Xavier de Oliveira.

Member of a family of New Christians, António Nunes Ribeiro Sanches was born in 1699. He began the study of philosophy at the University of Coimbra in 1716, transferred after three years to the Spanish University of Salamanca, where he studied civil law until 1720, and graduated in 1725, not in law but in medicine. He returned to Portugal briefly. Having been denounced to the Inquisition as a practicing Jew, he left Portugal again in 1726. We find him in London in 1727, engaged in the practice of medicine among the Portuguese colony and studying mathematics with Jacob Sterling. After visiting Paris, Marseille, Montpellier, and Bordeaux, he settled for the time being in Leiden. Here he studied medicine with Herman Boerhaave, experimental physics with Jacob Gravesende, anatomy with Bernard Albinus, and humane letters with Peter Burmann.

When the Russian College of Physicians asked Boerhaave to send them three of his pupils, he chose Ribeiro Sanches as one. Leaving for Russia in 1731, the talented Portuguese served at various times as physician in Moscow and St. Petersburg. As physician of the imperial armies, he visited Turkey, the Ukraine, Tartary, and other remote parts of the Russian territories. It was during this time that he was probably elected to the Academy of Sciences of Paris. He reached the heights of court physician. The palace revolution of 1741, which brought Elizabeth Petrovna to the throne, was unfortunate for Sanches, since the new czarina was anti-Semitic. In 1747, after it became known that Sanches was a Jew, he was dismissed from the imperial service. En route to Paris, where he established his home, he is said to have been received in Berlin by Frederick the Great. His financial situation at this time was precarious, and from 1759 until 1761 he received a pension from the King of Portugal, renewed in 1769. In 1762, following the death of Elizabeth Petrovna, Catherine the Great came to his rescue with a pension too. From these resources and from his practice he maintained himself in the French capital until his death in 1782.[111]

Ribeiro Sanches was on as good terms with French intellectuals as he was with the Portuguese, and with those who served Portugal in various capacities abroad as well as with those who had stayed in the homeland. He was wise enough not to let matters of religion stand in the way of his friendships, and it is indeed likely that he gave up the practice of Judaism. Later he declared himself a Christian and in favor of the assimilation of the Jews, but Coimbra Martins does not believe that he really meant it.[112] For Diderot, he wrote an article on venereal disease for the *Encyclopédie*.[113] Buffon mentions the by now celebrated Portuguese physician in the third volume of *Histoire Naturelle*.[114]

As a scientist he left an important corpus that makes it apparent why he enjoyed during his lifetime an enviable reputation.[115] His first published study, *Dissertation sur l'origine de la maladie vénérienne, pour prouver que ce mal n'est pas venu d'Amérique, mais qu'il a commencé en Europe par une epidémie*, appeared in Paris in 1750. A second French edition appeared in 1765, an English translation in 1751, and a German translation in 1775. For his fellow Portuguese he composed a *Tratado da conservação da saude dos povos: obra util, e igualmente necessaria aos Magistrados, Capitaens Generais, Capitaens de Mar, e Guerra, Prelados, Abbadessas, Medicos, e Pays de Familias*, to

111 For the life of Ribeiro Sanches, I have made use of Maximiano Lemos, *Ribeiro Sanches a sua vida e a sua obra escripta sobre novos documentos, no desempenho de uma commissão do governo portuguez* (Porto, 1911); the biography by António Coimbra Martins in *Dicionário de história de Portugal*, III, 736–40; and Barbosa Machado, *Bibliotheca Lusitana*, IV, 56–58.

112 Martins, *Dicionário*, p.739.

113 See Luís de Pina, *Verney, Ribeiro Sanches e Diderot na história das universidades* (Porto, 1955).

114 Cidade, p.55.

115 Maximiano Lemos, *Ribeiro Sanches*, pp.291–310, lists 26 published items and 138 unpublished, including some that have been referred to by other authors but never found.

which he added an appendix on earthquakes, *Consideraçoins sobre os Terremotos, com a noticia dos mais consideraveis, de que fas mençaô a Historia, e dos ultimos que se sintiraô na Europa desde o 1 de Novembro 1755* (Paris, 1756). The purpose of his treatise, as he says in the prologue, is "to show the necessity that each State has of laws, and of regulations to preserve itself from many illnesses, and to conserve the Health of its subjects."[116] The book is an eminently practical one for those who have the responsibility for the "conservation and increase of the People,"[117] and useful for superiors of convents, abbesses, directors of hospitals, and heads of families. Since architects do not concern themselves with such matters, he indicates how one goes about choosing a healthy site for the construction of a city, church, convent, hospital, or public prison. He touches upon the health of soldiers and sailors, and includes commentaries on diet and exercise. Although he felt that the reader had the right to know "the method of studying Medicine, and how Physicians, and Surgeons should study it in the Schools, and the Universities,"[118] he waited until 1763 to discharge that obligation. In that year, and again in Paris, he published the *Metodo para aprender a estudar a medicina, illustrado Com os Apontamentos para establecerse huma Univercidade Real na qual deviam aprender-se as Sciencias humanas de que necessita o Estado Civil e Politico.*[119]

For our purposes, what interests us most about Ribeiro Sanches is not his accomplishments as a physician, as a man of science, but his writings on education (of which the 1763 book is an example), on economics, politics, and colonial policy. Sanches was a philosopher in the sense that the Century of Light understood the word, a *uomo universale* in the sense of the Italian Renaissance, and he had much to say on many subjects. Insofar as education was concerned, the reorganized School of Medicine of the University of Coimbra that was shaped by the Statutes of

[116] Page 6; I have used the copy in the Oliveira Lima Library.
[117] *Ibid.*, p.vii.
[118] *Ibid.*, pp.viii–ix.
[119] There is a copy in the Oliveira Lima Library.

1772 followed some of the ideas advocated by Sanches, as for example the obligatory use by the students of some of the works of Boerhaave, his former mentor.[120]

His most important work on education is in the form of a series of letters addressed to Monsignor Pedro da Costa de Almeida Salema, the Portuguese representative in France, dated Paris, November 19, 1759, and published in the following year in the same city under the title *Cartas sôbre a educaçaõ da mocidade*.[121] As he says at the beginning of his work, the law on the reform of education in Portugal, i.e., the law of June 28, 1759, which abolished the classes and colleges conducted by the Jesuits, which Monsignor Salema had called to his attention, gave him the excuse to jot down on paper and to publish his thoughts on the education of youth.[122] To him the subject was of extreme importance. "If we consult the monuments of History, we will find that the glory and increase of Kingdoms did not result from their numerous armies, nor from riches; we will find that they were illustrious because of the Education of their Monarchs and their Subjects."[123]

What were Ribeiro Sanches' ideas on education and on the state? First and foremost, he favored the secularization of education, transforming education into the exclusive function of the state. The "supreme Pontiffs and the Bishops" had "arrogated the absolute power of the Education of the Schools of Christendom" when actually the right to promulgate laws "for the Education of his loyal Subjects, not only in the primary Schools but also in all [schools] where youth learns" belongs to His Most

120 Boerhaave is mentioned a number of times in the section on medicine of the *Estatutos da Universidade de Coimbra do anno de MDCCLXXII*, II (Lisbon, 1773), 39 *et seq.*

121 On the title page of the rare 1760 first edition—the copy in the Oliveira Lima Library at one time belonged to the monastery of Santa Cruz of Coimbra—the place of publication is given as Cologne. Maximiano Lemos, in *Ribeiro Sanches*, says that the book was published in Paris. I have used the new edition, *Cartas sôbre a educação da mocidade*, edited by Lemos and published in 1922 by the University of Coimbra Press. This edition will hereafter be cited as *Cartas*.

122 *Cartas*, p.1.

123 *Ibid.*, p.207.

Faithful Majesty.[124] Since a state is truly constituted as the result of a mutual swearing of fealty, between the sovereign and the subjects, tacitly or openly, and since Portugal was constituted in this "so free and so excellent" a manner, it follows that the kings of Portugal enjoy supreme power within their realms. As he is the First General, the First Judge, the Father and Conservator of his states, so also is he their First Schoolmaster and their First Priest of natural religion.[125]

The principal obligation of the Catholic Christian monarch was the preservation of the civil state. Each subject was in turn obliged to do unto others as he would want others to do unto him. Yet in order for a society to function, the subject had perforce to surrender to the sovereign the voluntary actions he had once enjoyed. Only two things remained inviolate: the property of his goods, with the obligation of supporting the state with a part of his income, and his interior freedom, i.e., "to wish, not to wish, to love, to hate, to judge, or not to judge, to see, or not to see."[126] A civil society so constituted will establish equality among its subjects and subordination to the magistrates. To function on a day-to-day basis, it will require affability, truth, faith, and punctuality, and laws whose ultimate aim is a public utility accompanied by decency.

If the civil authority allows ecclesiastics to govern the civil and political state, and if Christian intolerance becomes civil intolerance, the civil state will be dissolved and ruined. The interference of the ecclesiastical power in the affairs of the state ought not to be countenanced. At the University of Coimbra, the new doctor must swear "that he will always be faithful and constant in defending the Rights of the University, and of the *Doctrine that is taught there.*"[127] In 1717 the secular and ecclesiastical doctors of the University formally approved the power of the Pope and his jurisdiction when they swore to uphold the bull

124 *Ibid.*, p.17.
125 *Ibid.*, pp.19–20.
126 *Ibid.*, p.21.
127 *Ibid.*, p.63.

*Unigenitus Dei Filius.* What this meant, according to Ribeiro Sanches, was that the monarch "does not have, nor can he have a Councillor, a Judge, or a Procurator of the Crown who is not bound by oath to defend everything that has been decreed by a Foreign Power, a Power that established in his Monarchy another [power] that achieves the same effects as those plants that are called *parasites* which sustain themselves from the sap of the tree to which they are attached."[128]

Catholic universities are ecclesiastical institutions which teach only the subjects that preserve and increase the authority and primacy of the ecclesiastics. Insofar as Coimbra is concerned, the study of theology and canon law ought to be physically separated from the University and taught in three colleges in Braga, Lisbon, and Évora.[129] Instead of these disciplines, the universities should teach the human sciences, such as physics, natural history, mathematics, astronomy, moral philosophy, international law, and Portuguese law. To the King belongs the authority of organizing these studies, and to lay teachers the right to teach them, just as ecclesiastics alone should teach and study theology, scripture, and canon law.[130]

The privileges and immunities of the nobility and clergy, as expressed in the Ordinances of the Realm, destroy the subordination, equality, and justice of the civil state. As the result of the privileges they enjoy, ecclesiastics feel that they belong to a monarchy whose head is the Pope, independent of the King. The existence of these two special classes of society is pernicious to the best interests of the state: "In Portugal everyone who was not born Noble, or is not an Ecclesiastic, wants to become a member of these two respectable Bodies, where convenience, honor, distinction, and profit have their seat; the farmer, the laborer, the craftsman work day and night to produce a Cleric, an Abbot, a Knight of the Habit of Christ; a widow and three or four daughters weave day and night to make a Friar out of a son,

128 *Ibid.*, pp.63–64.
129 *Ibid.*, p.65.
130 *Ibid.*, p.73.

because of the honor that will come to the family, and because, if he becomes a Preacher or Provincial, will endow it with honor and abundance."[131]

Slavery as it is practiced in Portugal is also pernicious to the state because the country does not "recover through the Slaves, the Subjects that it loses in the conquest, navigation, and establishments that it has in Africa."[132] To Ribeiro Sanches it was inconceivable that children born of a slave mother or father in the Portuguese dominions and in the bosom of the Catholic church should not be free. If the faithful are equal so long as they observe the commandments of the church, why do ecclesiastics allow the distinction between slave and free among Christians? It is impossible to expect humanity in a slave society, and impossible to provide a good and perfect education.[133]

Ribeiro Sanches speaks favorably of the principle of freedom of conscience on the basis of what he observed in Holland and in Russia. The history of almost three hundred years, he says, has demonstrated two principles that were considered incredible and even absurd during the reigns of the Emperor Charles V and of Philip II. The first is that subjects of kingdoms that enjoy freedom of conscience daily give up their nonconformist religions to embrace the dominant one; the second, that in kingdoms that do not permit religious liberty, the reverse is true.[134] Even so, he does not advise the King to allow freedom of conscience in Portugal at this time; what he asks is that civil tolerance be allowed to exist side by side with ecclesiastical intolerance. "The Ecclesiastical Power is and ought to be exer-

---

131 *Ibid.*, pp.85–86.

132 *Ibid.*, p.88.

133 *Ibid.*, p.88 *et seq.* Was Ribeiro Sanches familiar with and influenced by Manoel Ribeiro Rocha's *Ethiope resgatado; empenhado, sustentado, Corregido, instruido, e libertado. Discurso theologico-juridico, em que se propoem o modo de comerciar, haver, a possuir validamente, quantos a hum, e outro foro, os Pretos cativos Africanos, e as principaes obrigações, que correm a quem delles se servir* (Lisbon, 1758), the first book on behalf of slaves? On unnumbered page 7 Rocha says that "the greatest infelicity, to which a rational creature may reach in this world, is that of slavery." There is a copy in the Oliveira Lima Library.

134 *Cartas*, p.93.

[181]

cised upon the Christian who spontaneously offers himself to the Church to satisfy his conscience; but it has no right whatsoever over that Christian, or Gentile who does not wish to enter the Church."[135]

The Portuguese monarchy was able to preserve itself during the Age of Discovery and conquest with an educational system oriented along ecclesiastical lines. Now that the period of conquest is over, that kind of education is no longer sufficient.[136] Today the problem is to hold on to the colonies with farmers, craftsmen, merchants, mariners, and soldiers, but the life which these men represent

> is not preserved with the privileges of the Nobility, with the immunities and civil jurisdiction of the Ecclesiastics, with slavery, and with civil intolerance.
>
> It is not preserved with the education of knowing how to read and write, the four rules of Arithmetic, Latin, and the mother tongue, and for all science the catechism of Christian doctrine; it is not preserved with leisure, dissolution, horseback riding, playing black sword, and hunting; another kind of education is now needed, because the State needs Subjects with other knowledge; it no longer needs in all of them that haughty, warlike spirit, aspiring always to be noble and distinguished, until they become a Knight or an Ecclesiastic.[137]

Ribeiro Sanches defined education in these words: "The Education of Youth is no more than that habit acquired by the culture and direction of the Masters, of carrying out easily and joyfully actions that are useful to them and to the State where they were born."[138] He was not in favor of education for everybody, for the poor as for the rich, because literacy kept people from enjoying menial labor. No schoolmaster on the primary level should be a celibate; all salaried functionaries of the state should be married. He was not in favor of many Latin schools,

135 *Ibid.*, p.92.
136 See *Cartas*, p.96 *et seq.*
137 *Ibid.*, pp.100–101.
138 *Ibid.*, p.109.

especially free ones, because they produced in effect ecclesiastics without vocations. And these schools should be prohibited altogether in the colonies in order to discourage farmers, merchants, and craftsmen from abandoning their respective callings. Where they did exist, the schoolmasters should be obliged to spend four or five years in Holland, Germany, England, and France to observe high standards of scientific education. A select number of qualified pupils should be sent abroad also. In Portugal "Latin is the passport to enter the terrestrial Paradise, where one eats without working."[139]

Ideally, the sciences that are necessary for the welfare of a modern state could be taught in three schools. The first would teach the history of universal and human nature, i.e., natural history, botany, anatomy, chemistry, metallurgy, and medicine. The second, the specific knowledge required for the maintenance of the political and civil state, i.e., universal history, both sacred and profane, moral philosophy, international law, civil law, Portuguese law, and civil economy. The third, everything that pertains to the Sacred Religion and its practice.[140] The Schools of Theology and Canon Law of the University of Coimbra should be separated from the University and combined to form a new Ecclesiastical University, to be erected by the King in a convenient city of the realm. These schools alone should be controlled by the church.

Ribeiro Sanches suggested the kind of middle schools that would best prepare students for higher education, indicated what should be done about the education of the nobility, described military colleges, and proposed the establishment of a Royal Portuguese School for the education of the nobility and aristocracy. The curriculum for the Royal School, which was in reality a military school, should include religion, physical education, military science, dancing, fencing, horseback riding, swimming, modern languages (Castilian, French, and English), Portuguese, mathematics, geography, history, hydrography, nautical science, moral

139 *Ibid.,* p.150.
140 *Ibid.,* p.154.

philosophy, international law, legal principles, political economy, and Latin.

Another work from the prolific pen of Ribeiro Sanches, dedicated to Dom Vicente de Sousa Coutinho, written in 1763 and never printed, is a series of essays with the inconclusive title of "Discursos sobre a America Portugueza."[141] Although some of the ideas that he expresses here on the Portuguese dominions were earlier broached in the work that we have just discussed, the "Discursos" offer fresh data on Sanches' theory of empire, additional light on economics, the Catholic church as it was then structured (always his *bête noire*), and on Brazil. What he says about America, as he confesses in his dedication, "is neither new in present-day Portugal nor do I believe that it is unknown to anyone who might have some knowledge of the *public utility* of Monarchies." All that he wishes to do is to incite his countrymen to show their ancient glories, not through conquests but through work, industry, and intelligence.

In his introduction, Ribeiro Sanches elaborates upon the idea of the ecclesiastical Universal Monarchy, which he had already touched upon in his *Cartas sôbre a educação da mocidade*. The conquest of Ceuta in 1415, he said, "and of the rest of Africa that we hold, and still control," is "an extension of the Crusades." During the Middle Ages, Portugal was brought up to believe in the expansionist ideals of the Papal Monarchy, and these ideals became the country's ideals. Portugal became "a *Devout* and *Warlike* nation" dedicated "to the conversion, or the destruction of the Enemies of the faith."

> . . . reflecting upon the evils that Portugal suffered and suffers still, from this insatiable thirst to extend the faith, to oblige conquered peoples to observe the Catholic Religion, to destroy

141 The manuscript copy in the Oliveira Lima Library is obviously item 33 of Maximiano Lemos' list of Sanches' unpublished works (*Ribeiro Sanches*, p.300). Lemos, who gives the title as "Sobre as colonias," describes the manuscript in these words: "Innocencio [Francisco da Silva] viu este manuscripto cuja conclusão tem a data de 3 de dezembro de 1763. Pelo *Journal* sabe-se que era dirigido a D. Vicente de Sousa Coutinho." Folios 24 through 71 are missing from the Oliveira Lima Library copy.

and lay waste the Nations that rejected it; and reflecting upon the shipwrecks, the evils that have stemmed from the discovery of the Mines, the bloody business of the Slaves; the Subversion of so many Kingdoms in Asia, the destruction of so many Portuguese in the three parts of the world, I say . . . that the cause of so many evils had its origin solely in the pretensions of Gregory VII and of his successors, who were the Lords of the World in matters Temporal and Spiritual; that all of their Kings and Monarchs are their subjects; wherefore the *Intolerance* and *Inhumanity* with the Inhabitants of Africa. Wherefore the evils caused by the *gold*, and the *silver* of America; and of our weakness, and Castile's.

The rest of the text, while not as virulent as the introduction, is full of the impatience of a man of the eighteenth century, of suggestions that were intended to bring prosperity to the Portuguese colonies, of the nature of colonies, of the relations between mother country and colonies. Basically, colonies are meant to be agricultural. To ensure the success of their efforts, farmers need transportation, i.e., navigation, and personnel such as the military to defend their property, craftsmen to supply their personal wants, and merchants to buy their produce. There is no place for privilege, aristocratic or ecclesiastic, and neither the aristocracy nor the church should be allowed to own property. The colonies furnish the raw materials for the manufactures of the mother country. Under the circumstances, education in the colonies must be of the most elementary kind; there is no place for the classical languages, for science of any kind, or for the arts and crafts that require a knowledge of mathematics.

The colonies should be the haven of refuge for the unwanted people of the mother country: "The Colonies ought to be the General Hospital of every man twenty years of age who does not have a trade, or a benefice, or does not live from his industry. . . . They ought to be the General Hospital of the Hermits, of all those accused of witchcraft, of *Mourismo*, of Judaism, of Calvinism, and of every visionary and false prophet."[142] But not at the

142 "Discurso sobre a America Portugueza," fol.19.

[185]

expense of the native population. The principle that the Portuguese followed in America for 200 years, that an unbaptized man is worthy of death or of slavery, aroused the bitterest enmity of the Indians and forced them to abandon the coastal areas of Brazil. Ribeiro Sanches applauded the laws that emancipated the Indians of Maranhão and Brazil in 1755 and 1758.

> When I consider carefully the consequences of this pious and just Law not only do I congratulate myself for having been born a Portuguese, and living in this Century, but I also predict that my compatriots in a few years will see broken the shackles with which humanity and reason had bound us. In a few years we shall not see bands of Domestic and Foreign Apostolic Missionaries filling merchant Ships, being masters of the Villages of the Indians, ordering them to work, dominating them with slavery, ordering and conducting bands of Portuguese to capture and assault wild Indians, conquer them, make them Christians before knowing that they are men.[143]

If agriculture were truly encouraged in Brazil, the income from the land alone would be more than from mining.[144] He pointed out the importance of forest products and the need for a policy of reforestation. "It would not be absurd in our days to restore the law of the Ancient Persians . . . *that every man plant a tree, and have a son.*"[145] As regards sugar, the industry had declined in Brazil for three reasons: the competition of the French and English colonies, the discovery of gold in Minas Gerais and Mato Grosso, and the imprisonment of New Christians by the Holy Office.[146] He said that he was opposed to the fleet system, whereby trade between Brazil and Portugal was limited to ships that sailed in convoy. He felt that "our Americans" should be allowed to sell their tobacco to foreigners and not be obliged to sell it to Portuguese buyers.[147] He advocated free trade and the

143 *Ibid.*, fol.24.
144 *Ibid.*, unnumbered fol.77.
145 *Ibid.*, fol.82.
146 *Ibid.*, unnumbered fol.85.
147 *Ibid.*, fol.97.

abolition of monopolies. The *Côrtes* or Parliament of Portugal had not been called because of "trade monopolies, privileges, and the income from the Bull of the Crusade," the secularization of the Order of Christ, and the wealth that came to Lisbon from the conquests and the Orient.[148] He spoke out against the ecclesiastical establishment in Portuguese America, and believed that Brazil was governed by the "Ecclesiastical Hierarchy."[149] He was opposed to the privileges of the clerical state, felt that "what constitutes essentially the Sacred Ministry of Religion is a *curate* and a Bishop";[150] nothing else was needed, not convents, not monasteries, not cathedral chapters. His criticisms, he said, were animated by love of country. As a Portuguese, it was painful to realize that Portugal, master of the best territories and ports in the world, had not reached its potential. With the proper management of the resources under its control, Portugal would be able to improve itself in the concert of European powers and attain at least second-class status.

Ultimately, the question that he poses must be applied to him also. Was Ribeiro Sanches' contribution to the Enlightenment of his country significant or was it mediocre? We know that his book on the reform of medical education was read, and he had some influence, as we have seen, in shaping the new School of Medicine of Coimbra that came into being in 1772. He may not have been responsible for the creation of the Royal College of Nobles of Lisbon in 1761, as Rómulo de Carvalho maintains,[151] but there is no doubt that some of his proposals, as elaborated in his *Cartas*, were in fact carried out in the school for the aristocracy.

António Coimbra Martins, his latest biographer, is not impressed with his total achievement. Martins sees him as a man who rejected the old prejudices, yet he accuses him of being at the same time guilty of gross ingenuousness and premature en-

---

148 *Ibid.*, fols.101–102.
149 *Ibid.*, fol.103.
150 *Ibid.*, fol.105.
151 Rómulo de Carvalho, *Dicionário*, p.49 *et seq.*

thusiasms. He was surely a precursor of the Enlightenment in Portugal and Russia, but he garnered his fame precisely in the two countries that were behind the times. Martins believes that Ribeiro Sanches occupied a "decent" position in the culture of his day, but again finds him neither advanced nor original in his thinking. "Whenever he happened to be more original, he also happened to be wrong."[152]

For a man as interested as he was in education, it is strange to find no mention in his writing or in the catalog of his library (at the time of his death in 1782 Ribeiro Sanches owned 2,020 volumes)[153] of a controversial compatriot, the Reverend Luís António Vernei, author of the most stinging criticism of Portuguese education that was published in the eighteenth century. Sanches was the older man, but Vernei's work appeared thirteen years before the *Cartas sôbre a educação da mocidade*. He was not reticent about Martinho de Mendonça de Pina e de Proença's pioneer book on education, *Apontamentos para a educação da mocidade* (Lisbon, 1734), and indeed praises it highly. At any rate, Ribeiro Sanches and Vernei, the scientist and the humanist, despite their faults, were part of the offensive against the Baroque system of education, and they both lived to see the day when the system was overthrown.

Vernei followed pretty much the pattern of the *estrangeirados* of his day.[154] Born in Lisbon in 1713, he graduated in theology and the arts from the University of Évora. He left for Italy in 1736, at the age of twenty-three, to further his studies in speculative and dogmatic theology and in law, and in time was awarded the degree of doctor of theology. Though he never returned to Portugal, he was named in 1742 to a living in Évora as archdeacon of the cathedral church, seven years before his ordination to the priesthood. In 1750 he became a knight of the Order of

152 Martins, *Dicionário*, p.738.

153 Maximiano Lemos, *Ribeiro Sanches*, pp.206, 353–55.

154 The most exhaustive study of Vernei and his times is by Andrade. Although diffuse and in some ways badly organized, the work is a monument to patient scholarship. Barbosa Machado mentions him in *Bibliotheca Lusitana*, III, 58. There is an excellent chapter on Vernei in Cidade, p.91 *et seq.*

Christ. He served his country in various capacities, as secretary, for example, of Francisco de Almada e Mendonça, who was sent by the Marquis of Pombal on a special mission to the Roman Curia, but always from his residence in Italy.

In 1746 and 1747 he published under an assumed name a work entitled *Verdadeiro Método de Estudar*,[155] the single most influential study by a Europeanized Portuguese of the Enlightenment. Sometimes unfair, this more than withering critique of the educational system of Portugal, which it ridiculed and made fun of, was an open attack against the philosophy of the Schoolmen, an appeal for the study of nature, past and present, through scientific history and scientific observation. Being a humanist rather than a scientist, as many of his fellow *estrangeirados* were, Vernei was particularly concerned with the human rather than with the severe sciences, and in particular with theology and canon law.

Vernei believed that theology was wretchedly taught in Portugal: "The first harmful thing that the student learns from the Scholastic method is to convince himself that the Bible is of no use to the theologian. The second is to convince himself that there is no other theology in the world except the four questions of speculative theology, and that everything else is superfluous quarrels and lazy ruminations of foreigners."[156] He objected to Scholastic philosophy, to Thomas Aquinas, John of St. Thomas, Suárez, the Salamanca School, Aristotle, and the Arabs. He protested against the memorizing of formulas, the repeating of traditional arguments in university classes in theology and canon law. He advocated a return to the Bible, much in the manner of the heretical Protestants of the north. Scripture was basic to the theological program, not a literary exercise designed to furnish quotations from the Bible for preachers of the gospel. He complained against the teaching of theology without any relation to

---

155 The latest edition, which I have used, is edited by António Salgado Júnior, in five volumes, published by the Livraria Sá da Costa of Lisbon (1949–1952) in the Colecção de Clássicos Sá da Costa; hereafter cited as Vernei.

156 Vernei, IV, 229.

history. Vernei insisted upon history, the history of the popes, the history of the universal church; and upon the original languages, Hebrew and Greek, not simply Latin. In place of medieval philosophy, Vernei would teach natural philosophy, i.e., the observation of nature. Since logic, metaphysics, and the like were mere exercises in reason, the new learning out to be pragmatic and scientific. Man would now study nature instead of the venerated authorities of the past, and through this kind of study would find what he needed to give meaning to life. And he wanted the students of the School of Law to learn Portuguese law; Justinian's *Corpus Juris Civilis* and the traditional texts of Roman and ecclesiastical law were not enough.

Before his death in 1792, Vernei, whose work was avidly read in Portugal and found its way into conventual and other libraries, had the satisfaction of knowing that his attack had proved effective. The reform of education, which his patron King John V had already begun by imposing the first restrictions against the Jesuit monopoly of the school system, began in earnest with the reign of Joseph I (1750–1777). The expulsion of the Society of Jesus from Portugal and the Portuguese dominions, the closing down of their classes and schools, were momentous events of 1758 and 1759. In 1761, as we have mentioned elsewhere, with the approval of the statutes of the Royal College of Nobles of Lisbon, the reform of the middle schools got under way. Finally, in 1772, with the reorganization of the University of Coimbra— the most thorough job of academic housecleaning of eighteenth-century Europe—Portugal, so far behind the rest of the Continent on the educational front, moved dramatically forward.

## V

A final group of Portuguese cosmopolites remains to be touched upon, members of the Portuguese intelligentsia who were born in Brazil. To be a Brazilian in Portugal was to suffer from some form of alienation, and the sensitive were particularly subject to it. Most Brazilians, when they came to the mother country, probably knew that they would never return to the land of their birth, never again see the friends, the family, the scenes of their childhood. Many must have retained throughout their lives the nostalgia for Brazil, the feeling that somehow their lives were not of one piece. Coming as they did from the New World, where social lines were less sharply drawn and man was essentially freer, the rigidities of Portugal, where the force of the Inquisition and of tradition made itself felt in sometimes rigorous and inhuman ways, the Brazilian-born intellectual, no matter how well received in the mother country, must have experienced severe moments of homesickness.

There is record of a triduum in honor of Our Lady of Exile that the overseas students of the University of Coimbra promoted, and of the sermon that Bartolomeu Lourenço de Gusmão, a Brazilian, preached on January 9, 1718, on the afternoon of the third day of the religious celebration.[157] The choice of Mary as their patroness is to be expected at a university that was so Marian-minded that its graduates were obliged to uphold the Immaculate Conception as an article of faith. But the choice of Our Lady under her title of Exile is, as Jaime Cortesão observes, "eloquent."[158] Gusmão's sermon was significantly impregnated with *saudade*, filled with an unsatisfied longing for Brazil. The preacher praised the students for the sacrifice that they had made in abandoning their homeland, spoke of the dangers of the Atlantic crossing, and recalled to them the delights of their younger days, in the bosom of their families. ". . . the conversations, the

---

[157] *Sermam que na ultima tarde do triduo, com que os Academicos Ultramarinos festejaõ a nossa senhora do Desterro, Prègou o Muyto Reverendo Padre Bartholomeu Lourenço de Gusmam na Parochial de Saõ Joaõ de Almedina aos 9. de Janeyro deste anno, estando o Santissimo Sacramento exposto. Dedicado ao senhor Manoel de Mattos Collegial no Real Collegio de Saõ Paulo, Lente de Leys na Universidade de Coimbra, Desembargador dos Aggravos na Relaçaõ do Porto, Conego de Sé de Viseu, & Deputado do Santo Officio. Pelos Estudantes naturaes do Brasil que cursaõ na mesma Universidade* (Lisbon, 1718), from the photograph of the title page published by Divaldo Gaspar de Freitas, *A vida e as obras de Bartolomeu Lourenço de Gusmão* (São Paulo: Serviço Estadual de Assistência aos Inventores, n.d.), p.104. This excellent work on Gusmão, the latest thing on the subject, was received only after my own text had been sent to the printer.

[158] Cortesão, p.108.

friends, the excursions, the amusement, everything appears before our eyes, everything gives us pain! This air was more benign, the waters more pure, the winter was not so severe, the trees I never saw without leaves, the fields there were never without fruit! How sad the fountains now flow and how happy have I already seen them flow. . . . Oh, Homeland, Homeland, how far are you? Your very stones, your very woods, what consolation could they now not give me if I could cast my eyes upon them! Why must I live so many years in exile? What breast is there, as hard as bronze, that does not explode with pain and nostalgia?"[159] If expatriates like the Chevalier de Oliveira in London and Ribeiro Sanches in Paris kept the memory of Portugal so nostalgically in their hearts, and spent their lives wrestling with the reality of the country they had abandoned, how much more real must the separation of the Brazilians have been, the Atlantic an unbridgeable chasm between themselves and the land of their hearts' desire, so close to their homeland sentimentally, and yet so far.

The problem of the Brazilian, already acute enough in Portugal itself, was obviously compounded when he added the further experience of a residence in Europe. Such a person was bound to suffer what Jaime Cortesão has called a "double foreignness."[160] The Brazilian Portuguese in eighteenth-century Portugal have never been studied in depth from the point of view of their influence as an element of change. I suggested this when I wrote in another connection that "the influx of Brazilians into Portugal throughout the eighteenth century coincided with, and possibly contributed to, movements of economic modernization and religious *aggiornamento*,"[161] but I did not say more. It does seem likely that they served to an undefinable extent as a catalytic agent, for they were present in great numbers in Portugal during

159 Affonso d'Escragnolle Taunay, *A vida gloriosa e trágica de Bartolomeu de Gusmão* (São Paulo, 1938), p.128.

160 Cortesão, p.111.

161 Manoel Cardozo, "Azeredo Coutinho and the Intellectual Ferment of His Times,"*Conflict and Continuity in Brazilian Society*, ed. Henry H. Keith and S. F. Edwards (Columbia, S.C., 1969), p.73.

the eighteenth century. Belonging as many of them did to the
governing elite, filling high positions in society, the Brazilians
gave the Enlightenment in Portugal an overseas or American
dimension that the Enlightenment in France and England did
not have.

At least 1,752 Brazilian-born students enrolled in the University of Coimbra during the eighteenth century.[162] How many
more attended the colleges and the University of Évora before it
closed in 1759 is not known. Another 215 Brazilians "read" at
the Court Royal (*Desembargo do Paço*), a requirement for ap-
pointments to the judiciary.[163] By the eighteenth century Brazil
had truly become Portugal's milk cow, and the impact of Brazil
upon the mother country, economically, intellectually, and cul-
turally, was enormous. Certainly this will help to explain why it
was possible for the Brazilian-born Alexandre de Gusmão to
become, as private secretary of King John V, one of the most
powerful men of his time; for another Brazilian, Dom Francisco
de Lemos de Faria Pereira Coutinho, later in the century, to be
rector of the University of Coimbra at the time of the drastic
curriculum reforms of 1772; for still another Brazilian, Dom
José Joaquim da Cunha de Azeredo Coutinho, to serve as the
last Grand Inquisitor of Portugal; for José Bonifácio de Andrada
e Silva to have a distinguished career in the mother country before leaving to achieve the independence of Brazil. In poetry,
drama, and music a Brazilian presence was also felt. During the
reigns of John V, Joseph I, and Mary I, that is to say, during the
major part of the eighteenth century, the Brazilian *lundum* was
the favorite music of Lisbon, an ancestor perhaps of the Portuguese *fado* of today.[164]

In point of time, the first of the cosmopolite Brazilians to suffer

[162] Francisco de Morais, "Estudantes na Universidade de Coimbra nascidos no
Brasil," *Brasília*, supplement to Vol.IV (Coimbra, 1949), p.75 *et seq.*

[163] Luiza da Fonseca, "Bacharéis brasileiros. Elementos biográficos (1635–1830),"
Instituto Histórico e Geográfico Brasileiro, IV Congresso de História Nacional
21–28 Abril de 1949, *Anais*, XI (Rio de Janeiro, 1951), 113 *et seq.*

[164] Rodney Gallop, *Portugal: A Book of Folk-ways* (Cambridge, 1961), especially
Chap.XI.

from "double foreignness" was the priest we have already mentioned, Bartolomeu Lourenço de Gusmão.[165] Born in Santos probably in 1685, Bartolomeu was an elder brother of Alexandre, John V's private secretary. He was first educated in Brazil, where he demonstrated an interest in science and technology. He came to Portugal for the first time in 1701. Returning to Brazil, he invented a process by which water could be made to rise to any height, and he made it work sometime before 1706. When he got back to Portugal in 1708, he had already been ordained to the priesthood. He enrolled in the School of Canon Law of the University of Coimbra but he never finished the course, perhaps, as his biographer Luís Ferrand de Almeida says, to devote himself to the experiments that would make him famous.[166] Barbosa Machado, his first biographer, praised his abilities: "Right from the first years he gave manifest indications of the great talent that nature had given him with liberality, not only in the admirable quickness with which he understood the difficulties of Philosophy, and of Mathematics, but also in the prodigious memory with which he retained the most recondite information in Sacred, and profane history."[167]

In 1709 he petitioned King John for what in effect was a patent for "the instrument that he invented to go through the air," which the monarch granted on April 19. Gusmão's experiments in aerial navigation—he must be considered the inventor of the aerostat[168]—were given wide publicity, and he was nicknamed

---

165 The Oliveira Lima Library has the following first editions of works by Bartolomeu Lourenço de Gusmão; *Petição do Padre Bartholomeu Lourenço, sobre o instrumento que inventou para andar pelo ar, e suas utilidades* (Lisbon, 1709), *Varios modos de esgotar sem gente as naos que fazem agua* (Lisbon, 1710), *Sermam da Virgem Maria* (Lisbon, 1712), and *Sermam pregado na festa do Corpo de Deos* (Lisbon, 1721).

166 Luís Ferrand de Almeida, "Gusmão, Bartolomeu Lourenço de," *Dicionário de história de Portugal*, II (Lisbon, 1965), 408–409.

167 Barbosa Machado, *Bibliotheca Lusitana*, I, 463–64.

168 In this connection see Visconde de Faria, *Le précurseur des navigateurs aériens Bartholomeu Lourenço de Gusmão "L'Homme Volant" portugais, né au Brésil (1685–1724)* (Paris, 1910), and Affonso d'Escragnolle Taunay, *Bartolomeu de Gusmão, inventor do aerostato. A vida e a obra do primeiro inventor americano* (São Paulo, 1942).

"The Flyer" (*O Voador*). In 1713 he left for Holland, "with the hope of carrying out some of his projects there and holding on for dear life to the dream of flying."[169] Apparently disillusioned, he returned to Portugal in 1716, enrolled again at the University of Coimbra to finish the course of study that he had interrupted, and in 1720 received the degrees of bachelor, licentiate, and doctor of canon law. He already enjoyed a certain prestige as a preacher and man of letters. When the Royal Academy of Portuguese History was founded in 1720, he was elected to membership. King John showered him with other favors, finding a place for him in the Secretariat of State, appointing him to the post of gentleman-chaplain of the Royal House, and guaranteeing him an income from Brazil. He was so favored by the King that according to a contemporary "he had an open door to the palace and a ready seat at table."[170]

Gusmão was at the height of his popularity when he fled to Spain, where, having become ill during the journey, he died in Toledo in November 1724. What motivated him to abandon Portugal precipitously? His fear of the Inquisition, for his name had come to the surface in a complicated case of witchcraft. Today we also know that he had become a convert to Judaism, at least by 1722. In a country of stringent and policed orthodoxy, as Portugal was, the embracing of Judaism and therefore of the risks involved in being a formal heretic was the supreme act of defiance.

Bartolomeu's brother, Alexandre de Gusmão, in spite of the scandal of his sibling, scaled the heights of Portuguese society and achieved a reputation that made him preeminent among the cosmopolite Brazilians of Portugal.[171] Barbosa Machado, his con-

---

169 Almeida, "Gusmão," p.408.

170 *Ibid.*, p.409.

171 For Alexandre's biography, I have followed for the most part what Luiz Ferrand de Almeida has written about him in *Dicionário de história de Portugal*, II, 405–407. Gusmão is listed in Barbosa Machado, *Bibliotheca Lusitana*, I, 97. The Oliveira Lima Library has the manuscript "Cartas De Alexandre de Gusmaõ, Ministro de Estado particular De S. Magd.e Fideliss.a O Senhor D. Joaõ 5.°" and another manuscript collection of his works with the binder's title of "Collecção de

temporary, said that the "sharp talent and penetrating comprehension with which nature profusely endowed him, made it easy for him to acquire the knowledge of humane letters, and of Poetry, in which he was eminent."[172] He is better known, however, for his achievements as a diplomat and statesman.

Like his brother Bartolomeu, he was born in Santos. The year was 1695. After studying in Brazil, he sailed for Portugal, possibly in the company of his brother in 1708, with whom he learned modern languages and mathematics. In 1712 he enrolled in the School of Canon Law of the University of Coimbra. He interrupted his studies in 1714 to serve as secretary of the Count of Ribeira Grande, the Portuguese ambassador to France. Gusmão spent almost five years in Paris, and was undoubtedly affected by the cosmopolitanism, rationalism, and licentiousness of the period of the regency. He studied law at the Sorbonne and certainly became aware of the intellectual currents of the times, from Cartesianism to empiricism. He was appointed agent in Paris in 1717 and two years later returned to Portugal where, by special decree of King John, he was permitted to finish the law course at Coimbra. In 1720 he was appointed secretary of the

cartas." In the latter codex, the following Gusmão items are of particular interest: (1) "Apontamentos discursivos Sobre o dever impedir-se a extracçaõ da nossa Moeda p.ª fóra, e Reinos Estrangeiros, por cauza da ruina, que d'ahi se segue. A cujo Papel, vulgarm. te se chama O Cálculo de Gusmaõ. Exposto ao Fidelissimo Rey o Senhor Dom Joaõ 5º Pelo d.º Author Alexandre de Gusmaõ," (2) "Oraçaõ ou Elogio Natalicio dedicado ao Sereniss.º Princepe do Brazil Dom Jozé o I.º Nosso Snr̃," (3) "Genealogia Geral Para desvanecer a errada Opiniaõ Dos Senhores Puritanos," (4) "Ecologa A huma Pastora, taõ formoza como ingrata, &.ª," (5) "A Jupiter, Suprêmo Deos do Olimpo Sonetto," (7) "Dissertaçaõ ou Discurso Em que se manifestaõ os interesses que rezultáraõ A Sua Mag.e Fidelissima Dom Jozé I.º E aos Seus Vassallos Da execuaçaõ do Tractado dos Limites d'America ajustado com S. Magd.e Catholica," and (8) "Reprezentaçaõ Que ao Fidelissimo Rey O Senhor Dom Joaõ 5.º Fez Al. de G. Expondo-lhe os importantes continuados Serviços, que pelo decurso de muitos annos elle tinha feito á Corôa; rogando-lhe a maior, e mais correspondente Remuneração dos mesmos Serviços." A number of Gusmão's letters were published by J. M. T. de C., *Collecção de varios Escriptos ineditos politicos e litterarios de Alexandre de Gusmão* (Porto, 1841), and by Albano Antero da Silveira Pinto, *Complemento dos Ineditos de Alexandre de Gusmão* (Porto, 1844). The best comprehensive biography is by Cortesão.

172 Barbosa Machado, *Bibliotheca Lusitana*, I, 97.

Portuguese delegation to the Congress of Cambrai, but before he left John V decided to send him to Rome instead. The mission to Rome lasted seven years.

He returned to Portugal in 1728 when John broke diplomatic relations with the Holy See, and at least as early as 1730 began to serve as the King's secretary. In 1732 he was elected to the Royal Academy of Portuguese History. He concerned himself in a special way with the affairs of the country of his birth as with the foreign policy of Portugal, and his appointment to the Overseas Council in 1743 particularly benefited Brazil. Diplomatically, his greatest achievement was the Treaty of Madrid of 1750, which for the first time defined the boundaries of Portuguese America. The treaty was obviously not of his exclusive making but he had an important hand in it. With the death of John V in 1750, Alexandre de Gusmão suffered an eclipse of power, but he continued to serve on the Overseas Council despite his growing opposition to the Marquis of Pombal, the new master of Portugal. His death in 1753 brought to an end the career of a man who has been considered "one of the most lucid and daring spirits of his time in Portugal"[173] and a precursor of liberalism.

Among Gusmão's circle of close friends, the family of a fellow Brazilian, Teresa Magarida Silva e Orta, meant very much to him, and with Teresa and her husband, Pedro Jansen Moler van Praet, he maintained intimate contact. Teresa was born in São Paulo in 1712, the daughter of a Portuguese immigant father and a Brazilian mother who belonged to an old colonial family. She came to Portugal in the company of her parents and two siblings, Catarina de Horta and Matias Aires Ramos da Silva de Eça, probably in 1716 or 1717. Although Teresa, unlike her brother, never had the advantages of a European trip, she may be considered among the Brazilian *estrangeirados*, if only because of the close ties that throughout her long life she maintained with the cosmopolitan set of Lisbon.

Her internationalism is reflected in a special way in her book of fiction, published for the first time in 1753, *Aventuras de Dió-*

---

[173] Almeida, "Gusmão," p.407.

*fanes,* under the anagrammatic pseudonym of Dorothea Engrassia Tavareda Dalmira,[174] a work of anti-absolutist propaganda, and the only one of its kind. Jaime Cortesão finds it significant that it should have been written by a Brazilian.[175] Of all the writings by the cosmopolitan Portuguese contemporaries of Alexandre de Gusmão, none has the political character and importance of Teresa Margarida's. Its greatest merit (since literarily it is not distinguished) is that it must be placed in the movement of reaction against absolutism, of which, as Cortesão again says, there are many indications during the reign of John V.[176]

Actually, the *Aventuras de Diófanes,* a self-admitted imitation of Fénelon's voyage of Telemachus, is a precious "historical source to appraise the political scene in Portugal during the middle of the [eighteenth] century and the influence of Gusmão upon his world."[177] The author's internationalism is apparent in such passages as "the admirable men, that have existed in the world, nearly all of them developed themselves with labors, with books and in foreign countries. . . ."[178] She invokes reason from time to time, e.g., "Human laws ought to be based upon reason."[179] And she expresses her political views clearly. "There is no wealth in human life that is equal to liberty." Or again, liberty is to be earned, bought, searched, succored, and defended, but it must be used with reason and therefore with moderation. The sovereignty of the King is not divine because the King is not above the law. (Queen Maria Ana of Austria, the wife of John V,

---

174 The work is generally known by the abbreviated title of the edition of 1777, as I have used it in the text. The full title, according to Cidade, p.330, is *Aventuras de Diófanes, Imitando o Sapientíssimo Fénelon, na Sua Viagem de Telémaco.* The title of the first edition (Cidade, p.330) is *Máximas de Virtude e Formosura em que Diófanes Climena e Hemirena, Príncipe de Tebas, Venceram os mais Apertados Lances da Desgraça.* The most recent edition of the work, published in Rio de Janeiro in 1945, has a preface and bibliographical study by Rui Bloem.

175 Cortesão, p.115.
176 *Ibid.*
177 *Ibid.*
178 Bloem edition, p.119.
179 *Ibid.,* p.263.

defined the limitations of absolutism in substantially the same way: "Kings are the Executors and the most illustrious vassals of the Laws of the Realm.")[180] This being the case, it followed that it was legitimate to disobey the King "in order to carry out a higher law."[181] Teresa Margarida falls short of justifying regicide, as the Spanish Jesuit Juan de Mariana did in a book that she must have known about.[182] She is not in favor of an aristocracy of blood exclusively: since sciences ennoble men, society must reward those who through their study have placed themselves above others in order to inspire in everybody the love of letters.[183]

Teresa Margarida's brother, Matias Aires Ramos da Silva de Eça, was not on friendly terms at this time with his sister (who had married at sixteen against the wishes of their father), and there is no evidence to show that he maintained with Alexandre de Gusmão the cordial relations that the latter maintained with Teresa Margarida; yet it is logical to suppose, as Jaime Cortesão has supposed, "that between the two men, born in the same captaincy of São Paulo, one of them Secretary of the King and since 1743 Councillor of the Overseas Council, and the other superintendent [*provedor*] of the Royal Mint since 1742, both residents of Lisbon and both not only Europeanized but also Frenchified, almost inevitably there must have coexisted side by side with their official relations, intellectual relations that were, if not intimate, at least cordial."[184]

Matias Aires was born in São Paulo in 1705. Years later, when he applied for a knighthood in the Order of Christ—membership

---

[180] Cláudio da Conceição, *Gabinete Historico*, XII, 214, cited by Alfredo Pimenta, *Elementos de história de Portugal*, 5th ed. (Lisbon, 1937), p.398.

[181] Bloem edition, p.123.

[182] Juan de Mariana, *Del Rey de la institución de la dignidad real*, trans. E. Barriobero y Herrán (Buenos Aires, 1945).

[183] Bloem edition, p.114.

[184] Cortesão, p.110. For the life of Matias Aires and to a more limited extent of his sister, see especially Ernesto Ennes, *Dois Paulistas Insignes José Ramos da Silva e Matias Aires Ramos da Silva de Eça (Contribuição para o estudo crítico da sua obra) (1705–1763)*, *Brasiliana*, Vol.236 (São Paulo, 1944), hereafter cited as Ennes. Matias Aires is listed in Barbosa Machado, *Bibliotheca Lusitana*, IV, 254.

in the Order would have publicly attested to the purity of his blood, the quality of his family, and the orthodoxy of his ancestors—it was pointed out by the examiners that although his mother was descended from good stock, his father had begun life as a manservant and had later kept a store in Rio de Janeiro, while his paternal grandfather had been a farmer who had always lived poorly, presumably from the sweat of his brow.[185] The charges were undoubtedly true, but to make an issue of them at a time when Matias Aires' father was serving as superintendent of the Royal Mint, a high government post, and had been given the same kind of knighthood that his son coveted, was patently absurd.

Despite the recommendation of the examiners, the King overruled his councilors and declared Matias Aires eligible for the honor,[186] but obviously the establishment had had its say and the harm was done—all of which dramatizes the problems Brazilians sometimes faced whenever they wanted to find a place for themselves in the system. Coming as they did from a freer society, where the cult of the past meant less than it did in the mother country, where a poor immigrant from Portugal, if he was industrious and sober, enjoyed possibilities of advancement and marriage beyond those that he enjoyed at home, Brazilians who had to fight their way through a system that was prepared to be ruthless and unrelenting must have experienced the frustrations of their efforts and feelings of estrangement.

Matias Aires, despite whatever wounds remained from his encounters with the system, found his way in it, after all, and succeeded his father as superintendent of the Royal Mint.[187] He was on friendly terms with the Infante Dom Manuel, the wayward brother of John V. The Infante caused the greatest royal scandal of the age by fleeing Portugal in 1715 without the permission of the Court and, after serving in the Austrian imperial

---

185 Ennes, p.84.

186 *Ibid.*, p.86.

187 He served in his father's place from 1742 until 1744, when he was appointed to the post in his own right (Ennes, pp.108–109, 119–20).

army—he was a Neuburg on his mother's side—living a Bohemian life in various parts of Europe (to the great embarrassment of his family), and unsuccessfully plotting to be King of Poland, returned to Portugal in 1734.[188] The Count of Tarouca was the godfather of one of his two children, both products of his illicit relations with a woman of inferior social standing.[189]

Matias Aires died prematurely in 1763, but Teresa Margarida survived until 1787, almost to the end of the regime to whose downfall she contributed in innumerable indirect ways. She frequented the palace and had friends in important places just as her brother had. She was on excellent terms with Alexandre de Gusmão, knew the future Marquis of Pombal, who controlled Portugal during the reign of John's son, and Francisco Xavier de Mendonça. John's brother, the Infante Dom Manuel, was the godfather of one of her twelve children, as were the Count of Tarouca; Joaquim Jansen, the Inquisitor of the Holy Office; and Gusmão himself.[190]

Fortunately for Matias Aires and Teresa Margarida, their father was immensely wealthy, and although she was provided with no more than a convent education (as it happened, an excellent one, however), her brother was given every advantage. José Ramos da Silva had great aspirations for his only son and was determined to educate him properly. Matias Aires studied at the College of Santo Antão of Lisbon and then on October 1, 1722, enrolled in the School of Law of the University of Coimbra.[191] His first year was spent in preparing for his university course, and on April 6, 1723, he received the bachelor's degree, required for admission to the Major Schools (*Escolas Maiores*).[192] At the same time he qualified for the degree of master in arts, which was conferred upon him on May 9 of the same year,[193] followed on May 18 by a grand ceremony in

[188] Ennes, pp.86–89, 95 *et seq.*
[189] *Ibid.*, pp.122, 130.
[190] *Ibid.*, p.82.
[191] *Ibid.*, p.73.
[192] *Ibid.*, p.76.
[193] *Ibid.*, p.77.

the Royal Chapel of the University attended by the Reverend
Dom António de Santa Teresa, vicar of the Royal Convent of
Santa Cruz and Vice Chancellor of the University. In the presence also of Francisco Carneiro de Figueiroa, Rector of the University, and of the faculty, the new master in arts was given a
thesis to defend, which he did, after which he swore to uphold
as doctrine of the Church the Immaculate Conception of Mary.
The insignias of the degree were then imposed upon him by his
sponsor, the Reverend Paulo Amado of the Society of Jesus, who
brought the impressive event to a close with the customary
laudatory oration.[194]

Matias Aires, who had been a haphazard student, interrupted
his studies in 1728 and left for Madrid. From Madrid he went
to Bayonne, in southern France, where he found the Infante
Dom Manuel, then on a visit, as it is supposed, to his aunt,
the dowager Queen of Spain. Here, according to Barbosa
Machado, he was magnificently received by His Serene Highness
and by his aides.[195] From Bayonne he went to Paris, where he
studied civil and canon law, graduating in both, and attended
lectures by Godin and Grosse on mathematics and physics. He
studied Hebrew with the celebrated Phourmond, whose knowledge of twenty oriental languages was a source of learned amaze-
ment. After a stay of five years in France, Matias Aires returned
to Portugal, possibly in 1733. He did not establish his residence
in Lisbon but instead went to live in Agualva, where his father
had built a magnificent house.

The return of the Infante Dom Manuel to Portugal in 1734
eminently pleased him, for the King's brother, who was assigned as his residence the palace and gardens of the Counts of
Pombeiro, in the town of Belas, would be his relatively close
neighbor. Among the members of His Highness' household were
Manuel Teles da Silva, the future Count of Tarouca, his old
friend from his French days, and Henrique Jansen Moler, none
other than his sister's father-in-law. The death of his father in

194 *Ibid.*, pp.77–78.
195 Barbosa Machado, *Bibliotheca Lusitana*, IV, 254.

1743 and his permanent appointment as superintendent of the Royal Mint in 1744 obliged him to abandon the pleasures of his country seat and establish another residence in Lisbon. In 1744 he bought the palace of the Counts of Alvor, a handsome large house on a bluff overlooking the Tagus.[196] Here he lived until the earthquake of 1755, when the shortage of housing for people of quality encouraged him to rent it.

Solidônio Leite, the Brazilian scholar, called Matias Aires Ramos da Silva de Eça a forgotten classic, and he remained so until Leite resurrected him.[197] For a long time authors of standard histories of Portuguese literature had nothing to say about him, not even literary historians of the stature of Fidelino de Figueiredo and Aubrey F. G. Bell; yet Matias Aires is an excellent disciple of La Rochefoucauld, Pascal, and La Bruyère. His reflections on vanity, which he published in Lisbon in 1752,[198] are more perceptive and epigrammatic than the famous letters on secular conventions and morality by the fourth Earl of Chesterfield.

As I have said in another place, it was difficult, in a disciplined country like Portugal, to maintain a rigorously independent stance. One could criticize the establishment, including the church, provided that one's intention was to support the absolutism of the crown or to improve public morality.[199] Matias Aires, already buffeted severely by life, chose to do the latter, and he appeared before the public at an opportune time, when Portugal "burned with the fury of sacred lasciviousness,"[200] when making love to a nun, as John V did, was looked upon as

---

196 The house is today known as the Palácio das Janelas Verdes, a part of the Museum of Ancient Art of Lisbon. It was at one time the property of the Marquis of Pombal; see Ennes, p.121.

197 Solidônio Leite, *Classicos esquecidos* (Rio de Janeiro, 1914), pp.159–71.

198 Matias Aires Ramos da Silva de Eça, *Reflexões sobre a vaidade dos homens, ou discursos moraes sobre os effeitos da vaidade* (Lisbon, 1752). I have used a facsimile of this edition.

199 Manoel Cardozo, "Azeredo Coutinho," p.74.

200 L. Cabral de Moncada, "Mística e racionalismo em Portugal no século XVIII," *Boletim da Faculdade de Direito* (Coimbra), XXVIII (1952), 32.

the height of amorous sensitivity.[201] Matias Aires, whose two sisters were educated by the fashionable nuns of the Convento das Trinas of Lisbon—Catarina later joined a community of nuns in Odivelas—undoubtedly knew what he was talking about when he said sharp things about convent life.

> . . . what a great difference there is between a woman, who professed through force, and one who professed through an act of will! The latter truly left the world; the former merely changed houses. Both entered the Temple, but one entered to profane it. One was called by God, the other was sent by men. One went to find a divine spouse; the other, because she did not find a man. Both entered Religion, yet only one became a Religious. Both professed but in opposite ways, because what one professed, the other did not. Both said the same thing, but one only mouthed it, while the other also said it from the heart. One made a sacrifice, the other a ceremony. . . . Finally, both were on the path of virtue, but both were not necessarily virtuous."[202]

A decade later, in a letter to his son, then a young man of sixteen, he warned him not to have commerce with nuns. They were, he wrote, "female devils whom Providence Itself has already condemned in this world to live in the Hell of the cloister." They were "rational mermaids"—have you ever heard of a male mermaid? he in effect asks him—and they were "birds of prey."[203]

He said equally harsh things about the nobility and the idea of nobility. "Men," he said with the conviction of a moralist who knew what he was talking about, "were born equal." In a passage reminiscent of Francis I's famous retort (conveyed to the Emperor Charles V by the Cardinal of Toledo),[204] Matias Aires declared further that "the sun rises for everybody; dawn awakens everybody for work; the silence of the night announces the period of rest for everybody. . . . The world was not made for the

201 *Ibid.*, p.29.

202 Matias Aires, *Reflexões*, pp, 233–34.

203 Ennes, p.139; the letter is dated April 24, 1763.

204 H. P. Biggar, *A Collection of Documents Relating to Jacques Cartier and the Sieur de Roberval*, Publications of the Public Archives of Canada, XIV (Ottawa, 1930), 190.

greater benefit of some than of others."[205] Men are not born "wise, just, prudent, virtuous, good; and in the same way they are not born noble; it is here that they find nobility."[206] The censor, who was rector of the Jesuit College of St. Patrick, saw nothing offensive in these and similar remarks. On the contrary, the book "seems to me to be very useful to awaken men engulfed in the pride of the world, from the lethargy, and forgetfulness of life eternal, and to make them deaf to the deccitful adulations of vanity, a vice as old as the world itself, and as universal as mankind, which follows them in life, and ordinarily does not abandon them in death."[207]

Matias Aires must have borne in mind the struggles of his father to attain status in the society of his times when he wrote his book on vanity, and he must have reflected on his own life, on the cost to him of the illusions that he pursued. His father could not have reached the heights that he managed to scale without the enormous fortune he had acquired in Brazil. And it was indeed a feat to hold the position that he held in the Baroque Portugal of the eighteenth century, a penniless immigrant to Brazil who began his career as a manservant and kept a store in Rio de Janeiro, ending his life in the mother country as a professed knight of the Military Order of Christ, a familiar of the Holy Office, and superintendent of the Royal Mint, the father of a son and a daughter who had achieved a name for themselves and were accepted everywhere. He had built a luxurious country seat in Agualva complete with private chapel, as was customary with aristocratic families, and, as a final touch of irony, which must surely not have escaped the son, in June 1743, not quite six months before his death, received the royal grace of a coat of arms for himself and his descendants, inscribed for all time by the King's herald in the Register of Shields of the nobility of Portugal.[208]

---

205 Matias Aires, *Reflexões*, pp.117–18.
206 *Ibid.*, p.400.
207 *Ibid.*, preliminary unnumbered pp.23–24.
208 Ennes, pp.112–15, 173.

Virtually on the eve of his own death, which occurred in December 1763, Matias Aires, in his fifty-eighth year, wrote a touching letter to his younger son, then away at school, which reveals the changes that had overcome the aging *estrangeirado* and affords glimpses of the social life of which he was so much a part. Keep to yourself, he advised him, flee from the plague of friends and comrades

> because bad companions are the world's worst plague . . . the more retired you live, the surer you will live. . . . Do not fraternize with boys, no matter how quiet they may appear, or with some old men who are still boys. I know that to live alone is sad, but it is very convenient; because nobody has repented for his solitude. Nearly everybody regrets commerce with people. . . . Men are devils to each other; and women are other little devils. . . .
>
> Do not apply yourself in learning the Arts of dancing, musical instruments, sports, fencing, and others like that; they are useless arts as I know from experience . . . if you want to amuse yourself, apply yourself to Poetry, and Portuguese Oratory: because poetry is the Art of expression with elegance. . . . If I had had somebody to advise me, things would have been different; I wasted my time in those ridiculous studies. . . .
>
> Comport yourself well; because comporting oneself well does not cost anything and is worth much; and comporting oneself badly costs much, and is worth nothing. Good works make nobility; bad ones unmake it; if you are not virtuous at least show that you are in some fashion; because even the shadow of virtue is estimable. Hypocrisy is in my opinion a praiseworthy vice, because to deceive the World with the cloak of virtue does not cease being a kind of virtue; to pretend to virtue is not a great evil, because in that very act, one recognizes its value, and he who represents it even though he may not take it seriously at least takes it accidentally. There are certain things so excellent that even the exterior form is precious; the same skin of a dead lion is respectable and if it does not instill terror for what it is, instills some fear for what it was.
>
> Shortly I will send you some books from my library; those ought to be your friends. Talk with them, and fear nothing from

such an Association. Dead men are even more useful than living ones; the latter you will always distrust, the former you may take to bed with you without qualms."[209]

## VI

During the eighteenth century, in conclusion, a variety of forces of dissolution and renovation, subtle and complex in their operation, were at work in a Portugal that was still essentially Baroque and largely traditional. Yet within the larger society, paraphrasing the luminous words of Jaime Cortesão, an active nucleus of cosmopolitan and internationally minded Portuguese, the *estrangeirados*, existed and moved about. These *estrangeirados*, some of the more interesting of whom we discussed above, were faithful for the most part to a universalist ideal of nation, of a people who had created other peoples and assimilated other cultures, and *a latere*, "between Portuguese and foreigners, without a focus, deviant, already pointing in the direction of other destinies, the group of Brazilian Portuguese, [men] who evolve, like stars in formation, in the nebulous spiral."[210] During that extraordinary period of contradictions and incoherences, fanaticism existed side by side with an amiable tolerance, traditional aristocracy with an egalitarian cosmopolitanism. An exterior intransigence was somehow mitigated by an interior freedom, reminding one of "majestic organisms, whose foundations a hidden malady undermines," but still "tremble with a voluptuous excitement that precedes the fever and death."[211]

[209] Published by Ennes, pp.138–41. I have taken a number of liberties with the text without, I believe, disturbing the author's meaning.
[210] Cortesão, p.119.
[211] *Ibid.*

# III

*Latin America*

# VII

# "Las Luces" and the Enlightenment in Spanish America

## LUIS MONGUIÓ

"Modern philosophy recognizes reason and the experience of the most enlightened men of all nations as its only foundation"; "as to the natural sciences, God has commended the world to the disputes of the philosophers," proclaimed the eighteenth-century *Gazeta de Literatura de México*, which however qualified these words with the following statement: "What God has revealed to us, what the Church—and the authority of the legitimate interpreters, that is to say, the Fathers and the Councils—proposes to us as an object of belief, all this—held as in a closed hand—we must blindly believe."[1]

Ought we to say then (perpetuating the misinterpretation of a Cervantine phrase), "Con la iglesia hemos dado, Sancho"? (*Q*, II, ix). What we read in the above quotations seems to be an acceptance of the tenets of modern philosophy, of reason, of the experience of man, of science, of the Enlightenment, yes, but within the boundaries set by orthodox belief; but we can also

---

[1] *Gazeta de Literatura de México*, November 7, 1789, and February 15, 1788, respectively. I quote from *Gazetas de Literatura de México, por Don José Antonio Alzate Ramírez* . . . reimpresas en la Oficina del Hospital de San Pedro, a cargo del ciudadano Manuel Buen Abad (Puebla, 1831), I, 230, and 17–18. All translations in the text are mine.

read in them an attempt to separate matters "de tejas arriba" from matters "de tejas abajo"; and as the separation of philosophy from theology is the fulcrum of the Enlightenment, those quotations appear to be then—within the purview of a Christian Enlightenment—characteristically enlightened dicta.

What other Enlightenment could we really expect to find in the colonies of Catholic Spain? Within this enlightenment we shall discover, nonetheless, plenty of scope for modernity, for—to use a currently fashionable word—"modernization" of the thought and life of Spanish America in the eighteenth century.

Let us remember, as Otis Green has recently reminded us, that reason was considered by the Spaniards of the sixteenth and seventeenth centuries "as a positive, a creative, force"; and he continues in terms akin to those of our eighteenth-century Mexican quotations: "Though she [reason] is not autonomous and must move within the limits of a doctrine which she receives from above as set forth in the 'book' of Scriptures and in the declarations of the Church—in spite of all these qualifications—reason is one of the two highest gifts of God to man, by some held to be nobler than her sister, the will. . . . That which is approved by 'right reason' cannot fail to be salutary for mankind."[2]

It should not appear strange, then, that much before the "Age of Reason" we should find in the Spanish Indies a tradition of rationalism, "right rationalism" if you wish, from which the enlightened eighteenth-century American Spaniards could draw sustenance and a sense of continuity, even when they added to that tradition the findings of modern European philosophy.

In fact since the earliest monuments of Spanish writing in the Indies and on the Indies, we can discover a considerable amount of scientific observation and its philosophical elaboration and interpretation according to rational and rationalist criteria. Observation of nature, for example, can be found as early as 1526 in Gonzalo Fernández de Oviedo's *Sumario* and

2 Otis H. Green, *Spain and the Western Tradition*, II (Madison, 1964), 207–208.

in his *Historia General y Natural de las Indias* of 1535; rationalist interpretations of the data of observation and experience we find, to mention one illustrious instance, in Father José de Acosta's *Historia Natural y Moral de las Indias* (1590). In this book, as he had done already in his Latin treatise *De Natura novi orbis* (1588–1589), Acosta did not hesitate to state that he was dealing with matters that had not been known to the old philosophy; that no one ought to be offended, nor should anyone scorn the Church Fathers, if, on some point of philosophy and natural science, they wrote differently from what was now received and approved by good philosophy. After all, they had searched for and served the Creator, which is what really matters, and it should not be deemed very important if in their views of what He had created they did not always hit the mark. Neither did Acosta hesitate to assert that, in difficult matters on which he did not have appropriate authorities to rely on, he would follow the thread of reason.[3]

From among sixteenth-century native American writers it will perhaps suffice to recall the famous sentence of the Inca Garcilaso on the validity of that reason which illuminated the mind of pre-Conquest wise men: "Besides adoring the Sun as a visible God . . . the Inca Kings, and their 'amautas,' who were philosophers, perceived through natural reason [*con lumbre natural*] the true supreme God, our Lord, who created heaven and earth . . . whom they called Pachacamac."[4]

In the seventeenth century, in her *Primero sueño*, Sor Juana Inés de la Cruz's soul, freed by her body's sleep from the duty of watching over her senses, attempted a soaring flight toward an intuition not only of all terrestrial things but also of all abstract concepts and pure spirits. Such an attempt at a cosmic vision

---

[3] José de Acosta, S.J., *Historia Natural y Moral de las Indias* (Seville, 1590). See "Proemio al lector," p.9; Book I, Chap.i, p.15; and Book I, Chap.xvi, p.57. See also his *De Natvra novi orbis libri dvo et De Promvlgatione evangelii apvd Barbaros sive De Procuranda Indorum salvte libri sex* (Salamanca, 1589 [but 1588 in the colophon]), Book I, Chap.ii, p.3; and Book I, Chap.xxi, p.43.

[4] *Primera parte de los Commentarios reales que tratan del origen de los Incas* [1609], 2ª impresión, enmendada (Madrid, 1723), Book II, Chap.ii, p.34a.

passes human possibilities, and it imposed upon her the realization that understanding and reason demanded that she acquire knowledge through the logical and step-by-step study of all classical categories and degrees: from mineral to vegetable, to brute animal, to man, angel, and God. Then she awakened in the bright sunlight, her passion for knowledge thus placed in the right perspective. That passion for rational knowledge was Sor Juana's dominating trait cannot be denied. She herself tells us: "I do not study in order to write, and even less in order to teach (this would be an impertinent presumption on my part), but only to see if by studying I become less ignorant." Let us not forget that even when, for a time, her books and her scientific instruments were forbidden her by an innocent and ill-advised mother superior, she found subject for study and reflection in the most ordinary, everyday circumstances: she could not help noticing that the lines of the walls of a large refectory run visually straight but not parallel, or that a spinning top described not a perfect circumference but a spiral figure; she could not avoid making chemical observations even while cooking in the convent kitchen. All this may seem to some, in our sophisticated days, mere pastimes, but as Sor Juana said, quoting Lupercio Leonardo de Argensola, "One can philosophize and also prepare supper."[5] If we can admire Blaise Pascal, who when he was twelve rediscovered geometry because of his thirst for knowledge, Sor Juana, a woman and a nun at that, with an equal thirst for knowledge, deserves our admiration also, because she too *studied* geometry among the other sciences.

Again let us not forget that her contemporary, compatriot, and friend, Don Carlos de Sigüenza y Góngora, was no mean rationalist and scientist. His *Libra astronómica y philosóphica* (1690), for example, is a polemic about the 1681 comet, a criticism

---

5 See "Primero sueño" in *Obras completas de Sor Juana Inés de la Cruz*, ed. Alfonso Méndez Plancarte, I (Mexico City, 1951), 335–59, and nn., pp.575–617. See also "Respuesta de la poetisa a la muy ilustre Sor Filotea de la Cruz," *ibid.*, ed. Alberto G. Salceda, IV (Mexico City, 1957), 440–75. The quotations are at IV, 444, 459.

of astrology as a false science, an undeceiving of the superstitious, a ridiculing of their beliefs on the significance of comets and their influence upon man, an astronomical and scientific book in the modern sense of these words. In this treatise Sigüenza quotes Pierre Gassendi at least twelve times, and direct quotations from John Kepler and Tycho Brahe are also quite numerous in it; they leave no doubt that he had their books before him as he wrote.[6] Moreover, his last will and testament prove his scientific outlook: in this document he asked that his body be dissected after death, so that the cause of his last disease might be better understood, and this knowledge be of help to future patients.[7]

These are only a few examples of the use of reason, right reason, in pre-eighteenth-century Spanish America. These examples, these lessons, these "luces," were not unknown to the American Spaniards of the eighteenth century. Their awareness of this tradition and of the acceptability of rational discovery, within the bounds of Christian belief, could not but sustain them in their eager acceptance of the new knowledge that was being so rapidly spread throughout the Western world by the natural philosophers of the seventeenth and eighteenth centuries. We know now, thanks to the work of a number of scholars (pre-eminent among them in this country are Arthur P. Whitaker and John Tate Lanning),[8] that modern philosophy and science

[6] *Libra astronómica y philosóphica en que D. Carlos de Sigüenza y Góngora, Cosmógrapho y Mathemático Regio en la Academia Mexicana, examina no sólo lo que a su Manifiesto Philosóphico contra los Cometas opuso el R. P. Eusebio Kino de la Compañía de Jesús, sino lo que el mismo R. P. opinó y pretendió haver demostrado en su Exposición Astronómica del Cometa del año 1681. Sácala a luz D. Sebastián Guzmán y Córdova, Fator, Veedor, Proveedor, Iuez Oficial de la Real Hazienda de Su Magestad en la caxa de esta Corte* [drawing: Pegasus with motto "Sic itur ad astra"] (Mexico City, 1690), [24]-188pp.

[7] Irving A. Leonard, *Don Carlos de Sigüenza y Góngora, a Mexican Savant of the Seventeenth Century* (Berkeley, 1929), p.181.

[8] Arthur P. Whitaker *et al., Latin America and the Enlightenment* (New York, 1942); 2d ed. (Ithaca, N.Y., 1961). John Tate Lanning, *Academic Culture in the Spanish Colonies* (New York, 1940); *The University in the Kingdom of Guatemala* (Ithaca, N.Y., 1955); *The Eighteenth-Century Enlightenment in the University of San Carlos of Guatemala* (Ithaca, N.Y., 1956).

was known, received, and expounded in the eighteenth-century schools and universities of the Spanish colonies in America. We know that the names and the works of Descartes, Leibniz, Newton, and Condillac, Copernicus and Kepler, Musschenbroek, Buffon, Boerhaave, Linnaeus, and Franklin, Heineccius and Filangieri, Raynal and Robertson, Montesquieu, Voltaire, and D'Alembert were as well known as those of the more familiar Feijoo, Jorge Juan, Antonio de Ulloa, and Piquer, Campomanes, Campillo, Macanaz, Floridablanca, and Jovellanos; and that this academic enlightenment was fostered by the crown and by a number of vice-roys.

There seems no need to gloss the findings of recent investigators, who have done their job well. I want, though, to see how far and in what ways the academic Enlightenment spread outside the walls of the schools. The periodicals of the eighteenth century may give us some idea of the possible diffusion of the enlightened doctrines among the general reading public, so I have looked into a few of them from the Mexican and Peruvian viceroyalties in search of information on this subject.

The appearance of periodicals of some substance, published at regular intervals, is in itself a sign of the interest on the part of publishers and of readers in the novelties of the times. The *Gazeta de Lima,* for example, in its first number of December 1, 1743, saw itself as being a sort of "summary of the novelties with which the polity of the peoples is formed and cultivated. Common utility is often derived from this political invention [a periodical] because thanks to it news of all events circulates throughout the rational world."[9] This early gazette did not fail to inform its readers about cultural events, for example the appointment of Louis Godin to the University of San Marcos as professor of mathematics (he was one of the French scientists who had come to America in La Condamine's expedition to measure a degree at the equator); it reported the pub-

9 John Carter Brown Library, Providence, R.I., *A Facsimile of the First Issue of the Gazeta de Lima. . . . with a Description of a File for the Years 1744–1763* (Boston, 1908).

lication of a letter of Eusebio Llano Zapata, and indicated that
other works of this Peruvian scientist, then residing in Spain,
were for sale at the *Gazeta's* printing shop.[10]

These periodicals were quite conscious of their function as
complements to the schools' instruction in the new knowledge.
In 1772, for instance, in the first issue of his *Mercurio volante*,
Dr. Bartolache stated that his journal was destined to comple-
ment in Mexico the reform of the schools undertaken by the
crown, "according to the ideas that are held today, for the greater
utility and good of the State," particularly if these reforms were
not carried out in the Indies as quickly as one might wish. "Let
us then commence—he said—to communicate to the public, in
our common Spanish tongue, some important and curious news
on matters of Physics and Medicine."[11] He obviously considered
his function not unlike that of Father Feijoo, "one of the first
undeceived authors; one who dared with the greatest fortitude
and indefatigable constancy, throughout almost half a century,
vigorously to resist the multitude, and to banish its prejudices";
but, since Feijoo had written some time previously, Bartolache
would try to improve on him by incorporating also the results
of later and new scientific knowledge.[12]

Bartolache did of course make the appropriate disclaimer
about dealing with theological matters: God, the angels, and
the soul are spirits; physics studies only bodies.[13] He would not
touch either of these, he said, or other subjects such as belles
lettres and politics, as they fell outside his competence.[14] But
within his fields of endeavor he would quite freely express any
opinions: Aristotle was a great philosopher, provided one did
not base this belief on his *De Physica auscultatione*; Descartes

10 *Ibid., Gazeta de Lima*, Nos.8 (November–December 1744) and 14 (September–
October 1745).

11 *Mercurio volante con noticias importantes y curiosas sobre varios asuntos de
Física y Medicina por D. Josef Ignacio Bartolache, Doctor Médico, del Claustro de
esta Real Universidad de México*, No.1 (October 17, 1772).

12 *Ibid.*, No.5 (November 18, 1772).

13 *Ibid.*, No.2 (October 28, 1772).

14 *Ibid.*, No.1 (October 17, 1772).

was a good geometer, and could have been a good physicist, except that he wanted to construct a complete system of physics on *a priori* concepts. The glory of philosophizing with solidity and of knowing the very Nature that God created, without having recourse to imaginary systems, of demonstrating with evidence the connection of the most admirable effects with their respective causes, of making himself master of the physical universe, this glory was reserved to Sir Isaac Newton. His is the only physics, the only true one, the one that must be followed.[15]

It might be curious to compare what Bartolache was saying in Mexico in 1772 with what Ernst Cassirer has said in our century about the eighteenth. In *The Philosophy of the Enlightenment*, Cassirer explained how the eighteenth century no longer vied with Descartes for the prize of systematic rigor and completeness, but attempted to solve the central problems of philosophic method by having recourse to Newton's *Rules on Philosophizing* rather than to Descartes's *Discourse on Method*; so that eighteenth-century philosophy took a completely different direction from that of the seventeenth century. Instead of starting from a highest, intuitively grasped certainty or axiom and, by proof and inference, adding other propositions to the first original certainty (thus linking and piecing together the chain of all possible knowledge), the Newtonian method was not one of pure deduction but of analysis: observation produces the datum of science and, contrary to the Cartesian method, the principle and the law is not the beginning but rather the end product of the investigation.[16] This is exactly what we have seen Bartolache say in his *Mercurio volante*: Descartes with his *a priori* concepts was a false guide; Newton, who, without any imaginary systems, connected effects to their causes, was the master of the physical world. Cassirer quoted some sentences of D'Alembert, published in 1759, about the effects of the new analytical method

---

15 *Ibid.*, No.2 (October 28, 1772).

16 *The Philosophy of the Enlightment* (Boston, 1955), pp.6–8 (English trans., first published by Princeton University Press, 1951, of *Die Philosophie der Aufklärung* [Tübingen, 1932]).

of philosophizing.[17] Our Mexican, in 1772, was saying much the same things, not of course in Paris but in Mexico City, capital of half an American world.

In holding those philosophical views the editor of the *Mercurio volante* was by no means an exceptional case. Alzate's *Gazeta de Literatura de México*, of November 7, 1789, for instance, printed a letter addressed to a Franciscan friar who had defended an "acto de conclusiones" of Aristotelian philosophy. The letter, signed pseudonymously but whose author was José Mariano Mociño, the naturalist, was a brutal review of the poor friar's work. After correcting some of his many errors in Latin grammar, it attacked his willful confusion of deistic and libertine heretics with modern Christian philosophers; a man of good faith ought not to do this. After all, modern philosophers did not confuse traditional Catholic philosophy with the innumerable errors of Aristotle and the Aristotelians. Mociño agreed that the works of a Gassendi, a Descartes, a Newton ought not to be put in the hands of beginners, but mature scholars should be able to find in them food for thought: "the object of an honest man possessed of love of truth must be to examine all works with impartiality and to take from each of them what is most probable and most in agreement with Reason."[18]

The same Mociño (again under the pen name of José Velázquez) published in the *Gazeta de Literatura de México* of February 20, 1790, a partly autobiographical article in which he states that in his early years he had studied Scholastic philosophy only to perceive, after completing his arts course, that he was as ignorant of true philosophy as when he began. Soon he realized that only the Newtonians had founded their philosophy on the incontrovertible principles of mathematics, and his love of mathematics had led him to the enjoyment of the natural sciences, which are either exact themselves or have a very close

[17] *Ibid.*, pp.3–4.

[18] *Gazeta de Literatura de México*, November 7, 1789, cit. by 1831 reprint (see n.1, above), I, 223–30; the quotation at p.227. The identification of José Velázquez as José Mariano Mociño in I, 417.

relationship with the exact sciences. He was now delighted to see that the popes had banished Aristotelian philosophy from their colleges De Propaganda Fide and replaced it by the philosophical works of Jacquier; that the kings of Spain in the universities of the Peninsula, the Inquisitor General in his Tridentine seminary, and the Archbishop of Mexico in his own college, had done the same. Also that the Commissioner General of the Franciscans, when he was Provincial of Andalusia, had also done away with Aristotelianism and caused "good taste" and the useful sciences to flourish in the schools of his order.[19]

Similar philosophical views did not remain mere speculation but were often translated into the practical world of public education, as the periodicals instantly reported. Thus, for example, a Supplement to Manuel Antonio Valdés' *Gazeta de México* of September 21, 1790, printed in extenso the text of a new Plan of Studies for the Royal and Most Ancient College of St. John Lateran, in Mexico City, a plan proposed by its Rector, Dr. Francisco Antonio Marrugat y Boldú, a Royal Chaplain, and a Substitute Professor of Sacred Theology at the University. As the plan details the authors to be used in each field and level of study, we can appreciate the modernity that informs it, particularly at the upper levels. There we meet with the philosophical books of Jacquier, of the Dutchman Musschenbroek, and the German Ernesti, with the Physics of Father Almeyda, with the Civil Law of Vinnius and the Natural Law of Heineccius. Just one year later, the same *Gazeta de México* of September 27, 1791, reported that Marrugat's plan had caused a number of protests because it was thought too advanced and progressive, but experience had shown its excellent results.[20]

At the other end of the Spanish Empire, in Peru, an article in the *Mercurio Peruano* of July 17, 1791, tells us that when in the Peninsula, Salamanca and Alcalá were resisting the King's or-

---

19 *Ibid.*, I, 285.

20 *Gazetas de México, Compendio de noticias de Nueva España, que comprehenden los años 1790 y 1791 . . . por Don Manuel Antonio Valdés, Tomo IV* (Mexico City, 1791), 456pp. and Index.

ders to reform their studies, the University of San Marcos of Lima had done so with alacrity, submitting a new plan of studies in 1771, another in 1779, and a third one in 1788.[21] Another long article in the *Mercurio Peruano* of November 17, 1791, reports that "Aristotle has little by little fallen into an excessive disrepute," that the "implacable partisans of Descartes and Newton crossed the oceans," and that if it is true that the Cartesians did not gain great advantages, "the Newtonians multiply with rapidity," and finally that, in the school acts and conferences "one hears the Stagirite's name only when he is being disparaged." All this just as a preface to the report that the Rector of the College of San Carlos of Lima, Dr. Toribio Rodríguez de Mendoza, had informed the Vice-Roy of the absurdity of a situation in which his students found themselves. In San Carlos the students were free to select their philosophy, and in general they selected systems other than the Peripatetic, but in the examinations they were required to expound Aristotle. This was illogical and irrational. Rodríguez further pointed out to the Vice-Roy that the college of the Augustinians and that of the Fathers of the Good Death, of Lima, also taught philosophies other than the Aristotelian. A solution to the San Carlos quandary would be to draw up from Aristotle a list of useful points of logic, metaphysics, physics, and moral philosophy but to allow the students to expound them in their examinations according to whatever philosophy they might have adopted. The Oídor Don Ambrosio Cerdán y Pontero, Judge Protector of San Carlos, informed the Vice-Roy that this seemed to him a feasible solution, since in his opinion, although Aristotle's *Politics, Poetics,* and *Rhetoric* deserved respect, and his *Logic* was exact, his *Ethics* was mediocre, his *Physics* ridiculous, and his *Metaphysics* quite murky. The Vice-Roy agreed to the new system of examinations.

We should notice that in the capital of the Peruvian viceroyalty, not only the new College of San Carlos, but the colleges

21 *Mercurio Peruano de Historia, Literatura y Noticias Públicas que da a luz la Sociedad Académica de Amantes del País de Lima y en su nombre D. Jacinto Calero y Moreira,* 12 vols. (Lima, 1791–1795).

of the Augustinians and the "Agonizantes" were anti-Scholastic and taught modern philosophy. On this point we have further proof upon perusing the review (printed in the *Mercurio Peruano* of November 24, 1793), of a philosophy textbook published by Father Isidoro Pérez de Celis for his students in the monastery of Saint Mary of the Good Death, in Lima.[22] Again we find that Father Celis explained physics, as a matter of course, by the Newtonian system, and that in astronomy he accepted the Copernican system "as that which conforms the most to astronomical observations and to the general law of nature, gravity."[23] Note here that the Copernican system is accepted by a priest as a matter of scientific evidence, not as a mere hypothesis as it had been the practice in earlier times when the church resisted its acceptance because of scriptural scruples.

Apparently then matters of philosophical doctrine, inside and outside the schools, were deemed by the editors of these journals to be of sufficient interest to the reading public to be reported in the detail shown in the above-mentioned examples. This was true not only in the viceregal capitals, Lima and Mexico, but also in smaller administrative centers: a glance at the *Primicias de la Cultura de Quito*, for instance, shows the same philosophical preoccupation, although in this case its editor, Dr. Santa Cruz y Espejo, seems to show more inclination toward the sensibility of a Rousseau, mixed with the sensorialism of a Condillac, than toward pure scientism. He is exemplary, however, in his interest not just in the higher reaches of knowledge, but with children's education. A Supplement to No.1 of the *Primicias* includes a letter addressed to primary school teachers about

[22] The book in question is *Elementa Philosophiae quibus accedent principia mathematica verae physicae, prorsus necessaria, ad usos academicos scholares ac religiosae juventutis Collegii Limani Sanctae Mariae Bonae Mortis, CC. RR. ministrantium infirmis accomodata, in tres tomos digesta. . . . Auctore R. Patre Isidoro de Celis, Europae nato, ejusdem Collegii Philosophiae ac Theologiae Lectorem* (Madrid, 1787), 3 vols. of 327, 253, and 336pp. See José Toribio Medina, *Biblioteca hispano-americana*, V (Santiago, 1902), 238–39, #5220.

[23] The review published by the *Mercurio Peruano*, November 24, 1793, had appeared first in the *Gazeta de Literatura de México* (see 1831 reprint, I, 347–53).

the means of leading children toward the discovery of the most important truths. He proposes the teaching of Castilian grammar, moral and religious principles, and the development of the children's reason, the latter to be done particularly by means of long conversations, by inspiring them to ask questions—although he acknowledges that at first perhaps not a single boy would dare to ask them, because of the bashful or timid nature of the people of his country "in which the climate and an education appropriate to slaves had a great part."[24]

Phrases like this notwithstanding, Santa Cruz and the other editors of eighteenth-century periodicals were at the same time much incensed at the disregard shown by European scholars for American cultural achievements. Santa Cruz was irritated by De Pauw, Robertson, Raynal, and all the others who had stated that the Americans were incapable of scientific knowledge. To disprove this he gave a long list of American scholars (Nos.6 and 7, March 17 and 29, 1792, of the *Primicias*). The *Mercurio Peruano* of January 2, 1791, had also protested that foreigners, French and English, because of their national prejudices, ignorance, or caprice, had described a Peru that seemed to its inhabitants entirely different from the one they knew from personal experience. On other occasions this same journal did not fail to give a long list of Peruvian botanists (May 29, 1791), or to mention the authorities—Feijoo first of all, Juan, Ulloa, Alcedo—who had vindicated Peru and the American Spaniards from the insults proffered by foreign envy (February 13, 1794). The *Gazeta de México,* in its turn, when reporting the inauguration of the Cabinet of Natural History of José Longinos Martínez, pointed out that eleven local gentlemen, whose names it listed, owned private scientific collections in Mexico City, and had made available to Longinos their duplicate specimens

---

[24] Supplement to No.1, of January 5, 1792. See *Primicias de la Cultura de Quito, por Francisco Javier Eugenio de Santa Cruz y Espejo* (Quito, 1953), p.19. The *Primicias* consisted of an "Instrucción previa" published in 1791, and seven numbers, January 5–March 29, 1792. There are several other modern reprints of this periodical.

(April 27 and August 24, 1790).[25] Finally, Alzate in his *Gazeta de Literatura de México* (July 18, 1789) said that in the viceregal capital there were ten or more bookshops: "Whom do they serve? the Apaches, the Kalmucks?" Weren't there in Mexico City a number of university professors, some two hundred lawyers, and a sufficiency of physicians, as well as mathematicians, experimental physicists, and naturalists?[26] American pride in American culture breathes through these expressions.

And so secure in their learning must these men have felt that, despite their disclaimers about not wanting to touch upon matters of faith, they would often deal with religious matters. To give just one example, in a description of Chicha and Tarija, published in the *Mercurio Peruano* (May 12, 1791), it was plainly stated that instead of reasonably explaining the presence of an old wooden cross, discovered in the latter valley, by the simple fact of the post-Conquest presence there of early Spanish expeditions and inhabitants, some people wished to consider that discovery a miracle, and to believe that the cross was one planted by the Apostle Thomas in his supposed visit to the American continent. The writer found these suppositions untenable. To support his own skepticism he mentioned Father Feijoo's well-known discourse on false miracles, and referred the reader to Macanaz' specific impugnation of the American voyage of St. Thomas. He indicated that he had deemed it indispensable to elucidate this point through the use of common sense, as one ought to do in historical matters; and he ended his argument with a quotation from Montengón's *Eusebio*: "De las cosas más seguras, lo más seguro es dudar"[27]—an ironical call to methodical doubt, if ever we saw one.

25 *Gazeta de México,* IV, 68, 152–54.

26 *Gazetas de Literatura de México,* 1831 reprint, I, 161.

27 The *Mercurio Peruano* documented its authorities: For Rafael Melchor de Macanaz the reference is to *Semanario erudito,* VIII, fol.32 (i.e., Antonio Valladares de Sotomayor's *Semanario erudito, que comprehende varias obras* [Madrid, 1788], VIII, 32); for Pedro Montengón to *El Eusebio,* II, fol.3 (i.e., *El Eusebio, Parte primera [-quarta] sacada de las memorias que dexó él mismo,* 4 vols. [Madrid, 1786–1788], II, 3). Father Feijoo's discourse is the sixth in Vol.III of his *Teatro crítico* (1729), which went through several editions.

Not only in these matters of high importance are the eighteenth-century Spanish American periodicals spreading enlightened information among their readers. The same is true in more pragmatic fields, economics, for example. It is not rare to find in these gazettes high praise for the new policy of free or open trade: old-fashioned people might say that there no longer existed the enormous fortunes that prevailed at the beginning of the century, but no one could deny that with free trade the general welfare had improved—food, home furnishings, means of conveyance, clothing, the amenities of life, all were cleaner, more comfortable, more colorful in the 1790's than they had been twenty years before. "El estado medio de los ciudadanos," the middle class, the artisan, the small merchant, the trader enjoyed greater prosperity than they ever had before.[28]

If from these subjective or empirical statements we go on to read more ponderous articles, such as Baquíjano y Carrillo's "Political and Historical Dissertation on the Commerce of Peru," or his "History of the Discovery of the Hill at Potosí," we shall find the same progressive views expressed; but his observations, analyses, and opinions will be bolstered with learned references not only to Spanish authors such as Ulloa, Bernardo Ward, Campillo, or Campomanes, but also to a number of works by important foreigners such as Montesquieu, Lavateur, Rousseau, Raynal, Hume, or Josiah Child, and even to some less familiar, for example, Bertrand and Calm (*sic*, for John Bartram and Peter Kalm), authors of a natural and political history of Pennsylvania (Paris, 1768).[29] Finally, when economics touches im-

---

28 *Mercurio Peruano*, February 2, 1791.

29 José Baquíjano y Carillo's article on Peruvian commerce runs through several numbers of the 1791 *Mercurio Peruano*; his article on Potosí is in three numbers of the same periodical, beginning with that of January 10, 1793. The so-called natural and political history of Pennsylvania by Bertrand and Calm (*sic*) must be: *Observations on the inhabitants, climate, soils, rivers, productions, animals, and other matters worthy of notice. Made by Mr. John Bartram in his travels from Pensilvania to Onondago, Oswego and the Lake Ontario in Canada. To which is annex'd a curious account of the cataracts at Niagara. By Mr. Peter Kalm, a Swedish gentleman who travelled there* (London, 1751). I have seen a modern facsimile edition (Geneva, N.Y., 1895), vii–94pp. I have not found the

mediately upon humane values, eighteenth-century philanthropy together with Christian charity shine in these American writings. I have in mind, for instance, an article on Negro slavery published in the *Mercurio Peruano* of June 16, 1791. The philanthropism expressed in it does not need to be based, as the author specifically states, on the principles of the "infamous treatises" of a Fréret, a Helvétius, or a Diderot (which he details in a footnote), because our will and our reason joined by a single principle consider humanity as inseparable from evangelical charity. This is all that man needs in order to feel concern for the situation and the treatment of the hacienda Negro slaves, "children of the Almighty . . . our brothers . . . like us vessels of immortal souls . . . co-heirs with us of the most precious blood of Christ . . . who are considered bundles of merchandise and who are sometimes treated worse than the donkeys that work the same fields alongside them."[30] We are again confronted here with an expression of the Christian Enlightenment, but I fail to see how the moral wrongs of Negro slavery could have been presented any more cogently, any more convincingly to the Catholic conscience and the humane mind of Spanish American eighteenth-century readers.

Coming now to belles lettres, it must be acknowledged that they play a minor role in the eighteenth-century periodicals perused. To the men of the Enlightenment, Literature, with a capital L, was a matter of natural and moral philosophy; belles

---

presumed French translation (Paris, 1768). John Bartram (1699–1777) was the father of American botany. Peter Kalm (1716–1779) was a Swedish botanist, a pupil of Linnaeus, who traveled in America from 1747 to 1751.

30 The writer does not hesitate to challenge his readers' Catholic conscience in stating that on the subject one cannot read without admiration and pity some reflections on Negro slavery by Schwartz: "The frozen mountains of Switzerland, inhabited by the sectaries of Zwingli and Oecolampadius," had thus done for the Negroes what ought more appropriately to be done by Catholics. The allusion is to a book entitled *Réflexions sur l'esclavage des Nègres, Par M. Schwartz, pasteur du Saint-Evangile à Bienne, membre de la Société économique de B\*\*\*\*\** (Neufchâtel, 1781), xii–99pp., with a *nouvelle éd., revue et corrigée* (Neufchâtel, 1788), iv–viii–86pp. "Schwartz" is the pseudonym used in this work by the Marquis de Condorcet.

lettres were more of a pleasing entertainment than real literature, even if they contained as much moral and utilitarian subject matter as could be managed to comply with the Horatian
dictum "omne tulit punctum, qui miscuit utile dulci / lectorem
delectando pariterque monendo" (*De Arte Poetica*, 343–44). As
Hugh Blair said in 1783, belles lettres stood "in a middle station
between the pleasures of sense and those of pure intellect. We
were not designed to grovel always among objects as low as the
former; nor are we capable of dwelling constantly in so high a
region as the latter."[31] Some eighteenth-century poetry books
with the apologetic title of *Ocios de mi juventud* (Cadalso, Jovellanos, for example) bear witness to a similar attitude in the
Hispanic world; but in the journals examined, belles lettres, if
not the most important of their components, are also included
in their purview for the purpose indicated. We shall mention
some examples.

A problem typical of these times, the question of the theater,
is treated in these journals in completely Neoclassic terms. The
*Diario literario de México*, No. 8, of May 10, 1768, for instance,
stated that, as to the stage, "in Italy and France, Reason triumphed; in England, art and caprice were joined together, and
produced monsters; and in our Spain, preoccupation triumphed,
inverisimilitude persists, and bad taste reigns."[32] The elder
Moratín could have subscribed to these lines.

Then in the *Mercurio Peruano* the public could read occasionally a poem in hendecasyllabic couplets on the history of
the Inca emperors (September 7, 1792), or a poem on the disasters of the French Revolution (May 18 and 22, 1794), or a
review of a didactic poem by Father Celis, *Filosofía de las costumbres* (July 17, 1794).[33] The same periodical did include an

---

[31] *Lectures on Rhetoric and Belles Lettres* [1783] (Edinburgh, 1813), I, 13.

[32] *Diario literario de México, dispuesto para la pública utilidad, a quien se
dedica, Por D. Joseph Antonio de Alzate y Ramírez* (Mexico City, May 10, 1768),
No. 8.

[33] Isidoro Pérez de Celis, *Filosofía de las costumbres* (Madrid, 1793), x–354pp.
See Antonio Palau y Dulcet, *Manual del librero hispano-americano*, 2d ed., XIII
(Barcelona, 1961), 419, #220037.

article on the public amusements available in Lima: comedy (and it boasted that the local theater was better appointed than many European ones), ball games, cockfights, bullfights, promenades, and coffeehouses (January 13, 1791). To the coffeehouses it devoted a special article (February 10, 1791), justifying their study with the allegation that there is no object too small for the consideration of the true philosopher: Reaumur had anatomized the fly, Malpighi had studied the egg, Duhamel had reflected upon sewers. We can perceive then that the authors of the lighter articles liked to reveal as wide and critical a reading of modern works, national and foreign, as the authors of heavier disquisitions.

One may be allowed to wonder if this combination of scientific and literary interests did not really justify a statement in the *Gazeta de México* of February 2, 1790, to the effect that "the fondness for the Sciences, or rather the fashion of a varnish of learning, much more general now than in other times, is [a] cause of the greater frequency of nervous complaints, which are the consequence of the application of the intellect and the inaction of the body," another cause being apparently "the prodigious proliferation of novels in the last hundred years."[34]

Be this as it may, allow me to mention one more instance attesting to the wide reading of belletristic writers, an instance somewhat seasoned with the flavor of literary scandal. The editor of the *Gazeta de Literatura de México* printed in his issue of December 16, 1788, a letter he had received, and which reads in part as follows:

> I sent urgently for a copy of the drama that was played for the entertainment and celebration of the birthday of His Excellency the Vice-Roy; it was entitled *La Elmira*, written, or so it is reported, by Sr. Pisón [i.e., Don Juan Pisón y Vargas]. I received it; I read it, and although I immediately noticed that it was not the first time that I had read it, I could not remember where. . . . This perplexity did not last for long, because rummaging through my little library I found the *Americans* [i.e.,

34 *Gazetas de México . . . por Don Manuel Antonio Valdés*, IV, 23–24.

*Alzire, ou les Américains*] of Mr. de Voltaire, which I had already read, and comparing Sr. Pisón's *La Elmira* with Mr. de Voltaire's *Americans* I found that the former was a translation of the latter, as anyone can easily discover by making the same collation.[35]

This shows, of course, that Voltaire's play was in the critic's library, that he took it for granted that it must also be in those of many of the *Gazeta*'s other readers, whom he invited to compare it with *La Elmira*, and that this fact could be broadcast in Mexico, without danger, in the public prints. By the way, the play is an unacknowledged translation of *Alzire* (1736).

As late as 1794, while the horrors of the Terror in France were being constantly reported in the Spanish American periodicals, a *Retrato de Voltaire*, together with the *Reflexiones de Marat*, and the *Decretos de la Convención* were being advertised for sale in the *Gazeta de México* (March 16, 1794). Of course, in the same issue were also advertised works that might be considered as antidotes to this revolutionary literature: a defense of Louis XVI, a treatise on his virtues, etc.[36]

Soon, however, one can notice a tightening of the prohibitions of politically subversive works. For example, the same *Gazeta de México*, in its issue of November 13, 1794, printed an inquisitorial decree forbidding a book by Santiago Felipe Puglia, *Des-*

35 *Gazetas de Literatura de México*, 1831 reprint, I, 91. See *La Elmira, Tragedia moderna, en cinco actos, Por Don Juan Pisón y Vargas: con la segunda parte de Los Abates Locos, y su Loa: en celebridad de los años del exmo. señor D. Manuel Antonio de Florez, &. &. &. y dedicada al señor Don Joseph de Florez, &.* (Mexico City, 1788), 18–96–28pp. The play was produced on May 22, 1788, and repeated the following Sunday (see Enrique de Olavarría y Ferrari, *Reseña histórica del teatro en México*, 2d ed. [Mexico City, 1895], I, 74). Pisón was the author of *La Perromachia, Invención Poética* (Madrid, 1786), 104pp. (See Palau, *Manual*, 2d ed., XIII, 287a, #227444), and of *El Rutzvanscadt, o Quixote trágico, Tragedia a secas sin dedicatoria, prólogo ni argumento para no molestar a los aficionados* (Madrid, 1786), 71pp. (See Gabriel-Martín del Río y Rico, *Catálogo de la Sección de Cervantes de la Biblioteca Nacional* [Madrid, 1930], pp.721–22, #1524). Other than a passing allusion, it has nothing to do with the *Quijote*, being a burlesque tragedy on "Chinese" subject matter.

36 *Gazetas de México . . . del año de 1794 . . . por Don Manuel Antonio Valdés, Tomo VI* (Mexico City, 1794), p.324.

*engaño del hombre* (Philadelphia, 1794), as blasphemous against God, Religion, and the Monarchy," and this prohibition was coupled with a reminder of a decree of March 13, 1790— obviously, as we have seen a moment ago, more respected in the breach than in the observance—forbidding French and other books that might instill a spirit of sedition.[37] As the thought of the French Revolution is perpetuated, we find the prohibitions becoming more insistent and more comprehensive. A Mexican inquisitorial decree of June 30, 1804, for example, covers quite a range of works,[38] from those of Mably and Voltaire, "impious, sacrilegious, and heretical," to novels such as *Rosalía, o la joven seducida*, by Arnaud (Madrid, 1797), and *Les mille et une heure* [*sic*], *contes péruviens* (Lille, 1778), "inducing to sensuality."[39]

These latter-day prohibitions notwithstanding, our brief look at some eighteenth-century Spanish American periodicals, dat-

[37] *Ibid.*, pp.640–42. I have also seen a separate printed broadside with the inquisitorial decree. The book in question is *Desengaño del hombre compuesto por Santiago Felipe Puglia* (Philadelphia, 1794), x–113–xvii–1pp. See Palau, *Manual*, 2d ed., XIV (Barcelona, 1962), 288a, #241277. The previous year Puglia had published *A Short Extract concerning the Rights of Man and Citizen from the Work entitled Man Undeceived, written in Spanish by J. Ph. de Puglia, Translated from the Original by the Author and corrected by a Democrat* (Philadelphia, 1793), 16pp. Puglia published a number of works, in Spanish and in English, in Philadelphia between 1790 and 1822. On Puglia see A. Owen Aldridge, "A Spanish Precursor of the Age of Reason," *Papers on French-Spanish Luso-Brazilian Spanish-American Literary Relations, Discussed at Conference 8, Modern Language Association of America, New York, December, 1968* (Elmhurst, Ill., 1969), pp.1–4. Professor Aldridge is preparing an extended study of this interesting writer.

[38] A broadside with this decree is extant at the Lilly Library, Indiana University, Bloomington. I owe the communication of a Xerox copy of it to my friend, Professor Edward M. Wilson, of the University of Cambridge, England.

[39] François Thomas Marie de Baculard d'Arnaud, *Rosalía o la joven seducida*, trad. *por* L. P. (Madrid, 1797). See José F. Montesinos, *Introducción a una historia de la novela en España, en el siglo XIX*, 2d ed. (Madrid, 1966), p.160; and *Rosalie, anecdote* [1775], in *Oeuvres d'Arnaud, III, Les épreuves du sentiment* (Paris, 1815), pp.432–522. Of *Les mille et une heure, contes péruviens*, apparently from the pen of Thomas Simon Gueulette, I have consulted the first edition (Amsterdam, 1733), 2 vols. of [10]–372 and 384pp. There are also other editions, of different places, dated 1734, 1759, and 1782.

ing from the 1740's to the 1790's, shows that the ideas of the Enlightenment were harbored by the editors of the gazettes and the writers who contributed to them; that these men conceived it to be their function to supplement the activities of the schools in spreading modern philosophy among the cultured reading public; and that until the very end of the century this was not only permitted but fostered by the authorities (the list of subscribers to the *Mercurio Peruano,* for example [see its January 6, 1793, issue among others] includes the King in Madrid, and in Peru the Vice-Roy, bishops, magistrates, canons, and other public and church officials, as well as a number of private citizens). It is a fact that must be understood, however, that at least the public expression of enlightened ideas did not go beyond the limits allowed by Catholic orthodoxy, limits that were by this time quite wide. We saw that a rationalist tradition could be perceived in Spanish America throughout the sixteenth and seventeenth centuries for, within that orthodoxy, the thread of reason, natural reason, right reason, was conceived to be a gift of God to man for the latter's appropriate use. We have also seen that in the eighteenth century the recognition of reason and experience as the foundations of philosophical knowledge, education, polity, and policy, for the common utility of the rational commonwealth and the state, could be propounded on the basis of that Catholic tradition, reinforced now by the new learning; and that it could be so propounded precisely because, as the *Mercurio Peruano* of June 16, 1791, quoted above stated, "our Will and our Reason joined by a single principle" of divine guidance could accept it.

How far in the ways of modernization of Spanish American thought and life this Christian Enlightenment could go is not difficult to document. Recently I happened to be reading a volume published in Lima in 1812 in memory and honor of Don Vicente Morales Duárez. It contains his biography, the description of the funeral services celebrated in the Cathedral of Lima by order and at the expense of the city's municipality on November 7, 1812, and the text of the funeral oration pronounced by the Magisterial Canon. Morales was born in Lima in 1755, in an aristocratic family. Educated first at the Royal Seminary of St. Toribio, he was then selected to be among the first pupils of the new Convictorio de San Carlos, where "the happy revolution of our literature" was to be carried out. Trained later in civil and canon law, he was appointed by different vice-roys to a number of important official positions, and to several chairs at the University. He was also a member of the "Sociedad de Amantes del País." Having traveled to Spain in 1810, he became a member for Lima of the Cádiz Cortes (of that "August Congress," the "Sovereign National Congress"). In the Cortes he was chosen to be a member of the commission that wrote the text of the constitution of 1812, and a Vice-President of the Parliament from November 1810 to March 24, 1812, when he was elected its President. Unfortunately, he died a few days later, on April 2. He is described in his obituary in terms fitting an enlightened man: he was a "genio benéfico," characterized by his "distinguido aprecio a la sabiduría," a man "útil a la sociedad." And he learned to be all this, as I mentioned before, in the College of San Carlos of Lima, where

> by superior command it was endeavored to improve our plans of study by means of promoting a more fine and delicate taste, of banishing the vain subtleties and the arbitrary systems that had before, in great part, occupied the schools to the neglect of useful knowledge. To this purpose it became necessary to introduce in these schools the mathematical sciences, and a solid and luminous philosophy, conservative of the ancient truths and productive of new ones dictated by experimentation, mechanics, and calculus; a healthier morality; a serious and majestic theology, cleansed of the aridity and strange argumentations that had so irritated the critical temper of a Vives, a Cano, and so many others, a theology illuminated by the lights of Scripture, Tradition, and History, comprehensive of Dogma and Antiquity; the legitimate laws of the Church; its true discipline; the rights of man, the privileges of the people, and the authority of the sovereign.

"Los derechos del hombre, los fueros del pueblo y la autoridad del soberano."[40] When these words could be preached in the metropolitan church of Lima, in the presence of the Vice-Roy, the Audiencia, the Archbishop, the Municipal Cabildo, the University, the constituted bodies, and the people, it must be realized that the ideas that fostered the concepts of independence and liberty in the nineteenth century had not been born *a nihilo* or in secret: the Spanish American eighteenth century, combining the tradition of "las luces" with the novelties of the Enlightenment, had done its work well.

[40] *Honores patrios consagrados a la tierna memoria del Señor Don Vicente Morales y Duárez, Presidente del augusto congreso de Cortes, por el Excmo. Cabildo de esta capital de Lima, en VII de Noviembre de 1812* (Lima, 1812), lii-52pp.; see pp.8-9, 13-14.

# VIII

# Félix Varela and Liberal Thought

## LUIS LEAL

Félix Varela (1788–1853) is the first modern Cuban thinker. Unlike other Cubans, for instance José Martí, Varela is hardly known outside of his own country. Only the Cubans themselves have been concerned enough to read his works and write about his philosophy. His contributions to the development of Latin American liberal thought have been ignored; if the histories of Spanish American philosophy and the histories of the essay are examined, it is discovered that Varela is dismissed with a sentence or two.

Cuban critics, on the other hand, have not forgotten Varela. Rather, they have rediscovered his importance in the history of ideas, not only philosophical but also political. As early as 1878 the Cuban José Ignacio Rodríguez, writing in Washington and New York, published the first biography of Varela, reproducing some of his articles, letters, and speeches, which otherwise would have been lost.[1]

A study of the philosophical reforms introduced by Varela cannot be made without mentioning the preparatory work done in Mexico by Juan Bautista Díaz de Gamarra (1745–1783) and

---

[1] José Ignacio Rodríguez, *Vida del Presbítero Don Félix Varela* (New York, 1878).

in Cuba by Varela's own teachers, José Agustín Caballero and Bernardo O'Gaván. These men represent the pioneers in the revolt against Scholasticism in Latin American thought. Gamarra, born in Mexico, received his doctorate at the University of Pisa, where he became acquainted with the new philosophy. Back in Mexico, he published in 1774 his *Elementa recentioris philosophiae* (*Elements of Modern Philosophy*), in which he declares that the philosopher should eagerly investigate the truth without adhering to any sect, be it that of Aristotle, Plato, Leibniz, or Newton.[2] He should pursue the truth without acknowledging any authority. Antonio Caso, commenting upon this statement of principles, has said: "Here we have the highest devotion to the liberty of thought expressed in the classrooms of the Colonial university."[3] In 1781 Gamarra published, under the pseudonym Juan Bendiaga, his *Errores del entendimiento humano* (*Errors of Human Understanding*), and it is known that his works definitely influenced Varela, for in 1840 he wrote to a friend: "I can affirm that when I studied philosophy at the College of San Carlos in Havana I was a *cousiano* [a follower of Cousin], as were all the students of my illustrious teacher José Agustín Caballero, who always defended pure intellectual ideas, following in the steps of Jacquier and Gamarra."[4]

It is not known if Varela actually read Gamarra himself or learned about his ideas through his teacher Caballero, who used Gamarra's book. Caballero represents, in Cuba, the point of transition between Scholasticism and the new philosophy. He did not, however, break away completely from Scholasticism, although the title of his notes, written in 1797, was *Eclectic*

[2] J. B. Díaz de Gamarra y Dávalos, *Elementos de filosofía moderna,* ed. Bernavé Navarro (Mexico City, 1963), Part II, Chap.III.

[3] Freely translated from the Spanish: "¡He aquí la más alta consagración de la libertad de pensamiento en las aulas de la Universidad de la Colonia!" (*México; apuntamientos de cultura patria* [Mexico City, 1943], p.45).

[4] This letter was first published by José Manuel Mestre in his monograph *De la filosofía en la Habana* (Havana, 1862). This essay and letter may be found in José Manuel Mestre, *Obras,* introducción por Lolo de la Torriente (Havana, 1965), pp.177–260; quotation, p.240. The letter may also be found in Rodríguez, *Vida,* pp.337–46.

*Philosophy.* He was, however, the first one to introduce reforms in the teaching of philosophy in Cuban universities.[5]

Caballero's reforms were continued by Bernardo O'Gaván, with whom Valera completed his study of philosophy. O'Gaván rejected Cousin's ideas and praised those of Locke and Condillac. His articles of 1808 in the newspaper *La Aurora*, reproduced by Mexican periodicals, were condemned by the Inquisition. Varela, in the same letter of 1840, says: "Mr. O'Gaván, who succeeded him [Caballero], and with whom I completed my course in philosophy, changed this doctrine [Cousin's doctrine], adopting what today, in fashionable terms, they call *sensualismo*, which I, who succeeded him [O'Gaván], always taught, although without so much *aparato*."[6]

Varela succeeded O'Gaván in the teaching of philosophy at the University in 1811 and immediately set out to reform the courses by introducing Descartes's ideas and abandoning Scholasticism. His first *Elenco* was printed in 1812, and it served as an outline for the teaching of the subject. This pamphlet has been called "the first essay on modern philosophy by a Cuban writer."[7] The *Elenco*, lost until 1873, when Bachiller y Morales found a copy in New York City, is made up of 226 propositions and is written in Latin. Proposition 13 states that the Cartesian method should always be admitted, and Proposition 14 that the best philosophy is the eclectic. In the propositions regarding the physical sciences it is stated that experience and reason are the only sources of knowledge in the sciences.[8]

This *Elenco* served as the basis for the writing of the *Institutiones philosophiae eclecticae (Principles of Eclectic Philosophy)*, a work in four volumes, the first two, in Latin, having appeared

---

5 See Mestre, *Obras*, pp.181–83. Also A. Hernández Travieso, *Varela y la reforma filosófica en Cuba* (Havana, 1942), pp.36–39. Caballero's notes on eclectic philosophy were never published.

6 Rodríguez, *Vida*, p.341; about O'Gaván see Hernández Travieso, *Varela*, pp.42–46.

7 Rodríguez, *Vida*, p.18.

8 *Ibid.*

in 1812.[9] The third and fourth volumes, written in Spanish, appeared in 1813 and 1814, respectively. This book gave the death blow to the teaching of Scholastic philosophy in Cuba. In the academic year 1813–1814 Latin was discarded as the language of the classroom. The natural sciences were taught for the first time in Spanish, using the experimental method. Thus Varela precedes other thinkers in Latin America, as the reforms introduced by Juan Crisóstomo Lafinur in the Argentine began in 1819, and the same can be said of other countries.

Varela's first work on philosophy was to be followed by his *Lecciones de filosofía* (1818) and his *Miscelánea filosófica* (1819), both written in Spanish.[10] In the last one Varela reaffirms his opposition to Scholasticism and his belief in the experimental sciences. "There is no other way," he says, "except to proceed by observation of the facts, examining with attention the relations, and having great care in forming ideas that contain exact elements, and trying not to alter those ideas while formulating our deductions" (p. 37). It is interesting to note that Varela, like the contemporary behaviorists, believed that in order to think one must make use of signs. He said:

> In the present state of our knowledge, all acquired through sensations, and closely attached to signs, it is impossible to think without their help. No matter what effort we may make to exclude them, we are not able to do it, and experience proves that whenever we think, it seems to us that we hear ourselves talk, and often we pronounce the words aloud without being conscious of it, and that's why it is said that *we speak to ourselves*. From this it is deducted that to think is the same as to use signs, and to think well is to use signs correctly.[11]

[9] Volume I of this work, *Lógica*, has been translated by Antonio Regalado González and published in a bilingual edition: *Instituciones de filosofía ecléctica* (Havana, 1952).

[10] The fifth edition of the *Lecciones de filosofía*, in two volumes, was published by the Editorial de la Universidad de la Habana in 1961. A new edition of the *Miscelánea filosófica*, with a "Prólogo" by Medardo Vitier, was published by the same house in 1944.

[11] *Miscelánea filosófica*, pp. 55–56.

This book also contains an essay on the doctrines of Kant, perhaps the first one on the German philosopher by a Latin American writer. No less interesting is his essay on patriotism, one of the finest pages of Varela.

Hernández Travieso has expressed very well the transition in Cuban philosophy from Scholasticism to *sensualismo*:

> We shall consider Caballero as the necessary link between Scholasticism and the new ideas, without breaking definitely with tradition, which language he uses in his text, and O'Gaván as the first who broke with the medieval-theological version of Aristotle in a conclusive way, to the point of having defied, in spite of being a clergyman, the powerful Tribunal of the Holy Inquisition. In Varela we see how the early attack of Caballero and the passionate one of O'Gaván upon Scholasticism become a vocation. He will become the philosophy teacher of future Cubans.[12]

It must be observed that although Varela follows, in the formulation of his philosophical concepts, the ideas expressed by Locke in his *Essay Concerning Human Understanding* (1666), Condillac's *Traité des sensations* (1754), and Testutt de Tracy's *Eléments d'ideologie* (1804), he does not follow them as to religious ideas. Varela, an ordained priest, managed to retain his religious beliefs and never broke away from the church. Nevertheless, his philosophy undermined the religious beliefs of his disciples, as they paid no attention to his declarations of faith. At the same time, his ideas prepared the way for political independence. Varela has often been called the precursor of Cuban independence.[13]

Félix Varela, like most of the Latin American *pensadores* of the period of independence, was interested not only in philosophy and science, but also in social and political affairs. His contributions in this aspect of Cuban life are just as important

---

12 *Ibid.*, p.46.

13 See the "Prólogo" of Roberto Agramonte to the 1940 edition of the *Lecciones de filosofía*. Also Vitier's "Prólogo" to the *Miscelánea filosófica*.

那 those in the field of ideas. In Spain, in 1820, General Riego's liberal pronouncement brought about the implementation of the forgotten liberal constitution of 1812. By royal decree special courses were to be established to teach the people the meaning of the constitution. In Havana Father Varela was designated to teach this new course; he began his classes in 1821 and had about 100 students. This class came to be known as "the class of liberty, of the rights of man, of national guarantees and the regeneration of Spain." His notes for the course were published the same year under the title *Observaciones sobre la constitución política de la monarquía española.*[14] In the first observation, titled "Soberanía," Varela says: "To be sure, all men, by nature, have equal rights and equal liberties" (p. 11). His course was so successful that the following year Varela was appointed, with his friends Tomás Gener and Leonardo Santos Suárez, as representative to the Spanish Cortes for the period 1822–1823.

Varela's activities in the Cortes during 1823 demonstrated that he was a great patriot and a man of vision. He participated actively in the debates and presented several projects, all of them motivated by his desire to save Spain from disaster. He presented, among others, proposals for the reorganization of the clergy, for the abolition of slavery,[15] and for the reorganization of the American provinces. He was, of course, defeated. Slavery was a profitable, if degrading, business for the Spanish government, and recognizing the independence of the American provinces was in 1823 out of the question. Defending his thesis for the granting of independence, Varela wrote: "No matter what happens, Spain can only lose what she cannot keep . . . but if she recognizes their independence, she will not lose their friendship. . . . If Spain waits, she can only benefit other countries, as she will

[14] This book has been published by the Editorial de la Universidad de la Habana (1944) with a "Prólogo" by Rafael García Bárcena.

[15] "Memoria que demuestra la necesidad de extinguir la esclavitud de los negros en la Isla de Cuba, atendiendo a los intereses de sus propietarios," Félix Varela y Morales, *Ideario cubano* (Havana, 1953), pp.53–61.

forego all cooperation with [Spanish] America."[16] The members of the Cortes decided that there was no reason why they should consider Varela's proposal. Soon Ferdinand VII was to abolish the Cortes, and the liberal members fled to Seville and from there to Cádiz. Here some of them, including Varela, signed a document, proposed by Alcalá Galiano, declaring Ferdinand incapable of governing and replacing him with a *Consejo de Regencia*. All those who signed the document were condemned to death in absentia. With the help of the English, Varela and others were able to take refuge in Gibraltar. From there they came to the United States, arriving in New York December 17, 1823. After a short time Varela went to Philadelphia, where he was to remain for some time. He was never to leave the United States; he died in St. Augustine, Florida, in 1853.

While in Spain Varela did not advocate that Cuba be granted independence. Following in the steps of his teacher Caballero, he was in favor of autonomy for the island, and in 1823 prepared a *Proyecto de gobierno autónomo*,[17] a document that was ignored by the Spanish government. As a result of his experiences in the Cortes, Varela changed his attitude and ideas and became a fervent advocate of independence for Cuba. To promote this cause he published the periodical *El Habanero* in Philadelphia, considered to be Cuba's first revolutionary paper.

In Philadelphia Varela was not alone in his fight for Cuban independence. There he found a group of liberals who sympathized with his ideas—the Philadelphia of that time was a center of conspirators.[18] Among others working with Varela, or sympa-

16 *El Habanero, papel político, científico y literario*. Estudio preliminar por Enrique Gay Calbó y Emilio Roig de Leuchsenring (Havana, 1945), "Prólogo," p.xxi. For the whole text see *Ideario cubano*, pp.73–77.

17 This document was first published by José María Chacón y Calvo in the *Homenaje a Varona* (Havana, 1935), and reproduced by García Bárcena in the *Observaciones*. It is also included in the *Ideario cubano*, pp.65–69.

18 See Vicente Lloréns Castillo, *Liberales y románticos, una emigración española en Inglaterra (1823–1834)* (Mexico City, 1954), pp.248–51. Ernest E. Moore, "José María de Heredia in the United States and Mexico," *Modern Language Notes*, LXV (1950), 41–46. Luis Leal, "*Jicotencal*, primera novela histórica en castellano," *Revista Ibero-americana*, XXV (1960), 9–31.

thizing with his ideas, were his two friends, Tomás Gener and Leonardo Santos Suárez, who had come with him from Gibraltar; José de la Luz Caballero, nephew of Varela's teacher; the writer Domingo del Monte; the poet José María Heredia; the restless Ecuadorian Vicente Rocafuerte; the Colombian man of letters José Fernández Madrid; the Venezuelan Nicanor Bolet Peraza, and the Argentinian José Antonio Miralla. They all published original works, or translations into Spanish, either in Philadelphia or New York. Varela himself translated Jefferson's *Manual of Parliamentary Practice* and Davy's *Elements of Chemistry Applied to Agriculture*.[19]

Of the seven numbers published of *El Habanero* three appeared in Philadelphia between 1823 and 1824, and the last four in New York between 1824 and 1826. The last number, without place of publication or date, is unknown, as not a single copy has been found, either in Cuba or the United States.[20] In spite of the severe censorship in the island, Varela managed to put the paper in the hands of his friends in Cuba, where its effect, because it was the first to advocate independence, was sensational. The Spanish government denounced the paper, and a royal order was issued to prohibit its circulation.[21] They even tried to assassinate the publisher, an act that Varela condemned in the strongest terms. In a supplement to the third number of *El Habanero* (1825) he wrote: "In La Habana the government's only worry seems to be to persecute my poor *Habanero* and to send a man to assassinate its author. I have just heard that as a consequence of the effect caused by the second number they have called for a donation to pay a man to assassinate me. *¡Miserables! ¿Creen destruir la verdad asesinando al que la dice?*" (p. 152).

Varela is at his best in the pages of the *Habanero*, fighting for a cause he sincerely believed to be right, expressing his ideals with

---

[19] See Hernández Travieso, *Varela*, p.122.

[20] See Enrique Gay-Calbó, "Varela y *El Habanero*," in *El Habanero* (Havana, 1945), pp.xxix–xxxi.

[21] Varela reproduced this royal order, with comments, in *El Habanero*, I, 6 (1825); see 1945 edition, pp.203–206.

fervor, and writing in a style that, without being oratorical, is very effective in moving the reader to act in favor of the cause he is advocating. Here are found some of his best essays; from the first, "Máscaras políticas," to the last, "Consecuencias de la rendición del Castillo de San Juan de Ulúa respecto de la Isla de Cuba," they reflect the author's liberal ideas, humanism, and patriotism. He did not hate Spaniards *per se*. He hated only those who were against liberty, against human rights, against freedom of expression. With good reason the essays of *El Habanero* have been compared to the tolling of the bells that woke the Cubans from their colonial slumber.

Half a century was to pass before José Martí would take up where Varela left off, also, like Varela, fighting for Cuban independence with that powerful arm, the written word. But the initiator of this chain of events was Félix Varela, whose liberal ideas became an inspiration for later Cuban thinkers.

# IX

# Primitivism in Latin American Fiction

## CARMELO VIRGILLO

L'enfant de la nature abhorre l'esclavage;
Implacable ennemi de toute authorité,
Il s'indigne du joug; la contrainte l'outrage;
Liberté c'est son vœu; son cri c'est liberté.
Au mépris des liens de la société,
Il réclame en secret son antique apanage.

*Les Éleuthéromanes*—1772[1]

These lines, written over two centuries ago, on the eve of the French Revolution, upheld the Indian as the product of a happy primeval society—a tangible dream for the freedom-starved European who longed to cut the bonds of social injustice. Today it is difficult to think of anybody who has been more abused and enjoys less autonomy than the American Indian, who, far from having impressed anything on the white man, remains, no doubt, the least recognized and understood inhabitant of the New World. This tragic fact is particularly true of most of Latin America, where the primitive who once was absolute master of his surroundings is today either extinct or excluded, a stranger in his own country. Ironically, his survival depends largely, if

---

[1] Paul Hazard, *European Thought in the Eighteenth Century* (New Haven, 1954), p.389.

not exclusively, on his giving up the little land still in his possession and on his merging into the mainstream of modern, urban-
minded civilization which refuses to understand the primitive's
plight for his freedom and independence.

In spite of the efforts of today's writers to present a realistic
picture of the Indian, most of us still rely on the stereotyped
version fashioned by nineteenth-century romantic literature,
and this, in general, has been the downfall of the oldest native
American.

After briefly outlining the earliest misconceptions surround-
ing the primitive, and discussing the role France played in creating the myth of the Noble Savage, we shall examine four
representative romantic Latin American novels in an effort to
show this distorted image and the consequences of such a distortion. The novels are José de Alencar's *O Guarani* (1857) and
*Iracema* (1865, Brazil), Juan León Mera's *Cumandá* (1879,
Ecuador), and Zorrilla de San Martín's *Tabaré* (1886, Uruguay).

As far as we know, the misconceptions about the Indian date
back to 1492, when Columbus returned to Spain with six tribal
dignitaries dressed in full regalia and presented this stereotyped
group as the definitive image of the native inhabitant of the New
World. In the ensuing years, the primitive was paraded through
Europe, where he came to be regarded as a real curiosity, while
reports from the New World were so subjective and far-fetched
as to create more confusion than anything else about the Indian.[2] France, from the start, took a special interest in the primitive, and soon the poets of the Pléiade were singing the praises
of the "enfant de la Nature," idealizing him but not really shed-
ding any light on him or his society. Montaigne, however, was
to take a more realistic look at the primitive, and, after meeting
some Tupinambá Indians from Brazil at the court of Charles
IX in Rouen, was so impressed with their wisdom and simplicity
that he came to regard the American aborigine as the epitome of
instinctive goodness, which he claimed resulted from an ideal

---

[2] For further considerations on this topic, see Peter Farb, "The American Indian: A Portrait in Limbo," *Saturday Review*, October 12, 1968, p.27.

free society close to God because it was close to Nature. Thus began the myth of the Noble Savage, and there are those who report that Montaigne, inspired by his encounter with the savages and by their account of society in the wilderness, was to trace a clear outline of what was later defined as "class struggle" and "social revolution."[3]

It wasn't, however, until the Enlightenment that the primitive and his society became the center of much interest, particularly in France, where, by the middle of the eighteenth century, the original sketch of Montaigne had become the blueprint of a real social revolution in the works of the enlightened *philosophes*. In Rousseau's *Discours* (1750) and three years later in his *Discours sur l'inégalité parmi les hommes* the primitive appears definitely established as the embodiment of natural goodness and representative of an ideal equalitarian society from which the white civilized man had much to learn. Obviously, what Rousseau really advocated was not that civilized man adopt the savage and his society but that the distorted product of an unjust, unnatural society become undistorted, keeping all the virtues of civilization but at the same time returning to the simplicity of the primitive. Unfortunately, Rousseau was taken literally, and a generation of *éleuthéromanes*, or nature maniacs, came into being. As we all know, many of these fled the shores of Europe to seek shelter in the world of the savage, only to return to their native countries shocked and disillusioned by cold reality. As I see it, the situation did not become critical for the primitive until this disillusionment affected the arts, particularly literature. We see this in Chateaubriand, who, upon his return from North America, disenchanted with the natives and with the perils of his journey to the wilderness, refashioned in his works both the primitive and his environment to fit his neurotic self in search of an imaginary world. Thus begins the systematic destruction of the oldest native American. For, too intent on recreating the beauty of the exotic settings in which he had wished to become lost but had failed, and set on forget-

[3] *A Literatura no Brasil* (Rio de Janeiro, 1955), I, No.2, 664–65.

ting the primitive he had actually met, Chateaubriand turned the native into a prop whose main purpose was to highlight the scenery and give vent to the writer's "mal du siècle." In short, Rousseau's happy Indian had been replaced by a sad would-be Indian whose only real identity lay in his feathers and moccasins.

In American primitivist fiction this image is paramount in the works of James Fenimore Cooper and other Indianist writers inspired by him in whose hands the Noble Savage becomes the tool of sentimentalism. Conforming to romantic tradition, the primitive is cast as a rebel fighting the oppressing forces of civilization, namely the white man, who wants to enslave him and deprive him of his natural freedom.[4] As one might have expected, the Indian hero is fashioned after his white European counterpart, thus conforming to the white man's standards of valor, intelligence, and physical prowess. However, alongside this "noble" savage there appears a "savage" savage who couples the worst elements of the white villain of romantic European tradition with the least desirable traits of his own race. He is deceitful, animalistic, ignorant of the white man's ways, and unwilling to bow to the *conquistador*. He is labeled as a bad Indian, therefore a nonentity.

In the same tradition of his North American brother, the Latin American primitive appears in nineteenth-century fiction as possessing the instinctive natural goodness attributed to him by Rousseau and the fatalistic, hypersensitive, and quasi-pathological personality created for him by Chateaubriand. Unreal as this fictional primitive might sound, he fulfilled an urgent need for the Latin American countries, which had just achieved independence from Spain and Portugal. A national literature had to be created to unite the indigenous elements in each country. In view of the fact that no one had been subjected more to the treachery of the European colonists than the Indian, he was the logical choice for a symbol of national identity

4 George Ross Ridge, *The Hero in French Romantic Literature* (Athens, 1959), pp.97–98.

in the struggle against the foreign invader. What better opportunity to clear the conscience of the wealthy oligarchy and forge a national tradition at the same time than to turn the clock on the mistreatment of the primitive and place the blame for this on the founding fathers—the European *conquistadores* who had started abusing the primitive centuries before! Ironically, it was the powerful land-owning intellectuals of Latin America, converted for the occasion into romantic writers, who brought the Indian skeleton out of the closet hoping to redeem him artistically. The result was the creation of an unbelievable Indian who might be called a combination Tonto and René.

Thus a literature was born filled with disconsolate, frustrated primitives whose main problem seemed to stem from their inability to mix with the white race. This sentimentalism appealed, no doubt, to the sensitive feelings of the lady of the mansion who would while away her time enthralled by heart-warming tales of ill-fated friendships between Indians and whites. She had plenty of time to do this, for in her household and out in the fields numerous Indians slaved away to provide her with wealth and leisure. In Brazil many hearts among the land-grabbing upper classes must have been stirred by José de Alencar's sentimental novels filled with touching scenes of brotherly love between white Portuguese noblemen and their Indian companions. Taking a closer look at this relationship one notices, however, that the Noble Savage as portrayed in these works, though physically compatible with his natural environment, is otherwise fashioned after the white man's conception of the romantic hero. In short, on the outside he may be a primitive, but inwardly he is a European with all the attributes of white nobility. In *O Guarani*, Indian Peri, a handsome son of the wilderness, saves the life of Cecília, daughter of the Portuguese *fidalgo* Dom Antônio de Mariz, who therefore befriends the Indian because down deep Peri is a nobleman in the body of a savage.[5] On another occasion the Indian's intelligence is praised: vigorous as

[5] José de Alencar, *O Guarani* (Rio de Janeiro, 1964), p.69.

the vegetation of his native soil, says Alencar, Peri is guided by common sense and prudence worthy of civilized man.[6] After another act of supreme altruism, Dom Antônio is carried away by his enthusiasm and tells Peri that his deeds would classify him as a veritable *fidalgo*, then throws his arms around the Indian and assures him that his savage heart should not feel ashamed to beat over the heart of a Portuguese nobleman.[7] As can be seen here, contrary to the enlightened man's concept that true nobility, symbolizing virtue, comes naturally to the unspoiled savage, it would appear that it is instead an attribute associated with civilized man in general and white European aristocracy in particular. At best all the primitive can expect is to equal it.

If in the romantic Indianist novel, supposedly fostering national unity, the author's intention was to advocate a harmonious coexistence of all the inhabitants of his country, no trace of this can be seen in the four works representing the very best in their genre. Definitely not in *O Guarani*, where Indian Peri is portrayed as a misanthrope who prefers to live a sad and lonely existence in a cabin near the white settlement of Dom Antônio. Peri saves Cecília from the hostile Indians at whose hands her family perishes but declines her invitation to go live with her in Rio, certain that he could not survive in the world of civilized man. In *Iracema* Martim marries an Indian maiden and settles in her world. He soon discovers, however, that the wilderness and the accompanying bucolic life are not meant for a civilized Portuguese. He returns to civilization with his child and his Indian companion, proving that if the Indian cannot get along in the white man's world, the same is true of civilized man, who has no alternative but to put up with the ills of his complex white world.

In Harriet Beecher Stowe's *Uncle Tom's Cabin*, happiness for the American Negro is defined as being sheltered by a devout

6 *Ibid.*, p.149.
7 *Ibid.*, p.173.

white patriarch who teaches him how to sing religious hymns, behave like a child, and learn what is good for him. Thus Thomas Paine's *The Rights of Man* is reinterpreted to mean the rights of the nonwhite to imitate the white. What started as a sentimental novel has come to mold the Negro's image in the eyes of the majority of white Americans. May we suggest that the Latin American counterpart, the romantic Indianist novel, did just as great an injustice to the primitive south of the border.

In Juan León Mera's *Cumandá*, one is shown what happiness means to the Záparo tribesmen inhabiting the *reducción* of Fray Orozco. The once-proud Indian warriors appear as a community of zombies who have switched from an Indian *cacique* to blind obedience to a white Dominican friar of whom they must ask permission before they can take one step. As we recall, attending pagan tribal festivities for the Záparos becomes a major issue until Orozco's son Carlos decides to attend and the Indians are allowed to go. Let us remember that such Dominican *reducciones* were a very poor substitute for the Jesuit Latin American utopias which Spain and Portugal had seen fit to eliminate for a number of reasons. Foremost, it would seem, was the threat which the enlightened Christianity of the Society of Jesus posed to those two powers who, far from wishing to educate the savage and bring about his self-sufficiency, preferred instead to make him dependent on them to better exploit him.

According to the pattern of the primitivist novel in Latin America, the difference between a human being and an Indian is almost always determined by the savage's acceptance of the orthodox Christian faith, which will raise him from the rank of *tigre* to that of *hermano*. This is not really saying that he is elevated to the status of the white man. In military terms one might call an Indian convert a noncommissioned officer. Spain's destiny, claims Zorrilla de San Martín in *Tabaré*, was to fight the savage monster that lurked in the New World and bring Christianity into the wilderness.[8] *Tabaré* is outstanding among

[8] Zorrilla de San Martín, *Tabaré* (Barcelona, 1927), pp.58–59.

his tribesmen, not because he is a blue-eyed mestizo, but more because deep inside his savage body there beats a Christian heart, for his white mother was a Christian. Likewise, Cumandá's Christian faith sets her apart from the Indians who raised her, and she remains unbelievably pure and angelical in the midst of the wildest savages a writer's mind could possibly conceive.

Christian salvation invariably serves as the *deus ex machina* of the sentimentalist novel, providing the author with the opportunity of gathering the loose ends of his plot while carrying the melodrama to its inevitable climax. In *Iracema* Martim, realizing that becoming an Indian warrior has brought down a divine curse upon him and his Indian bride, who eventually dies, rejoins Christianity more fervently than ever, and for good measure converts even his good Indian friend Poti. In *O Guarani* Peri accepts conversion to Christianity on the spot in order to escape from his master's burning home and be allowed to carry Cecília with him to safety. Christianity plays an important role also in the dénouement of *Cumandá*. The heroine, really Fray Orozco's daughter Julia, loses her life in a horrible sacrifice while Orozco, whose timely arrival could save her, gives top priority to converting Indian Tongana, spending precious hours to save his soul.

As one can see, the Enlightenment's Noble Savage—instinctively good, naturally free, and socially independent—is reshaped in Latin American fiction to fit the image of an animal on trial whose redemption depends on serving God in Heaven and white man on earth, being protected and guided by both. Having come to this conclusion, one naturally assumes that under such tutelage the Indian lived happily ever after.

In much the same fashion as television and movie writers nowadays create productions filled with Negro neurosurgeons and Oxford-educated Indians, Latin American landowner-writers filled their books with noble, disproportionate Indian chiefs suffering from *mal du siècle* and not necessarily social injustice. This expedient is an easy way out because it allows the sentimentalist writer to blame everything on fate without having to suggest any solution to the racial conflicts that were the core of his plots. Moreover, the writer points to the revolt of the oppressed—the primitive—as a source of divine as well as human punishment, thus advocating the status quo in a genre that should suggest revolutionary measures. This is evidenced in *Cumandá,* in which the 1790 Indian uprising in Ecuador is seen by Mera as having brought down the wrath of God upon thousands of innocent people, among whom are some of his characters. From this it would appear evident that the Latin American Indian is doomed and his fate considered inevitable and quietly accepted as such.

If one examines closely the ill-fated, marked-for-death protagonists of a romantic primitivist novel one cannot help but notice the following cliché: to be an Indian, to have any Indian blood, or to become involved with an Indian engenders cataclysmic results, as it brings down divine wrath. In reality, this can only be interpreted as the social stigma placed upon the primitive by the writer. It is quite interesting to note how consistent this cliché is in Latin American primitivist fiction. Indian Peri's love for Cecília causes her death as God suddenly sends down a horrible deluge that drowns the ill-fated lovers just as they are about to fulfill their dream. In *Iracema* Martim's love for the Indian vestal is the cause of the near extermination of her family as well as the cause of her own death.

If love between the members of two cultures—the Indian and the white—leads to disaster, no better fated is the fruit of that love: the mestizo. While in romantic European literature the hero is ordinarily forced by fate to pay for an unintentional yet unpardonable sin, in Latin American romanticism this victim of fate is the mestizo, and his unforgivable sin is his mistake of racial integration. As we see, the primitivist who claims to be writing a national epic based on the union of the two cultures, the European and Indian, is actually doing no more nor less than painting a bleak picture of such a union. It would appear

from this genre that the Latin American hybrid race has resulted from an unfortunate set of circumstances which could
not be avoided or helped since they were predetermined by destiny. While on the one hand the North American James Fenimore Cooper does not try to conceal his disapproval of racial
integration, the Latin American primitivist shows greater sub-
tlety in dealing with this issue. According to Leslie A. Fiedler,
Cooper rejects the idea of marriage even in Heaven between
white Cora and Indian Uncas in *The Last of the Mohicans*, thus
making his position quite clear.[9] Hypocritically, Cooper's Latin
American counterpart will strongly endorse the union of his
racially incompatible lovers after death, although seldom if ever
allowing them to marry on earth. This is evidenced in *O Guarani*
where Isabel, the sensual, illegitimate mestizo daughter of Dom
Antônio, shows the indelible traits of her race: she is madly in
love with a white nobleman, Dom Álvaro. When he reciprocates
this feeling, he is immediately punished by José de Alencar,
who sends him off to die at the hands of non-Christian Indians.
Isabel then chooses to poison herself and lies down next to
Álvaro to achieve in death what was impossible in life. Dom
Antônio also pays with his life for having loved the Indian
maiden who was Isabel's mother. Similarly, Tabaré's blond,
blue-eyed mother dies as the result of her abduction and physical
union with the mighty Indian chief Caracé. Tabaré makes the
mistake of falling in love with a white girl, and this is enough to
bring upon him the usual curse that marks him for inevitable
death. In *Cumandá* the heroine dies as a result of her marriage
to Indian warrior Yahuarmaqui.

The fear of miscegenation seems to haunt the Latin American primitivist writer. Poorly concealed behind unfulfilled love,
this fear is evident in almost every plot and could not fool even
the least-aware reader. Death, however, is the writer's check
valve, and he uses it generously to prevent physical union from

[9] Leslie A. Fiedler, *Love and Death in the American Novel* (New York, 1960),
p.205.

occurring while he appropriately remains within the boundaries of romantic tradition. When Christianized Peri is finally alone in the jungle with his beloved Cecília, death surprises them in the form of a deluge which, with biblical implications, cleanses the evil which is about to be committed on earth. The pair die unfulfilled but pure. Julia Orozco also dies by water before her marriage to Yahuarmaqui is consummated. Mestizo Tabaré and Blanca will never be joined in marriage because a sword puts an end to Tabaré's life at the very moment when Blanca might have been able to make a plea for her noble savior. However, Tabaré is allowed to die in Blanca's arms in the presence of a sympathetic monk, which should be of some consolation to him. An unusual circumstance is employed in Alencar's *Iracema* to justify physical union between two races. Martim first implores Christ to save him from succumbing to the Indian maiden Iracema's passionate advances. When this fails to work Martim then begs the maiden herself to put him to sleep with her magic potion that can induce wishful dreams. This precursor of LSD eventually accomplishes what Martim's conscious mind would never have allowed.

Undoubtedly the Latin American primitivists all agree on the strong attraction between the Indian and the white man, and this is made obvious by the contrast between the physical characteristics of the lovers. To be sure, the white maidens are depicted more along the lines of Sir Walter Scott's fair lasses than the rugged, southern, dark-skinned Spanish and Portuguese belles. Peri is spellbound by the divine features of Cecília, the stereotyped white *conquistadora*—very blond, blue-eyed, and ethereal. For her he rejects his most beautiful Indian maidens and even leaves his mother. Isabel, half-Indian and quite dark, confesses that she envies Cecília's fair features and deep inside hates the Indian in herself, a hatred which she turns against Indian Peri. Peri, recognizing why he is hated, cannot help but hate her. By the same token, chief Yahuarmaqui chooses white Cumandá over hundreds of maidens to be his favorite wife. Writer Mera states openly that Cumandá's superior beauty sets her apart from her fellow tribesmen. Zorrilla de San Martín would have one believe that Tabaré feels attracted to Blanca because he sees in her the Virgin Mary–like image of his own mother. Actually, what the writer has in mind and is afraid to express is the plight of the unfortunate mestizo who would like to forget the Indian half of him and is desperately attracted to the fair race.

Reinforcing our proposition that the Noble Savage in romantic Latin American literature is but a mere artistic creation of little human consequence, Emilio Carilla states: "El indio aparece—literariamente—defendido, idealizado, pero no exactamente como ideal de vida o cultura."[10]

In short, the Indian is seen as a tool of the sentimentalist writer who uses the primitive as a bad copy of the white man. The Noble Savage's salvation, as nineteenth-century romantic Indianist fiction suggests, is seen as his adaptation to the world of his white master, whose characteristics he must inherit if he is to survive. For it is the Noble Savage who must conform to the distorted society of the European and not the other way around, as Montaigne and later the French encyclopedists advocated. To be sure, the corrupt and class-conscious society which the eighteenth-century *philosophes* condemned so vehemently appears to have been transplanted to the once-peaceful wilderness of the New World. The native American described by Diderot and his fellow encyclopedists as the "implacable ennemi de toute authorité" would appear in the works discussed in this paper as a subculture resigned by fate to play second fiddle to blond, blue-eyed *conquistadores*, envious of the master's white skin and desperate to lose its native traits. These traits, sentimentalist novelists would have one believe, the Noble Savage would gladly relinquish for the chance to be a little less dark, less pagan, less instinctive, less free, less natural, less Indian. The Noble Savage, as portrayed in Latin American primitivist fiction, is an

[10] Emilio Carilla, *El romanticismo en la América Hispánica* (Madrid, 1967), I, 159.

allegory rather than a human being of flesh and blood. He is an abstraction symbolizing both evil and virtue, as some fictional Indians are made out to be more savage than others, but always stereotyped and unreal. In the melée it is difficult to imagine what the Noble Savage is really like, and, since most of us have still to understand him as an individual with his own particular needs and desires, it is easier for us to keep on destroying him physically just as he has been destroyed artistically.

# X

# Concerning the Transmission and Dissemination of the Enlightenment in Brazil

## E. BRADFORD BURNS

THE ENLIGHTENMENT which swept across Europe in the eighteenth-century entered Portugal hesitantly during the first half of that century and more boldly in the latter half. The isolation characteristic of seventeenth-century Portugal broke down during the "enlightened century" as the Lusitanians entered into closer diplomatic, commercial, and intellectual contact with the rest of Europe, especially with England and France. Intrigued by the changes overtaking the rest of Europe, members of the Portuguese elite questioned some long-accepted concepts and reasoned new answers to old questions. In some cases clandestinely, in others openly, they read the works of those authors most associated with the ideas of the Enlightenment, d'Alembert, Condillac, Diderot, Helvétius, Kant, La Mettrie, Locke, Montesquieu, Rousseau, Smith, Voltaire, et al.[1] The frown of the censor

---

[1] Most writers on the intellectual history of eighteenth-century Portugal assert that the principal philosophers of the European Enlightenment had an eager reading public in Portugal. For example, see António Ferrão, *A Academia das Sciências de Lisboa* (Coimbra, 1923), pp.32 and 46; José Augusto França, *Lisboa Pombalina e o Iluminismo* (Lisbon, 1965), p.163. For one fascinating relationship between the Enlightenment in Portugal and in the United States, see the informative monograph of Richard Beale Davis, *The Abbé Correa in America, 1812–1820* (Philadelphia, 1955).

and the Inquisition failed to prevent the importation and reading of the latest books from abroad. Some Portuguese scholars have observed that the stronger the condemnation of a book by the censor the more eager were the curious to locate and read it.[2] In the last half of the eighteenth century at least six French bookdealers resided in Lisbon to cater to the tastes of the reading public.

Portuguese writers too reflected the spirit of criticism and inquiry and none better than Father Luís António Vernei of the Congregation of the Oratory.[3] In his principal work, *Verdadeiro Método de Estudar*, published in 1746, he scoffed at the Scholasticism dominant in Portugal and advocated a renovation of studies based on observation, experimentation, and questioning. His work stirred a heated controversy and served as a major impetus to the Portuguese cultural renaissance of the last half of the century. A second significant writer of the Portuguese Enlightenment was António Nunes Ribeiro Sanches, a physician obsessed with reforming education in Portugal. His *Cartas sobre a Educação da Mocidade*, first published in Paris in 1760, summarized his pedagogical philosophy: education should be

[2] For example, see António Ferrão, *A Academia*, p.46; and J. Lúcio de Azevedo, *O Marquês de Pombal e sua Época*, 2d ed. (Rio de Janeiro, 1922), p.341. There is evidence that the bookdealer Jorge Rey, a French national resident in Lisbon, ordered books from France in the 1770's and marked with an asterisk those works prohibited by the Inquisition so that they could be shipped to him in different covers. Angela Maria do Monte Barcelos da Gama, "Livreiros, Editores e Impressores em Lisboa no Século XVIII," *Arquivo de Bibliografia Portuguesa*, Ano XIII, Nos.49–52 (1967), p.59. See also Georges Bonnant, "Les Libraries du Portugal au XVIIIᵉ Siècle Vus à travers leurs Relations d'Affaires avec leurs Fournisseurs de Genève," *Arquivo de Bibliografia Portuguesa*, Ano VI, Nos.23–24 (1960), pp. 195–200. For an excellent intellectual history of Portugal in the eighteenth century, consult Hernani Cidade, *Lições de Cultura e Literatura Portuguesas*, Vol.II, *Da Reacção contra o Formalismo Seiscentista ao Advento do Romantismo* (Coimbra, 1968).

[3] The literature on Vernei is extensive. Two valuable short studies are: L. Cabral de Moncada, *Um 'Iluminista' Português do Século XVIII: Luiz António Verney* (São Paulo, 1941) and António Alberto de Andrade, *Vernei e a Filosofia Portuguesa* (Braga, 1946). Without doubt, the foremost study is the recent and lengthy *Vernei e a Cultura do seu Tempo* (Coimbra, 1965) by the above-mentioned António Alberto de Andrade.

lay, administered by the state, and based on "analytical reason."[4] It is a curious commentary on both Portugal and its Enlightenment that both of those intellectuals felt safer living abroad, although their books circulated in Portugal.

At least three events put Portugal in close harmony with the European Enlightenment: the foundation of the Royal Academy of Portuguese History in 1720, the reform of Coimbra University in 1772, and the establishment of the Academy of Sciences of Lisbon in 1779. On each successive occasion, the nation identified more closely and enthusiastically with broader European intellectual trends. The Academy of History founded by João V imitated French and Spanish academies.[5] It encouraged devotees of Clio to base their writing of the history of Portugal and its overseas conquests on primary sources. An entire school of historians emerged from the Academy—José Soares da Silva, José Barbosa Machado, António Caetano de Sousa, Diogo Barbosa Machado, *et al.*—well versed in the study of primary sources. Their extensive use of such material made them critical of previous historical interpretations and assertions.[6] The shaping of a critical mentality encouraged by the Academy contributed significantly to Portugal's intellectual development in the eighteenth century.

The omnipotent Portuguese prime minister, Sebastião José de Carvalho e Mello, better known by his title, the Marquês de Pombal, prepared the empire for educational innovations by expelling the Jesuits in 1759.[7] For two centuries they had dom-

---

[4] The most recent edition of *Cartas sobre a Educação da Mocidade* appears in António Nunes Ribeiro Sanches, *Obras*, I (Coimbra, 1959). Selections from the *Cartas* with annotations and a preface were published by Joaquim Ferreira (Oporto, n.d.). His long preface furnishes a meaty study of Ribeiro Sanches. The influence of Ribeiro Sanches on educational reform is well summarized in Rómulo de Carvalho, *História da Fundação do Colégio Real dos Nobres de Lisboa (1761–1772)* (Coimbra, 1959).

[5] The objectives of the Academy are clearly set forth in Vol.I of *Collecçam dos Documentos, Estatutos, e Memórias da Academia Real da História Portuguesa* (Lisbon, 1721).

[6] António Ferrão, *A Teoria da História* (Coimbra, 1922), p.305.

[7] A highly controversial figure in history, Pombal has been the subject of many

inated Portuguese education and imposed Scholasticism and classical texts on their students. In the mid-eighteenth century, they stood accused of—among other things—retarding Portugal's intellectual development. With their influence removed, Pombal hoped to invigorate and update studies in the manner suggested by both Vernei and Ribeiro Sanches. He implemented many of their suggestions in 1772 by reforming the ancient Coimbra University. He introduced Cartesian methods into the teaching of all subjects and substituted experiment and practice for dogmatic doctrine and speculation. He allocated funds to build a new observatory, a medical amphitheater, a botanical garden, and physics and chemistry laboratories. He hired the most intelligent men of the empire as professors and induced a number of Italian scholars to come to Coimbra. The philosophy of the French physiocrats enjoyed considerable popularity among the faculty.[8] Ideas of the Enlightenment radiated outward from Coimbra to distant parts of the far-flung Portuguese empire. Since there was no university overseas, any inhabitants of the colonies who desired advanced education had to go to Coimbra for it. There they imbibed contemporary European ideas, which they carried back home with them. In more than one respect, the reforms of Coimbra prepared the Lusitanian world for the Enlightenment.[9]

The idea of creating a scientific academy had circulated during the Pombaline period, but not until 1779, two years after the fall of the powerful prime minister, were the statutes of the Academy of Sciences of Lisbon approved. At its inaugural ses-

polemical biographies. Considered to be one of the best biographies is the previously mentioned *O Marquês de Pombal e sua Época* by J. Lúcio de Azevedo.

8 Moses Amzalak, "Les Doctrines Physiocratiques au XVIIIe et au Début du XIX Siècles au Portugal" in *Mélanges Économiques*, ed. René Gonnard (Paris, 1946), p.1 *et passim*. For an example of the influence of physiocrat ideas on the thought of one of the professors at Coimbra, consult José António de Sá, *Compêndio de Observaçöens que formão o plano de Viagem Politica e Filosófica, que se deve fazer dentro da Pátria* (Lisbon, 1783).

9 Manoel Cardozo, "Azeredo Coutinho and the Intellectual Ferment of His Times" in Henry H. Keith and S. F. Edwards (eds.), *Conflict and Continuity in Brazilian Society* (Columbia, S.C., 1969), p.79.

sion in 1780, Father Teodoro de Almeida proclaimed, "This Academy is ample testimony to one and all that we have awakened from centuries of lethargy."[10] The Academy, through its meetings and *Memórias*, disseminated the latest scientific knowledge. The members paid particularly close attention to the advances made in natural sciences and agriculture. In good physiocrat tradition, the Academy sought to gather both data on and samples of the riches of the empire.[11] Such information would lead to the better exploitation of that wealth.

These events suggest a part of the intellectual change Portugal experienced in the eighteenth century, particularly during the Pombaline years, 1750–1777. The innovations inspired one poet of the period to muse:

> So much change has been wrought among us
> That rustic Portugal one day
> Among the nations of the world will be known
> As the faithful disciple of France.[12]

As Portugal attuned itself to innovations and reforms, so did its principal overseas possession, Brazil. The cultural lag between the overseas colony and the metropolis was slight and diminished to insignificance by the end of the eighteenth century. The new ideas were transmitted to South America either through Portugal or directly from those two nations, England and France, whose intellectuals contributed most to the brilliance of the century. They arrived in Brazil by a variety of routes. As one means, a distinguished group of officials brought with them to the New World the ideologies of Europe. Throughout the century, the monarch appointed many enlightened men to posts in Brazil. The King sent Martinho de Mendonça de Pina e de Proença, an admirer of John Locke and a member of the *estrangeirados* ("foreignized")

10 Christovam Ayres, *Para a História da Academia das Sciências de Lisboa* (Coimbra, 1927), p.98.

11 *Breves Instrucções aos Corespondentes da Academia das Sciências de Lisboa sobre as Remessas dos Productos, e Notícias Pertencentes à História da Natureza, para Formar hum Museo Nacional* (Lisbon, 1781).

12 The poem is quoted in França, *Lisboa Pombalina*, p.182, n.34.

in Portugal, to enforce tax laws around 1730. José Mascarenhas Pacheco Coelho de Melo arrived in Salvador in 1758 to set up several tribunals, and at once he participated in the foundation of one of those scholarly academies which became characteristic of the Brazilian Enlightenment. With second thoughts, Pombal regarded that official as pro-French in his outlook and ordered his imprisonment. One of the secretaries of the crown in Minas Gerais, José João Teixeira, wrote a splendid treatise on enlightened government in which he discussed as part of his political philosophy the concepts that governments were established for the good of the people, that a contract existed between the government and the people, and that a government should be one of laws rather than the whims of the governors.[13] His views reflected some of the most advanced political thought of his day. Throughout the 1790's, Manuel António Leitão Bandeira, *ouvidor* and member of the Junta de Comércio in São Luís do Maranhão, spent long hours writing essays on the French Revolution and its meaning for Europe and Portugal. He quoted from a wide variety of European authors, including Hobbes, Buffon, Locke, and Rousseau, and physiocrat doctrine permeated his writing.[14]

Foreigners, too, introduced European thought into eighteenth-century Brazil. Portugal never sealed Brazil as hermetically as Spain closed its American colonies. In fact, throughout the eighteenth century, the Portuguese monarch dispatched a large number and variety of scientific expeditions to Brazil, many of whose members were foreigners, as the names Reverend, Cronsfeldt, Schwebel, Galluzi, Hestcko, Rorich, Goltz, Hatton, Havelle, Brunelli, Capassi, and Landi testify.[15] Occasionally foreign ships

13 José João Teixeira, "Instrucção para o Governo da Capitania de Minas Gerais," *Revista do Instituto Histórico e Geográfico Brasileiro* (cited hereafter as *RIHGB*), XV (1852), 257–58.

14 His correspondence is scattered through caixas 60–72 (caixas pertaining to Maranhão) in the Arquivo Histórico Ultramarino, Lisbon. Of particular interest is caixa 64, which contains a group of ten documents. I am indebted to Professor Colin M. Maclachlan for directing my attention to those curious documents.

15 An indication of the number and objectives of those expeditions appears in Aurélio de Lyra Tavares, *A Engenharia Militar Portuguesa na Construção*

visited Brazilian ports. For example, in 1759, both French and English squadrons dropped anchor in Salvador. One of the French officers was admitted into the local academy at that time. Toward the end of the century, such naval visits became commonplace. Between 1792 and 1805, eighty-three ships flying the stars and stripes of the newly independent and fiercely nationalistic United States called at Brazilian ports.[16] At the same time, North American whale fishers appeared in Brazilian waters and on occasion in the ports as well.[17] When the prince-regent officially opened Brazilian ports to international trade in 1808, fleets of foreign ships entered. The port of Rio de Janeiro alone registered the entrance of 90 foreign ships in 1808; 83 in 1809; 122 in 1810; 217 in 1815; and 354 in 1820. Foreigners who visited Brazil at the end of the colonial period and left accounts of their visits often commented on the eagerness of the Brazilians to hear about events in Europe. One such visitor observed of the Brazilians in 1792, "They seem to enquire, with an uncommon degree of interest, into the progress of the French Revolution, as if they foresaw the possibility of a similar event among them-

---

*do Brasil* (Rio de Janeiro, 1965), Sousa Viterbo, *Expedições Científico-Militares Enviadas ao Brasil*, 2 vols. (Lisbon, 1962 and 1964), and Rodolfo Garcia, "História das Explorações Científicas," *Diccionário Histórico e Geográfico Brasileiro* (Rio de Janeiro, 1922), I, 856–910. An excellent résumé of this activity of the crown can be found in the essay by Fidelino de Figueiredo, "O Aspecto Scientífico na Colonização da América," *Estudos de História Americana* (São Paulo, 1928), pp.79–122.

16 C. L. Chandler, "List of United States Vessels in Brazil, 1792–1805," *Hispanic American Historical Review*, XXVI (1946), 599–617.

17 Dauril Alden, "Yankee Sperm Whalers in Brazilian Waters and the Decline of the Portuguese Whale Fishery (1773–1801)," *The Americas*, XX (January 1964), 267–88. The appearance of the whalers in Brazil recalls the comments of Herman Melville about their impact on Spanish America and makes one wonder if the following statement from *Moby-Dick* cannot be applicable in part to Portuguese America as well: "Until the whale fishery rounded Cape Horn, no commerce but colonial, scarcely any intercourse but colonial, was carried on between Europe and the long line of opulent Spanish provinces on the Pacific coast. It was the whaleman who first broke through the jealous policy of the Spanish Crown, touched these colonies, and, if space permitted, it might be distinctly shown how from those whalemen at last eventuated the liberation of Peru, Chile, and Bolivia from the yoke of Old Spain, and the establishment of the eternal democracy in those parts" (New York, 1950), p.108.

selves."[18] Thomas Lindley detected a similar fascination during his enforced stay in Salvador in 1802–1803.[19] By the end of the colonial period an increasingly large number of foreigners resided in Brazil. Between 1808 and 1820, more than 300 Frenchmen lived in Rio de Janeiro alone.[20] In that same city resided about 100 British merchants by the end of 1808. Officials registered 601 foreigners living in Maranhão, Pernambuco, Minas Gerais, São Paulo, and Rio Grande do Sul in the period between 1777 and 1819.[21] Of course not all those foreign residents were paradigms of the Enlightenment, but at least a representative number—John Luccock and Henry Koster serve as excellent examples[22]—could easily have conveyed the ideas of the Enlightenment to their Brazilian neighbors.

Brazilian university graduates, returning to their native land after studying in European universities, brought back with them the latest thoughts. For obvious reasons, most of them chose to study in the venerable Coimbra University—approximately 3,000 Brazilians received degrees from there during the colonial period. The number of Brazilians graduated from the reformed Coimbra who went on to play important roles in the formation of an independent Brazil is impressive.[23] A smaller number matriculated in foreign universities, of which Edinburgh and Montpellier seemed to be the most popular.[24] Crown officials in the

[18] G. Stanton, *An Authentic Account of an Embassy from the King of Great Britain to the Emperor of China . . . Taken chiefly from the Papers of His Excellency the Earl of Macartney* (London, 1797), I, 181.

[19] *Narrative of a Voyage to Brazil* (London, 1805), p.154 *et passim*.

[20] Arquivo Nacional, *Os Franceses Residentes no Rio de Janeiro, 1808–1820* (Rio de Janeiro, 1960).

[21] Arquivo Nacional, *Registro de Estrangeiros nas Capitanias 1777–1819* (Rio de Janeiro, 1963).

[22] Both left superb accounts of their impressions of Brazil: Henry Koster, *Travels in Brazil* (Carbondale, Ill., 1966) and John Luccock, *Notes on Brazil* (London, 1820).

[23] Ministério da Educação, *Estudantes Brasileiros na Universidade de Coimbra 1772–1872* (Rio de Janeiro, 1943); Francisco Morais, *Estudantes da Universidade de Coimbra Nascidos no Brasil* (Coimbra, 1949); and Divaldo Gaspar de Freitas, *Paulistas na Universidade de Coimbra* (Coimbra, 1958).

[24] On the Brazilian students at Montpellier there are three articles: Robert Reynard, "Recherches sur Quelques Brésiliens Étudiants en Médecine à Montpellier

New World suspected many of those graduates of propagating seditious ideas. The governor of Minas Gerais, the Visconde de Barbacena, acidly expressed that suspicion in a letter to Maria I after nipping in the bud a local conspiracy against Portugal: "I cannot help believing that the ideas came from Coimbra . . . because in that matter I found very dangerous the sentiments, opinions, and influence of the Brazilian university graduates, who have returned to their own land . . . aware of the self-interests of Europe. They know too well the wealth of their own land. Even more dangerous were those who studied in foreign universities, as some have done without sufficient reason."[25] On other occasions as well, the university graduates would find themselves in difficulty because of their ideas.

Books formed yet another bridge for the migration of ideas. The urban elite bought increasing numbers of books during the last half of the eighteenth century and disregarded the censor's efforts to prohibit the importation and reading of books on the Index. Henry Koster remarked that in order to import his library from England to Pernambuco in 1809 he needed the permission of the governor, but noted that the most common practice was to smuggle books in.[26] A French visitor to Pernambuco a few years later commented on the ease with which the censor's prohibitions on book imports could be evaded.[27] Despite obstacles, books arrived in and were disseminated throughout Brazil.

---

à la Fin du XVIII^me Siècle," *Languedoc Médical* (Faculty of Medicine of Montpellier), No.98 (May–June 1954), pp.162–66; Xavier Pedrosa, "Estudantes Brasileiros na Faculdade de Medicina de Montpellier no Fim do Século XVIII," *RIHGB*, CCXLIII (April–June 1959), 35–71; Carlos da Silva Araújo, "Médicos Brasileiros Graduados em Montpellier e os Movimentos Políticos da Independência Nacional," *Revista do Instituto Histórico e Geográfico de Minas Gerais*, VIII (1961), 125–41. These authors all affirm that those students returned to Brazil with very liberal ideas.

25 Quoted in João Camillo de Oliveira Torres, *História de Minas Gerais* (Belo Horizonte, n.d.), III, 685.

26 *Travels in Brazil*, p.84.

27 L. F. de Tollenare, "Notas Dominicaes Tomadas durante uma Viagem em Portugal e no Brasil em 1816, 1817, e 1818," trans. Alfredo Carvalho, *Revista do*

(None was printed there until the first press was set up in 1808.) The books imported came in a wide variety of languages: Portuguese, French, English, Latin, Spanish, and Italian. Portuguese and French predominated. As impressive as the number of languages was the great variety of cities in which the books were published. All the major and many of the minor European cities were represented. Paris ranked as the most important. Such diversity spoke well for the book agents of the period, who were able to gather volumes from all over Europe and market them in Brazil.

Unfortunately almost nothing is known of the book trade in colonial Brazil. An occasional visitor mentioned *en passant* the presence of some bookdealer in one or another of the ports. The *Almanaques* for Rio de Janeiro prepared by Antônio Duarte Nunes reveal that for the years 1792 and 1794 there was a bookseller in the viceregal capital. In 1799 there were two. The most extensive documentation available thus far on a colonial bookdealer concerns Manuel Ribeiro Santos, who imported books from Portugal and sold them in Vila Rica, Minas Gerais, between 1749 and 1753.[28] He ordered works on medicine, law, literature, history, geography, and classics. Apparently his service was fast (the imprint date on the book and the arrival date of the book in Minas Gerais were sometimes only one year apart) and frequent (he spoke of books arriving with every fleet).[29]

Part of our knowledge about early libraries in Brazil comes from the accounts of foreign travelers who on occasion mentioned the literary tastes they encountered or particularly impressive libraries they visited. Thomas Lindley remembered in Bahia Father Francisco Augustinho Gomes, whose library was, to use Lindley's expression, "very complete" in English and French works. He mentioned by name Buffon, Lavoisier, and d'Alem-

*Instituto Archeológico, Histórico, e Geográphico Pernambucano* (cited hereafter as *RIAHGP*), XI (March 1904), 436.

28 Sílvio Gabriel Diniz, "Um Livreiro em Vila Rica no Meiado do Século XVIII," *Kriterion* (Belo Horizonte), XII (January–June 1959), 180–98.

29 *Ibid.*, p.196.

bert.[30] In Pernambuco, the Frenchman L. F. de Tollenare commented on the literary preferences before the Revolution of 1817, "The French works are the most sought after and among those all the writers . . . of the philosophy of the eighteenth century."[31] John Luccock spoke of the brisk book trade in Rio de Janeiro in 1818 where "French books are in demand."[32] And in Minas Gerais in 1828, the visitor Robert Walsh admired the large selection of foreign books in evidence, calling special attention to the works of Voltaire, Rousseau, Raynal, and Adam Smith and mentioning "many which appeared in the early part of the French Revolution."[33] John Armitage, a resident of Rio de Janeiro, mentioned the *Social Contract* of Rousseau and some of the writings of Voltaire and Raynal as being known to some urban intellectuals.[34] It is apparent from this scattered information that, as one Brazilian historian concluded, the French philosophers in particular became "the political Bible" of the enlightened Brazilians.[35] Their works penetrated even into the interior of Minas Gerais.[36] As late as the 1840's one can still find references in the writings of the foreign travelers which indicate that books were one of the main bridges over which the ideas of the European Enlightenment migrated to the New World. This quaint statement from Daniel P. Kidder sums up the point: "Book auctions, indeed, are of very frequent occurrence. Europeans who are about to retire to their native country, and Brazilians who go abroad, generally dispose of their libraries by public sale. It is often painful to witness, on these occasions, the vast amount of infidel literature in circulation. The works

30 Lindley, *Narrative of a Voyage*, pp.66–67.

31 "Notas Dominicaes," p.436.

32 *Notes on Brazil*, p.575. During the First Empire, several Frenchmen opened bookstores in Rio de Janeiro. Francisco de Assis Barbosa, *Alguns Aspectos da Influência Francesa no Brasil* (Rio de Janeiro, 1963), p.xxiii.

33 *Notices of Brazil in 1828–1829* (Boston, 1831), p.84.

34 *The History of Brazil* (London, 1836), I, 9.

35 Francisco Muniz Tavares, *História da Revolução de Pernambuco em 1817* (Recife, 1917), p.44.

36 Joaquim Felício dos Santos, *Memórias do Distrito Diamantino*, 3d ed. (Rio de Janeiro, 1956), p.200.

of Voltaire, of Volney, and of Rousseau, are offered almost daily to the highest bidder, and bidders are always found."[37]

A more thorough investigation of the libraries at the close of the colonial period promises to give both a revealing intellectual profile of Brazil's tiny literate class and a further indication of the availability of enlightened ideas to that privileged minority. Thus far, such studies are few. One of the best is Eduardo Frieiro's *O Diabo na Livraria do Cônego* (Belo Horizonte, 1957), a witty essay on the library of Canon Luís Vieira da Silva, a participant in the *Inconfidência Mineira*. His magnificent collection of nearly 800 books and 270 titles represented all of Europe's foremost thinkers of the seventeenth and eighteenth centuries. The implication was—and the Portuguese government did not hesitate to draw it—that he was influenced enough by what he read to conspire for Brazil's independence. A similar connection between a man's library and his political activities can be found in the cases of Resende da Costa, Senior and Junior, both owners of large libraries of liberal European thinkers and also participants in the same *Inconfidência*. I examined their books, along with those of Batista Caetano de Almeida, a liberal reformer of the First Empire and Regency period, in "The Enlightenment in Two Colonial Brazilian Libraries," *The Journal of the History of Ideas*, XXV (July–September 1964), 430–38. The list of authors represented in those rich libraries reads like a roll call of the European Enlightenment. In his book *A Sabinada* (Rio de Janeiro, 1938), Luiz Viana Filho connected the books a man owned with his political activity. Francisco Sabino Alvares de Rocha Vieira's library contained nearly 1,000 volumes among which were the works of Voltaire, Say, Tocqueville, Montesquieu, Meguiné, Morat, Rousseau, Locke, Condillac, *et al.* Their owner led one of the liberal revolts of the Regency period, the Sabinada. Sílvio Gabriel Diniz in his "Biblioteca Setecentista nas Minas Gerais," *Revista do Instituto Histórico de Minas Gerais*, VI (1959), 333–44, spoke in general terms of libraries in that region of gold-mining fame and then listed books which

[37] *Sketches of Residence and Travels in Brazil* (Philadelphia, 1845), I, 116.

belonged to some churchmen during the eighteenth century. His footnotes reveal the existence of other documentary material in the Arquivo Público Mineiro for the study of colonial libraries. For example, on page 338, he mentioned a manuscript classified among the miscellaneous books of the Delegacia Fiscal, Seção Colonial, which "gives as the property of the deceased some lists of books which constituted their libraries." A revealing book inventory can be found in "Seqüestro Feito em 1794 nos Bens que Forão Achados do Bacharel Mariano José Pereira da Fonsêca Extrahido do Respectivo Processo," *Revista do Instituto Histórico e Geográfico Brasileiro*, LXIII, Part 1 (1901), 14–18. Many of the works were in French. In the catalog *A Coleção da Casa dos Contos de Ouro Preto* compiled by Herculano Gomes Mathias (Rio de Janeiro, 1966) there is information (p. 145) about the library that the physician Antônio Teixeira da Costa brought to Minas Gerais in 1791. The names of Voltaire, Montesquieu, Raynal, and Rousseau figure prominently in that document.

The religious libraries would provide another bibliothecarial perspective of eighteenth-century Brazil. Serfim Leite has given this subject the most attention so far in his monumental *História da Companhia de Jesus no Brasil*, 10 vols. (Rio de Janeiro, 1938–1950). In Volume IV, he listed the inventory of the Jesuit Library at the Casa da Vigia, Pará, and commented, "That library, shining like a spotlight in the colonial forest of Brazil, contained a little of everything" (p. 410). In Volume V, he discussed the library of the Jesuit College in Bahia (pp. 92–95).

Some very good sources for a knowledge of the reading preferences of colonial Brazilians still remain unexploited. None of the hearings on the various conspiracies against Portuguese authority has been fully studied for bibliographic information, although the documents from them have been published for some years now: *A Inconfidência da Bahia. Devassas e Sequestros*, 2 vols. (Rio de Janeiro, 1931), reprinted from Volumes XLIII, XLIV, and XLV of the *Annaes da Biblioteca Nacional*; the *Autos de Devassa da Inconfidência Mineira*, 7 vols. (Rio de Janeiro,

1936–1937); and Volume LXI of the *Annaes da Biblioteca Nacional*. The latter contains the hearing on the so-called "Conspiracy of the Intellectuals," uncovered in Rio de Janeiro in 1794. Another promising depository of information on colonial libraries is the *inventários* drawn up after the death of men of property. If the deceased owned a library, the *inventário* enumerates the author and the title of each book. The director of the Arquivo Público da Bahia informed me that his archive contained many such inventories. I checked the one left by the statesman-physician José Lino Coutinho (1784–1836) and found a list of the books in his extensive library. A few of the many European authors present were Jean Duplan, Johann Spurzheim, Henry Thorton, Condorcet, d'Alembert, Jeremy Bentham, Montesquieu, Paul Henri Holbach, Mirabeau, Pradt, Racine, and Voltaire. Also there were two titles by the chief representatives of the Enlightenment in North America: *The Works of Dr. Benjamin Franklin*, 2 vols. (London, 1793), and Thomas Jefferson, *A Manual of Parliamentary Practice* (Washington, 1801).[38] If my understanding is correct, the archives of the major Brazilian states hold numerous such *inventários*. An analysis of the book lists in those *inventários* will provide an informative intellectual profile of the educated elite in the late colonial period, when the Enlightenment flowered in Brazil.

Books, foreign visitors, enlightened colonial officials, and returning university graduates on the one hand introduced into Brazil the latest ideas from Europe and on the other diffused them among the literate minority. The new gospel spread effectively also through the various academies which sprang up, flourished briefly, and disappeared in Salvador and Rio de Janeiro during the eighteenth century. The academies drew inspiration from European models which they frankly imitated. Some information—surprisingly little in at least one case—exists about six of them: Academia Brasílica dos Esquecidos (Bahia, 1724–1725), Academia dos Felizes (Rio de Janeiro, 1736–1740),

---

[38] Arquivo Público da Bahia, "Inventário de José Lino Coutinho," Document No.357.919.62/M157/d4.

Academia dos Selectos (Rio de Janeiro, 1751–1752), Academia Brasílica dos Renacidos (Bahia, 1759–1760), Academia Scientífica (Rio de Janeiro, 1771–1772), and Sociedade Literária (Rio de Janeiro, 1786–1794).[39] A variety of archives in both Rio de Janeiro and Lisbon (and possibly other places as well) contain unpubished and apparently unstudied documents on these academies. They constitute an obvious field of research which as yet has been virtually unexplored. While most Luso-Brazilian

[39] There is some published material on the academies but superficiality characterizes it. A general conclusion easily deduced after reading the material is that original research has been kept to a minimum and that what has been done has not been digested. J. Lúcio de Azevedo, "A Academia dos Renascidos da Bahia e seu Fundador," *Revista de Língua Portuguesa*, XIV (November 1921), 17–29; Moreira de Azevedo, "Sociedades Fundadas no Brasil desde os Tempos Coloniaes até o Começo do Actual Reinado," *RIHGB*, XLVIII, Part 2 (1885), 265–322; "Estatutos da Academia Brazílica dos Académicos Renascidos," *RIHGB*, XLV, Part 1 (1882), 49–67; José Vieira Fazenda, "Academia dos Felizes," *RIHGB*, CXLIX (1943), 433–37; Max Fleiuss, "As Principaes Associações Literárias e Scientíficas do Brasil (1724–1838)" in *Páginas Brasileiras* (Rio de Janeiro, 1919), pp.381–456; Barão Homen de Melo, "O Brasil intelectual em 1801," *RIHGB*, LXIV (1901), i–xxxi; Augusto da Silva Carvalho, *As Academias Científicas do Brasil no Século XVIII* (Lisbon, 1939); J. C. Fernandes Pinheiro, "A Academia Brasílica dos Esquecidos. Estudo Histórico e Literário," *RIHGB*, XXXI, Part 2 (1868), 5–32, and "A Academia Brasílica dos Renacidos. Estudo Histórico e Literário," *RIHGB*, XXXII, Part 2 (1869), 53–70; Visconde de São Leopoldo, "O Instituto Histórico e Geográfico Brasileiro he o Representante das Ideas de Illustração que em Differentes Épochas se Manifestarão em o nosso Continente," *RIHGB*, I (1839), 66–86; Lycurgo Santos Filho, "Sociedades Literárias do Século XVIII," *RIHGB*, CCLXVII (1965), 43–60; José Joaquim Norberto de Souza e Silva, "Litteratura Brasileira: as Academias Litterárias Scientíficas no Século Décimo Octavo. A Academia dos Selectos, "*Revista Popular* (Rio de Janeiro), XV (1862), 363–76; Alexandre Passos, "Academias e Sociedades Literárias nos Séculos XVIII e XIX. Sua Influencia na Vida Cultural Bahiana," *Anais do Primeiro Congresso de História de Bahia* (Salvador, 1951), V, 7–51; Joaquim Jozé de Atahide, "Discurso em que se Mostra o Fim para que foi Estabelecido a Sociedade Literária do Rio de Janeiro . . . ," *RIHGB*, XLV (1882), 69–76.

There is only one book on the subject, Alberto Lamego de Campos' brief *A Academia dos Renacidos, sua Fundação e Trabalhos Inéditos* (Paris, 1923). Fidelino de Figueiredo treats the academies at some length in his *Estudos de História Americana* (São Paulo, 1927), and most literary historians discuss them, some in considerably more detail than in others. Alexander Marchant discussed them briefly in English in his "Aspects of the Enlightenment in Brazil," in Arthur P. Whitaker (ed.), *Latin America and the Enlightenment*, 2d ed. (Ithaca, N.Y., 1961), pp.95–118.

scholars agree on the importance of the academies, none has done a meaningful study of them which could in any way compare to the splendid monographs published on comparable institutions in Spanish America.

The first academy held eighteen sessions in the colonial capital under the patronage of the viceroy, the Conde de Sabugosa. Strongly influenced by the recently established Portuguese Academy of History, the Esquecidos decided to write the history of the colony, a goal achieved in 1730 with the publication of *História da América Portuguesa* by Sebastião da Rocha Pita. At one of the sessions of the Academy that Bahian historian also recited his symbolic poem "The Shift of the Sunrise," in which he boasted that the sun "is born with greater brilliance in the West." This nativism, pervading both the history and the poem, characterized all the academies. Examples of it are numerous. At least four other distinguished members of the Esquecidos, Luiz de Siqueira da Gama, Ignácio Barbosa Machado, Padre Gonçalo Soares da França, and Chancellor Caetano de Brito Figueiredo, contributed long nativistic--and Gongoristic— discourses on Brazilian history. With the baroque flourish typical of those sessions, Chancellor Figueiredo rhapsodized, "Golden Brazil is the depository of the most priceless metal, fertile producer of the sweetest sugar canes, and generous cultivator of the most useful plants. Let me say it boastfully: Brazil is the most precious jewel of the Lusitanian sceptre, the most valuable stone of the Portuguese crown, which of itself possesses much majesty and beauty."[40] The others concurred fully and expressed similar sentiments. Sessions of succeeding academies seemingly dedicated much of their time to Brazilian subjects too. At the meeting of the Felizes, the thirty members discussed such questions as "Was Portuguese America the best part of this continent?" (they unanimously decided it was) and "Which is the better

[40] "Dissertações Académicas e Históricas, nas quais se trata de Histórias Natural [*sic*] das Couzas do Brasil pelo Desembargador Chanceler Caetano de Brito e Figueiredo no anno de 1724," located in the manuscript collection of the Sociedade Geográfica de Lisboa, Mss. no. Res.43–C–148, p.36.

political virtue: prudence or temperance?" (they favored temperance). The Renacidos returned to the theme of writing history. The Academy's noble aim was to prepare a "secular, ecclesiastical, political, military, and natural history of Brazil," accompanied by a bibliography. In truth, a number of important and productive colonial historians were associated, directly or indirectly, with that Academy: José Mirales, Antônio de Santa Maria Jaboatão, Gaspar da Madre de Deus, Antônio José Vitorino, Borges da Fonseca, and Domingos de Loreto Couto. The members of the last two academies, the Academia Scientífica and the Sociedade Literária, through research and discussion tried to know their own land better. Sessions were devoted to the study of local diseases, plant life, water supplies, the characteristics of cochineal and the possibilities of producing it in Brazil, etc.[41] The Academia Scientífica maintained its own botanical garden. In their environmental studies and emphasis on improving agriculture, the South American academicians endorsed those aspects of physiocrat doctrines popular in Portugal. Before very long, however, some Brazilians turned their thoughts to the more controversial parts of physiocrat doctrines such as the reduction or abolition of taxes and duties and greater freedom of trade.[42] João Rodrigues de Brito boldly called for complete liberty for the Brazilian farmers to grow whatever crops they wanted, to construct whatever works and factories necessary for the good of their crops, to sell in any place, by any means, and through whatever agent they wished to choose without heavy taxes or burdensome bureaucracy, to sell to the highest bidder,

41 The president's report of the activities during the first year of the Sociedade Literária has been translated into English and appears in E. Bradford Burns (ed.), *A Documentary History of Brazil* (New York, 1966), pp.170–77.

42 The first stages of this new thought will be found in two essays by José Joaquim da Cunha de Azeredo Coutinho, *Memória sobre o preço do assúcar* (Lisbon, 1791) and *Ensaio económico sobre o commércio de Portugal e suas colónias* (Lisbon, 1794). There is an English translation of the latter, *An Essay on the Commerce and Products of the Portuguese Colonies in South America* (London, 1807).

and to sell their products at any time that best suited them.[43] Brazilian thought had come a long way from the nativistic rhapsodizing of the early eighteenth century.

A reformation of the limited educational system in Brazil after the expulsion of the Jesuits further contributed to the spread of new ideas within the colony. Critical of Scholasticism, the Franciscans updated the curriculum of their Province of the Immaculate Conception of Rio de Janeiro in 1776 to place a new emphasis on geometry, natural history, and experimental physics.[44] Professor of rhetoric Manoel Ignácio da Silva Alvarenga, one of the graduates of the reformed Coimbra, came to the attention of crown officials investigating the "Conspiracy of the Intellectuals" in Rio de Janiero in 1794, partly because of his radical teaching. The professor's library contained a copy of Gabriel Bonnet de Mably's *Direitos do Cidadão* (to use the title given in the court testimony), a book which seemed to particularly upset viceregal officialdom. Found among his papers were notes expressing ideas similar to those of the Frenchman. Further, the crown charged that he had taught such ideas to at least one of his students. According to one judge, Professor Alvarenga was too much a Francophile.[45] At the end of the century in Salvador, the Benedictines taught philosophy using, among others, the texts of Antonio Genovesi, Johann Gottlieb Heineccius, and Pieter van Musschenbroek.[46] A sort of itinerant philosophy

[43] João Rodrigues de Brito, *Cartas Económico-Políticas sobre a Agricultura e Commércio da Bahia* (Salvador, 1924).

[44] *Estatutos para os estudos da província de N. Sra. da Conceição do Rio de Janeiro, ordenados segundo as disposições dos estatutos da nova universidade* (Lisbon, 1776). See the discussion in Manoel Cardozo, "Azeredo Coutinho and the Intellectual Ferment of His Times," pp.87–88.

[45] Antônio Diniz da Cruz e Silva to Conde de Rezende, Rio de Janeiro, June 18, 1797, reprinted in *RIHGB*, XXVIII, Part 1 (1865), 159.

[46] Antônio Joaquim das Mercês, "Do Archivo do Instituto. Carta Escripta na Bahia, em 12 de Agosto de 1851, pelo Cônego Dr. Antônio Joaquim das Mercês ao Padre Mestre Amaral a Respeito dos Primeiros Professores da Philosophia da Bahia, Alagoas, e Parahiba," *Revista do Instituto Geográfico e Histórico da Bahia*, No.58 (1932), pp.84–85.

professor between 1818 and 1823, Antônio Joaquim das Mercês lectured in Bahia, Alagoas, and Paraíba, where he too used Genovesi and Heineccius, in addition to Etiene Bezout and Rousseau's *Social Contract* (the latter apparently he used only in Paraíba).[47] A participant in several revolutionary plots, Mercês found himself in considerable difficulty with officialdom. Somewhat more conventional was Silvestre Pinheiro Ferreira, a Portuguese disciple of Condillac, who delivered public lectures on philosophy in Rio de Janeiro in 1811 and 1812.[48] His lectures later appeared in book form under the title *Preleções Filosóficas* (Rio de Janeiro, 1813).

Bishop José Joaquim da Cunha de Azeredo Coutinho, contributed significantly to educational reforms through the establishment of a seminary in Olinda, Pernambuco, in 1800.[49] The school reflected some of the Pombaline reforms of Coimbra. In the first place, the curriculum emphasized the sciences. The traditional classes in Latin, philosophy, ecclesiastical history, dogma, and morals were taught but they competed with such novelties as chemistry, physics, natural history, universal history, geography, geometry, and design. The courses aimed to make the student more adaptable to Brazilian surroundings, needs, and orientation, which were shifting ever so slightly from patriarchal agriculture to incipient industrialization and more diversified agriculture. In the second place, the influence of the reformed Coimbra on Azeredo Coutinho could be seen in the

47 *Ibid.*, pp.86–87.

48 João Cruz Costa, *Panorama of the History of Philosophy in Brazil* (Washington, D.C., 1962), p.31; Miguel Reale, *Filosofia em São Paulo* (São Paulo, 1962), pp.19–20.

49 There is a growing interest in Azeredo Coutinho. For recent studies of him see E. Bradford Burns, "The Role of Azeredo Coutinho in the Enlightenment of Brazil," *Hispanic American Historical Review*, XLIV (May 1964), 145–60; the essay by Manoel Cardozo previously cited, "Azeredo Coutinho and the Intellectual Ferment of His Times," as well as his "Dom José Joaquim da Cunha de Azeredo Coutinho, Governador Interino e Bispo de Pernambuco, 1798–1802," *RIHGB*, CCLXXXII (January–March 1969), 3–45; Sérgio Buarque de Holanda has re-edited four of the Bishop's major essays on Brazil, *Obras Econômicas de J. J. da Cunha de Azeredo Coutinho* (São Paulo, 1966) and has written a superb introductory essay to preface the work.

method of teaching adopted at Olinda. It broke sharply with the traditional pedagogic methods of the Jesuits, strongly influenced by Aristotelian theory, and introduced innovations based on Cartesian doctrines.[50] The third reform of Coimbra noted in the Bishop's educational measures was the effort exerted to hire an outstanding faculty to staff the seminary. Azeredo Coutinho persuaded several intellectuals to accompany him to Pernambuco to teach, and in the captaincy itself he attracted some of the most learned men, both lay and clerical, to his seminary as professors. Because of the notable faculty, the use of the latest European teaching methods, and the new emphasis on science, the Seminary of Olinda, in its own modest way, considered itself as the "new Coimbra."[51]

That the seminary saw and appreciated its own innovative role was apparent in the speech delivered by Professor Father Miguel Joaquim de Almeida e Castro at the school's opening. He called for a new enlightened age of glorification of the sciences and arts to replace the "dark centuries" of the past.[52] Quoting from and referring to Lacombe, Voltaire, Millot, Fleury, and a host of other Frenchmen, Almeida e Castro told his audience that only the sciences could "illuminate the darkness" and dispel the ignorance and superstition of the past.[53] Instead of the customary blind acceptance of life, he supported the principal concepts of the Enlightenment and urged the students to explore through science the world around them. All testimony concurs that the seminary succeeded in spreading the ideas of the Enlightenment within Brazil.[54]

[50] Manoel de Oliveira Lima, *Pernambuco e seu Desenvolvimento Histórico* (Leipzig, 1895), p.216.

[51] *Annaes do Seminário* (Recife, 1921), p.61. Some of the praise of the seminary exaggerates its noble achievements beyond recognition. As a case in point see Aníbal Fernandes, *Idéias Francesas em Pernambuco na Primeira Metade do Século XIX* (Recife, 1957), p.13.

[52] Miguel Joaquim de Almeida e Castro, "Orasam Acadêmica," *RIAHGP*, XXXV (1937–1938), p.180.

[53] *Ibid.*, p.174.

[54] As examples, see José do Carmo Baratta, *História Ecclesiástica de Pernambuco* (Recife, 1922), p.72; Koster, *Travels in Brazil*, I, 50; Tollenare, "Notas Dominicaes,"

The printing press provided yet another means—albeit a belated one—of disseminating ideas in colonial Brazil. The first, the Régia of Rio de Janeiro, was set up only after the arrival of the royal family in the New World in 1808.[55] During the first eight years of its existence, it published a number of European authors in translation: Leonhard Euler, Adrien Marie Legendre, Alexander Pope, Sylvestre François Lacroix, René Just Haüy, Adam Smith, Gaspard Monge, Edmund Burke, Marie François Xavier Bichat, Louis Benjamin Francoeur, Nicolas Louis de Lacoille, Guy de Vernon, Jean Herrenschwand, and Antoine François de Fourcroy. In addition, the Régia Press put out works by Luso-Brazilian authors, such as José da Silva Lisboa and Silvestre Pinheiro Ferreira, who popularized European thought. In 1811 the city of Salvador witnessed the installation of the second Brazilian printing press.

The spread of the Enlightenment among the Brazilians produced many effects. Warmly embracing physiocrat doctrine, some Brazilians—and some Portuguese living in the New World as well—interested themselves in their surroundings and discussed the most practical means of mastering their lush environment.[56] They undertook a wide variety of projects to study Brazil. José Vieira Couto wrote a long monograph on Minas Gerais; José de Sá Betencourt left studies on cotton farming; Bernardo Teixeira Coutinho Alvares de Carvalho prepared a treastise on the manufacture of ink from local resources; and Joaquim Amorin de Castro wrote a natural history of Brazil as well as monographs on the tobacco and cochineal industries. The botanists ranked among the most active students of Braziliana and at least two first-rate scholars emerged. Alexandre Rodrigues

---

p.436; Francisco Muniz Tavares, *História da Revolução de Pernambuco em 1817* (Recife, 1917), p.44.

[55] For a history of early Brazilian printing see Carlos Rizzini, *O Livro, o Jornal e a Tipografia no Brasil, 1500–1822* (Rio de Janeiro, 1946), pp.309–426.

[56] Thales de Azevedo points out the acceptance of physiocrat doctrine in Bahia in his *As Ciências Sociais na Bahia, Notas para sua História* (Salvador, 1964), p.35.

Ferreira, a native of Bahia who received his doctorate in natural history from Coimbra, perambulated through Amazonia for a decade, 1783–1792, collecting specimens, sketching, and writing reports in an investigation of the potential of that neglected basin. Surveying the scene, he gasped, "The land is a paradise; it produces so much that I do not know which way to turn."[57] Reflecting the temper of his times, he entitled his unpublished masterwork on the wealth of the Amazon "Viagem Filosófica." José Mariano da Conceição Velloso, a Franciscan from São João del-Rei in Minas Gerais, devoted eight years (1782–1790) to his major study, the *Flora Fluminensis*, the collection and classification of 1,640 different plants from the captaincy of Rio de Janeiro.

Encouraging interest in their surroundings, the local representatives of the Enlightenment helped to make Brazilians more acutely aware of the colony's wealth and potential. Like the literati who sang the praises of the land and its inhabitants in prose and poetry, they aroused native pride. Indeed, as the Brazilians turned their attention increasingly toward themselves, as they studied themselves and their environment, their pride in and esteem of Brazil grew. That nativism—the exaltation of all things Brazilian—burst into full bloom in the last half of the eighteenth century. It contributed decisively to Brazil's spiritual formation. The Brazilians became ever more conscious of the widening differences between themselves and the metropolis. By the end of the century the elite and probably other elements of society were well aware of the uniqueness of Brazil. That awareness in turn intensified their devotion to their own land, traditions, and experiences.

The increased awareness of the potential of the land and the failure to realize it made the Brazilians more critical of metropolitan policies, particularly the economic ones against which there was a long history of protest. In 1799, a Portuguese who

[57] Quoted in Arthur Cézar Ferreira Reis, *Aspectos da Experiência Portuguesa na Amazônia* (Manaus, 1966), p.207.

had resided twelve years in Salvador posed the intriguing and challenging question: "Why is a country so fecund in natural products, so rich in potential, so vast in extent, still inhabited by such a small number of settlers, most of them poor, and many of them half-starved?"[58] Frankly answering his own question, he put the blame on slave labor, latifundia, and inefficient or obsolete agricultural methods. We have already noted the bold reforms João Rodrigues de Brito advocated. Another group of reformers, under the sway of Adam Smith and led by José da Silva Lisboa, favored freer trade with the consequent reformation of mercantilist philosophy and the establishment of banks to further encourage commerce.[59]

In the three decades before Brazil declared its independence, at least four Brazilians, José Joaquim da Cunha de Azeredo Coutinho, João Rodrigues de Brito, José Acúrcio das Neves, and José da Silva Lisboa, wrote treatises on economic reform within the empire which influenced the royal government. Here, then, was a fascinating example of Enlightenment in the colony influencing the metropolis.[60] The flow of ideas went both ways across the Atlantic. The suggestions of those Brazilian econo-

[58] Luís dos Santos Vilhena, *Recopilação de Notícias Soteropolitanas e Brasílicas* (Salvador, 1922), II, 926.

[59] José da Silva Lisboa's *Princípios de Economia Política* (Lisbon, 1804) bears the stamp of Adam Smith. In his *Memória dos Benefícios Políticos do Governo de El-Rey Nosso Senhor D. João VI* (Rio de Janeiro, 1818), he quotes Montesquieu, Bentham, and most frequently Adam Smith. A Portuguese translation of *The Wealth of Nations* was published in Rio de Janeiro in 1811. Some Brazilian disciples of Smith, in addition to Silva Lisboa and João Rodrigues de Brito, were Claudio Manoel da Costa, Januário da Cunha Barbosa, Gonçalves Ledo, Hipólito José da Costa, Rodrigo de Souza Coutinho, José Bonifácio de Andrada e Silva, and Martim Francisco de Andrada e Silva. Thomas Lindley noted among the inhabitants of Bahia in 1803 a strong desire "to embrace the advantages that a free unrestricted trade would afford" (*Narrative of a Voyage to Brazil*, p.279).

[60] Manoel Cardozo suggested another way in which Brazil influenced Portugal: "In the eighteenth century no other colonial country, in proportion to its human and physical resources, may have exerted so great an influence upon the Mother Country. . . . The influx of Brazilians into Portugal throughout the eighteenth century coincided with, and possibly contributed to, movements for economic modernization and religious aggiornamento" ("Azeredo Coutinho and the Intellectual Ferment of His Times," pp.72–73).

mists illustrated one important aspect of the Brazilian Enlightenment which eschewed revolution for reformation.[61]

But ideas from Europe's enlightened writers also helped to stir some Brazilians to revolutionary action. It was no mere coincidence that the plotters in the two major conspiracies against Portugal, the Inconfidência Minera, 1789, and the Inconfidência Bahiana, 1798, and the rebels in the Revolt of 1817 in Pernambuco had read Europe's most liberal thinkers and embraced their ideals. In some cases, the new thoughts provided convenient and well phrased logic to express festering grievances; in others, they offered previously unconsidered alternatives to increasingly unpalatable laws or situations.

Of the several revolutionary uses to which the Enlightenment was put, the most curious and intriguing was the Bahian conspiracy, the unique example of the penetration—imperfect as it may have been—of the Enlightenment into the masses. Salvador alone furnishes an example of the plebian elements thinking in terms of economic, social, and political reforms and even of independence. The conspirators were simple folk: common soldiers, workmen, artisans, and so large a number of tailors that the movement often is referred to as the "Conspiracy of the Tailors." The statistics tell the tale. Of the forty-nine arrested, forty-six were men, forty were freemen, almost all were literate, all were between seventeen and thirty years old, all had modest backgrounds, all were Mulattoes. A poster affixed by the conspirators to a public wall summed up local grievances: "Each soldier is a citizen, principally the brown and black men who live abused and abandoned. All are equal. There is no difference. There will only be liberty, equality, and fraternity."[62] The

[61] Carlos Guilherme Mota, "Mentalidade Ilustrada na Colonização Portuguesa: Luís dos Santos Vilhena," *Revista de História*, No.72 (October–December 1967), p.405.

[62] Quoted in Braz do Amaral, *Fatos da Vida do Brasil* (Salvador, 1941), p.44. Francisco de Assis Barbosa speculated that the ideas of the Enlightenment were passed on by word of mouth since Brazil imported relatively few books and had no printing press and since few Brazilians were literate (*Alguns Aspectos da Influência Francesa*, p.xxi).

French influence was patent. Under questioning the humble conspirators spoke in vague but eloquent terms of free trade which would bring prosperity to their port and of equality for all men without distinctions of color and race. Their courtroom testimony garbled many of the ideas of the Enlightenment but did not mask the fact that in this unique case the latest European thought had reached the common people.

When Brazilian independence did come, it arrived quietly. A Braganza ascended the new imperial throne in 1822 and two years later handed down a constitution which embodied many of the ideas of the Enlightenment. It separated the various branches of government, promised personal liberties, civil freedom, and religious toleration, applied a uniform system of laws, and guaranteed property rights. Its attention to individual freedoms fit well within the liberal ideology of the nineteenth century.[63] At the time of the constitution's promulgation, a new group of French writers, the heirs of the Age of Reason, exerted influence on the political thought of the Brazilians. Most authorities credit Benjamin Constant de Rebecque, whose works, particularly his *Cours de Politique Constitutionelle*, were widely read and discussed in Brazil in the early 1820's, with significantly influencing the creation of the liberal constitutional monarchy which would govern Brazil until 1889.[64] Many of the political ideas which he, his contemporaries, or his predecessors also suggested were the basis for protracted debates throughout the nineteenth century. During a dynamic three-year period toward the end of the century, 1888–1891, many of the key goals of the political enlightenment were realized: slavery was abolished, a

---

63 Richard Graham concluded that the core of Brazilian liberal ideology in the nineteenth century was "the belief in the freedom of the individual" (*Britain and the Onset of Modernization in Brazil* [Cambridge, 1968], p.353). For an analysis of Brazilian liberal ideology in that century see Roque Spencer Maciel de Barros, *A Illustração Brasileira e a Idéia de Universidade* (São Paulo, 1959).

64 Constant made a strong impression on Spanish Americans as well. For Mexico, see Charles A. Hale, *Mexican Liberalism in the Age of Mora, 1821–1853* (New Haven, 1968), pp.55–61; for Argentina, see Mario C. Belgrano, "Benjamin Constant y el Constitucionalismo Argentino," *Boletín del Instituto de Historia Argentina "Doctor Emilio Ravignani,"* VI (1961), 1–57.

republic established, the government decentralized, and church and state separated.

As these suggested effects of the Enlightenment indicate, the new ideas radiating from an enlightened Europe enjoyed considerable influence in Brazil and produced a variety of results. Of course ideas alone did not propel events; they only can be fully appreciated and understood within the wider political and economic scopes of the Portuguese empire at the dawn of the nineteenth century and of a Europe altered first by the French Revolution and then by Napoleon. As no one should consider events in Brazil shaped solely by the importation of ideas, neither could anyone fully explain those events without recourse to the migration of ideas.

# XI

# On the Enlightenment in Central America

## T. B. IRVING

DURING THE REIGN of Philip V, the Spanish empire's first Bourbon ruler, there appeared in 1729 the first newspaper in Central America, *La Gazeta de Guatemala*. It was a monthly publication which at first consisted of four pages and was later expanded to eight. This served as a calendar or notice board for official and church events, and it was read throughout the isthmus of Central America. *La Gazeta* lasted for about two years, disappearing from the scene in 1731. It had not represented distinguished journalism, but it did reflect its times.

Sixty years later at the very close of the colonial period, publication of *La Gazeta de Guatemala* was resumed. This time it ran for a quarter of a century, from 1793 until 1816, except for a brief period from 1796 till 1797, when it was suspended temporarily for lack of paper due to the blockade which the British fleet enforced at sea. A study of the contents during both runs tells us a great deal about Central American culture and the changes that had occurred in the meantime.

Printing had been introduced to Guatemala in the middle of the previous century under circumstances which reflect the paternalistic intellectual conditions existing during the middle colonial period. The first press had been painstakingly pieced together by hand from woodblocks in 1641, almost like Guten-berg's, or perhaps more in the style of linoleum printing today, by Juan de Dios del Cid. This effort was quickly broken up by the authorities, however, showing how jealously the government of the kingdom of Guatemala controlled cultural expression throughout the colony.

Two decades later, in 1660, a press was officially sanctioned. José de Pineda Ibarra (1629–1680) was the first printer to be licensed in Central America. Permission was extended by Bishop Payo Enríquez de Ribera (who later became bishop of Michoa-cán and then archbishop of Mexico) because he wanted to print some of his own sermons. Ibarra came from Mexico, although some sources say he was a Spaniard. His press was subsequently used for printing sermons which chiefly concerned the doings of the royal family in Spain, events which could be commented upon safely. In 1663 he printed his first book, not surprisingly, on theology. Most works printed were official publications for either the government of the kingdom or the church. Three years later Diego Sáenz de Ovecurri recounted the exploits of Thomas Aquinas, the thirteenth-century Scholastic, in *La Thomasiada*, which Menéndez y Pelayo has called "un monumento de mal gusto"; its Gongoristic verses read like a dull *Pilgrim's Progress* while several cantos which leave out different vowels are even worse. These verbal gymnastics were products of the Baroque period in Central American letters. Pineda Ibarra's effort came rather late, as happened in other Spanish colonies and in New France, for he worked a century and a half after the colony was founded.

Nevertheless some beautiful examples of the printer's art were turned out, as we see in the lovely *tarjas* or university diplomas decorated with woodcuts which are preserved in the National Archives in Guatemala City. The printer who published these and the first series of *La Gazeta de Guatemala* was Sebastián de Arévalo (1727–1772). His most notable work was a Cakchiquel grammar by Ildefonso José Flores in 1753 called *El arte de la lengua metropolitana del reyno cakchiquel*, for which he was obliged to design four new letters to represent differing palatal sounds in that Mayan dialect. Since the Chilean scholars José Toribio Medina and Juan Enrique O'Ryan have documented this activity, we will merely comment on trends now.

The seventeenth and early eighteenth centuries were a period of Baroque expression in both Europe and the Spanish colonies overseas. In America its visible remains are to be found largely in architecture, but the volcanic nature of Central America restricted it to special forms; the charming Rococo of Guatemala is modest because they feared earthquakes. This can be seen in the church of Carmen, the Capuchin convent, and the University of San Carlos in Antigua, which all cling to the earth dreading what was coming. Perhaps in San Cristóbal de las Casas in Chiapas, Comayagua in Honduras, Sonsonate in Salvador, and León in Nicaragua it achieved a higher expression. Central America has moreover been a neglected area for literary research; the region remains a backwater, not merely in itself but also in the eyes of the world, which generally neglects it; only Rubén Darío has a secure place in most histories of literature. Nonetheless the Mayab, as it was called before Columbus explored its north coast, or the kingdom of Guatemala as it was known under the Spanish crown, is the most venerable cultural complex of America, where the zero was invented centuries before the Hindus or the Europeans knew it. This region still contains some of the most spectacular monuments on this continent. The Mayas lived an urban and urbane life in a climate that gave the people leisure to pursue cultural objectives. They used it well, and as a result the Mayas produced Baroque long before the Spaniards intruded upon the area.

The conquest by don Pedro de Alvarado and his Tlaxcalan soldiers might be viewed as the end of the ancient Mayab and the beginning of a new era, a sort of middle age anticipating modern times and the imposition of a new language. This is when men like Bernal Díaz del Castillo settled down to enjoy the

climate. His great-grandson Fuentes y Guzmán (1642/43–c. 1700)
shows the type of mind which developed there, inquisitive and
lush like the title of his major work, the *Recordación Florida*,
which records Central American history from its most ancient
period. Baroque means a working out of endless symbolic values,
and Fuentes understood that Central America was heir to both
the Mayas and the Spaniards, set as it is amid the lush tropics
and nervous geology which give it its special traits. Baroque
influence can be sensed in the writings of Sor Juana Inés de la
Cruz despite her clear, inquiring mind. Her contemporary
Fuentes y Guzmán was a different man from the Mexican nun,
although both were inquisitive by temperament; he belonged to
the dominant military caste rather than to any aristocracy, and
the privilege of law and "order" which he enjoyed conceded
scant justice to the Indian and Ladino (or mestizo) masses.

Most histories following his ancestor Bernal Díaz had been
compiled by monks and recounted the so-called spiritual conquest of the Indians. For this reason, Fuentes felt constrained
in the 1690's to write a defense of history as an avocation, which
he called the *Preceptos historiales,* when his friends and acquaint-
ances reproached him for having such an undignified hobby.
This remarkable study anticipates European interest in history
during the eighteenth century as well as our own current appreciation of historiography. Some monkish chronicles were
excellent, for instance the work of Francisco Ximénez (1666–
1729/30), who preserved the *Popol-Vuh* or Mayan Bible within
his greater *Historia de Chiapas y Guatemala* when he served as
parish priest at the last Kiché capital of Chichicastenango in the
early eighteenth century. With these historians we perceive
the intellectual climate in which Central America approached
the end of her private middle ages. It was one of mild curiosity
though not quite of enlightenment, for the kingdom had not
been in touch with the great ideas of either the Renaissance nor
the Reformation which had developed in France and Britain,
nor had the Indian languages been allowed to expand within

their frame. Attempts at doubt were childish during the Spanish colony: dissent was not well reasoned. The Inquisition fought loose morals and witchcraft chiefly; the greatest crime seems to have been bigamy, and most of the Inquisition's victims were demented folk. It was also against dirty books, as is censorship whenever it plays to the gallery, and afraid of "Lutherans, Moors, and Jews," who faced persecution if they had managed to survive into the eighteenth century. A certain fear of Jansenism came with the Bourbons. The theater was pietistic too, and displayed none of the restlessness which we associate with the stage. The cult of Mary which we find in the plays of the Guatemalan playwright Antonio Paz y Salgado (c. 1700–1757) was typical, for the Indians were still being proselytized and the outdoor theater was largely directed toward them.[1] However Paz y Salgado wrote some satires which reflect relaxed morals.

In any case, the kingdom of Guatemala possessed most of the institutions necessary for civilized living, if not for full political expression. If the Hapsburgs did not leave a progressive economy in the isthmus, they also did not exploit Central America as thoroughly as they had Mexico and Peru. There was little gold in this colony, for jade and feathers had formed the Mayas' wealth. The capital of Antigua Guatemala, or Santiago de los Caballeros as it was officially styled, was a city of from 50,000 to 80,000 people in its heyday. Thomas Gage has described its busy life during the 1620's, a century after its founding. The first archbishop was appointed in 1734, five years after *La Gazeta* appeared, and this shows Central America's growing importance to the Spanish crown. By the mid-eighteenth century, the capital had four boys' schools and three girls'. The colleges which had been founded two centuries earlier by the first bishop, Marroquín, and the various religious orders eventually collected around the new University of San Carlos, which had received a belated charter in 1676, and whose lovely cloister in *mudéjar* style was then rising across the street from the cathedral.

[1] See Walter D. Kline's article on Paz y Salgado in *Hispania*, XLI (December 1958), 471–76.

The late eighteenth century was not destined to remain stagnant but was one of impending change. Under Charles III (1759–1788) a desire to study and reform institutions is noted. The Bourbons founded academies and sponsored the spread of French ideas to their overseas realms, especially a taste for natural science, which is exemplified by Buffon in France and Linnaeus in Sweden. If we today need to describe the mechanical and physical discoveries of the space age, the eighteenth century felt an urge to catalogue and classify the flora and fauna of the New World, and this before cameras were invented. The importance of this curiosity on the development of language should not be overlooked, for accurate descriptions required minute discrimination as to shape, color, and other distinguishing features. Thus La Condamine went straight to the equator at Quito in order to measure the circumference of the earth accurately; Mutis studied plant life around Bogotá in New Granada and trained a whole generation of patriots as he did so; and the greatest natural scientist of them all, Humboldt, traveled widely over the Spanish empire in America toward the end of the century. Central America was not behind the times, as we shall see, but slow in responding, as it still is even in this century despite the labors of UNESCO to spread knowledge into the high schools and colleges of the isthmus. In Guatemala this trend was spread by the botanist José Longiños Martínez, who spent the years 1794–1802 there after working on the flora of California and Mexico. He penetrated the kingdom via Soconusco, or the south coast of Chiapas.

We should mention, however, the cultural shock which came in 1767 with the expulsion of the Jesuit order. We are often told this expulsion was cruel and hampered higher education. In Central America such an effect was only momentary. The *Rusticatio Mexicana* by the Jesuit poet Rafael Landívar (1731–1793) is generally mentioned as a first fruit of the expulsion. He is one of the first Central American exiles, and during his banishment in Bologna he felt homesick for the American landscape, just as Andrés Bello was to feel four decades later in London. His intense feeling for nature anticipates the Romantics and such descriptive works as Bello's *Silva a la agricultura de la zona tórrida* or Gutiérrez González' *Memoria sobre el cultivo del maíz en Antioquia*: all three writers expressed American reality, but Landívar's poem has remained dead, somewhat like the Paraguayan missions of his order which soon went back to jungle. The poem is Virgilian, and Landívar wrote in Latin, a classic and medieval tongue, instead of Spanish; so for most purposes his effort has been lost for today.

The departure of the Jesuits brought a change in intellectual standards. All through the previous century, the different religious orders had carried on a running battle aimed at founding their own university in Central America, and thereby controlling higher education in the kingdom. Now with the exit of the Jesuits, who had been the keenest in this struggle, the other orders were able to work in peace. Amazingly, they responded. The Cartesian method was finally introduced, a century late. Natural philosophers like Newton, Descartes, and Locke were given a place in the curriculum; all the modern thinkers were favored except Spinoza, whom for some reason they did not like, and Kant, who was possibly too contemporary to be appreciated. If we observe the University of San Carlos, its great lack was in textbooks, which threw the students upon memory learning and may have led to a dearth of original ideas. Once more we notice a medieval aspect to Central American culture (which continues till today, in every school where the teacher has to function without textbooks). The printing press had thus not fulfilled its function; in 1808 Juarros' great six-volume history of Central America took eight years to come off the press. There was some research however in linguistics, studies of the Indian languages for missionary purposes: the sounds of Cakchiquel, for instance, were described as well as they have been till the present day.

Shortly after the expulsion of the Jesuits, a Spanish Dominican called Fermín Aleas brought forward a new plan of studies in higher education. He wanted twelve new chairs established at the University, in mathematics, geometry, optics, natural science, anatomy, and so forth. Another educational figure was José

Antonio Liendo y Goicoechea (1735–1814), who was born in the Costa Rican city of Cartago, was orphaned at the age of nine, and first taught in Chiapas. He became an excellent teacher who worked for modern thought to replace that of Aristotle. Goicoechea was a man of science and of action who wrote a clear prose; in his later newspaper articles he signed himself "el viejo Licornes." In 1767 there were seventy-four students enrolled in physics at the University of San Carlos. Two years later when Goicoechea was asked to fill this important chair, he introduced the experimental method. He was interested in the principle of fluidity, and this may have started the fad for electricity which continued into the following century in Guatemala. This change occurred four years before the Great Earthquake. In 1782, following that disaster, he pushed for the same reforms which Aleas had proposed from within the university cloister. In 1787 Goicoechea left on a visit to Spain. He traveled via Veracruz, which he reached three months after leaving Santiago de los Caballeros. He was eventually called back to his chair at San Carlos, even though many other people who left for Europe never returned. He brought visual aids for teaching physics and experimental science. Practical university reform thus reached Guatemala ahead of Mexico, as we can check by reading Humboldt, who preferred the new School of Mines there over the University.

The Great Earthquake of 1773 led to the transfer of the capital from the valley of Panchoy to the valley of the Hermitage 25 miles to the northeast, where it still stands. The move created a heavy need for working capital just when the onset of the troubles which attended the French Revolution caused tax revenues to decline.[2] The University became especially short of funds, as we learn from Irisarri, who attended it at the turn of the century, although family business kept him from graduating. The

---

[2] The robbing of the *situado* or state subsidy sent from Mexico is one of the dramatic episodes described in José Milla's *La historia de un pepe*. There were few taxes to support the state, just as today the wealthy classes fight against the income tax and expect support from other countries.

new building, now the Law School, was not as impressive as the old building in Antigua; but its *Salón de Actos* was now ready to receive the first National Assembly of Central America, and still later the National Library. We may remember the poet Arévalo Martínez and others who served as directors there in this century. The cathedral and government buildings were less spectacular than in the former capital: New Guatemala was not pretentious and by the turn of the century had only 18,000 to 20,000 inhabitants. Many stayed on to enjoy the fine climate in Antigua, mostly poor Ladino families who defied the government's evacuation order and squatted among the ruins, as John Lloyd Stephens describes them sixty years later in 1839.

Despite this natural disaster and the ensuing depression, the revived *Gazeta de Guatemala* served as a vehicle for new ideas starting in 1793. In its second phase, the *Gazeta* was edited in good prose and ran serious articles. Many gazettes were published at this time, in Mexico, New Granada or Colombia, Ecuador, and Montreal; the last is the only one which has survived to the present day. Pen names were often formed in anagrams. The first editor was Ignacio Beteta. Alejandro Ramírez, the next one, who came to Guatemala in 1794, was a modernist in philosophy.

After 1797 and the paper shortage, the *Gazeta* seems modern. An article by Mutis, the Spanish botanist working in Bogotá, was published in 1802. Lanning has observed, however, how they talked of the Nootka Indians of what is now British Columbia during the exploration of the North Pacific which we associate with the name of Captain Cook, while local Indians walking the streets or working in the villages or countryside were overlooked.[3] All of this shows an active alliance between the liberal

---

[3] *The Eighteenth-Century Enlightenment in the University of San Carlos de Guatemala* (Ithaca, N.Y., 1956); this recalls the fad for linguistics in Guatemala City in 1946, which the government supported for a time with an office and magazine, but they were studying Max Muller in Argentine reprints and not Kiché or Cakchiquel.

professors at the university and progressive elements within Central American society. Yet, although several persons went to Spain, few went on to France, as Miranda and Bolívar did from Venezuela.

An event which paralleled the rebirth of the *Gazeta* was the founding of the Sociedad Económica de Amigos de la Patria. This society came into existence in 1796 under the patronage of Jacobo de Villaurrutia, an *oidor* or appeal judge (and was thus a semi-official act). The visiting botanist Longiños became an honorary member. This led to important experiments in agriculture and also to investigation on economic topics. New varieties of cinnamon, pepper, camphor, mangos, and breadfruit (which directly recall the expedition of Captain Bligh) were brought in from Jamaica by an expedition which was sent there. Yarn from Pinula and textiles from Quezaltenango were studied; it is rarely stressed sufficiently how the Highlands of Guatemala possess an incipient industrialism which goes back to Mayan times. Seventy years later with the advent of the Reform movement when the conservative republic fell, the Economic Society and its library became the nucleus for the new Ministerio de Fomento or Development set up by the liberal president Justo Rufino Barrios.

A third institution introduced was the Protomedicato or Medical Board set up in 1793 to regulate the practice of medicine in the isthmus. The kingdom had suffered from a dearth of doctors, and under the later Bourbons, French physicians and barbers, who functioned as primitive surgeons for bleeding, tooth pulling, and minor operations, began to immigrate to the colony. They may have been another focus for French ideas. Dr. Narciso Esparragosa, who dominated intellectual circles till his death in 1819, became the Protomédico. He published research on smallpox in 1815 (as early as 1780 a book on the same disease and vaccination had been printed and distributed in these same circles). His teacher was the famous physician José Felipe Flores from Ciudad Real in Chiapas, who graduated from San Carlos in 1780; he operated on cataracts and experimented with meatballs made from Amatitlán lizards or newts as a possible cure for cancer. More important, he built anatomical models, possibly inspired by Professor Goicoechea, which could be taken apart to show the structure of the human body. Both Flores and Esparragosa instituted the practice of vaccination in Central America. Dr. Flores emigrated, traveled through the new United States, settled down for a time in London, and finally died in Madrid after serving as physician to the King.

With the slow infiltration of French thought, literary change came as well, especially a vogue for fables. The first native writer was José Domingo Hidalgo from Quezaltenango in the Mayan highlands; the most famous was Rafael García Goyena (1766–1823), who came to Guatemala from Guayaquil at the age of twelve. He wrote thirty-four fables in all; *Una yegua y un buey* offers the rationalistic theme that a proud mare's colt will only be a brute without training. More enterprising was his contemporary Matías de Córdoba (1768–1828), a Dominican from Tapachula in what is now Mexico. His story *La tentativa del león*, telling how a lion tried to overcome man, is a small epic in the same rationalistic vein. In 1800, after taking his doctor's degree in theology, he went to Spain, where he later witnessed the 2nd of May. He was modest, but ahead of his time: he advocated phonetic spelling just when these changes were being brought about by the Royal Academy, and later founded normal schools in Chiapas. He suggested that Indians be encouraged to wear European-style clothes, which it has required industrialization to effect. In 1821 he served as parish priest in the town of Comitán on the Mexican border facing Guatemala. Fray Matías is the last eminent Central American to hail from Chiapas, before Iturbide swept that state into Mexico, and so physically and symbolically he was lost to Central America. His student Tomás Ruiz, however, returned to Nicaragua, where he taught in the newly established university in León.

The most interesting writer at this time, both for his promise and his frustration, was Simón Bergaño y Villegas (1781–1828).

His real name was Simón Carreño, and he was born near the city of Escuintla in the hot country on the coast south of Guatemala City. He was endowed with a good mind but a serious physical handicap: as a boy, Bergaño was crippled by a fall from a jocote tree where he was gathering the plums. He became as sour and peevish as jocotes, but a talented and spirited writer who was fascinated with French ideas. He learned French, which is not hard for Latin Americans, and was styled a "Voltairean heretic" in his later indictment, which shows an improvement in the style of dissent then prevalent. Bergaño in fact had daring ideas for his time. He poked fun at the philosophy he had learned in Mexico, for Aristotle represented authority to him. He longed to live in Philadelphia, where he could express his mind, and one wonders what would have happened to him there; probably like Heredia, who did reach the States, he would have been unhappy with the climate and the language.

Central America by this time was infected with French ideas; Bergaño was "empapado" in the concepts of Diderot's *Encyclopédie*, just as thirty years later the poet Pepe Batres would run down the *Britannica* so he could study mathematics. Yet despite his progressive plans, Bergaño died unfulfilled. He had projects for schools, although there was not enough money to support these. He was hard on businessmen, claiming they only parrot knowledge without really understanding what they are saying. However, he himself liked horses, since being lame he relied on them to get around.

In 1805 Bergaño was appointed editor of the *Gazeta*. This was now a weekly which appeared on Mondays and consisted of sixteen pages. He wrote a variety of articles for the paper; his *Silva de economia politica* is a livelier document than one might suspect from its title, and he supported vaccination in another poem called *La vacuna*, which however does not measure up to Quintana's similar ode. Bergaño wrote original fables, and some say that García Goyena may have been credited with some of his; in one on *El poeta y el loco* we find a predecessor to the poor poet who died on the music box in Darío's *El rey burgués*. In all of this he tried to cultivate a "forma amena," which shows a real sense of journalism.

After serving for three years as editor, he was arrested in 1808 by the Inquisition and deported to Cuba, one more exile. He was allowed to take no manuscripts with him to Havana—only his crutches, razor, cane, and cloak. His books were sold at auction to pay for the expenses of his trial. Many people poke fun at him, but I cannot help but feel sorry for poor Simón Bergaño. What would one of us have done under the same circumstances? He is typical of the intellectual exile, and if he later edited hack newspapers in Havana, that was to earn a living. When the victims had to pay for their own repression, we can understand how Spain lost so much capital and initiative over the centuries: families were broken up in this way, their breadwinner killed or intimidated, and wealth and enterprise squandered. It shows one reason why Central America did not prosper, the very question which the Economic Society was raising. The British blockade was also having its effect; cochineal and indigo, the two dyes which were then the staples of Central American trade, rather than coffee and bananas, could not be shipped abroad. Eventually it forced an accommodation with British shipping, which brought them into the Mosquito coast of Nicaragua and Honduras as well as to Belize.

The Holy Office was destined to disappear from Central America in 1813. The Inquisition had performed mostly silly chores like hunting down witches during its career there, and in later years in watching out for sedition, as it did with Hidalgo in Mexico. This institution has left its trace on the Central American character with its hypocrisy and fear of committing oneself.

In 1816 the *Gazeta* was suppressed too, after a quarter of a century's service. The authorities were afraid, for this marked the reaction under Ferdinand VII; but within a few months other newspapers were appearing to carry on the process of public information and communication. The publishers of these new sheets which appeared at Independence had been prepared in the atmosphere we have been describing. In 1820 there was *El Editor Constitucional*, which in 1821 changed its name to *El Genio de la Libertad*, while the Honduranian José Cecilio del Valle founded his conservative *El Amigo de la Patria*.

In this last colonial phase, the University of San Carlos managed to produce a distinguished group of graduates. This circle was not as unique as the one which Mutis fostered in Bogotá during the same years, but these men were equally well trained and alert. It was the Creole maturity, although the generation did not quite fulfill its promise. The most outstanding was Fray Antonio Larrazábal, who represented the cabildo of Guatemala City in the Cortes of Cádiz and served that body loyally from 1812 till 1814. When Ferdinand VII returned to the throne, Larrazábal was arrested and sent home to Guatemala as a prisoner; but in 1820 he was elected president of the University. Another was Simeón Cañas from Salvador, the Wilberforce of Central America. In 1806 he too became rector of San Carlos, and later speaker of the assembly. José Cecilio del Valle from Cholutcca in Honduras (1780–1834) edited his own newspaper. José Francisco Barrundia, who spent a term as prisoner from 1813 to 1819, wrote *El Coliseo*; born in 1787, he died in Washington in 1834 while on a diplomatic mission to this country. Don Pedro Molina was the great link between the colony and the republic. Born illegitimate, in 1792 he was admitted to the University because of his superior talent. He studied under Flores and Esparragosa but outshone them for his universal qualities. In 1830 his Academia de Ciencias showed the French inspiration under which the University was superseded, as happened also in Mexico; but this new academy was essentially the same institution, down to the buildings of the Law School and its professors. The equipment which Goicoechea and Flores had introduced to the lecture halls had gone to pieces by 1810, according to our information. In 1812 it is interesting to note that Negroes were admitted to the University; many had already been druggists, just as Indians became herb doctors. Everybody nevertheless still had to subscribe to religious dogmas in order either to register or to graduate.

Through all of this we can sense a common thread running from Fuentes y Guzmán to Pepe Batres and Irisarri. These men were plutocrats rather than aristocrats, as Arqueles Vela and Humberto Alvarado have pointed out. Many had not even attended university and were more interested in money and social position. The Creoles did not revolt from Spain; outside events like the Enlightenment, the French Revolution, and the industrial and commercial revolutions forced Central America to change. The last decade of the eighteenth century and the first two of the nineteenth had been intense; but the government itself was powerless except to obstruct, as we saw in its treatment of Simón Bergaño, since it could levy so few taxes. When Pepe Batres could not break with his own order even in the 1840's, despair led him to commit suicide. The class as a whole, when it could not export the products of the country because the Napoleonic wars and consequent sea blockade were upsetting their trade patterns, ended up in an alliance, either open or covert, with British shipping. Neither had there been much popular discontent within Central America until 1820. The leaderless Indians, captive within the culture that had been imposed upon them three centuries before, found no justice. They still had some memories however: in the highland city of Totonicapán, one revolt led to the appointment of diarchs, in the manner of the ancient Mayan city states, whom they called "king" and "president."

It was the injection finally of French secularism which really broke up Central America even before this issue ravaged Mexico. French ideas were reinforced with President Morazán from Honduras, the last head of the still-united though moribund federation, who injected the issue of secularism into Central American politics. The influence of his background has never been properly studied, although his family came from the French Antilles. The federal republic was founded on the inadequate institutions which did not provide for a modern political life, and as this occurred in the 1820's and 1830's, well within the new century of independence and civil wars, we shall leave it for a future investigation.

# XII

# Rafael Landívar and Poetic Echoes
## of the Enlightenment

### GRACIELA P. NEMES

THE EIGHTEENTH CENTURY saw the publication of chronicles, travel books, personal letters, and histories that furnished European readers with information concerning the New World. In Spain and Portugal, chronicles and polemical histories served as the principal vehicles. Only rarely did a poet attempt to use his art as an instrument of propaganda or information, as Virgil and Lucretius had done in classical times. A large measure of useful knowledge, topographical and biological description, however, constitutes the subject matter of a didactic poem in Latin, *Rusticatio Mexicana*, written by a Guatemalan Jesuit, Rafael Landívar, during his exile in Italy.

His work was first published in Modena, in 1781, in an edition of 133 pages now known merely through a bibliographical notice.[1] The oldest existing edition is the second, a book of 238 pages published in Bologna one year later.[2] This edition con-

---

[1] "Rusticatio Mexicana, seu rariora quadam ex agris mexicanis decerpta atque in libros decem distributa a R. Landívar. Mutinae, apud Soc. Typographicam, 1781. 8⁰–133 pages. 1 hoja s.f." In J. Toribio Medina, *Noticias bio-bibliográficas de los jesuitas expulsos de América in 1767* (Santiago, 1914), p.201.

[2] Raphaelis Landívar, *Rusticatio Mexicana* (Bonomiae, 1782).

tains a "Salutation to Guatemala" and a preface by the author indicating, among other things, that the poem is based on fact and that certain parts have been revised and others added. It consists of fifteen parts or books, plus an additional unnumbered part in which Landívar renders homage to the Christian faith. Three translations in Spanish and one in English have been made of this edition.

Alexander von Humboldt read *Rusticatio Mexicana* and mentions it in his *Political Essay on the Kingdom of New Spain*. Referring to a volcano that was born in Michoacán the night of September 29, 1759, he says: "This remarkable phenomenon was sung in hexameter verses by the Jesuit father Rafael Landívar."[3] Humboldt notes that in spite of the fact that the abbé Clavigero also mentioned the volcano in his ancient history of Mexico, the phenomenon "remained unknown to the mineralogists and naturalists of Europe, though it took place not more than fifty years ago, and within six days' journey of the capital of Mexico." This seems to indicate that most Europeans paid insufficient attention to books written by Americans containing authentic information about America, since the second part of *Rusticatio Mexicana* is devoted entirely to the volcano which Humboldt later visited and described. It took Hispanic criticism over a century, moreover, to make a value judgment of the work although the book was obviously read and cited.[4] The first person who wrote at length about its merits seems to be Marcelino Menéndez y Pelayo in his *Antología de poetas hispanoamericanos*, of 1893. He attributes to Landívar outstanding qualities as a descriptive poet and declares that if he had written *Rusticatio* in the vernacular instead of Latin, he would have

---

[3] London, 1811, Vol.II, Chap.VIII, p.211.

[4] Menéndez y Pelayo originally encountered some verses of *Rusticatio Mexicana* in Juan María Maury's notes to his poem "La agresión británica": "Desde que casi en nuestra infancia leímos algunos versos de este poema en una de las notas que pone Maury á su espléndido canto de 'La agresión británica,' entramos en gran curiosidad de adquirir y leer la *Rusticatio*." In *Antología de poetas hispanoamericanos* (Madrid, 1893), p.clxvi.

surpassed all other American poets in the genre. The place of the poem, according to this critic, is between Bello's "La agricultura de la zona tórrida" and Balbuena's "Grandeza mexicana."[5]

In 1942 Octaviano Valdés, author of a third Spanish translation of the poem,[6] stressed its superiority over the works of Bello and Balbuena, praising the plastic quality of the verses and the ability of the author to give luster to the different facets of any one theme, in particular, his ability to sustain the poetic vein in the books about industries, livestock, and similar topics. Valdés does not dwell on these aspects of the poem. In 1950 José Mata Gavidia finally called attention to Landívar's particular approach, to his praise of industry and the working habits of the native man.[7] In 1956 Federico de Onís mentioned Landívar in the Introduction to the *Anthologie de la poésie ibéro-américaine* published by UNESCO.[8] He called him one of the great American poets of all times; in his opinion, *Rusticatio Mexicana* is equal and often superior to subsequent descriptions of the most authentic and picturesque aspects of American life and nature. Other well-known Hispanic critics, among them Pedro Henríquez Ureña and Gabriel Méndez Plancarte, have extolled the work for its truly American character. Graydon W. Regenos, the author of an excellent prose version of the poem in English, also praises it as a descriptive poem but, like critics before him, finds some fault with the form. In his opinion, the poem lacks the sustained spark of genius found in Virgil; he notices, as does Octaviano Valdés, an occasional forced metaphor, a wearisome repetition of the same figure, or a choice of words

[5] *Ibid.*, p.clxix.

[6] Rafael Landívar, *Por los campos de México*, trans. Octaviano Valdés (Mexico City, 1942), p.xiii. (A second edition of this work with the Latin text was published by the Editorial Jus, Mexico City, 1965.) The other two Spanish translations are by Federico Escobedo, *Versión métrica del poema latino del P. Rafael Landívar, S.J., Rusticatio Mexicana* (Mexico City, 1924), and by Ignacio Loureda, *Rusticación mexicana* (Mexico City, 1924).

[7] *Landívar, el poeta de Guatemala*, I (Guatemala City, 1950), 16.

[8] Compiled, with Introduction and notes, by F. de Onís (Paris, 1956), p.21.

at times strained. He concedes that the character of the subject matter together with the restriction of meter places heavy demands on the poem. Regenos leaves to others the decisive appraisal of its literary qualities.[9]

Whatever reminiscences there are of the classical Latin poets in Landívar are, as Regenos points out, incidental. Menéndez y Pelayo and Octaviano Valdés have dwelt at length on the Virgilian aspects of *Rusticatio Mexicana*, but have taken pains to stress the originality of the poem and its independence from Virgil's *Georgics*. Regenos also notices in his Introduction that "the work, while certainly inspired by Virgil's *Georgics*, is far more than a pastoral poem."

Although it may be true that the Latin idiom of Landívar's poem has kept it from exerting any profound influence on later generations, it should not be dismissed as a mere poetic exercise. It is a document of historical significance revealing the conscious attempt of a colonial Spanish American intellectual to incorporate himself into the new European currents of thought at a time when colonial tradition still weighed heavily on him.

Most of the phenomena described in *Rusticatio Mexicana* are a result of Landívar's direct perception, a result of his education in the colonies in the current Scholastic tradition. The author was the product of the best education the colonies offered prior to the changes brought about in Guatemala by men like Jacobo de Villaurrutia, or Father Antonio de Liendo y Goicoechea. His teachers were eminent men within the intellectual framework of the colony; they taught in Latin and defended tradition and Scholasticism.[10] Yet they could not have been indifferent to the type of knowledge which characterized the Enlightenment. In

---

[9] *Rafael Landívar's Rusticatio Mexicana* (Mexican Country Scenes). The Latin text with an Introduction and an English prose translation by Graydon W. Regenos. *Philological and Documentary Studies*, I, No.5 (1948), 159–60 (reprinted from Publication No.11, pp.155–314).

[10] Biographical information is found in J. Antonio Villacorta C., *Estudios bio-bibliográficos sobre Rafael Landívar* (Guatemala City, 1931). (This work is based on documentation in the Colonial Archives of Guatemala.)

his study of *The Eighteenth-Century Enlightenment in the University of San Carlos de Guatemala,* Lanning has called attention to the fact that the zeal for research in botany and astronomy, for example, existed long before it was formally established at San Carlos in 1793.[11] Roland D. Hussey notices that the Jesuits taught Descartes, Newton, and Leibniz.[12] As a postulant and newly ordained Jesuit priest in Mexico, Landívar had to familiarize himself with the customs of the various people to whom he was going to preach.[13] The Jesuits had schools where they learned the native tongues and taught the Indians Spanish, and they had, especially in Mexico, cattle ranches, mines, mills, tanneries, and country stores. Landívar, in the Preface to *Rusticatio Mexicana,* states that he relates only things that he saw or which were told to him by trustworthy eyewitnesses. He also says that he confirmed the more unusual things written on the authority of others. We know that he lived in Michoacán about the time of the appearance of the spectacular volcano described in his poem; that he made trips to Oaxaca and Antequera where cochineal was produced, and that he saw in Mexico the cultivation of sugar cane and the manufacturing of sugar.

That Landívar wrote for the European reader is indicated by the first words of his "Author's Preface": "I have entitled this poem *Rusticatio Mexicana,* not only because nearly everything contained in it relates to the fields of Mexico, but also because I realize that it is customary in Europe to call the whole of New Spain, Mexico, without taking into account the different countries." His desire to reach the European public probably accounts for his having written the poem in Latin, a language known by the educated. It is doubtful, moreover, that he could have written in a European language other than his native Spanish. In the first stanza of the poem he indicates his intention to be under-

[11] Ithaca, N.Y., 1956, p.161.
[12] "Traces of French Enlightenment in Colonial Hispanic America," in *Latin America and the Enlightenment,* ed. Arthur P. Whitaker (New York, 1942), p.35.
[13] Villacorta, *Estudios bio-bibliográficos,* p.63.

stood rather than to conform to prevailing literary tastes. In an obvious reference to the conceptualism of the Baroque period which dominated the literary production of Spain and Spanish America during the first half of the eighteenth century, he states: "Let another conceal his thoughts in obscure figures whose hidden meaning no one would venture to interpret or worry his mind with the thankless task." Setting himself apart from the most common tendencies, he refuses to join ranks with the imitators of Aesop or La Fontaine or with those Hispanic poets who exalted the armed victories of a nation long in a period of military decadence: "Let another bestow reason and pleasant discourse upon dumb animals, let him cover the fields with armies, the earth with death, and let him vanquish entire nations by armed force." Particularly noticeable in the second stanza of the poem are his love for his native land and his great interest in pragmatic knowledge.

Any doubt concerning Landívar's didactic intention is dispelled by the following words in the Preface: "I confess that more is to be desired in this poem on the subject of mines, for I have not proposed to display a very exact knowledge of this industry since that would require a very large volume, but I give only the important facts and those things worth knowing." Yet he conformed to the conventions of Latin verse by adorning his work with pagan deities. "In order that you, my gentle reader, may read this poem inoffensively, I would have you know that I am going to speak in the manner of a poet whenever mention is made of the false deities of the ancients. I solemnly realize and devoutly confess that such fictitious deities have no understanding, much less any power and might."

Few critics have called attention to the significance of *Rusticatio Mexicana vis-à-vis* the Enlightenment. Menéndez y Pelayo, who called this movement "Enciclopedismo," dwells on the novelty of Landívar's themes and yet he attributes his particular approach to mere nostalgia for his native land. Placing great importance on the local color of the poem, he dismisses the enlightened character of its content by implication and with humor, saying that it belongs to the descriptive-didactic Jesuit school responsible for so many capricious and ingenious meters about tea, coffee, gunpowder, magnets, earthquakes, clocks, the art of conversation, the consorting of plants, the silkworm, fishing and game, comets, the rainbow, the aurora borealis, the barometer, the game of chess, and even tarwater.[14] This so-called descriptive-didactic Jesuit school, according to Mariano Picón Salas, was an expression of Jesuit humanism, considered to be one of the eighteenth-century bridges that joined the Baroque age to the pre-revolutionary period. Referring to those aspects of colonialism which influenced and shaped modern Latin American thought, Picón Salas observes that while European influence injected "the virus of insurrection into the slothful body of the colonies from the eighteenth century on," the native organism itself was slowly evolving toward that new ideology which led to revolutionary thought.[15]

Landívar represents the intellectual man who was breaking away from colonial tradition. He was not a reformer, much less a revolutionary, but as the member of the Jesuit order, a major cultural, economic, and political force in the colonial Spanish world, he was slowly moving toward a new spirit characterized by a rational approach to learning and a concern for economic development and progress.

In spite of quandaries which reveal a conflict between the old ideas and the new, the most noticeable trait of *Rusticatio Mexicana* is its scientifically oriented approach, providing precise explanations of industrial and agricultural processes, of natural and human phenomena, and of natural and human resources. The book contains illustrations of a mule-drawn and a water-run sugar mill and of a flying pole, their different parts lettered to serve as a guide to the reader. The footnotes which follow each part of the poem explain the origin and development of certain

14 *Antología*, p.clxvi.

15 *A Cultural History of Spanish America*, trans. Irving A. Leonard (Berkeley and Los Angeles, 1962), p.130.

autochthonous words used, e.g.: "*Centzontle* ... a corrupted word from the ancient *centzontlatolis* which means 'countless voices' " (note 5, p.175). Then Landívar quotes other writers who have written about the bird called "centzontle." Most notes expand the information contained in the poem, giving ample bibliographical data.

The manner in which Landívar concludes his work merits particular attention. In the reverent garb of the religious man he admonishes youth to embrace the new scientific spirit, *to abandon old ideas and adopt the new, to uncover the mysteries of nature*, and to search with *the full vigor of their mind*. The *new ideas* are implicit in *Rusticatio Mexicana*, which attests to a new alertness, to a zeal to enlighten and to promote new knowledge about its author's native land. Landívar attains his purpose without sacrificing the artistic quality of his poetic genre.

If Landívar had stayed in the colonies, he might never have written his scientific American poem. It is a widely accepted fact that the writings of the exiles, directly influenced by European thought, were the best fruits of eighteenth-century Jesuit humanism. In Bologna Landívar enjoyed the company of many illustrious Spanish American exiles devoted to the task of writing about their beloved America. The historian Francisco Javier Clavigero wrote there his now classic *Historia antigua de México*. Distance is said to have given these exiles a clearer perspective of their native land. Besides having each other to supplement and verify their knowledge, they also had the support of Italian intellectuals and access to private files and good libraries. As Picón Salas has observed, "The fact that the Jesuits had lost their ascendancy in America, so that all that was left to them was to write and to die in a proper Christian manner, serves to underscore their noble effort to be truthful and their nearly always detached line of thought."[16]

Landívar does not rank among the liberal thinkers who led the way to political and cultural independence in Spanish America, men like Santa Cruz y Espejo, Antonio de Nariño, Camilo

[16] *Ibid.*, p.134.

Henríquez, but he was, psychologically, a precursor of independence. In his efforts to make his country known in Europe in a manner befitting the times he revealed the same "hospitality to scientific inquiry" which distinguishes the leading thinkers of the Enlightenment.

# IV

## Anglo-America

# XIII

# The Younger John Winthrop,
## Precursor of the Scientific Enlightenment

ROBERT C. BLACK III

Anyone with the most rudimentary knowledge of New England in the seventeenth century is sure to acknowledge that John Winthrop, Jr. (1606–1676) was a remarkable person. Eldest son of the renowned senior John Winthrop of Massachusetts Bay, an important participant himself in the early development of that colony, a vital influence in the legal establishment and subsequent expansion of Connecticut, a primary factor in the bloodless English conquest of New Netherlands, the younger Winthrop commands notice as possibly the most accomplished politician of his region and era. Yet his reputation notably transcends the public sector. It is as an alchemist, a physician, a savant, a natural philosopher that he has been most widely recognized. Winthrop was the first resident of North America to be elected a Fellow of the Royal Society of London. Indeed, we may rank him with confidence among the most humane spirits of his time. But his role as a major influence has yet to be certified, nor has his place in the Western intellectual community of his day ever been perfectly assured. Probably they never will be.

Winthrop was a man of exceptional gifts—of perception, of imagination, and of understanding. The range of his curiosity was vast. Yet he always suffered from a lack of staying power; his attention span ran short. As a youth he afforded a classic example of a late bloomer; as an adult he barely escaped becoming a dilettante. However, these weaknesses were regularly concealed by his personality, which was altogether extraordinary.

Winthrop's growth into the man he became is still a matter for wonder. Though he was the offspring of an over-committed Puritan father, his sympathy for dialectical systems was always minimal. The leader, over decades, of a heavily Puritan community, he exhibited an unwavering disinterest in religious controversy. The influence chiefly responsible for these unusual attributes is anyone's guess. Perhaps it was his abbreviated undergraduate experience (between 1622 and 1624) at Trinity College, Dublin, which at the time was much under the influence of the ideas of Peter Ramus. Possibly it was his occasional residence, in 1625, with an uncle, Thomas Fones, who was a London apothecary. More probably it was his friendship with a certain Thomas Howes, a student at the Inner Temple, but less a lawyer than a master of intelligent discourse.[1]

Most likely of all, he simply responded to his own instincts. In June of 1628, he was sent off by his father upon what amounted to a Mediterranean cruise, a piece of undeserved indulgence which was carefully disguised as a search for prospects. The journey, which carried him to Tuscany, Constantinople, and Venice, occupied more than a year; its career consequences were nil but its influence upon him was noteworthy. In Tuscany, Winthrop became absorbed, not in artistic treasures, but in botanical gardens. At Constantinople, he became interested in current diplomatic affairs. From Venice he wrote of political matters and the intricacies of foreign exchange. Everywhere, it

[1] Constantia Maxwell, *A History of Trinity College, Dublin, 1591–1892* (Dublin, 1946), pp.28–29; W. B. S. Taylor, *History of the University of Dublin* (London, 1945), p.219; Allyn B. Forbes (ed.), *Winthrop Papers, 1498–1649*, 5 vols. (Boston, 1929–1947), I, 333ff., 514 note; Robert C. Winthrop, *Life and Letters of John Winthrop, Governor of the Massachusetts Bay Company*, 2 vols. (Boston, 1869), II, 240 note; *Dictionary of National Biography*, XXVIII, 119.

is plain, he charmed the local English colony. But his most satis-
fying friendship was with a Dutch scholar named Jacobus
Golius, a specialist in oriental languages, but most of all another master of good conversation.[2]

The elder John Winthrop departed—as governor—for Massachusetts Bay in the spring of 1630, and the younger followed
somewhat more than a year later. It is to be noted that he took
with him a barrel of books, chiefly "chimical." He furthermore
undertook to record, at sea, the daily wind direction; simul-
taneous observations were to be made in eastern England by
yet another learned friend, the Reverend Henry Jacie. No permanent results came from these data, but they suggest an inspired theory of temperate zone weather.[3]

Winthrop's first years in New England were a season of training, mainly political and by osmosis. He did maintain a fairly
steady correspondence with Howes and Jacie, and during a semi-
official journey to Britain in 1634–1635 he established a significant friendship with a pair of Germanic brothers, Abraham
and Johann Sibert Kuffler, both doctors of medicine, but more
particularly devotees of alchemy.[4] The most interesting features
of this period, however, were his attitudes toward public questions. As an "assistant" of Massachusetts Bay he was thrust close
to the center of the doctrinal furors occasioned by the deviations
of Anne Hutchinson, the Reverend John Wheelwright, and Dr.
Robert Child. Yet he consistently side-stepped any public position in such matters—even to the point of nonattendance at court
sessions. In fact, his personal repugnance for the more rigid
aspects of Massachusetts' religious policy is clear. But he dis-

---

[2] *Winthrop Papers*, I, 267–68, 402 and note, 403, 406, 408–409, 417–18; II, 72–74;
IV, 155–56; R. C. Winthrop, *Life and Letters*, I, 263–65, 268, 270–71; Massachusetts
Historical Society, Ms. Winthrop Papers, Vol.V, fol.91; Hugh James Rose (comp.),
*A New General Biographical Dictionary*, 12 vols. (London, 1857), VIII, 58–59.

[3] *Winthrop Papers*, III, 31ff., 58, 226–27.

[4] *Ibid.*, pp.55–127, *passim*; *Collections*, Mass. Hist. Society, Series 5, I, 382–83;
Basil Valentine, *Von den Naturlich und Obernaturlich Dingen* (Leipzig, 1624),
Title No.254 in Winthrop Library, New York Society Library.

played another characteristic: he had no instinct for martyrdom. Never would he defy a situation which he felt to be inevitable.[5]

Winthrop was not a man who found it easy to settle down. His abounding energy was of a distinctively nervous kind. Even in mid-career he continued to tack erratically about, from salt-works to iron-works to graphite mines and on to ventures in real estate. He did not settle upon a semi-permanent residence (at New London) until 1647, and he would not undertake a lasting political association (with Connecticut) for yet another decade. Such personal uncertainties were not, of course, inconsistent with his curiosity, and it was during these years that his penchant for "natural philosophy" became most pronounced. A second semi-official voyage to Britain (1641–1643) led to a noteworthy series of extracurricular activities, including a lengthy visit to Hamburg and the Low Countries, where he sought out promising luminaries of the intellectual community, including Dr. Johannes Tanckmarus, Augustinus Petraeus, Johann Rudolf Glauber, and Johannes Amos Comenius.[6] It was probably at this time also that his existing interest in alchemy was modified into a commitment to Paracelsian medicine, and Winthrop's reputation as a physician (though without a degree) continued thereafter assured.

It is difficult nowadays to assess his true contribution to medicine and, in particular, to alchemy. His emphasis upon chemical specifics suggests a willingness to experiment. On the other hand, he was much devoted to an all-purpose nostrum of his own compounding, a rather violent purgative which he called "rubila powder."[7] (One is inclined to believe that the most effective of

[5] See Robert C. Black III, *The Younger John Winthrop* (New York and London, 1966), pp.104–107, 130–32.

[6] *Ibid.*, pp.114–16.

[7] R. H. Shryock, *Medicine and Society in America, 1600–1860* (New York, 1960), p.51; Williams Haynes, *American Chemical Industry, a History*, 6 vols. (New York, 1945–1954), I, 91; C. A. Browne, "Scientific Notes . . . of John Winthrop, Jr.," *Isis*, XI, 335; Ms. Winthrop Papers, 20a and 20b; Walter R. Steiner, M.D., "Governor John Winthrop, Jr., of Connecticut as a Physician," *The Connecticut Magazine*, IX, 34; *Collections*, Mass. Hist. Society, Series 3, X, 15–18; undated notes on Winthrop, Ms. Winthrop Papers, 5.205.

his healing arts was his bedside manner!) His position in the
jealously guarded shadow-world of alchemy may have been of
yet greater consequence; his alchemical library was one of the
century's most extensive, and there is strong evidence that Winthrop was in fact the elusive "Eirenaeus Philalethes," author of
*Introitus Apertus, or Secrets Reveal'd.* On the other hand, his
enthusiasm for the strictly occult did not prove permanent.[8]

Winthrop's efforts in the securing of the remarkable Connecticut Charter of 1662 have been widely applauded. (It was an
intricate business, requiring a visit to England that lasted almost
two years.) But the historian will be most interested in his con-
current intellectual activities, which included an association
with an impressive array of savants and his election, in January
1662, as an Original Fellow of the Royal Society of London.

Winthrop already enjoyed an effective entrée to such a group.
He had long corresponded, upon a great variety of topics, with
the widely respected Samuel Hartlib, and Hartlib had subsequently brought him to the attention of young William Brereton.[9] Brereton now conducted Winthrop into the chambers of
Gresham College to be presented to the assembled Fellows, and
it is a commentary upon Winthrop's unusual character that he
was immediately received as one of them.[10] He grew particularly
close to Robert Boyle and Henry Oldenburg; he delivered a
number of papers upon North American topics; and he became,
following his departure, the Society's principal trans-Atlantic
correspondent. It was an activity much to his liking and one that
he never wholly abandoned.[11]

[8] R. S. Wilkinson, "The Problem of the Identity of Eirenaeus Philalethes," *Am-
bix*, XII, 24–43, and "The Alchemical Library of John Winthrop, Jr.," *Ambix*, XI;
J. W. Hamilton-Jones to author, September 19, 1964; Black, *The Younger John
Winthrop*, pp.155–57.

[9] *Proceedings*, Mass. Hist. Society, LXXII, 36–67; *Proceedings*, American Anti-
quarian Society, new series, III, 267–73.

[10] *Proceedings*, Mass. Hist. Society, XVI, 215; Ms. Winthrop Papers, 5.30;
Ms. Journal Book, Royal Society Library; "Extracts from the Journal of the
Royal Society," Additional Mss.4447, fol.25, British Museum; Egerton Mss.,
fol.218, British Museum.

[11] Register Book of the Royal Society (Ms. copy), I, 182–87, 209–11, 292–305,

Whether Winthrop can be regarded as a significant influence, either upon the "reason" of his own century, or upon the "enlightenment" of the next, must remain an open question. As with so many of the intelligently knowledgeable of his era, his position was two-sided: backward-drawn toward the traditional, forward-seeking toward the inductive. He frequently displayed a startlingly modern viewpoint. "I wish," he wrote Hartlib in 1660, "you could prevail with Dr. Kuffler to bury that firework [an experimental submarine mine] in oblivion. . . . There are means enough known to the world of ruin and destruction to mankind both by sea and land." He chided Hartlib himself for experimenting with a perpetual-motion machine—on the ground that it would be abused by the rich to deprive the poor of gainful employment. Moreover, the pressures of the New England frontier set him to considering the benefits of artificially cheap money; indeed, he forsaw the possibility of a monetary system that could be managed without any fixed standard at all.[12] His reports to the Royal Society were, however, a mixed bag. Though more than casual, they were distinctly spasmodic, and their undisciplined qualities still are obvious to anyone who will take the trouble to examine them. He dispatched to England, with commentaries, a perfect hodgepodge of American specimens, some of authentic interest, others not; included were common barnacles, dwarfed white oaks, hummingbird nests, starfish and horseshoe crabs. He did provide certain very perceptive data upon the planet Jupiter and three naked-eye comets. But he also took pains to record certain dubious phenomena of a miraculous nature (which he had not observed himself), and he suggested that the catastrophic "wheat blast" which was afflicting contemporary New England might indeed be the result of "blasting from heaven."[13]

It must be admitted that the Royal Society itself could exhibit

Royal Society Library; Boyle Letters, 5.197–202, Royal Society Library; Ms. Winthrop Papers, 5.208; Black, *The Younger John Winthrop*, pp.232–33, 307–19.

12 See note 9 above.

13 See Black, *The Younger John Winthrop*, pp.307–17 and notes.

similarly un-Linnean procedures. A number of its Fellows were openly willing to acknowledge the impulsive interventions of the Deity, and the Society made no objection when Winthrop ascribed the waterspouts of the Caribbean to the actions of sea monsters. It made no clear distinction between the natural and the political; it sought as enthusiastically to develop the English economy as to investigate the heavenly bodies. Winthrop's own inconsistencies were reflected accurately in the uncertainties of his colleagues overseas—and in the profoundly transitional character of the seventeenth century itself.[14]

Any serious evaluation of the younger John Winthrop must always consider his effect upon subsequent attitudes, both in America and in Europe. Politically, he left behind much that was useful, and his public services—so curiously subtle, practical, and humane—afford examples that still are worthy of contemplation. His intellectual impact has been less obvious. Though he is undoubtedly to be numbered among the more perceptive minds of his day, he contributed no *system* of thought, no disciplined philosophy, no ordered morality. So far as the record can inform us, he never even tried. It is clear that he was highly regarded by a number of major thinkers, but his influence upon them was probably slight. And he developed few associations south of the Low Countries in Europe and none at all south of the Hudson in North America.

Winthrop in fact never quite fulfilled the requirements for "enlightenment" as established by subsequent commentators. He unquestionably would have disappointed the abbé Morellet. He was too frequently lazy, and sometimes he failed to grapple with what he obviously regarded as erroneous. His library was crammed with slightly used books. He nursed a basic distrust of personal commitments, and he characteristically avoided open hostility toward those established institutions with which he was confronted.

Most of all, he appears to have believed that a too-perfected body of theory can, when applied to the ordinary business of

14 *Ibid.*, pp.314–16.

living, be dangerous. Perhaps that is why he has never been reckoned "important"; so frequently is intellectual stature associated with the disposition to overturn. Winthrop was, in a word, too tolerant to be enlightened—at least in the sense accepted by the following century.

But that he was extraordinary no one can deny.

# XIV

# Literary Ecumenicalism of the American Enlightenment

## LEWIS P. SIMPSON

THE THEORY that American literature and thought are fundamentally governed by a quest for nationality is an almost axiomatic assumption by historians of that literature. This has unfortunate consequences—it restricts perspectives on the cosmopolitan sources of our literature and literary life, surely nowhere more so than in the virtually irresistible tendency to regard the Enlightenment in North America (the part of North America which became the United States of America) entirely in the context of the eruption of a colonial people into the novelty of revolution and unique nationhood. Indeed at times we get the impression in studies of the eighteenth century in America that it assumed a wholly indigenous character. I should like here to present a few notes on the irony of this kind of literary isolationism—and, I suppose, of isolationism generally in the study of American letters—by calling attention, briefly and schematically, to a relationship between literary nationalism and the literary ecumenicalism of the American Enlightenment. I employ the term *literary ecumenicalism* together with the more common term *literary cosmopolitanism* because I want to convey the idea of a metaphysical sensibility of universal literary order present in the minds of American men of letters in the eighteenth century. This sensibility was a basic force in their way of thinking and feeling about the life of the lettered mind (the educated mind) in America; to be sure, it shaped the imagination of literary order in America. I mean it furnished to American men of letters the symbolic structures, the images, of secular literature (in the broad-ranging sense of the term before the advent of specialization of knowledge) as an autonomous realm of existence.

And yet ironically the ecumenical sensibility of letters had the effect in America of encouraging the nationalistic bias. How, we may ask, did this happen?

## I

Possibly the most famous imagining of the possibilities of America as a novel dominion in history, a work endlessly appealed to by American literary nationalists, is to be found in St. Jean de Crèvecoeur's *Letters from an American Farmer* (1782). This is notably true of Letter No. III, the one which asks the leading question, "What is the American, this new man?" Here is part of Crèvecoeur's response:

Americans are the Western pilgrims who are carrying along with them that great mass of arts, sciences, vigour, and industry which began long since in the east; they will finish the great circle. The Americans were once scattered all over Europe; here they are incorporated into one of the finest systems of population which has ever appeared, and which will hereafter become distinct by the power of the different climates they inhabit. The American ought therefore to love this country much better than that wherein either he or his forefathers were born. Here the rewards of industry follow with equal steps the progress of his labour; his labour is founded on the basis of nature, *self-interest*; can it want a stronger allurement? Wives and children, who before in vain demanded of him a morsel of bread, now, fat and frolicksome, gladly help their father to clear those fields whence exuberant crops arise to feed and clothe them all; without any part being claimed, either by a despotic prince, a rich abbot, or a mighty lord. Here religion demands but little of him; a small voluntary salary to the minister, and gratitude to God; can he refuse these? The American is a new man, who acts upon new principles; he must therefore entertain new ideas, and form new opinions. From involuntary idleness, servile dependence, penury, and useless labour, he has passed to toils of a very different nature, rewarded by ample subsistence.—This is an American.[1]

This passage from Crèvecoeur suggests concepts with opposing implications for the life of the mind in America. On the one hand, the author asserts, the Americans are carriers of letters and learning who will complete the bringing of arts and sciences to the world. This is their historical mission, one begun far back in ancient times in the distant East and now to be fulfilled by Europeans transported with all of their inherited baggage of knowledge to the New World wilderness. Such a conception gives the Americans both a culminating role in the long history of intellectual endeavor and a heavy historical responsibility. On the other hand, and in the same breath, Crèvecoeur conceives that in America the European is altogether freed from the works of the mind in other ages. He has no obligation to intellectual and literary history—to any transmitted order of words or realm of letters. Entering into a new relationship with a bountiful nature in a pastoral economy, he is nearly free from the impositions of church and state. Economically and psychically independent and secure, he becomes a new man whose responsibility is purely to "form new ideas" and "new opinions," not to perpetuate the "great mass" of intellect from a superseded past. The American lives at the beginning of the development of the human mind instead of at the end of it. The American mind, Crèvecoeur implies, freed from political, ecclesiastical, and literary forms of order as these have been construed, will create a singular autonomy of its own.

Crèvecoeur holds these contradictory notions so easily and simplistically that they seem to coalesce. This is because they are

[1] *Letters from an American Farmer*, ed. W. P. Trent and Ludwig Lewisohn (New York, 1904), p.55.

essentially related to literary conventions, poetic and metaphorical in nature, with a common source in the historical literary ecumenicalism of Western civilization. Both in fact are expressions of the symbolism of literary order which supports the ecumenical sensibility. This is to say the order of the "Third Realm," the realm of letters, which in the Age of the Enlightenment achieved, or was assumed by men of letters to have achieved, a status approximating independence from church and state.

To understand the nature of the Third Realm is one of the most difficult problems of intellectual and literary history. We must involve ourselves in a study calling for us as literary persons to examine the structure of a way of existence we may well assume without knowing we assume it. And we must be willing to follow the complicated struggle to symbolize the life of the mind under the aspect of letters for the past two thousand years and over. Realizing that Western civilization has been dominantly a verbal civilization—one which represents its meaning primarily through the artifice of words rather than through such artifices as music, painting, sculpture, or architecture—we must make an inquiry into the history of the symbolic differentiation of the literary realm from the realms of church and state (and, if we persist far enough, from the realm of science, once under the aspect of letters but now no longer so). Consequently, we confront a puzzling and vexatious task. But with some historical boldness and mobility we can proceed to it. To start at some point less remote than the age of stone tablets, or Egyptian antiquity, we can find the symbolic discrimination of the literary realm developing in Athenian times. This occurs in the literary definition of man by the Sophist rhetorician Isocrates (the powers of speech and persuasion disciplined by education sharply distinguished men from beasts and Greeks from barbarians); and in the withdrawal of Plato from the unhappiness and disorder of politics to the intellectual and verbal discipline of the Academy. If we cannot attribute to Isocrates or Plato a cosmopolitan outlook—for indeed they were Greeks, and Greeks in their age were not cosmopolites—we do find the symbolic basis of a literary ecumenicalism rising in later Grecian times and in the Roman appropriation of Greek letters and art. One major expression of this is the ideal cosmopolis of the Stoics ("the cosmopolis," as Eric Voegelin says, "to which men belong by virtue of their participation in the Logos").[2] Another major expression of ecumenicalism, if less obvious, is the Arcadia of Virgil's *Eclogues*. This poetic community of shepherds withdrawn from Rome and its politics and corruptions represents in general, as Bruno Snell convincingly demonstrates in *The Discovery of the Mind*, Virgil's finding in the pastoral mode an independent world of literary art.[3] We have established in classical times the idea of the life of the mind, the life of words as a dimension of existence, in the urban image ("the city of letters"—Athens, Rome, or later say, Florence, Paris); and we have set up the life of the mind in the pastoral image of Arcadia. One implies the collectivity of the literary existence, the other its relative isolation and solitude. But both enter into the creation of the independent identity of the literary realm; they become metaphors of the literary existence, serving to separate it symbolically from church and state, thus to make it the Third Realm.

In its unfolding distinction as a realm of being, however, the dominant image of the Third Realm is urban. Quite logically the realm of letters had a covenant with the city, the dominant expression of civility and civilization. This compact was encouraged by Christian ecumenicalism. Expressed in the symbols of the City of God and/or the Republic of Christ, Christian universalism nurtured the dynamic literary cosmopolitanism which began to emerge in the Middle Ages. In the rise of the concept of the university, associated closely with the urban image, the medieval "clerks" provided for a distinction of the realm of letters from church and state not before known. Eric Voegelin in *The New Science of Politics* describes how the church became the "historically concrete representation of spiritual destiny"

2 *The New Science of Politics* (Chicago, 1952), p.157.
3 *The Discovery of the Mind: The Greek Origins of European Thought* (New York, 1960), p.281f.

and the Roman Empire the "historically concrete representation of temporality."[4] With the creation of the university as a representation of literary power with ambivalent, perhaps ambiguous, yet independent relations to church and state, we see the definite establishment of the Third Realm in Western civilization. (I am saying this, I should say, not Voegelin.) At the same time we see emerging a more general symbol of literary order, the *res publica* of letters, the Republic of Letters, often used as a term for the university but a term embracing various embodiments and visions of literary and intellectual order.

Returning at this juncture in the discussion to the quotation from Crèvecoeur's *Letters from an American Farmer*, we may—employing the brilliant aid of Leo Marx in his *The Machine in the Garden: America and the Pastoral Ideal*—discover in Crève-coeur's depiction of the novelty of intellect in America a reversal of the urban image of literary order. In *Letters from an American Farmer*, Marx says, all "the traditional features of the pastoral are present in new forms supplied by the American experience." Crèvecoeur's "independent, democratic husband-man with his plausible 'rural scheme' " and "exuberant idiom," together with his tendency to make America and Europe resemble the antithesis present in the pastoral convention as city and country, nature and art, is a dynamic version of the shepherd of Arcadia. Like the Arcadian figure, he has his home in a literary landscape which, as a rural place of peace and plenty, is a reconciliation of "natural and civilized conditions."[5] Adapting Marx somewhat we may well argue, I think, that the farmer of the *Letters*, with his "fat and frolicksome" wife and children, together with all his notions about new opinions and new principles in an America affording maximum freedom from church and state, suggests a compelling extension of the pastoral myth of the autonomy of the literary mind. Because of the effect of the possibilities of America on the literary mind, after 2000 years the Arcadian sensibility in the imagination of literary order

4 P.110.
5 *The Machine in the Garden* (New York, 1964), pp.107–16.

takes on fresh meaning and power. But let me pass over the significance of this point to come back to it presently in a consideration of Thomas Jefferson.

Meanwhile, we may see in Crèvecoeur's statement another idea related to the Third Realm. This is the idea Crèvecoeur refers to in his remark about the pilgrimage of letters and learning from East to West, which may be identified as the concept of the *translatio studii*. This concept appears in embryonic form in the *Epistles* of Horace; and the Horatian mention of the transfer of letters from Athens to Rome serves as the model for the appearance in the ninth century of the full-fledged concept of the transfer of letters. It becomes a transfer of intellectual power which is coordinated with the older concept of the *translatio imperii*, the transfer of empire.[6] Literary power, like the power of empire (ecclesiastical and political), is conceived in the Carolingian Age as a part of a deterministic theory of history, offering an explanation of the decline of civilization in its ancient centers in the East and its transplantation to a succession of metropolises further west. This deterministic theory, however illogical, served to represent the providential continuity of civilization and to make literary power equal in history with that of church and state. The transfer of letters was less important as a theory of literary history than it was as another way of symbolizing the community of the urbane, lettered mind—the community of Athens with Rome, and of these classical cities (particularly Rome, the universal city) with Paris, London, or St. Petersburg.

By the time of the Renaissance, we may say, the Third Realm had become "historically concrete." By the time of the Enlightenment it was assumed to be a reality. The polity of letters was visibly expressed in the lives of the humanists and *philosophes* moving about in the urbane complex of the Republic of Letters: the interlocked world of universities, academies, and libraries; of clubs, salons, coffee houses, and taverns; of essays, books, and perpetual correspondence. In substance and power the Republic

6 See Ernst Robert Curtius, *European Literature and the Latin Middle Ages* (New York, 1953), p.29.

of Letters reaches a climax in the eighteenth century at its full tide; when, divided though they were by many animosities, men of letters, Augustan humanists, and radical *philosophes,* were united through their hostilities as well as their friendships; and men of letters as diverse as Samuel Johnson and Voltaire had, Peter Gay declares, a "consensus of ideals, and ways of thinking."[7] This was true in spite of the fact that Johnson called Voltaire the *philosophe* a villain and Voltaire called Johnson the Christian humanist a superstitious dog. The consensus rested in the notion that men of letters shared a feeling for their membership in a common realm of being—autonomous, secular, thoroughly moral—a realm illuminated by the use of letters to promote civilization. They shared a "cultural style"—the style of urbanity and urbane discourse descending from the Stoic image of a cosmopolis of lettered minds. "My dear David," Diderot exclaimed to David Hume, "you belong to all nations, and you'll never ask an unhappy man for his birth-certificate. I flatter myself that I am, like you, a citizen of the great city of the world." Edward Gibbon thought of the Europe of the man of letters "as a great republic, whose various inhabitants have attained almost the same level of politeness and cultivation."[8] In the middle of the eighteenth century Voltaire declared that the Republic of Letters had been consolidated in Europe; it was "a great fellowship of intellect, spread everywhere and everywhere independent."[9] From St. Petersburg in the Russia of Catherine the Great to Rome to Paris to London, the Third Realm found its image in the great city of letters, the literary ecumene.

## II

To what extent was this image realized across the Atlantic in the British colonies shortly to constitute the new Republic of the United States? Philadelphia, Boston, New York, Charleston—

[7] *The Enlightenment: An Interpretation* (New York, 1968), p.21.
[8] Quoted in *The Enlightenment*, p.13.
[9] *Age of Louis XIV* (London, 1926), p.380.

these colonial "cities in the wilderness," as Carl Bridenbaugh has called them—were in their intellectual life conscious and articulate areas of the Republic of Letters. Nothing, we know, is more prominent in the careers of Franklin, Jefferson, and John Adams than their involvement in the Western community of letters and learning. We recognize, moreover, how much American men of letters who had less opportunity to live abroad were involved in the "consensus of ideals, and ways of thinking" of the cosmopolis of letters and were formed by its cultural style. This was the style which governed the American Philosophical Society. Located in Philadelphia and drawing its membership from all of British North America, it was, as Daniel Boorstin observes, "truly continental in catholicity and influence." But, we must add, its catholicity was not of indigenous origin; the Society was a creature of the Republic of Letters. As a matter of fact, to some indefinable extent the new nation was a creature of the Republic of Letters, a conscious invention of the ecumenical Western mind. America, among all the other promises it held forth, promised to be the place in history for the fulfillment of the polity of letters. As the American Enlightenment appropriated and synthesized the symbols of literary order inherited from ancient and medieval times and from the Renaissance, it promised to achieve a balance of power among church, state, and letters, with the balance in favor of letters. Why this is so is not difficult to discern. The Jeffersonian doctrine of the separation of church and state rests on the autonomy of the Third Realm. The full recognition of the independence of the Third Realm is the necessary source of the separation of the first two; and such a recognition was clearly a possibility offered by the American Enlightenment.

Ironically we see the failure of this possibility in the same age. We detect in the consciousness of the Enlightenment in America—in the appropriation of the symbols of literary order—what amounts to a nationalization of the spirit, or the metaphysical power, of the literary ecumenicalism of the European Enlightenment. And in this we perceive a weakening of the autonomy, or potential autonomy, of the Third Realm in the United States.

The nationalization occurs to some extent because the Americans were more self-consciously aware of the symbolic transfer of letters and learning than the Europeans. The vision of America as the culmination of the mind was naturally appealing to American men of letters; it was a support to all who felt inferior to their fellows in Europe and who pridefully wanted to see the wilderness redeemed by arts and letters, no doubt mingling in their aspiration the *translatio studii* and the *translatio imperii.* John Adams documents the situation in the eighteenth-century American mind solidly: "There is nothing, in my little reading, more ancient in my memory than the observation that arts, sciences, and empire traveled westward; and in conversation it was always added since I was a child, that their next leap would be over the Atlantic into America."[10] The conversation, it may be added, might well have followed specific encouragement from the Old World. "The next Augustan age will dawn on the other side of the Atlantic," Horace Walpole said. Bishop Berkeley, combining the concepts of the transfer of empire and the transfer of studies, composed his well-known poem "On the Prospects of Planting Arts and Learning in America":

> There shall be sung another golden age,
> The rise of empire and of arts,
> The good and great inspiring epic rage,
> The wisest heads and noblest hearts.[11]

Still and all, stressing as it did the continuity of letters through Old World decline into New World renewal, the progress of letters from Europe to America was not an idea that lent itself strongly to the notion of an indigenous American achievement in the life of the mind. It did not forcefully support an integral literary nationalism. On the contrary, it logically repudiated

[10] Quoted in Benjamin T. Spencer, *The Quest for Nationality* (Syracuse, N.Y., 1957), p.22.

[11] *Works of George Berkeley*, ed. Alexander Campbell Fraser (Oxford, 1901), IV, 366.

the possibility of American intellectual uniqueness. What did
lend itself to the American nationalistic impulse was the image
of order the Americans tended to concentrate on in the transfer
of the European literary ecumenicalism into their historical
time and place. This was the recessive image of literary autonomy, the pastoral or Arcadian image. If Americans, hopefully
spreading the names Athens and Rome all over their geography,
by no means rejected the urban image of literary order, they
showed a marked affinity for the pastoral image. In America, the
attraction of Athens, Rome, and Paris as homelands of the mind
was distinctly subject to the appeal of Arcadia.

The reasons for this are quite complex. Let me inadequately
sum them up in two generalizations. For one thing, by the eighteenth century, life in America, and especially in the British colonies, had developed in the Western imagination, in the minds of
Europeans and colonials, more as a possible restoration than a
possible future. America was a unique and final chance for man
to redeem his life from the complicated misery of Europe by
entering into his lost pastoral state of simple happiness. This
imaging of America as the bucolic past of Edenic paradise was
capable of many variations. In it renewal and novelty became
thoroughly confused. Returning to a pastoral state and rising to
newness of life became equated notions, brought together in
the vision of the redemptive power of nature. In the second place,
as the scientific-industrial-technological revolution began to
manifest itself in eighteenth-century Europe, the literary imagination began to associate the city or the metropolis more and
more not only with the traditional evils of business and commerce, but to experience intimations of the dehumanizing influence of the industrial wasteland. In America the prospect of
the industrial city was more ominous than in Europe. Literary
opposition to the city was heightened not only by a close association between pastoralism and the destiny of the nation but by
an intimate association between pastoralism and the life of the
mind. In America, in short, the city seemed to be a menace to
the identity and autonomy of the literary realm.

[327]

## III

To illustrate this fear easily and directly is impossible. The thought of Thomas Jefferson is central to any effort to explain it, affording us, if we oversimplify considerably, the most important and dramatic illustration.

More than John Adams and as much as Franklin a universal man and major citizen of the Republic of Letters, known everywhere in the cosmopolitan fellowship of intellect in the West, Jefferson followed Franklin in making the American Philosophical Society of Philadelphia the embodiment of an urbane, transcendent literary ecumenicalism. "The republic of letters," Jefferson said, "is unaffected by the wars of geographical divisions of the earth."[12] And yet he was also responsible, primarily so it would appear, for providing an important basis for a nationalistic ordering of the life of the mind in America. He did this by at once identifying the American mind, obliquely but in a graphic, poetic way, with the pastoral mode of literary order and celebrating this in effect as the only mode appropriate to the American experience and destiny.

The key document may be located in Query XIX in the *Notes on Virginia* (1785), in which Jefferson deals with the state of manufactures and commerce in Virginia, his general comments, we may assume, applying to the whole of the new nation. In *The Machine in the Garden*, Leo Marx in a provocative close reading of the nineteenth query shows how in his argument Jefferson passes from the language of poetical economy to a language closely akin to the spirit of pastoral poetry. In this spirit he writes the famous words: "Those who labour in the earth are the chosen people of God, if ever he had a chosen people, whose breasts he has made his peculiar deposit for substantial and genuine virtue. It is the focus in which he keeps alive that sacred fire, which otherwise might escape from the face of the earth." Jefferson goes on to draw the contrast between the American husbandman

12 *The Writings of Thomas Jefferson*, ed. Andrew A. Lipscomb and Albert Ellery Berg (Washington, 1905), XIII, 87.

and the workers in Europe who belong to "the mobs of the great cities" with all their "subservience and venality." Implicitly identified in Jefferson's mythopoetic language, if with less concern for its sheer novelty, is the mythical role of the yeoman farmer in America. "He is," Marx observes, "the good shepherd of the old pastoral dressed in homespun."[13] But as in Crèvecoeur's depiction of the American farmer, there is another and more significant presence implied. We become aware of this presence the more readily in the *Notes on Virginia* because Jefferson does not, like Crèvecoeur, use the farmer-shepherd-narrator as an overt technical device. Whose voice really speaks in Query XIX? And to whom does he describe his vision of the American pastoral economy? Beneath the guise of the poet-farmer is the poet-*philosophe*, the cosmopolitan man of letters, the eighteenth-century citizen of the Third Realm; and he speaks to the fellowship of his peers. Identified in Query XIX is a poet—Jefferson, a man deeply read in the ancient poets, humanist and classicist, an American Virgil—speaking something like a passage from an American eclogue, and projecting for his fellow men of letters what becomes through metaphorical transformation a vision of a homeland of the literary spirit. That is to say, America. The poet speaks, moreover, not in the role of an urbane outsider (as Theocritus does in the Grecian pastoral), but, more like Virgil in the *Eclogues*, as an insider—for all his sophistication a genuine dweller in the garden and a keeper of the sacred fire of the virtue which reposes in it. The economy of Jefferson's garden is a literary economy, having nothing to do with agricultural productivity; it is in essence in metaphysical communion with the economy of spiritual leisure Virgil imagines in opposition to the corrupt and unhappy life of Rome. In Jefferson's affinity for the pastoral convention the transfer of the sensibility of the ecumenical literary order to America is defined fundamentally not as from Athens to Rome to Paris to London to Philadelphia but as straight from Arcadia to Monticello, Jefferson's beautiful rural

[13] *The Machine in the Garden*, p.127. Query XIX is quoted in its entirety, pp.123–25.

domain in Virginia. The American landscape is identified as Arcadia reborn, the redemption of the life of the mind from the sick Metropolis of Europe. Through Jefferson's profound poetic influence on the life of the mind in America, it is scarcely too much to assert, the American imagination of literary order broke the compact with the city and entered into a covenant with Arcadia.

By the time the American Enlightenment began to give way to American Romanticism, this covenant was historically realized. A significant incident in the early life of the noted American literary scholar, George Ticknor, occurs to me. When our first distinguished historian of Spanish literature began his well-known literary journey to Europe in 1815, he traveled with difficulty and danger all the way to Monticello. A Bostonian's Bostonian, brought up in a community which despised Jefferson, he yet felt a need to get the aging Jefferson's blessing on his literary mission and to secure letters of introduction from him to men of letters in Europe. The winding road up to Jefferson's mountain home—not like Voltaire's Ferney a place of exile but the one place in the world Jefferson ever really wanted to be—this road led, the ambitious and urbane young Ticknor knew, to the heart of the order of letters as this had been asserted in the United States. Ticknor had no intention of rejecting his native city, which would shortly come to be called the "American Athens," and he would be strongly instrumental in his city's achievement of literary renown. He commenced his important career in American cosmopolitan scholarship, nevertheless, by paying his tribute to the American Arcadia.[14]

I am of course making an exaggerated emphasis. George Ticknor's tribute was not in itself a definitive sign of a marked restriction on the ecumenical sensibility in America. For in the sum total of his career Jefferson did not reject Athens or Rome. As a matter of fact, when Ticknor called on him at Monticello, Jefferson was contemplating the establishment at nearby Char-

14 See George Ticknor, *Life, Letters, and Journals*, ed. G. S. Hillard, Mrs. Anna Ticknor, and Miss Anna Eliot Ticknor (Boston, 1877), I, 34f.

lottesville of the University of Virginia. He intended it to be a cosmopolitan, institutional "bulwark of the mind" in the Western hemisphere. In the shifting dialectic of thought and emotion which characterized Jefferson's wide-ranging mind, we may locate a productive tension between the Arcadian and metropolitan images of literary ecumenicalism.

But eventually the Jeffersonian, though I do not mean simply the Jeffersonian, identification of the life of the Third Realm in America with Arcadia resulted in a kind of pastoral subversion of the autonomy of the ecumenical order of letters in the new nation. If the world city of letters attained a certain fulfillment in Philadelphia and in Boston and New York, the values of the urbane literary realm were always suspect in the American imagination of literary order. Thus literary order could be preserved in moral purity and strength only if it found its truest image in, say, rural Concord village. The result, if hardly for this reason alone, was that the role of the man of letters—the versatile, inquiring, comprehensive mind seeking its meaning and identity in contact, in agreement and collision, with similar minds—was undercut in the United States. Because of the attraction to Arcadia, the cosmopolitan consciousness of the American Enlightenment was the more easily nationalized in the period of romantic nationalism that followed; the literary life in America the more easily reduced to parochialism. We cannot say that the Arcadian emphasis altogether promoted the decline of literary autonomy in America. The feeling for the independence of the literary realm as a realm of being would seem to be most completely expressed in this country by the image of Henry David Thoreau living in his hut by Walden Pond. In his absolutely pure devotion to literature and writing, Thoreau created a complex Arcadia which in modern literary history represents the autonomy of the Third Realm in an absolute way.

The cost of this creation to Thoreau was not less than Boston, one not more than he gladly paid. It was a cost greater than Emerson finally wanted to pay. He at length sought the society of Holmes, Lowell, Aggasiz, and others in the monthly meetings of the Saturday Club at Boston's noted Parker House. Thoreau refused all invitations and never went, even once. "The only room in Boston I visit with alacrity," he told his friend Harrison Blake, "is the Gentleman's Room at the Fitchburg Railroad, where I wait for the cars, sometimes for two hours, in order to get out of town." The train bore him back to "that glorious society called Solitude."[15] Had he not attended this society so faithfully, he would not now be so idealized as a uniquely American writer by our literary nationalists. But—and I speak as a longtime and sympathetic member of the Thoreau Society—we should consider, as the urbane James Russell Lowell did in his notorious attack on Thoreau, to what extent Thoreau's intensely personal representation of the literary life in America may have been a deprivation as well as an enrichment of it. In so doing we bring up the whole question of the rejection of Athens and Rome for Arcadia in the life of the mind in America.

[15] Thoreau to Harrison Blake, January 1, 1859, *The Familiar Letters of Henry David Thoreau*, ed. F. B. Sanborn (Boston, 1894), p.401.

ROBERT N. BECK is professor and chairman of the Department of Philosophy at Clark University. He is author and editor of a number of books including *The Meaning of Americanism, American Ideas,* and *Perspectives in Social Philosophy.*

ROBERT C. BLACK III is professor of history at Temple Buell College. He is the author of *The Railroads of the Confederacy, The Younger John Winthrop,* and *Island in the Rockies: A History of Grand County, Colorado.*

E. BRADFORD BURNS is associate professor of history at the University of California, Los Angeles. He has written or edited five books on Brazilian history, one of which, *The Unwritten Alliance,* won the Bolton Prize in 1967.

MANOEL CARDOZO is chairman of the Department of History and curator of the Oliveira Lima Library at The Catholic University of America. He is the author of more than fifty studies on the culture of the Iberian countries, particularly Brazil and Portugal. He has been twice decorated by the Brazilian government for his contributions to the history of Brazil.

T. B. IRVING is professor of Romance languages at the University of Tennessee. He has also taught at Berkeley and Minnesota and founded the Summer School at the Universidad de San Carlos, Guatemala. His recent publications include *Falcon of Spain* and *Paisajes del Sur*.

Luis Leal is professor of Spanish and Latin American literature at the University of Illinois. He is the author of several books including *Breve historia del cuento mexicano*; *Mariano Azuela, vida y obra*; *Historia del cuento hispanoamericano*; *Panorama de la literatura mexicana actual*; and *Literatura de Hispano-américa*.

Isaías Lerner is assistant professor of Spanish at the University of Illinois and co-editor of an annotated edition of *Don Quijote*, published by the Editorial Universitaria de Buenos Aires.

Juan Marichal is professor of Romance languages and literatures and chairman of his department at Harvard University. He also holds an honorary chair at the University of San Marcos in Lima, Peru. He is the author of *La voluntad de estilo: teoría e historia del ensayismo hispánico* and *El nuevo pensamiento político español* and has edited the works of Pedro Salinas and Manuel Azaña.

Luis Monguió is professor of Spanish at the University of California, Berkeley. He is the author of *César Vallejo*; *La poesía postmodernista peruana*; *Estudios sobre literatura hispanoamericana y española*; and *Don José Joaquín de Mora el Perú del ochocientos*.

Graciela P. Nemes is professor of Hispanic literature at the University of Maryland and well known for her definitive study *Vida y obra de Juan Ramón Jiménez*.

Russell P. Sebold is chairman of the Department of Romance languages at the University of Pennsylvania and co-editor of the *Hispanic Review*. He has published *Tomás de Iriarte: poeta de "rapto racional"*; *El rapto de la mente: poética y poesía dieciochescas*; and *Colonel Don José Cadalso*, and has edited Isla's *Fray*

*Gerundio,* Torres Villarroel's *Visiones,* and Lopez de Ayala's *Numancia destruida,* with extensive critical studies.

LEWIS P. SIMPSON is professor of English at Louisiana State University and co-editor of *The Southern Review.* He has edited *The Federalist Literary Mind* and has written several essays relating to the Enlightenment in Anglo-American culture.

CARMELO VIRGILLO is associate professor of Romance languages at Arizona State University and author of various essays on Latin American literature. He is editor of *Correspondência de Machado de Assis com Magalhães de Azeredo* recently published in Brazil by the Instituto Nacional do Livro.

ARTHUR P. WHITAKER is emeritus professor of history, University of Pennsylvania. He has published a dozen major books on Latin American history, including *Latin America and the Enlightenment.* His paper in the present collection was delivered both at the University of Illinois and at the American Philosophical Society and is published as well in the *Proceedings* of the Society.